RETHINKING BAKHTIN

To David —
with best wishes
Caryl
24.II.89

RETHINKING BAKHTIN

Extensions and Challenges

Edited by Gary Saul Morson and Caryl Emerson

NORTHWESTERN UNIVERSITY PRESS   EVANSTON, ILLINOIS

Northwestern University Press
Evanston, Illinois 60201

Library of Congress Cataloging-in-Publication Data

Rethinking Bakhtin : extensions and challenges / edited by Gary Saul
  Morson and Caryl Emerson.
     p.   cm.
    Bibliography: p.
    Includes index.
    ISBN 0-8101-0809-7. — ISBN 0-8101-0810-0 (pbk.)
    1. Bakhtin, M. M. (Mikhail Mikhailovich), 1895-1975.
2. Criticism. I. Morson, Gary Saul, 1948- . II. Emerson, Caryl.
PG2947.B3R48 1989
801'.95'0924 — dc 19   88-32263
                                                              CIP

To our first teachers,

Robert Louis Jackson
and
Sidney Monas

Contents

ACKNOWLEDGMENTS

Several of the essays in *Rethinking Bakhtin* were reprinted, some in revised form, from the following original publications and are used here by permission.

Gary Saul Morson, "Parody, History, and Metaparody." Excerpted and reprinted by permission of the University of Texas Press from *The Boundaries of Genre: Dostoevsky's "Dairy of a Writer" and the Traditions of Literary Utopia* (Austin, 1981).

Linda Hutcheon, "Modern Parody and Bakhtin." Excerpted from *A Theory of Parody: The Teachings of Twentieth-Century Art Forms* (London: Methuen, 1985).

Paul de Man, "Dialogue and Dialogism," in *Poetics Today* 4: 1 (1983).

Ann Shukman, "Bakhtin's Tolstoy Prefaces." Excerpted from "Bakhtin and Tolstoy," in *Studies in Twentieth-Century Literature* 9: 1 (Fall 1984).

Caryl Emerson, revision of "The Tolstoy Connection in Bakhtin," in *PMLA* 100: 1 (January 1985).

Aaron Fogel, "Coerced Speech and the Oedipus Dialogue Complex." Excerpted from *Coercion to Speak: Conrad's Poetics of Dialogue* (Cambridge, Mass.: Harvard University Press, 1985).

Gary Saul Morson
Caryl Emerson

Introduction: Rethinking Bakhtin

After one's death, Bakhtin once wrote, the creation of a coherent and "aesthetically whole" picture of one's life and work can begin. He was oversimplifying the fate of an author under Soviet publishing conditions.

During the last ten or fifteen years of Bakhtin's life, it had again become possible to publish his works, including many he had written forty or fifty years before. He was allowed to revise and republish his book on Dostoevsky in 1963 (first version, 1929); and in 1965 his book on Rabelais, which was originally written in the 1940s, at last appeared. In 1975, the year of his death, a large collection of his major writings of the 1930s was published. That collection was published soon after in Western European languages and in an English translation of the principal essays entitled (by the translators) *The Dialogic Imagination.* This translation decisively changed and enriched the image of Bakhtin.

But his archives were by no means exhausted. Another major collection of his unpublished work was issued in 1979. Some of these pieces have recently appeared in English under the title *Speech Genres and Other Late Essays,* and they, too, have begun to alter our sense of Bakhtin's achievement, not only because they address new problems, but also because they provide a new "dialogizing background" for already familiar earlier work. Each new text that appears seems to foreground different aspects of old ones, and to reveal concerns that were evidently central to Bakhtin but which have been only intermittently visible to his readers. Still untranslated from the 1979 collection are some of Bakhtin's earliest work, unfinished or unpublished manuscripts dating from the 1910s and eary 1920s. These pieces, too, seem likely to alter our sense of Bakhtin, primarily by calling attention to the centrality of ethics in his thought.

In 1986, yet another important early essay (or interrupted fragment) was published in the Soviet Union under the title "Toward a Philosophy of the Act." Although some of its formulations seem hazy and inadequate — which is possibly why he abandoned them — others, particularly those concerning ethics, are remarkably powerful. Even the weaker formulations, however, are important in helping us to understand what Bakhtin was striving after in his later work, by showing us the alternatives he tried out and then rejected. Bakhtin had evidently not discovered the controlling importance of language, and had not yet arrived at his concept of dialogue, when he composed this early essay; the image of Bakhtin before dialogue is especially intriguing. "Toward a Philosophy of the Act," along with the essays written in his last years, also illustrates one feature of his thought that appears constant — his lifelong dislike of Marxism.

This statement may seem strange because a number of his explicators have insisted, largely without substantial evidence, that Bakhtin was also the author of three avowedly Marxist books published under the names of his friends — Valentin Voloshinov's *Marxism and the Philosophy of Language* and *Freudianism: A Critical Essay*, and Pavel Medvedev's *The Formal Method in Literary Scholarship*. So categorical are the attributions of these works to Bakhtin that many American readers are unaware that among specialists the attribution is by no means uncontroversial. We ourselves long accepted assurances that convincing evidence would be forthcoming and consequently cited Voloshinov's and Medvedev's works, without adequate qualification, as evidence for what Bakhtin believed. We now tend toward the opposite view, and deem it unlikely that Bakhtin wrote these three remarkable books.

Voloshinov and Medvedev obviously owed a great debt to Bakhtin, but the use they make of Bakhtin's ideas clearly changes their import and the larger framework into which the ideas fit. We also believe that Voloshinov and Medvedev, far from being mere passive lenders of their names or scribes undertaking "the onerous

task of preparing a summary" of the master's thoughts, were vig-
orous, creative thinkers in their own right. The Marxism of their
books was in no sense mere window dressing to be removed by a
skillful reader, nor does it appear to us as Bakhtin's way of "ven-
triloquizing" his ideas into another idiom.[1] Rather, it is organic to
their central argument. The work of the Bakhtin group offers us a
real *choice* between a Marxist and a non-Marxist interpretation of
a new view of language and culture; readers can only lose by col-
lapsing this dialogue into an elaborate hoax to elude the censor.
Once we took seriously the divergence between Bakhtin and his
friends, it also became possible to consider the extent to which they
influenced *him* — by encouraging him to answer their challenge and
formulate a view of language and literature that was social without
being Marxist.

Thus, both additions and subtractions to the Bakhtin canon
have changed our view of him. When one relates *Problems of Dostoevsky's Poetics* to the early essay "Toward a Philosophy of the
Act," and "Discourse in the Novel" to the much later piece "Toward a Methodology of the Human Sciences," it becomes both
more plausible and more logical to see *Marxism and the Philosophy
of Language* as a work not only inspired by but also different from
Bakhtin's. In consequence, one's sense of all these works undergoes
a sea change.

Bakhtin himself was aware of another source of change in the
meaning of a thinker's ideas: the use to which they are put by later
commentators and theorists working on new problems. In his last
essays, Bakhtin considers at some length the relation of later interpreters to a received text. He tries to steer clear of two positions
that have defined recent debate. On the one hand, he insists that
reader reception is not a matter of unlocking a meaning hidden in
the text — in which case the relevant category for judging an interpretation would simply be correctness or error. Readers are never
passive, and understanding may be genuinely "creative." On the
other hand, he argues that the text is not mere putty to be shaped
however a given reader or "interpretive community" wishes. Both
of these alternatives, the "dogmatic" and the "relativist," collapse
two distinct voices into one, and thus make true dialogue impossible. Bakhtin finds the relativist view to be particularly pointless,
because it makes it impossible ever to encounter an *other*, inasmuch

as the other simply becomes a version of oneself. The "dogmatic" attempt to unlock the author's meaning usually impoverishes the text, but at least it may serve as a starting point for creative understanding at a later time.

How then are we to explain (as Bakhtin assumes) that great works grow, not just in significance, but also in real meaning, over time? Bakhtin's solution is to insist, as he does in other contexts as well, on the concept of "potential." The author may be aware of the presence of this potential — it is really in the work, and he may experience it when he reads the work over — but because any potential cannot be wholly actualized by any single reader, the author is only barely aware of its meanings. The concept of potential is central to Bakhtin's thought, which was always concerned with vindicating creativity and innovation as real. Only in such a way, he felt, could life be genuinely "unfinalizable."

Potential is realized through dialogue. A rich dialogic standpoint allows one to encounter the otherness of the text without sacrificing one's own position. As in all genuine dialogue, something unforeseen results, something that would not otherwise have appeared. The text allows for and invites this sort of interaction, but does not contain its results. Truly great works invite such interaction from countless diverse and unforeseeable standpoints — standpoints as diverse and unforeseeable as the multiplicity of peoples and cultures over what Bakhtin calls "great time."[2]

If the best work that has been written about Bakhtin is any indication, he has himself begun to show how great is the potential of his books and essays. A number of recent thinkers have responded dialogically to him, either by extending his ideas into areas he did not consider, or by challenging the conclusions he draws from his own premises. By "extensions" we do not mean mere "applications"; none of the critics in the present volume applies his thought in that way. Rather, each thinks *with* Bakhtin's ideas, and sheds light on current problems. As Bakhtin observed, agreement, too, is a dialogic relation. And disagreement can be something other than an empty rejection. The challengers presented here develop implications Bakhtin overlooked and question overly optimistic conclusions that his own arguments cannot sustain.

Before outlining the contents of this volume, we would like to offer the reader an opportunity to reconstruct the image of Bakhtin.

To this end, we will first describe in some detail the contents of "Toward a Philosophy of the Act" (henceforth "Act"), which has neither been translated into English nor extensively summarized. We will then indicate why we are now inclined to think that Bakhtin did not write the three books whose authorship is in dispute.

PART ONE: "TOWARD A PHILOSOPHY OF THE ACT"

A philosophy of life can only be a moral philosophy. — "Toward a Philosophy of the Act," 124

We see Bakhtin's work as a complex, and often haphazard, development that may be divided into four periods.[3] Bakhtin's earliest period, concluding roughly in 1924, consisted of largely philosophical writings about ethics and aesthetics. A decisive break that ushered in the second period of his thought appears to have been provoked by his encounter with Russian Formalism and his attempts to create an alternative model of language. In his first period, language was *not* a central category of his thought; in the second period, he arrived at his key notion of dialogue. The most important work of these years was *Problems of Dostoevsky's Creative Art* (1929), which introduced his new ideas on language and his concept of "polyphony." That concept enabled him to rethink problems central to his work before 1924.

Another discovery propelled Bakhtin into his third period, covering roughly the 1930s, 1940s, and perhaps the early 1950s. That discovery was the novel, and it quickly became a central category of his thought. Whereas the book on Dostoevsky describes that writer as fundamentally different from all who preceded him, including other novelists, "Discourse in the Novel" and other essays of the 1930s shift that focus by identifying the creation of the entire genre of the novel as the decisive break in European literature and thought. During these years, Bakhtin also developed his concepts of "chronotope" and "carnival."

In Bakhtin's last period, he returned to the philosophical concerns of the first period, now enriched by his long sojourn through literary history. He reworked (and retitled) the book on Dostoevsky; most of the lengthy fourth chapter of *Problems of Dostoevsky's Poetics* (on menippean satire, carnival, and the nature of literary

genres) belongs to this final period. So do several essays on the
nature of the humanities and the kinds of dialogic or creative understanding appropriate to those disciplines. Especially important are
his brief, meditative essays, "Response to a Question from the
Novy Mir Editorial Staff," "The Problem of the Text in Linguistics,
Philology, and the Human Sciences: An Experiment in Philosophical Analysis," and "Toward a Methodology for the Human Sciences." As in his earliest period, Bakhtin's most provocative
formulations are often his least elaborated and least prepared for
print: notes "Toward a Reworking of the Dostoevsky Book" and
a series of extracts "From Notes Made in 1970–71."[4]

A close reading of Bakhtin's early essay "Toward a Philosophy
of the Act" is not only rewarding in its own right, but also serves
to highlight themes of Bakhtin's better known work in a new way.[5]
A number of interesting features of this work are immediately apparent. First, in contrast to the later work, here language plays at
best a secondary role. The central category is the "act" (*postupok*),
not the "word" (*slovo*). Second, the center of Bakhtin's concerns
is clearly ethics: the essay is essentially a polemic with the dominant
trend (as Bakhtin describes it) of Western ethical thought since the
seventeenth century. Kant in particular is a target. Third, in contrast
to those Russian—and Russian Orthodox—admirers of Bakhtin
(including his editor Sergei Bocharov, and those Western commentators who have seen Bakhtin's thought as essentially religious) the
work barely touches on theology, except in one passage. A projected section was to deal with theological questions, but Bakhtin
stresses that ethics, his main concern, is no more a matter of formal
religion than it is a matter of law. It would seem hard to justify the
notion that Bakhtin's works are, at least in the Western sense of the
term, really a theology in code.[6]

Fourth, in contrast to Bakhtin's later work, this essay evinces
no special hostility to lyric poetry. Indeed, Bakhtin chooses a lyric
poem, rather than a novel, to illustrate his ideas on the interaction
of the ethical and aesthetic spheres. Fifth, the text is highly existential in tone, reflecting the Russian literary tradition in general and,
most likely, Dostoevsky in particular. And finally, Bakhtin aims
here to offer a theory not only of ethics and aesthetics, but also of

all human life — including politics and religion, literature and mythology, "love and death" — treated from an ethical standpoint.

"The Philosophy of the Act": Theoretism

It is a sad misunderstanding, the legacy of rationalism, that truth can only be
that sort of truth that is put together out of general moments, that the truth of
a proposition is precisely what is repeatable and constant in it. . . .   —"Act,"
110

Most of "Act" consists of a long attack on a style of thought
Bakhtin calls "theoretism." Theoretism is described as a way of
thinking that abstracts from concrete human actions all that is generalizable, takes that abstraction as a whole, transforms the abstraction into a set of rules, and then derives norms from those rules.[7]
But this process loses the most essential thing about human activity,
the very thing in which the soul of morality is to be found: the
"eventness" (sobytiinost') of the event. "Eventness" is always particular, and never exhaustively describable in terms of rules. Hume,
it will be recalled, argued that the mere existence of moral norms
and rules offers no reason why we should obey them. Bakhtin goes
further, contending that even if we did obey those rules, we would
still not necessarily be behaving ethically, for ethics is not a matter
of rules.

In his later work, Bakhtin was to argue that the opposition of
"social" to "individual" is a false one. In attempting to analyze
living phenomena, we incorrectly isolate out from life some elements that we call social and others that we call individual. Forgetting that the abstraction is our own, and reifying the opposing
categories, we then argue about the relation between the hypostas-
ized opposites, or else try to dissolve one of them into the other.
But what if the very act of abstraction is the problem; what if the
real phenomena of life are not reducible to these opposing categories? And what if life itself is not a synthesis of social and individual, but a "live entity" that precedes and transcends the synthesis?
Bakhtin was eventually to argue that dialogue was an example of
such a "live entity." In "Act," he constructs a related argument and
offers his concept of "the act" as a category that must always exceed
our "transcriptions" (theoretical and reductive descriptions) of it.

According to Bakhtin, different disciplines carve out of existence distinct realms (history, literature, science, art) and assume that the sum of these disciplines can in principle account for life. But because these disciplines all "transcribe" life and lose the "eventness" of events, they all, separately or in any possible combination, leave something essential out: "the singular world in which we create, become aware, perceive, in which we live and in which we die. . . . [As a result of the theoretical disciplines,] an act of our activity, of our experience, like a two-faced Janus, gazes in different directions: into the objective unity of the cultural sphere and into the unrepeatable unity of experienced life, but there is no unified and singular plane where both faces could mutually define themselves" ("Act," 82–83). Konstantin Levin, it might be noted, reaches much the same anxious conclusion in *Anna Karenina.*

Later in Bakhtin's life, "unrepeatability" became a characteristic of "the word" overlooked by linguists; in "Act," it is a characteristic of the act overlooked by all disciplines. The disciplines are content with "abstract meaning" (*znachenie*) and think that that is all there is; but to understand human acts, one must also take into account unrepeatable "contextual meaning" (*smysl*). The failure to take this step beyond theoretism is utterly fatal for any understanding of ethics.

Ethics for Bakhtin is a matter not of norms but of "oughtness."[8] The term "theoretical obligation" is in fact a contradiction in terms, according to Bakhtin; morality is a matter of "the historical concreteness of the individual fact, and not . . . the theoretical truth of a proposition." It is not "transcendental" or "categorical," as Kant believed, but concrete and particular. One cannot, in fact, even talk about moral, ethical norms, or about oughtness without any particular content. Oughtness can be found in no kind of theory—neither scientific nor aesthetic nor even ethical as it is usually understood. "There are no definite moral norms signifying in themselves, but there is a moral subject . . . on which one must rely" ("Act," 85). Bakhtin is unremitting in his attacks on Kant as the epitome of the wrong approach.

Should theoretists come to recognize some version of this problem, their natural move would be to try to overcome it *in* their theory—say, by providing rules of context. Later in his life, Bakhtin would see the same sort of impulse behind the futile attempt of some linguists to describe a grammar of situations, which is necessarily inadequate to the unsystematic, messy quality of real communicative situations.[9] In Bakhtin's view, "all attempts to overcome the dualism of cognition and life, of thought and singular concrete reality *from inside theoretical cognition* are absolutely hopeless . . ." He compares such activity with attempts "to lift oneself up by one's own hair" ("Act," 86).

Indeed, the attempt may even be dangerous. Faith in rules, norms, theories, and systems blinds us to the particular person and situation, which is where morality resides. In what might be an allusion to the Russian revolution and civil war, Bakhtin writes that blind faith in such "technical" systems and laws, unfolding according to their own immanent logic, is "terrible . . . and can from time to time invade the singular unity of life like an irresponsibly terrifying and destructive force" ("Act," 87).

Relativism is no answer to this threat, Bakhtin insists, because relativism is itself a form of theoretism. For relativism, no less than for other theories, life ceases to be an ethical, "responsive, risk-taking, open act-in-the-process-of-becoming" ("Act," 88). From a relativist, no less than from a dogmatic, perspective, "I" as a specific, unrepeatable person have no role; in principle, I do not even exist in such a context.[10] Indeed, if anything, relativism is the worst form of theoretism — worse than ethical and cognitive systematization — because real moral acts do at least take theoretical knowledge into consideration as a part of their ethical stance. Relativism deprives us of those aspects of theoretism that are helpful without supplying us with a sense of "eventness" in return.[11]

Bakhtin then briefly considers a few disciplines that "transcribe" existence and mistake their transcription for the real thing. He has two types of reductionism in mind here, one of which diminishes the cognitive realm and the other the ethical. Knowledge is mistakenly impugned when (let us say) economic materialists assess scientific theories on the basis of "class origins" or likely political effect.[12] And ethics is debased when real responsibility is replaced by the "laws" of a discipline.

Bakhtin illustrates both errors with examples from psychology. He appears to have in mind thinkers as different as Pavlov and Freud, or, to be more accurate, an image of the distilled essence of psychological thought of whatever school.[13] The theoretists of psychology, he argues, would transcribe the theoretical world itself into mere psychological phenomena. Believing that all knowledge is ultimately a psychological phenomenon, they may see the need for such disciplines as physics and mathematics as temporary. When psychology has progressed far enough, those disciplines will become mere subdivisions of it, for psychology will tell us what is really going on: processes in the brain of the physicist or mathematician. In the same way, economic materialists would tell us about the physicist's or mathematician's class interests. But all these claims are either inadequate or absurd, Bakhtin contends. Mathematicians working on a theorem neither do nor should function with an awareness that what they are doing is a mere psychological process. Psychology, likewise, must not mistake its proper role and pretend to be a sort of philosophical cognition.

Turning to ethics, Bakhtin argues that the attempt to reduce real-life, responsible "becoming-acts" to psychological categories is no less absurd. According to Bakhtin, "real acts" are always oriented "responsibly" to the particular context in which the acting person lives. But unwilled psychological processes are by definition never "responsible" in this sense. No less than mathematicians working on a theorem, moral agents performing an action neither do nor should consider the psychological and physiological processes they undergo to make their choices: "One can think [in that mode], but one cannot accomplish an act" in it, Bakhtin observes; "the act moves and lives not in the psychical world" ("Act," 90).

The same criticisms apply to biological, economic, and all other disciplinary transcriptions. All these approaches do is translate one theoretical vocabulary into another, without ever escaping the theoretical world. Bakhtin concludes that we can begin to remedy this problem not by devising some new theory but by attending to the reality of the specific act. "[Only by beginning] from the act itself, and not from its theoretical transcription, is there an exit into its meaningful content" ("Act," 91).

"Live Entering" and More False Dualisms

Bakhtin next introduces a concept essential to the ethical "act itself": *vzhivanie*, "live entering" or "living into."[14] Live entering, Bakhtin stresses, must not be confused with empathy (*Einfühlung*).

In empathy, one tries to merge totally with the suffering other and to experience the world entirely from the other's place. But even if such "pure in-dwelling" were possible, it would in any case be unproductive, because total identification precludes the capacity to contribute something new: "in someone else's place I am as without meaning as I am in my own place" ("Act," 95). Empathy is only a part of a truly helpful relation to another.

In *vzhivanie,* one enters another's place *while still maintaining one's own place,* one's own "outsideness," with respect to the other. "I actively live into [*vzhivaiu*] an individuality, and consequently do not, for a single moment, lose myself completely or lose my singular place outside that other individuality" ("Act," 93). From such a relation, something new and helpful can emerge. Later in his life, after language had become central to his thought, Bakhtin was to rethink this concept in dialogic terms as "creative understanding." Dialogic response, he came to write, depends on the irreducibility of both participants. In creative understanding, the reader or listener does not seek to merge with the author of the text. Respecting the author's "outsideness" and "otherness," the reader "lives into" the text and lives alongside the text. "Passive understanding," which is similar to empathy, simply reproduces what is already there; creative understanding, like "live entering," produces something new and enriching.

In short, real responsibility, according to Bakhtin, is necessarily misunderstood or precluded by two different conceptions of ethics. First, systematic ethics denies the particularity of both participants in an ethical relationship by making each of them generalizable and replaceable: in principle, an infinite number of other people could be in the same position as the participants, and only the rule that governs their interaction matters. Second, empathy tries to erase the "second person" by dissolving him into the "first person" (the sufferer). Systematic ethics respects no persons, empathy one person; only *vzhivanie* respects both persons.

Yet another relation to other people is possible: the aesthetic. In aesthetic living, one creates a sort of "double" to enter into life, while remaining oneself irresponsibly separate from it. Whereas empathy values only the sufferer and seeks to erase the position of the outside other, the aesthetic approach seeks to keep *only* outsideness by separating the one outside both from the sufferer and from any real, responsible involvement in the "event of being" and "the co-being of being."[15]

The sort of "theoretical" existence proposed by systematic ethics is impossible for a living person, but in Bakhtin's view one can indeed live "aesthetically." This form of living is in fact quite seductive. "It is quite possible to live, and people do live, in aesthetic existence, but it is really *other* people living and not me; it is a lovingly perceptualized past life of other people. . . . I will not find myself in that life, but only my double-pretender. I can do no more than play a role in it, i.e. clothe myself in the flesh-mask of another, of one who has [in effect] died" ("Act," 95). I create a hero and let him live in my place.

One way to imagine Christ, Bakhtin suggests, is to see the incarnation as an act of *vzhivanie.* According to this analogy, Christ did not empathize with people; rather, he became one of them while still maintaining his divine outsideness. What Christ offered was neither theoretical truth nor an example of aesthetic doubling, but a "living into" the world that left it a fundamentally different place. "The world from which Christ departed could no longer be that world in which he had never been, it became different in principle."[16]

Bakhtin now proceeds to an argument that to us reads like a lengthy gloss on Dostoevsky. Dostoevsky's hero from the underground describes a world in which people have become products made in a chemical "retort":

After all, we do not even know where living exists now, what it is, and what it is to be called! Leave us alone without books, and we will be lost and in a confusion at once — we will not know what to join, what to cling to, what to love and what to hate, what to respect and what to despise. We are even oppressed by being men — men with real *individual* body and blood. We are ashamed of it, we think it a disgrace and try to contrive to be some sort of impossible generalized man. We are still-born, and for many years we have not been begotten by living fathers, and that suits us better and better. We are developing a taste for it. Soon we shall somehow contrive to be born from an idea.[17]

The underground man's solution to this quandary is to try to live purely perversely, by spite; rejecting the theoretical realm, he lives according to everything it excludes. Indeed, the underground man contends, the perverse behavior so common in modern life results from a similar impulse among most people to escape from their usual condition as "generalized."

To return to Bakhtin: he claims in the early manuscripts that "contemporary man" lives in a world that theoretism has split in two. On the one hand, man is "confident, rich, and clear-eyed wherever, in essence, he is *not* — [that is,] in the autonomous world of culture and its immanent laws of development" ("Act," 96–97). Where he lives his real, singular, individual life, he "feels himself to be uncertain, impoverished and unclear" ("Act," 97). The result of this situation is that we have one world of ethical and cultural knowledge, with its abstract generalized norms and laws, and another, senseless world in which all the rest is left to dark, spontaneous, irresponsible forces. Because meaning and responsibility are given over to the theoretical realm, the world of action is impoverished in a perverse and highly dangerous way.

As Bakhtin further explains, "I" do not fit into theory — neither in the psychology of consciousness, nor the history of some science, nor in the chronological ordering of my day, nor in my scholarly duties. "All these contexts and possibilities of meaning wander in some sort of airless space, rooted in nothing" ("Act," 97). Henri Bergson's attempt to escape the crisis fails, because it merely reverses previous evaluation of the divided parts of life while still maintaining what Bakhtin later calls ("Act," 103) the "abstract partition" itself. The idea of *élan vital* brings us no closer to the responsible act. All divisions of the act or the self into the rational and nonrational are part of, not an alternative to, the problem. One may suppose for Bakhtin that Freud's division of the psyche is presumably both symptom of and contributor to the crisis.

All of these problems derive from the fundamental error of "rationalist" philosophy, even where it attempts, as vitalism does, to free itself from itself. The fatal flaw is the denial of responsibility — which is to say, the crisis is at base an ethical one. It can be overcome only by an understanding of the act as a category into which cognition enters but which is radically singular and "responsible."

Real ethics is never a matter of rules, Bakhtin repeats. Norms belong to law and religion, not to concrete responsibility. We may note here Bakhtin's principled refusal to make ethics a part of religion; he also declines to include it as part of philosophy in the usual sense. "Formal" and "material" ethics make responsibility a matter of rules and the concrete act a mere instantiation of the rule. Later in his life, Bakhtin was to object in much the same way to Saussurean linguistics, with its split of *langage* into *langue* and *parole:* such a view makes the utterance a mere instantiation, correct or incorrect, of linguistic rules. In "formal" ethics, too, such an approach "theoretizes . . . and consequently loses the individual act" ("Act," 100). Human will is reduced to a shadow of itself and "dies in its own product" ("Act," 101), whereas in fact human will, like the dialogic utterance, is "creatively active in the act, but in no sense does it generate a norm, a general proposition" ("Act," 101).

To paraphrase Bakhtin's thought, then: if ethics were a system of rules, a computer could be the most ethical agent. No one would have to think, care, or be responsible from one moment to the next. Each person could behave like Tolstoy's Ivan Ilych, who is such a fine jurist precisely because he never allows any personal responsibility to affect his dextrous application of legal categories to specific cases. Sharing a fundamental dislike of systems, Tolstoy and Bakhtin believed that neither culture nor ethics can be made into a set of rules and that in morality there is no substitute for an educated sensitivity to irreducibly particular people in unrepeatable particular circumstances.[18]

"The principle of formal ethics," Bakhtin writes, "is in no sense the principle of the act, but the principle of possible generalization from already completed acts in their theoretical transcription" ("Act," 102). The concrete act or event "cannot be transcribed in theoretical terms in such a way that it will not lose the very sense of its eventness, that precise thing that it knows responsibly and toward which the act is oriented" ("Act," 104). One must go within the concrete individual act to understand it, while at the same time remaining outside it. One must, in short, engage in "live entering."

Language, Tone, Signature

Bakhtin then briefly addresses the problem of language. Contrary to what one might expect from his argument so far, Bakhtin contends that language *is* more or less adequate for understanding responsibility — provided that we use not theoretical language, but rather ordinary, everyday language. Philosophical impatience with

everyday language and romantic insistence on the unspeakability
of experience are both mistaken: "I think that language is considerably more qualified to utter precisely [the truth of the event] and
not the abstract logical aspect in all its purity" ("Act," 105). "Purity" is usually a pejorative word for Bakhtin, who preferred to
emphasize the impure messiness of the world. These rather unsub-
stantial observations just about exhaust the problem of language in
this essay.[19]

The purpose of these passing comments on language is to lay
the groundwork for Bakhtin's discussion of "tone." Tone is, of
course, a feature of language, but that fact is almost coincidental;
for Bakhtin, tone is a much broader category of life, and only in
consequence is it a characteristic of language. For Bakhtin, acts have
tone; speech has tone by virtue of being a form of action. Again
we see how far Bakhtin was to develop, and how much he had to
rethink, when dialogue became central to his thought.

Bakhtin then introduces a distinction he was to use and refor-
mulate often in his life, that between *dannost'* and *zadannost'*,
"givenness" (that which we find) and "positedness" (that which we
posit as a task). For someone who acts, all material with which he
works—his knowledge, the situation in which he finds himself—
are "given." Likewise, all abstract theory is given. In acting and
transcending what he merely inherits—in *doing* something—he enters a realm of new particular meanings for which he is responsible,
the realm of the "posited." "[Truly] experiencing an object, I thereby
fulfil something in relation to it, it enters into a relationship with
positedness, grows within in my relationship to it" ("Act," 105).
In other words, Bakhtin writes, one imparts one's *tone* to the situation. Tone, therefore, is essential to the process of making a situation not abstract, of creating a situation in which one truly
"participates." Tone is always "emotional-volitional" and "evaluative." Even abstract theories, when they become meaningful "for
me," take on a tonality. "Emotional-volitional tone opens up the
locked-in, self-sufficient potential content of a thought, attaches it
to a unified and singular being-event. Every generally-signifying
value becomes truly signifying only in an individual context" ("Act,"
108–9).

Tone always pertains to an individual living consciousness *in
activity*. Never a "passive psychical reaction," tone is rather "an

obligation-laden [*dolzhnaia*] orientation of consciousness . . . a responsibly cognized *movement* of consciousness" ("Act," 109). It is both active and central to the act, the act understood in a way that theoretism never could understand it. Tone is what makes an act "mine," and, in reflecting the nature of my participation in an activity, tone is at the root of my active responsibility.

Modern philosophy of value, Bakhtin observes, tends to see value in abstract terms, either as a stability of transcendent judgments or as a "constant, self-identical principle of evaluation" ("Act," 110). Again, Bakhtin's criticisms apply to relativistic as well as dogmatic theories of value, both of which think away the ethical, responsible, and active character of an evaluative act. Both turn evaluation into a matter of "content." But "it is not the content of the obligation that obliges me, but my signature on it, the fact that I once acknowledged it, signed a given admission" ("Act," 110–11).

Signature—making an act one's own, taking responsibility for it—is, according to Bakhtin, another category unknown to theoretism. Theoretism concerns itself solely with the content of the act, which is only one aspect of action. But could not theoretism transcribe signature as well as content? Bakhtin cautions us that although such a transcription may at first look possible, it is not. "Of course it is possible to transcribe all this in theoretical terms and express it as a constant law of the act; the ambiguity of language permits us to do this, but we will end up with an empty formula" ("Act," 111). Theoretism could presumably say that unrepeatable acts are unrepeatable, but it cannot actually comprehend that unrepeatability, because its categories of comprehension are general.

The unrepeatability of the act makes possible the "absolutely new"; which is to say, there is a clear link between Bakhtin's approach to ethics and his lifelong concern with creativity. He verges here on what was soon to become a global concept of his thought, "unfinalizability."

Alibis for Being

Bakhtin insists on the radical singularity of each person at every moment. As he argues: "I am"—I alone occupy a particular place at a particular time, no one else can be in my place at my time. From the point of view of ethics, this means: "That which can be accomplished by me cannot be accomplished by anyone else, ever" ("Act," 112). This fact means in turn that moral "oughtness" is not a matter of a few important moments, nor is it a matter of big decisions. Rather, it is a constant fact of the most prosaic moments of life. Bakhtin calls the ineluctability of responsibility one's "non-alibi in being" (*ne-alibi v bytii*).

And yet there are many ways for us to act as if there *were* alibis for being. Most obviously for intellectuals, we can describe theoretically the fact of the "non-alibi," at which point we immediately begin to generalize. "And here we [already] have a theoretical formulation, striving to the limit of absolute liberation from any emotional-volitional tone" ("Act," 112). *This* position obligates me to nothing. "As soon as I think my singularity as an aspect of existence, shared by all existence, I have already exited from my singular singularity" ("Act," 112).

In the course of his discussion, Bakhtin does not consider whether this criticism could be leveled at his own highly theoretical and abstract treatment of the concrete and the singular. We may surmise that he came to sense the inadequacy of his discourse to his theme, and that he therefore came to look for a more adequate discourse. The search, it appears, led him eventually to celebrate the novel as the form best able to convey singularity and the non-alibi in being.[20]

What, then, is the proper orientation to theoretical knowledge? Bakhtin here draws a distinction between *znanie* (knowledge) and *priznanie* (acknowledgment). Neither should be collapsed into the other, he insists. The world of theoretical knowledge has its place, and it can neither be reduced to our own interests nor reformulated to accord with our moral sense. We must not remake facts to suit our interests or our principles. But by the same token, we must not be content to live only in the world of knowledge, or to pretend that the possession of knowledge absolves us of the responsibility to make it morally meaningful. We must assess the implications of knowledge for ourselves and for our relations to others. Having acquired it, we must impart a "tone" to it and "sign" it—that is, we must "acknowledge" it.

It is quite common, Bakhtin notes, for scholars to take knowledge itself as their alibi for being. The problem with this view is that the world of "unacknowledged" knowledge is a world of "empty potentiality." Bakhtin does not use a linguistic analogy to explain what he means, as he was later so fond of doing, but he seems to have in mind the sense that *znanie* is like a grammatical paradigm with many choices, whereas *priznanie* involves an actual choice among these alternatives, a bringing of knowledge toward one by attaching it to (*pri-*) one's self. That choice, necessarily made in a specific emotional-volitional tone, produces a real, responsible utterance. Real responsible action, then, involves a choice among the possibilities made available by knowledge. In the world of unacknowledged knowledge by itself, there is no "I" and no true responsibility: "The world of meaningful content is infinite and self-sufficient, *its* power to signify in itself makes *me* unnecessary, my act for it is accidental. It is the realm of endless questions. . . . Here it is impossible to start anything, every beginning will be arbitrary; it will drown in the sea of [possible but not actual] meaning. It does not have a center, and provides no principle for choice: everything that is could both be and not be, or could be differently" ("Act," 114).

Again, Bakhtin may have Dostoevsky's underground man in mind. Living in the pure world of theory, according to what he calls "the laws of hyperconsciousness," the underground man describes why he does not "act." Real action, he explains, requires a basis for acting, by which he means a theoretical principle. Such a principle is ultimately unavailable:

Where are the primary causes on which I am to build? Where are my bases? Where am I to get them from? I exercise myself in the process of thinking, and consequently with me every primary cause at once draws after itself another still more primary, and so on to infinity. That is precisely the essence of every sort of consciousness and thinking. . . . Oh, gentlemen, after all, perhaps I consider myself an intelligent man only because all my life I have been able neither to begin nor to finish anything. Granted, granted I am a babbler, a harmless annoying babbler, like all of us. But what is to be done if the direct and sole vocation of every intelligent man is babble, that is, the intentional pouring of water through a sieve?

Notes from Underground (pt. 1, chap. 6)

To use Bakhtin's term, the underground man lives a life of "absolute restlessness" ("Act," 114). He consciously takes to an extreme the possibility of life without "participation" and responsibility. Of course, most people who try to live in the theoretical realm are neither so thorough nor so aware of the meaning of that sort of life as is Dostoevsky's hyperconscious hero. The underground man fully embodies the life of "abstract content": he becomes a person of "pure and infinite function" (as Bakhtin was soon to say in the Dostoevsky book), avoiding any self-definition by participation at all. Condemned to knowledge and acknowledging nothing, he truly lives a life of "empty potential."

To understand Bakhtin's point it is crucial to distinguish "empty potential" from real potential, which can result only from acting out of one's singularity in an unfinalizable world. Real potential results from an act of commitment, albeit a tentative and open-ended commitment, and produces the genuinely new.

Bakhtin calls those who try to live with an alibi for being "pretenders." This use of the word "pretender" (*samozvanets*) is curious, because normally in Russian (as in English) the term means someone who tries to take another's place. The "false Dmitri" in the Boris Godunov story is a pretender; so were the rebel Emilyan Pugachev, who claimed to be the true tsar, and the hero of Dostoevsky's *Double*, where pretendership is used to describe the usurping of a mind in schizophrenia. In Bakhtin's vocabulary, however, a pretender is not someone who usurps another's place, but someone who tries to live in no particular place at all or from a purely generalized, abstract place. The mature Dostoevsky created just such a pretender in Stavrogin, the hero of *The Possessed*. People who live this way "pass meaning by" or "irresponsibly sneak meaning past existence" ("Act," 115). Each of their acts is a sort of "rough draft for a possible accomplishment, a document without a signature, obligating no one and obliged to nothing" ("Act," 115).

Another way in which people can become pretenders is to live lives that are "ritualized" or "represented." Bakhtin has in mind political or religious officials who so identify with their role that they lose any responsible orientation to it. "Attempting to understand our lives as hidden representation and our every act as ritualistic, we become pretenders" ("Act," 121). In a possible allusion to Russian Communism, Bakhtin criticizes the "pride" of those who become pure "representatives of some large whole." This forfeiture of singular participation in the name of representation is a constant temptation of political activity and has the potential for catastrophe.

Bakhtin seems to regard political ideologies as incorporating all the dangers of the categorical imperative, and adding a few of their own. All systematic ethics, and all attempts to dissolve personal responsibility into a general political system, deny the value of one's own particular moral obligation. "There is no person in general, there is me, there is a definite concrete other: my close friend, my contemporary (social humanity), the past and future of real people (of real historical humanity)" ("Act," 117).

From the perspective of the categorical imperative or of political ideology, all deaths are alike. Our "loving flesh" can signify only as "an aspect of infinite matter, indifferent to me," as an "exemplar of *homo sapiens*" ("Act," 120). "But no one lives in a world where all people are mortal in an axiologically equal way" ("Act," 118).

In one of his most remarkable passages, Bakhtin asks us to consider "the destruction and fully-justified shaming of a person beloved by me" ("Act," 128). From the point of view of abstract "content," norms, and rules, one might recognize the justice of the punishment. Nevertheless, the agony I experience suggests that this situation would *and should* be different from a similar situation in which the person were a stranger. Indeed, one would be behaving irresponsibly and immorally if one reacted the same way in both instances. Categorically, there can be no categorical imperative. The highest value is a human being, and the subordinated value is "the good," and not the other way around ("Act," 129).

Does this approach not fragment the world beyond the possibility of any unity? If we have a world in which there is an infinite multitude of individual centers of responsibility, each particular and not generalizable, do we not in effect deny all values? Indeed, Bakhtin answers, the multitude of value centers should lead us to *doubt* our values and to make our commitments to them provisional. But we do not end up with moral relativism. On the contrary, we arrive at a view that makes us continually and personally responsible for our actions and for assessing our moral responses — a world in which "everyone is responsible for everyone and everything," as Father Zosima says in *The Brothers Karamazov*. Precisely because responsibility is *not* generalizable, each of us is always responsible.

Nevertheless, it is still fair to ask what sort of unity could obtain with such a diversity of irreducible moral perspectives. Bakhtin does not really answer the question. But with the advantage of hindsight, we can see one way in which he was to try to answer it. As he describes the "polyphonic novel" in *Problems of Dostoevsky's Poetics,* Bakhtin offers us the image of a world made up of genuinely diverse and irreducibly particular moral centers but still possessing its own unity — albeit a "unity of a different order."[21]

If the moral world is viewed in this way, Bakhtin argues, we must *not* love others as ourselves; rather we must love others *as others,* without ceasing to be ourselves ("Acts," 116 – 17).

The "Architectonics" of Responsibility

Bakhtin now defines the fundamental goals of moral philosophy and projects a four-part study of it. As we might expect by this point, the goal is to describe "the world in which my act orients itself on the basis of its own singular participation in existence" ("Act," 122). The act "does not know" existence as a unified whole, it "knows" only concrete individual people, objects, and other acts, all given not objectively but in an emotional-volitional tone. "This is a world of proper names, *these* objects, and specific chronological dates of a life" ("Act," 122).

The first part of the study is to be general; it will deal with "the real world, not the world as it is thought but the world as it is experienced" ("Act," 122). Part two will concern "the aesthetic act of deed" from the point of view of moral philosophy — "as an act [taking place] not from within the product, but from the point of view of the author, as someone responsibly participating in it" ("Act," 122). In the third part, Bakhtin proposes to discuss the ethics of politics, and in the fourth, the ethics of religion.

In each of these parts, Bakhtin writes, it will be necessary to introduce one more concept, which he calls "architectonics." Bakhtin is rather obscure in his discussion of this crucial term, which has a distinctly paradoxical, and perhaps even self-contradictory, character. When he finally gets around to defining it, his definition is hardly transparent: "*Architectonics* — as a focused and indispensable, non-arbitrary distribution and linkage of concrete, singular parts and aspects into a finished whole—is possible only around a given person as hero" ("Act," 139).

The paradox is that "architectonics" is the generalized aspects of irreducibly concrete acts. Architectonics is not a matter of general concepts or laws. It is, rather, the general aspects of particular acts that nevertheless do not compromise their particularity. Bakhtin intends the concept as an alternative to the idea of system. For the problem with systems, Bakhtin everywhere implies in his early writings, is not only their inaccuracy, their artificiality, and their predictability. *Non*-system can exhibit those traits too. The problem with system is that it does not necessarily contain any human beings. And without concrete individual instances there is no obligation, because only the particular can obligate us.

It seems to us that "architectonics" is a tentative but interesting attempt to solve a problem that was to concern Bakhtin throughout his life: What can we say in general about particular things except that they *are* particular? What responsible discipline can be elaborated for the humanities, if the essential subject of those disciplines is all those things that are inevitably impoverished by being reduced to a system? The problem was to arise in different form when Bakhtin outlined his general theory of language, which he did not want to reduce to laws or grammar in the manner of structuralism; in his theory of psychology, which is to be neither social nor individual in the usual sense of those terms; and in his theory of the novel, as a class of works that are radically individual.

In hindsight, therefore, it is easier to see what Bakhtin was groping after in these early writings, but had not yet thought through. The concept of genre was to become central to that effort. Genres of speech and literature, he was later to argue, provide specific complexes of values, definitions of situation, and meanings of possible actions. They are complexes, clusters, or "congealed events" as opposed to systems;[22] they are themselves neither systematic nor parts of larger systems, as the Formalists tried to argue. These "complexes" provide a relative stability, but they do not exhaustively define the members of the genre. Each act of speech and each literary work uses the resources of the genre in a specific way in response to a specific individual situation. The genre is changed slightly by each usage; it "remembers" its uses, as Bakhtin was to put the point, anthropomorphically, in the Dostoevsky book. We need genres to understand specific acts, but in understanding genre we have not understood everything that is important about those acts. So Bakhtin was to argue about genres, but he is not nearly so lucid as he struggles with "architectonics."

What he does tell us is the sort of terms we should employ in an approach to "architectonics." We have already encountered some of these terms: participation, "live entering" (or "living into"), acknowledgment, signature, emotional-volitional tone, and responsibility. Bakhtin immediately adds three more—*I for myself, the other for me,* and *I for another*—and cautions us not to confuse the first of these with "selfishness," since "to live from oneself does not mean to live for oneself" ("Act," 119). He then introduces another complex of terms to play a major role in his subsequent discussion.

The first of these is the "value-center": each of us organizes the world in a complex of values different from that of every other person, each of whom has a specific value center, too. In order to understand the value center, it is necessary to distinguish between *okruzhenie* (surroundings) and *krugozor* (field of vision; literally, "circumvision"). A neutral third person observing "me," and describing my perspective as scientifically as possible, would see my surroundings but not my field of vision. For I inevitably see each object and person in my own emotional-volitional field, that is, in a "field of vision" unique to me. According to Bakhtin, one problem with "economic materialism" is that it understands the world entirely from the perspective of "surroundings."[23]

Each of us, therefore, perceives time and space in a different way, and all of us perceive it differently from the way it is described in abstract geometry. My value center is not a mere mathematical point.[24] Again reading retrospectively, we can see Bakhtin struggling toward the concept of the chronotope, but not reaching it. Chronotope and the dialogic situation of which the chronotope constitutes an intrinsic part were to replace architectonics when his thinking on these issues became more complex and precise.

From a purely theoretical view, Bakhtin argues, "the time and space of my life are insignificant . . . fragments of a unified time and space . . . but from within my participatory life these fragments receive a unified value-center that transforms actual space and time into a singular—albeit open—individuality" ("Act," 126). To be sure, mathematical time and space enables some sort of possible unity of opinions, but only *my* space and time "fills them with flesh and blood" ("Acts," 126). Individual value centers are the real primary data for ethical philosophy. "Rays fan out, as it were, from my singularity, [and] passing through time, affirm the humanness of history" ("Acts," 126).

In this way time and space are made human, enfleshed, given value, as they could not be if we were immortal. "All abstractly-formal aspects become concrete aspects of an architectonics only in correlation with the concrete value of the *mortal* human being" ("Act," 130, emphasis Bakhtin's). Rhythm can be meaningful for us because of the complex values that time takes on under the shadow of death.

Applied Architectonics: Bakhtin's Reading of Pushkin's Poem "Parting"[25]

Bakhtin now proposes to illustrate these ideas by considering a lyric poem. For what is a lyric poem but a compressed architectonics, a cluster of values around the "value-center" of the poet? Architectonics is often better viewed in art, Bakhtin explains, because art is closer to the act than is the world of abstract theory. In a poem, everything has an emotional-volitional tone. "The unity of a work of artistic visualization is not a systematic unity of meaning, but a concretely architectonic unity; it is distributed around a concrete value center, which is thought, and seen, and loved" ("Act," 128).

Only love, Bakhtin writes, can be aesthetically productive; only in love can one truly appreciate the complex and varied multiplicity of values in the act without leaving behind "a naked hull of basic lines and semantic moments" ("Act," 130). Of course, one normally does not respond to everything with such love; if one did, Bakhtin observes, it would be impossible to function in the world. In effect, indifference — "unlove" (*bezliubost'*) — makes life pragmatically possible; for much the same reason, we need not just to remember but also to forget.[26] Nevertheless, love is what one needs to understand the fullness of the act. "Unlove, indifference, never develop sufficient strength to *linger intensely* over the object, to strengthen it, to mould each tiny instance and detail of it. Only love can be aesthetically productive, only in correlation with the beloved is the fullness of multiplicity possible" ("Act," 130).

We will sketch only the broad outlines of Bakhtin's analysis of Pushkin's poem. The poem, one of the most famous Russian lyrics, is addressed to the poet's mistress who had left Russia for her native Italy; from that distant land the poet hears of her death. The poem begins:

Dlia beregov otchiznoi dal'noi
Ty pokidala krai chuzhoi . . .

[For the shores of your distant native country
You abandoned an alien land]

According to Bakhtin, the poem presents us with a complex of overlapping and interacting value-centers, in each of which time and space is experienced in a different way. The first two lines give *his* impression of *her* viewpoint: it is her "native land" (*otchizna*, a word with powerful emotional overtones in Russian), and it is she who sees Russia as "an alien land." The effect would have been entirely different had Pushkin written (as he did in one of his drafts) *chuzhbina* (foreign country) instead of *otchizna*. In the second line, we hear his own emotional-volitional reaction to his tone in the first line; this reaction is registered in the word "*pokidala*" (abandoned). She has abandoned him; her departure is an event in his life. Similarly, it is from his point of view that Italy is "distant"; she will be far *from him*. "Here we find a mutual interpenetration and unity of events in an axiological non-merging of contexts," Bakhtin observes ("Act," 132).

The next two lines shift perspectives again:

V chas nezabvennyi, v chas pechal'nyi
Ia dolgo plakal pred toboi.

[In an unforgotten hour, in a sad hour
I cried before you for a long time.]

The unforgotten hour and the sad hour are events for both him and her, figure in both their mortal lives. Nevertheless, his tone predominates over hers. In this way, Bakhtin goes through the poem to explore a complex interrelation and "mutual interpenetration" of tones and value-centers.

This interrelation is still more complex, however, because the entire drama we have so far described belongs to the author, who is the speaker at a later time in his life. "The whole concrete architectonics in its totality is given to the aesthetic subject (to the artist-perceiver) who is positioned outside it" ("Act," 135). Parting and anticipated events are components of his memory and anticipated future; he has chosen the rhythm of the poem, and he relates this event to his own life and to human experience. Moreover, in addition to the author-speaker, there is also an "author-creator," who has produced the poem; and to add yet another layer of complexity, the poem also belongs to a reader, in ways Bakhtin indicates only vaguely. The author-creator has performed an act of live entering, which the reader, too, is invited to perform. The creator and reader ultimately make the poem a poem, an aesthetic act; the "outsideness" of both parties is required. "Outsideness is the indispensable condition for bringing into one unified, formal-aesthetic value-context the various contexts that take shape around the several heroes" ("Act," 141–42).

Bakhtin next introduces a series of rather mechanical contrasts that nevertheless provide some insight into his working distinction between the aesthetic and ethical realms. Bakhtin first suggests that we call all that pertains to the reaction of the poem's heroes "realistic" and all that pertains to the reactions of the author "formal." Bakhtin does not explain this terminological choice, which he later abandoned, but it appears to be closely connected to a point he makes later in the essay. The author's primary role is to create a "finalized" aesthetic whole of the poem (or other artwork): the aesthetic is thus the "reaction to a [hero's] reaction." Should an author fail to separate himself from the hero in this way, the work would become an essay or a mere confession. In separating himself from the hero, the author transforms the world of the hero, which is (for the hero) "posited," into the "given." Only in this way is a sense of a whole possible.

Keeping in mind Bakhtin's other writings in his first and second periods, we may explain this distinction through Bakhtin's meditations on the relation of the aesthetic or finalizing impulse to death. When someone dies, he at last becomes fully available for a finalizing image because he can no longer change his self. Death, strictly speaking, is not an event in the life of a mortal being; it is an event

in the lives of those who survive and who contemplate and finalize
that being's life. Finalization is only possible from outside. In "Act,"
this distinction suggests that the hero lives, as real people do, primarily in the ethical realm: "The whole of a hero — the total expression of the hero — bears a purely ethical character . . . it belongs
not to a discursive but to an emotional-volitional order: shame,
insignificance, sacredness, authoritativeness, the rightness of a personality, love, etc." ("Act," 153). An outsider is needed to create
a finalizing image from an aesthetic standpoint.

Of course, Bakhtin concedes, even in life people are to a degree
aestheticized. "The ethical definition defines a *given* human being
from the point of view of the *posited;* it is enough to move the
value-center of the latter into the realm of the given, and the definition will already be completely aestheticized" ("Act," 153). Conversely, we should add, even the act of aestheticization has moral
import.

Bakhtin uses the term "a pure lyric" to refer to a poem in which
the ethical (or ethical and cognitive) energy belongs entirely to the
hero and the aesthetic energy to the author ("Act," 151). Lyrics of
this sort are "like the simple unmediated song, where experience,
as it were, sings itself. . . . [where it] both laments and sings its
own lament (aesthetic self-consolation) . . . the hero is not afraid
nor ashamed to be expressed, the author does not have to struggle
with him; they were born, as it were, in the same cradle, one for
the other" ("Act," 151).

Given these distinctions, what are we to say about other essential features of a poem, specifically "rhythm" and "intonation"?
First of all, we must distinguish between "realistic rhythm and intonation" (of the hero) and "formal rhythm and intonation" (of the
author). In practice, however, rhythm usually belongs mostly to
the author and intonation mostly to the hero. Conflicts between
(formal) rhythm and (realistic) intonation define to a great extent
the character of the given poem.[27]

Bakhtin turns to classical Greek drama to continue his argument. In drama there is no direct expression of the author and, in
this special sense, the form is wholly "realistic." Rhythm is one
way in which the author's presence is felt. Rhythm expresses the
"purely formal-aesthetic reaction of the author to the contradictory
realistic reactions of the heroes, to the entire tragic event taken

as a whole, aestheticizing it [the drama], severing it from reality (from cognitive ethical reality) and artistically framing it" ("Act," 145). A specific meter, of course, does not express the author's particular reaction to particular events, but it can express the author's overall orientation. Bakhtin also considers the author's voice in epic, an analysis that seems to look forward to his much more complex discussions of the author's voice in the novel in "Discourse in the Novel" and to Voloshinov's analysis of indirect speech in *Marxism and the Philosophy of Language.*

This long excursus on "The Philosophy of the Act" and on Bakhtin's reading of Pushkin's lyric illustrates two aspects of his theories relevant to reassessing and "rethinking Bakhtin." First, the early writings do not engage in the sort of "anti-lyricism" so prominent in the essays of the 1930s. Second, we learn something about Bakhtin's characteristic mode of constructing an argument. In Bakhtin's discussions, we often find an initial statement of an idea, followed by a series of expansions; we then come upon restatements, qualifications, and examples, after which new distinctions are drawn and further restatements are offered. In his writings both prepared and unprepared for publication, Bakhtin seems to think things through in front of the reader, or for himself, and so we experience both repetitiveness and a peculiar sense of intimacy.[28] It should not be surprising that at the very end of this fragment Bakhtin introduces yet another set of qualifications and distinctions.

In particular, Bakhtin asks us to differentiate between a "person" (*chelovek*) and a "hero" (*geroi*). The person is the "condition for the possibility" of the hero ("Act," 154); the hero is the person aestheticized, a process that can happen outside of art as well as in art ("Act," 155). Bakhtin offers this distinction in order to make a challenging point that may seem counterintuitive or flatly untrue: that every artwork of whatever sort demands a hero, the representation of a person with all his or her "emotional-volitional tones" and values, as finalized by an artist.

Bakhtin's whole ethical orientation toward aesthetic problems makes this point important to him. "Aesthetic creativity," he insists, "overcomes cognitive and ethical infinity and 'positedness' by relating all moments of existence . . . to a concrete human being — as an event of his life, as his fate. The given human being is a concrete value center of the architectonically aesthetic object" ("Act," 156). "Thus one can state positively that there is no aesthetic visualization nor artistic work without a hero" ("Act," 155).

Bakhtin is well aware that not all artworks have a hero: a hero is absent, he admits, from nature descriptions, ornament, arabesque, architecture, and music. In fact, the exceptions to Bakhtin's thesis seem to gobble up the rule. In addressing this problem, Bakhtin suggests that even if works do not have an actual hero, they have a *potential* hero, the emotional-volitional field in which a hero *could* live and act. "In this sense, every visualization includes within itself a tendency toward the hero, the potential of a hero; in each aesthetic perception of the object there slumbers, as it were, a specific human image, as in a block of marble for the sculptor" ("Act," 155). The hero is not so much absent *from* a work, as absent *in* the work. Thus in mythology — where nature is aestheticized — we may find evidence of this tendency: dryads, oreads from rocks, nymphs out of the water. Indeed, a great deal of language is anthropomorphized in this way; to a fair extent, language, too, could be said to have a potential hero ("Act," 156).

In offering these distinctions, Bakhtin occasionally interrupts to comment on the process of drawing them. He cautions us to recognize that the analytic approach has a tendency to separate phenomena that are in fact deeply fused. These observations appear to reflect Bakhtin's impatience with the analytic techniques at his disposal, and to anticipate his later appreciation of the novel, which he will describe not only as the greatest of genres, but also as the supreme form of philosophy in our time.

"Theoretism" and the Bakhtin Canon

Hostility to all forms of "theoretism," evident in "The Philosophy of the Act," was one constant in Bakhtin's long career. His many attacks on "dialectics," his criticisms of the Saussurean view of language, and his attempts to outline a theory of psychology inimical to both Freud's and Pavlov's all derive from his concern for the "eventness" of the event. They reflect as well his belief in the unsystematicity of culture, the "unfinalizability" of people, and the centrality of genuine responsibility to human experience.

Like Tolstoy, Bakhtin imagined himself as offering an alternative to the view that knowledge in the humanities must be modeled on the hard sciences and that culture, language, and the mind could ultimately be described as systems. According to Bakhtin, this view constitutes pseudoscientific reductionism, which was bound to lead to terrible moral consequences and to provoke a sterile relativism in response. To explain what sort of knowledge is possible without "theoretism," Bakhtin developed numerous conceptual alternatives: "live entering," "dialogue," "novelness," and "creative understanding."

In his "Notes of 1970–71," for instance, we find him rejecting Marxism (and "dialectics") along with semiotics and structuralism (with their concept of "code") as twin errors:

Semiotics deals primarily with the transmission of ready-made communication using a ready-made code. But in live speech, strictly speaking, communication is first created in the process of transmission, and there is, in essence, no code. . . .

Dialogue and dialectics. Take a dialogue and remove the voices (the partitioning of voices), remove the intonations (emotional and individualizing ones), carve out abstract concepts and judgments from living words and responses, cram everything into one abstract consciousness — and that's how you get dialectics.

Context and code. A context is potentially unfinalized; a code must be finalized. A code is only a technical means of transmitting information, but it does not have cognitive, creative significance. A code is a deliberately established, killed context.[29]

Readers of passages like these may wonder at the by now widespread ascription to Bakhtin of three other books — Valentin Voloshinov's *Marxism and the Philosophy of Language* and *Freudianism: A Critical Sketch* and Pavel Medvedev's *The Formal Method in Literary Scholarship* (as well as a number of articles by Voloshinov and Medvedev). Each of these books is avowedly and consistently Marxist, and Voloshinov's book on language is also a work of semiotics. On what basis, then, has Bakhtin been credited with works fundamentally at odds with his most cherished convictions?

PART TWO: THE DISPUTED TEXTS

What would I have to gain if another were to *fuse* with me?   —Bakhtin

It is now commonplace for critics to cite Voloshinov's and Medvedev's works as Bakhtin's, often without offering any qualification, but in fact the authorship of these texts is far from a settled question. In the United States the influence of Katerina Clark and Michael Holquist's pioneering biography, which takes a strong stand for Bakhtin's authorship of these books, has led to a widespread assumption by nonspecialists that an open question is in fact closed.[30]

For a number of years, we followed and contributed to this practice of attributing Voloshinov's and and Medvedev's works to Bakhtin.[31] The case finally offered in the Clark/Holquist biography, plus our own reading of the newly published manuscripts, led us to reconsider our previous assumption. In 1986, *Slavic and East European Journal* published a forum on Bakhtin in which the question was addressed by three contributors.[32] I. R. Titunik, a translator of Voloshinov and an advocate of Voloshinov's authorship, raised serious objections to Clark and Holquist's position.[33] Other scholars, including Nina Perlina and Edward J. Brown, have also objected on grounds of methodology and internal consistency to the double assumption that the works of the Bakhtin group can be treated as the product of a single author and that the author is Bakhtin.[34]

We have since come to the conclusion that, barring the presentation of new evidence, there is no convincing reason to credit Bakhtin with the authorship of the disputed texts.

In arguments of this sort, a good deal of skepticism is in order. Politics and academic politics color the issues, as do the economics of publishing and the "economics" of scholarly reputation on the professional marketplace. In this case, both Soviet and American politics have played a conspicuous role.

In the USSR, the rediscovery of Bakhtin in the early 1960s coincided with a lengthy debate over the emergence of semiotics, structuralism, and related methods of literary, linguistic, and cultural analysis. "Physicists" and "lyricists," semioticians and traditionalists, took varying and complex positions over such questions as the "mathematization" of literary studies, the use of cybernetics in the humanities, the place of linguistics in literary scholarship, the value of the Formalist heritage, the formalizability of "intuition" and "creativity," and the role of neurophysiology in aesthetics. Intense debates involved accusations of "reductionism," "scientism," "vitalism," and "vulgar sociologism."[35] Undercurrents of Russian nationalism and the revival of Russian Orthodoxy further confused the matter. Understandably in the Soviet context, opposing camps cited Marx and Lenin; equally understandably, opposing polemicists used Bakhtin, whose prestige was at its height, as a cudgel. Bakhtin was too significant for any side to abandon him to the opposition.

In this context, the attribution of Voloshinov's and Medvedev's works to Bakhtin offered various kinds of ammunition. If Bakhtin were allowed to be the author of works in semiotics, the semioticians stood to gain; if one stressed Medvedev's attack on Formalism, their opponents might profit. A more generous reading of events is also possible: that Bakhtin, now approved and even celebrated in his homeland, was being used as a conduit through which to reintroduce texts by his associates long banned or out of print.[36] The result was a kind of biographical imperialism, that is, the expansion of the Bakhtin canon to include powerful works by the other two scholars.

In the West, other interests have come into play. To state only the most obvious: Jakobsonians have endeavored to claim Bakhtin for structuralism and semiotics (despite Bakhtin's frequent attacks on both). Marxists have also claimed Bakhtin, and the attribution to him of the avowedly Marxist disputed texts has aided them in doing so. Scholars whose careers are linked to Bakhtin's stature have an understandable reason to accept arguments that magnify his legacy. The economics of effort has also played a role: in assembling a coherent account of the three theorists' ideas, critics often find it convenient to treat them as the product of one author, and to take advantage of claims tending to free their text from awkward qualifications. And, of course, publishers are clearly likely to sell more books with Bakhtin's name on the cover.[37]

To clarify the arguments on both sides, it would be useful to state what is *not* in dispute. There really were a Voloshinov and a Medvedev; nobody believes those names are pseudonyms in the sense that "Mark Twain" is a pseudonym. It is clear that Medvedev and Voloshinov were close friends of Bakhtin who exchanged ideas with him and with each other frequently. It is also clear to all that Bakhtin's ideas exercised a profound influence on his friends' books. Voloshinov and Medvedev appear to have been sincere Marxists. They were both dead by 1938. From the time of the publication of the works in question (approximately the late 1920s) until 1970, no one publicly disputed that Voloshinov and Medvedev wrote the books published under their names.

Because no one contests the influence of Bakhtin's ideas on his friends, the presence of important similarities between works signed by Bakhtin and works signed by Voloshinov and Medvedev is not germane to the argument. Because Voloshinov's and Medvedev's works are avowedly Marxist, the significance of the broader framework of their studies *is* relevant. Is the Marxism window dressing for the censor, and is it in fact compatible with Bakhtin's beliefs?

Vyacheslav Ivanov, the Soviet semiotician who claimed Bakhtin for his discipline, was the first to take a public stand for Bakhtin's authorship. In a lecture delivered in 1970 and published in an expanded version in 1973, Ivanov made the following statement, which we quote in its entirety:

The basic texts of works 1–5 and 7 [of the article's bibliography] are by M. M. Bakhtin. His students V. N. Voloshinov and P. N. Medvedev, under whose names they were published, made only small insertions and changes in particular parts (and in some cases, such as #5, in the titles) of these articles and books. That all the works belong to the same author, which is confirmed by the testimony of witnesses, is evident from their very texts, as one may easily convince oneself by the quotations presented [in Ivanov's article].[38]

As Voloshinov's defenders have noted, Ivanov offered no evidence to substantiate the assertion. The "witnesses" were not named. Similarity of ideas, as we have noted, would be entirely compatible with the assumption that Voloshinov's and Medvedev's books were influenced, but not necessarily written, by Bakhtin.

In their biography of Bakhtin, Clark and Holquist present the extant evidence for Bakhtin's authorship. According to them, Bakhtin wrote the works either entirely or almost entirely: "the disputed texts were written by Bakhtin to the extent that he should be listed as the sole author, Medvedev and Voloshinov having played a largely editorial role in each instance" (C&H, 147).[39]

Immediately after this assertion, Clark and Holquist advance a methodological argument that goes to the heart of the issue: "For one thing, nothing has established that Bakhtin could *not* have written the disputed texts and published them under friends' names." That is, the burden of proof is assumed to lie with the skeptics rather than with them. This argument is crucial, because in fact very little of Clark and Holquist's chapter on "The Disputed Texts" presents evidence that Bakhtin *did* write the works in question. The preponderance of the chapter either attempts to discredit arguments against Bakhtin's authorship or else offers motives why Bakhtin would have wanted to publish under others' names if indeed he did so.

It seems to us, however, that the burden of proof must lie with those who claim that Bakhtin wrote works signed by others. After all, Voloshinov's and Medvedev's names appear on the title pages, and their authorship was not disputed for some four decades. To our knowledge, no one has shown conclusively that the Earl of Oxford or Francis Bacon could *not* have written Shakespeare's works, but the burden of proof still lies with those who claim they did.

Refuting counterarguments is therefore largely beside the point unless convincing evidence for Bakhtin's authorship is first presented. What evidence has been offered?

Clark and Holquist cite four kinds of evidence. The first and "most important" (C&H, 147) is anecdotal, the reported testimony of "eyewitnesses" of Bakhtin and his wife "on private occasions." Most of this anecdotal evidence is presented in footnote 3 of the chapter, where we learn that "Bakhtin claimed authorship in a conversation with the American Slavist Thomas Winner in 1973" and that he made the same claim to his literary executor, Sergei Bocharov. Moreover, "in Ivanov's presence Bakhtin's wife once reminded Bakhtin that Bakhtin had dictated the Freud book to her," according to an interview of Clark and Holquist with Ivanov. "The American Slavist Albert J. Wehrle observed that when a copy of the 'Medvedev' book was produced in front of Bakhtin and his wife, Bakhtin said nothing, but his wife exclaimed, 'Oh, how many times I copied that!' " We are also told that the Formalist Victor Shklovsky "knew as early as the 1920s that Bakhtin was the sole author of the Medvedev book about his own group, the Formalists," according to Clark and Holquist's interview with Shklovsky in 1978.

In addition to the oral character of this evidence, which under any circumstances would be difficult to substantiate, Clark and Holquist indicate that there are other problems with it. In another footnote, they concede that "as a former Formalist, Shklovsky had reason for putting a negative construction on the affair" (C&H, 376n9). Moreover, when other people questioned Bakhtin about the disputed texts, Bakhtin did not confirm his authorship: "Indeed, during the 1960s and 1970s most people found that if they asked Bakhtin directly about whether he authored the disputed texts, he either avoided the question or was silent" (C&H, 148; no references are cited). "At first he [Bakhtin] did not even admit authorship to his literary executors, and when he later did admit it, he did not like to talk on the subject" (C&H, 148). Like Ivanov, the executors were deeply involved in polemics over the significance of Bakhtin's legacy. Finally, Clark and Holquist report that when the Soviet copyright agency (VAAP) asked Bakhtin to sign a prepared document that he wrote the three disputed books and one of the disputed articles, "he refused to sign it" (C&H, 147). The Soviet Union became part of international copyright agreements shortly before this document was prepared, and stood to profit from anything tending to raise Bakhtin's prestige in the West. In short, the anecdotal evidence is not only oral and mostly unverifiable but also far from unambiguous.

Another problem with this sort of evidence is that it is not always clear how precise the question was, or just what answer Bakhtin actually gave on the few occasions when he allegedly did speak about the matter. Was the question framed clearly enough to distinguish between Bakhtin's actual composition of the disputed texts and his influence on them? Did the question clearly distinguish between mere mechanical changes in Bakhtin's text (on the one hand) and (on the other) composition by Voloshinov and Medvedev after extensive discussions with Bakhtin? Since those are the only issues in dispute, the precision of the question is crucial. Many students and colleagues are profoundly influenced by a talented friend's ideas, but still digest those ideas, deploy them in a framework of their own, and creatively transform their overall significance in the process.

In our reading, Albert Wehrle's account of the anecdotal evidence would seem to indicate that information often taken to prove Bakhtin's authorship could be taken just as well to indicate his influence. Reporting a conversation he had with V. N. Turbin, Wehrle writes:

The few pieces of the puzzle we have now are hard to put together. Ivanov reports that Voloshinov and Medvedev "made only small insertions and changes in particular parts" of the books and articles in question and changed some titles. V. N. Turbin seems to support Ivanov when he quotes Bakhtin as saying, with regard to *The Formal Method:* "Pavel Nikolaevich [Medvedev] added to it, and not always for the better." According to Turbin, this was as much as Bakhtin ever said about the book. At other times he would confine himself to the remark that he "helped" with it. Knowing Bakhtin's reticence about the book, Turbin decided to conduct an experiment. In 1965, on a visit to Bakhtin, Turbin laid a copy of *The Formal Method* on the table without a word. Bakhtin said nothing, but his wife exclaimed: "Oh, how many times I copied that!" On the other hand, the latest published information, provided by Vadim V. Kozhinov, is that the problematic books and articles were written "on the basis of conversations with Mikhail Mikhailovich [Bakhtin]" ("Introduction" to *The Formal Method,* xvi).

Let us imagine that Medvedev wrote his own book "on the basis of conversations with" Bakhtin, but that, having thought profoundly about the issues, he transformed Bakhtin's ideas into a Marxist framework. Then Bakhtin might well have felt that he "helped" Medvedev but that Medvedev's additions "were not always for the better." Given the close relations of the Bakhtins with Medvedev, and given their considerable dependence on the largesse and protection afforded by Medvedev's influential position, Bakhtin's wife might well have copied the manuscript even if her husband had not written it (Bakhtin was unemployed at the time). Moreover, if Bakhtin was himself influenced by Medvedev's book, as we suspect, his wife may have copied extensive parts of it as notes.[40] In short, it is easy to imagine that people who had only recently learned that there was any connection among Bakhtin, Medvedev, and Voloshinov may have asked imprecise questions and leaped to conclusions, especially in the charged atmosphere of the time and given the importance of Bakhtin's newfound prestige to all groups.

Clark and Holquist's second type of evidence is also inconclusive. Because Voloshinov and Medvedev died more than three decades before the controversy began, American scholars, unable to consult them, interviewed their families. According to one scholar, Voloshinov's first wife attributed her husband's books to Bakhtin; according to another, Medvedev's son and daughter insisted that their father wrote *The Formal Method* and only "consulted with" Bakhtin (C&H, 148, 376n4).

The third type of evidence cited is dubious for several reasons, although it evokes our sympathy. In 1929, Bakhtin was arrested and faced imprisonment in a camp in the Soviet far north; because of his ill health, he appealed on the grounds that the sentence would kill him. According to Clark and Holquist, investigators called on Bakhtin to inquire about his possible authorship of the Medvedev and Voloshinov texts, since they knew he was familiar with "Marxist methods." The implication here, presumably, is that Marxist books written by Bakhtin could help the investigators contribute to a stronger defense of Bakhtin and so lighten his sentence. In these circumstances, it is said, Bakhtin admitted authorship (C&H, 143–44). No oral or written documentation is offered for this story; and, in any case, the circumstances would hardly allow for Bakhtin *not* to have admitted authorship. (Bakhtin's sentence was eventually changed to six years' internal exile, and his life thus saved.)

Finally, Clark and Holquist argue that examination of the texts themselves confirms Bakhtin's authorship. Their argument here depends on judgments of quality. According to Clark and Holquist, Medvedev's undisputed texts — that is, the ones they believe he really wrote, such as *In the Writer's Laboratory* — are of a much lower quality than *The Formal Method*. They also state that the texts that are genuinely Voloshinov's are, though better than Medvedev's undisputed texts, still not as good as the disputed Voloshinov texts. They conclude that Voloshinov, and especially Medvedev, were not intelligent enough to have written the texts they signed on their own, except, perhaps, for their poorest (and most Marxist) passages. So Shakespeare scholars used to argue that only the best passages of his plays were written by Shakespeare and that worse ones must have been written by someone else.

This argument assumes that a great writer must be consistently great, and a less great one consistently less great—an assumption it would be difficult to justify. Are Bakhtin's prefaces to Tolstoy, published in the present volume, as good as his study of Dostoevsky, published in the same year? Besides, if the argument were accepted, it could just as easily demonstrate that Voloshinov, rather than Bakhtin, wrote *The Formal Method*, because Voloshinov is also said to be intellectually superior to Medvedev. Above all, it must be noted that judgments about the quality of a work are profoundly disputable. We are persuaded by Wlad Godzich's observation in his foreword to the reprint of *The Formal Method:*

One must be wary of a phenomenon that seems to have grown quite strong in the Soviet Union in recent years: a veritable (though "unofficial") cult of Bakhtin, who thus becomes the recipient of all praise while the more questionable aspects of the works attributed to him are alleged to be the products of collaborators and name-lenders, especially when it comes to Marxist views. The rewriting of history is not the monopoly of state ideology in the Soviet Union today. (ix)

Proving Actions by Alleging Motives

In presenting their case, Clark and Holquist devote much of their attention to describing Bakhtin's motives for publishing under others' names. To us, this argument seems to put the cart before the horse. Of course, if it were shown that Bakhtin did write the works in question, one would want to know why he might have done so. But the fact that one can suggest possible motives for someone's having done something does not prove that he did it.

In the Soviet context, it is especially easy to discover possible motives, hidden meanings, and Byzantine strategies, because censorship, restrictions on publishing, and the fear of punishment are always a factor. As a certain kind of American critic can handle any passage that offers counterevidence to his interpretation by discovering "irony," so Slavists learn very early in their training to resort to the censor. And since original thinkers in Russia always do worry about the censor, this argument is always possible. But for that very reason, the argument is not sufficient, because it can in principle justify any interpretation of any text. Surely even in Russia people sometimes mean what they say.

In order to describe Bakhtin's motives, Clark and Holquist first need to answer a number of obvious objections to their account, some of which had already been raised and others of which were bound to occur. In 1929, *Marxism and the Philosophy of Language* appeared under Voloshinov's name; in the very same year, *Problems of Dostoevsky's Creative Art* was published under Bakhtin's name. How then can one argue that Bakhtin published under his friends' names because that was the only way he could get into print? Why would Bakhtin, who was a non-Marxist and a religious man (according to Clark and Holquist), labor to defend Marxism against its most powerful enemies?

To begin with, Clark and Holquist contend, Bakhtin was fond of "recherché jokes": "Bakhtin was himself a great lover of rascals and would have taken delight in pulling off so large-scale a hoax" (C&H, 151). In effect, Bakhtin was illustrating his own theory of "carnivalization." Paraphrasing a conversation with Vadim Kozhinov, one of Bakhtin's Soviet executors, Albert Wehrle endorses this explanation: "Vadim Kozhinov has observed that Bakhtin was associated with other people of the 'carnival' type. Perhaps the exchange of identities within the Bakhtin circle owed something to this carnival atmosphere, or at least was stimulated by Bakhtin's attraction to ambivalence, disguise, the 'unofficial,' and non-written popular tradition" (Wehrle, "Introduction" to *The Formal Method*, xxi).

Bakhtin's behavior, in short, is described as performing his theories. Elsewhere, Holquist has argued that pseudonymy was a way of dramatizing Bakhtin's lifelong concern with polyphony, dialogue, and the complexities of authorship.[41] Alternatively, Holquist argues that publishing Christian views in Marxist language was Bakhtin's way of dramatizing the incarnation.[42]

Of course, it is possible that such motives would have occurred to Bakhtin, if he did indeed publish under others' names. But as Titunik has observed, why then should the exchange of identities have been only in one direction?[43] If carnivalization was so characteristic of the Bakhtin group, then it is equally possible that *Problems of Dostoevsky's Creative Art* was written in whole or in part by Voloshinov. In any case, as Titunik observes, the concept of "carnival" had not yet appeared in any of Bakhtin's works at this time.[44]

Titunik also questions the implications of this account for Voloshinov's doctoral dissertation, which, according to Clark and Holquist, "was probably 'the problem of how to present reported speech' " (C&H, 110), that is, the very problem to which one-third of *Marxism and the Philosophy of Language* was devoted. If Voloshinov wrote his own dissertation, then surely he could have written the passages in *Marxism*. If Bakhtin wrote the dissertation, "then Baxtin and Vološinov perpetrated no mere 'hoax' but out-and-out fraud—again no mere laughing matter."[45]

As for the thesis that Bakhtin was dramatizing his concern with dialogue and incarnation by ascribing his works to others, Titunik objects that there is no necessary reason why someone would have to make scholarly works instances of their own theories ("The Bakhtin Problem," 94). The thesis, which seems to project current American critical practice onto Bakhtin, is suspiciously anachronistic. Moreover, this sort of false ascription of his work to others would not illustrate, but contradict, Bakhtin's key belief (stated in "Toward a Philosophy of the Act") that action must be ethical and "responsible." It will be recalled that for Bakhtin "signature" was a fundamental ethical act. And one might add that attributing books worked out in group discussion to a single person is a rather odd way to dramatize dialogue.

Are the Marxist Books Marxist?

One of the reasons that the authorship question matters is that it bears directly on the status of three books that have often been considered exemplars of sophisticated, nonreductive Marxist criticism. If Bakhtin was not a Marxist, and if Bakhtin wrote *Marxism and the Philosophy of Language, The Formal Method,* and *Freudianism,* then the Marxism of those books turns out to be mere "window dressing," as Clark and Holquist assert (C&H, 168). On the other hand, if Voloshinov and Medvedev were the real authors, albeit authors strongly influenced by Bakhtin, then the Marxism of the books may be taken seriously. The books become attempts to construct a sophisticated Marxist theory of culture. Rather than theology in code, they constitute alternatives to the rather unsophisticated Marxism prevalent in the Soviet Union at the time.[46]

In part, this argument depends on how one reads the disputed texts. "The Marxist aspects of *Freudianism,* which have been cited to prove that it was not written by Bakhtin, have been exaggerated," Clark and Holquist contend (C&H, 164). Regarding *Marxism and the Philosophy of Language,* Clark and Holquist assert that "the farther one reads in the book, the more the Marxist terminology fades from view" (C&H, 166). It does not fade from our view; we invite our readers to test theirs.

Clark and Holquist are committed to two views of Bakhtin's works that we believe are open to question. First, they argue that all of Bakhtin's key ideas were already present in his earliest writings (before 1924), after which he simply sought different ways to express or apply them; as Holquist puts it, Bakhtin's first work *"contains, in embryonic form, every major idea Bakhtin was to have for the rest of his long life"* ("The Politics of Representation," 171; italics in original). Second, they contend that Bakhtin's fundamental concerns were religious and that his works are a disguised theology. Because they characterize Bakhtin's early work as explicitly theological, the two contentions are closely linked. Their argument concerning the Marxism of the disputed texts is grounded in these premises.

To them, the question is why a "religious man," as they believe him to have been, would have allowed his ideas to be presented as a kind of Marxism, especially at a time when persecution of religion was at its height in Russia. In addition to the argument about "incarnation," they suggest that Bakhtin's version of religion was not inimical to Marxism, because his early neo-Kantian meditations on the relation of self to other were already "social" in character. But in this loose sense almost all cultural theories could be described as "social."

Clark and Holquist thus simultaneously maintain two premises: that the Marxism of the "pseudonymous" texts is mere window dressing, but that Bakhtin was nevertheless not hostile to Marxism. For example, they claim that the argument of the Dostoevsky book (or certain parts of it) "is in a general sense Marxist" (C&H, 154). As evidence, they cite a passage in which Bakhtin states that the polyphonic novel "could have been realized only in the capitalist epoch" because capitalism brought diverse and previously isolated social groups together and, of course, created an acute sense of individuality.[47] But one hardly has to be a Marxist even in a "general sense" to see a connection between the genre of the novel, the rise of the middle class, and concern for individual identity. In the West, the theme is a cliché of non-Marxist novel criticism, and in Russia it was a commonplace in non-Marxist Dostoevsky criticism. Clark and Holquist do not mention passages in the Dostoevsky book that are overtly critical of "dialectics."[48]

Clark and Holquist do mention the two texts of Bakhtin's that are overtly Marxist, the Tolstoy prefaces translated in the present volume. Wisely, they do not press the point. To just about all concerned, the Marxism of these essays does indeed seem like "window dressing" of some sort. It is as far from the sophisticated, flexible Marxism of the disputed texts as it is from the discursive openness of Bakhtin's other works. Clark and Holquist cite with approval (C&H, 377) an early version of the Shukman article included in the present volume, in which Shukman suggests that the Tolstoy prefaces may in fact be parodic.

The Debate Does Not Abate

In their 1986 reply to Titunik and Morson, Clark and Holquist not only went over some familiar ground but also made some new arguments, some of which Titunik seemed to have already anticipated.

First, Clark and Holquist concede that the "hearsay evidence" is provided by "witnesses with varying claims to direct knowledge and differing degrees of disinterestedness," and that it cannot stand on its own, although they also assert that it "cannot be dismissed out of hand."[49] They concede as well that the evidence of "the texts themselves" does not prove their case. They therefore present a new piece of evidence.

In their book, they claim that in addition to authoring works signed by Medvedev and Voloshinov, Bakhtin wrote an article published under the name of a third friend, I. I. Kanaev. Their book offers no evidence to support this assertion, and Titunik bypassed discussion of it: "One article by I. I. Kanaev is also attributed to Baxtin, but it is not a disputed text for the simple reason that only Clark and Holquist seem to know about it" ("The Baxtin Problem," 93). The article in question is Kanaev's "Contemporary Vitalism" (1926).

In brief, Clark and Holquist argue (1) that they have proof, which they cannot reveal, of Bakhtin's authorship of the Kanaev article and (2) that if Bakhtin wrote the Kanaev piece, he might well have written the Medvedev and Voloshinov works as well. In our view, the second statement does not follow from the first. In the Soviet context, as we noted, the censorship and the state control of publishing frequently produce complex scenarios. What is in question, however, is whether Bakhtin wrote Voloshinov's and Medvedev's works, not whether he ever shared in the Soviet practice of Byzantine publishing maneuvers.

To support the contention that Bakhtin wrote the vitalism essay, Clark and Holquist state that Kanaev himself "confirmed" Bakhtin's authorship of the article, although not to them personally (ACD, 96).[50] To explain why they cannot reveal to whom Kanaev credited Bakhtin's authorship, and why they cannot reveal certain other evidence about the authorship question, Clark and Holquist then mention the sensitivity of the issues involved, including Bakhtin's "Marxism" and "Christianity," and state that many people supplied them with information but asked not to be identified. In the Soviet context, such a situation is, of course, quite common.

One answer to this argument is already implicit in the Titunik essay to which Clark and Holquist reply. Titunik's central point is the responsibility of scholars to be skeptical, especially when information is impossible to verify and sources of information may not be disinterested. He also suggests that Clark and Holquist's evident enthusiasm for Bakhtin may have led them astray. Like a number of other commentators, Titunik discovers a strong element of "hagiography" in the Clark/Holquist biography. Its authors may have been convinced by their sources, but how are we to judge how skeptically those sources were evaluated or how precise were the questions asked?[51]

Titunik places special emphasis on the Clark/Holquist attempt to read Bakhtin's works as a kind of theology in code.[52] Whether or not Bakhtin was religious, it is quite possible to be religious without making all of one's writing a concealed theology. In particular, Titunik objects to the biography's characterization of Bakhtin's early works (which Clark and Holquist believe to be part of one large work to which they give the name "The Architectonics of Answerability"). The text on which Clark and Holquist concentrate, "Author and Hero," would appear from their characterization to be largely theological, but in fact "the 'Christological' passage of the fraction dealt with [in their account] — the key passage for the authors — is approximately a page and a half [out of 175]" ("The Baxtin Problem," 92). Moreover, the authors often do not distinguish their paraphrases of Bakhtin's ideas from their own "excurses and digressions" and so "it takes special acquaintance with the original text to discern what is and what is not paraphrase" ("The Baxtin Problem," 92). As this preface indicates, our own examination of the more recently published archival fragment "Toward a Philosophy of the Act" confirms Titunik's objections to the characterization of Bakhtin's early writing as primarily theological.

We also concur with one other point Titunik makes about these paraphrases. Titunik charges Clark and Holquist with a kind of biographical anachronism, that is, with paraphrasing the early manuscripts in terms of language and concepts not present in them but present in Bakhtin's later works — without indicating to the reader that later concepts are being invoked ("The Baxtin Problem," 93). The reader of the Clark/Holquist chapter on "The Architectonics" might well come away with the idea that "Author and Hero," "Toward a Philosophy of the Act," and "Art and Answerability" have lengthy discussions of dialogue similar to those in the Dostoevsky book and in "Discourse in the Novel." But that is not the case. We would add that the very use of the word "answerability" to translate *otvetstvennost'* (the Russian word for "responsibility," which contains the root word for answer or response) is itself a kind of anachronism, because it suggests that language and dialogue were central to Bakhtin's work at the time, but the available texts do not support that view.[53] The issue of anachronism is not crucial, of course, if one accepts Clark and Holquist's thesis that all of Bakhtin's later ideas are already present in the early texts; but that is itself one of the issues in dispute.

At the time Clark and Holquist made this "embryonic" assertion, they alone among Western scholars had access to "The Philosophy of the Act." (To date, none of these texts are available in English.) Titunik's central point is the possibility of interpreting texts in different ways, the consequent need for skepticism about unverifiable evidence, and the need to reassess conclusions when previously unavailable texts do at last appear. Readers of the present volume should keep in mind that our exegesis of "The Philosophy of the Act" reflects our view that Bakhtin underwent a genuine development in the course of his long career, and that the early texts do not contain all the important concepts of the later ones.

Nina Perlina raises a quite different objection to Clark and Holquist's attribution of "Contemporary Vitalism" to Bakhtin. It appears that the philosopher Nikolai Onufrievich Lossky (1870–1965), who was expelled from the Soviet Union in 1922, had published a brochure entitled *Contemporary Vitalism* shortly before his expulsion. Bakhtin was quite familiar with Lossky's work, to which he refers, very positively, in "Philosophy of the Act" ("Act," 92). "Including Lossky's brochure on Vitalism into the discussion of Bakhtin's vexing texts is like sowing the wind and reaping a whirlwind," Perlina observes. For the Kanaev (or Bakhtin) article "Contemporary Vitalism" repeats large sections of the Lossky brochure, which it would have been imprudent to mention (as the work of an exile) by 1926. Inverting Lossky's conclusions, Kanaev (or Bakhtin) managed "to drag several chunks of Lossky's writings, which had already stopped circulating in the country, through the machinery of Soviet censorship." Perlina comments: "Without denying the validity of Kanaev's statement that Bakhtin had published at least one text under his name, we still are not sure whether Bakhtin *had actually written the article.*" If Bakhtin "copied several parts of Lossky's brochure on Vitalism for his friend Kanaev," she asks, does that make Bakhtin the author? What precisely did Kanaev say when he admitted Bakhtin's authorship, and can he be trusted? The questions here are complex indeed, and, it would seem, derive from a situation quite different from the circumstances surrounding the Medvedev and Voloshinov books.[54] In any case, evidence about the Kanaev incident cannot go very far toward proving Bakhtin's authorship of *The Formal Method* and *Marxism and the Philosophy of Language.*

It will be recalled that Clark and Holquist concede that neither the anecdotal evidence nor the evidence of the texts themselves can demonstrate their claims. They then appear to claim that the Kanaev incident does demonstrate it. Since the Kanaev incident does not even concern the Voloshinov and Medvedev texts, it would seem that this new claim cannot rectify the deficiencies of the old ones. It is therefore hard to understand what basis there is for continuing to attribute the disputed texts to Bakhtin.

But why should the question matter?

What Is at Stake

The critics often invent authors: they select two dissimilar works — the *Tao Te Ching* and the *1001 Nights,* say — and attribute them to the same writer and then determine most scrupulously the psychology of this interesting *homme de lettres* . . .   —Borges, "Tlön, Uqbar, Orbis Tertius"[55]

Any thinker with original and challenging views is subject to degrees of misunderstanding, superficial readings, and careless appropriations of terminology. In Bakhtin's case, understanding has been impeded by delayed and inconsistent translations, by a lack of familiarity with the tradition of Russian critical and linguistic thought, and by the fact that comparatively few Americans can read his texts in the original. Add to these factors the charged Russian atmosphere from which the texts emerged and the charged American debates into which they were rapidly recruited, and it ceases to surprise us that his work has so often been read in disappointing ways. The debate over the disputed texts has added an extra and particularly obscuring layer to the already complex problem of interpreting his ideas.

As imperialist countries are often weakened, rather than strengthened, by territorial expansion, so imperialist biographers and interpreters, in our view, can harm the cause of understanding Bakhtin. More is not always better or stronger. The attribution to Bakhtin of works that Voloshinov and Medvedev signed seems to have obscured the meanings both of those studies and of Bakhtin's own works. Early attempts to present Bakhtin as a Marxist or a semiotician still affect large numbers of readers, who come to his texts with presuppositions that the texts themselves do not justify and often contradict. Alternatively, attempts to present the Marxism of Voloshinov's and Medvedev's works as "window dressing" lead to Byzantine reading strategies at the expense of real consideration of the import of those books. Confusion and diminution result, and the distinctive ideas of all three thinkers are lost in the attempt to treat them as one.

Voloshinov's and Medvedev's works are sincerely Marxist. In our view, they represent a particularly complex and rewarding form of Marxism, and are among the strongest works on language and literature of our century; that is especially true of *Marxism and the Philosophy of Language*. No disrespect is or should be incurred by the idea that Bakhtin did not write, but merely influenced, the books and articles of Voloshinov and Medvedev. The time has passed when the very mention of Bakhtin's name should evoke a talismanic aura.

Bakhtin was neither a Marxist nor a semiotician. Neither was he a Freudian or a Formalist. In his view — as the early manuscripts illustrate — all these approaches share the errors of "theoretism" in especially destructive ways. As we have seen, a fundamental tenet of Bakhtin's thought is that knowledge, to be genuine and valuable, does not have to be a system; neither does it have to describe its object as a system. On the contrary, the most important aspects of language, literature, ethics, the psyche, history, and culture are lost if one assumes that either there is a system or there is nothing. Bakhtin dedicated his intellectual life to finding a way around this mistaken belief. The description of him as a Marxist, a semiotician, a structuralist, or an adherent of any other -ism is therefore bound to result in a trivialization of his ideas.

In "Toward a Philosophy of the Act," Bakhtin accuses "theoretism" of "transcribing" events in such a way that they lose their "eventness." Later in his life, the concept of monologization replaced that of transcription: abstract systems, such as Marxist or Hegelian dialectics, remove the dialogue from dialogue, and monologize the world.

Bakhtin concedes that monologization and transcription have their legitimate uses. In the hard sciences, for instance, a researcher's interest may lie precisely in what is repeatable and statable as monologic propositions. Those who decipher dead, or even living, languages may be interested in what can be codified into a systematic grammar. But in most areas of the humanities, monologization destroys the essence of the object under investigation.

Evidently, Voloshinov and Medvedev did not share this hostility to systems of whatever sort. They appear to have taken some of Bakhtin's specific concepts and shown that they could be integrated into systems. Voloshinov described language as dialogic, but he incorporated this description into a Marxist, dialectical system. The fact that he effected this change so well indicates that Bakhtin's specific concepts are not necessarily dependent on the overall framework they were designed to serve. Voloshinov and Medvedev produced remarkable books about literature and language using Bakhtin's ideas. But the books as wholes, we suggest, are fundamentally alien to Bakhtin in their informing vision and in their very spirit. They are excellent books, but they are not Bakhtin's. They are highly sophisticated *monologizations* of Bakhtin's thought.

Oddly enough, defenders of the great proponent of dialogue have themselves monologized a deeply dialogic relationship. As Bakhtin often observed, real dialogue is destroyed by the attempt to make a "synthesis" (dialectical or otherwise) that conflates distinct voices. We believe that the relations among Bakhtin, Voloshinov, and Medvedev were genuinely dialogic.[56] Their readers can only be the poorer for losing the chance to choose among them.

It is hard to tell just how the attribution of the disputed texts to Bakhtin has obscured readers' sense of Bakhtin's own intellectual development. But it is clear that the resulting distortions are bound to be considerable. The attempt to create an image of a thinker who in the course of the 1920s wrote such disparate work as "Toward a Philosophy of the Act," "Author and Hero," *Problems of Dostoevsky's Creative Art, Marxism and the Philosophy of Language, Freudianism: A Critique* and *The Formal Method: A Critical Introduction to Sociological Poetics* could only make the outlines of Bakhtin's own concerns more imprecise and opaque. If it came to be believed that Chekhov had written Gorky's works, would our sense of Chekhov (or for that matter of Gorky) be more precise? In place of understanding, we have been given a Borgesian parable masquerading as reality.

Once one begins to think in terms of dialogue and influence, rather than identity and pseudonymy, other possibilities come into view. If Bakhtin influenced Voloshinov and Medvedev, why could they not have influenced him? In our view, that is what very likely happened. Bakhtin's early writings were emphatically *not* sociological, except in the trivial sense in which every meditation on selves and others is sociological. But his writings of the 1930s and 1940s (for example, "Discourse in the Novel" and the book on Rabelais) were deeply sociological. Is it not possible that the encounter with strong Marxist renditions of his own ideas provoked the change? Faced with the challenge of a sophisticated sociological poetics, based to a considerable extent on Bakhtin's own ideas, Bakhtin appears to have responded with theories of language and literature that were sociological without being Marxist; he answered the challenge of his friends with his sociology without theoretism. It is largely for this reason that Bakhtin came to show us that Marxism, for all its help in prodding thinkers to consider sociological questions, falls short in answering them.

PART THREE: THE PLAN OF THE VOLUME

Bakhtin's reception in the United States began with a great deal of uncritical hero worship, followed by rather mechanical applications and, at present, by considerable confusion. The contributors to the present volume all attempt to confront this confusion squarely by asking how, and under what constraints, Bakhtin's ideas can be used creatively. As "extenders" of Bakhtin's ideas, they often disagree with each other, in part because their own theoretical stands and concerns differ, and in part because they extend different Bakhtinian concepts. We have therefore organized their contributions in pairs.

Gary Saul Morson's essay on theory of parody describes parody as a specific type of dialogic utterance. Parody is one of many ways in which utterances, whether literary or nonliterary, verbal or nonverbal, situate themselves with respect to other utterances and with respect to their audiences. He describes parody "not simply as an interaction of two speech acts, but as *an interaction designed to be heard and interpreted by a third person* (or second 'second person'), whose own process of active reception is anticipated and directed." This approach permits Morson to discuss a number of questions of more general concern: the relation of parody to other "double-voiced" utterances, such as stylization, imitation, plagiarism, forgery, "false parodies," and "preemptive self-parodies"; the ways in which audiences may in effect "re-author" texts in the course of "actively receiving them"; and the role of literary history in changing the "dialogizing background" against which a given utterance is understood or identified as parodic.

Morson's discussion is directed explicitly at all formalist approaches to parody, which, by their very nature, locate the parodic in a specific set of textual features, elements, or devices. "We cannot parody words, syntax, or any other element . . . out of which utterances are made, but only utterances themselves — that is, speech acts as discourse in a context." Morson contends that even if parodies often use certain devices, no devices are essential to parody. Rather, what is essential to parody is function and a relation to context and to the audience. Noting that parodies may even be verbally identical to their targets, Morson observes that "parody aims to discredit an act of speech by redirecting attention from its text to a compromising context. That is, while the parodist's ironic quotation marks frame the linguistic form of the original utterance, they also direct attention to the *occasion* (more accurately, the parodist's version of the occasion) *of its uttering*." Parody is "the etiology of utterance." It follows that parodies may be directed not only at "texts" and "authors" but at readers of a text; "the etiology of utterance includes the pathology of reception." It also follows that utterances claiming transhistorical authority are especially vulnerable to parody: "denial of history is invitation to parody."

Morson extends his observations to a discussion of parodic genres (or antigenres) and to a class of texts he calls "metaparodic." Reserving the term "parody" for those texts where it is clear which of two views discredits the other, Morson then considers utterances where target and parody, parody and parody of parody, reverse places in a potentially endless succession. Metaparodic works and genres constitute a special type of "threshold" utterance, that is, utterances designed (or assumed to be designed) to be read according to contradictory sets of interpretive conventions.

Linda Hutcheon's discussion of parody takes issue with Morson's in a number of interesting ways. Grounding her discussion in a consideration of modern literature and art, Hutcheon objects to the characterization of parody as an utterance *discrediting* its target. According to Hutcheon, such a view in effect identifies parody with satire, an identification that is warranted only for certain historical periods.[57] But parody need not be satiric, it can even be "loving." We can appreciate the range of parodic modes if we regard it as "a form of imitation characterized by ironic inversion, not always at the expense of the parodied text." Alternatively, Hutcheon describes parody as "repetition with critical distance, which marks difference rather than similarity." In a Bakhtinian spirit, she writes that parody involves "a productive-creative approach to tradition."

Hutcheon's remarkable analytic strategy is deliberately to define parody in a broad and fluid way, so that she can then examine the specific forms of parody in particular cultures and periods. The breadth of the definition is dictated by a fundamentally historical outlook. According to Hutcheon, different forms of parody derive from different cultural attitudes; Hutcheon provides a number of examples that link a period's predominant parodies with its attitudes to tradition. She argues that although there are common denominators to parodies of different ages, "there are probably no trans-historical definitions of parody possible."

Hutcheon's historical orientation also leads to a sensitive probing of Bakhtin's notion of carnivalization as a parodic form. Using Bakhtin's paradoxical concept of carnival as an authorized transgression, Hutcheon explores the ways in which parody may be both conservative and revolutionary, depending on whether the emphasis is on the norms that are acknowledged in the very act of transgression or on the transgression itself. Parody "bifurcates" from author to author and age to age. "In Bakhtin's terminology, parody can be centripetal — that is, a homogenizing, hierarchizing influence. But it can also be a centrifugal, de-normalizing one. And I think it is the paradox of its authorized transgression that is at the root of this apparent contradiction."

The next two essays focus on the problem of "dialogism and absence" and, in a broader sense, on fundamental differences between deconstructive poetics and Bakhtinian dialogics. Paul de Man considers only one text of Bakhtin, a section of "Discourse in the Novel," and bases his views on mediations by Holquist and Tzvetan Todorov, but nevertheless manages to engage key problems of Bakhtin's theories in a profound way. Half an "extension" of and half a "challenge" to Bakhtin's ideas, de Man's essay draws a dotted line from two Bakhtinian premises until they meet in what may be a paradox, a synthesis, a dialogue — or a contradiction.

De Man shrewdly observes that Bakhtin's arsenal of techniques for analyzing the novel is often appreciated as "a formal method by which to conquer formalism itself." According to de Man, Bakhtin sometimes treats dialogue as a largely "formal" category, in the sense that it lends itself to use by " 'formalist' practitioners of American close reading." And yet, at other times, dialogue takes us beyond formalism, to a recognition of genuine otherness. Obviously relying on Todorov's study, de Man refers to Bakhtin's concept of exotopy, which is Todorov's rendition of the concept we prefer to translate as "outsideness." In this model, "the formal study of literary texts becomes important because it leads from intralinguistic to intracultural relationships." Bakhtin therefore appeals to those weary formalists and close readers who would like to move "beyond form by way of formal analysis" into "the practical sphere of ethics and politics." De Man then asks whether this move, however appealing it may be, is legitimate. The question whether Bakhtin actually effects "a passage from dialogism to dialogue," or whether that passage remains only a desire, must in his view be central to the interpretation of Bakhtin.

De Man also briefly alludes to another key argument in "Discourse in the Novel": the distinction between the dialogic language of novels and the monologic language of poetic tropes. Ultimately, this distinction implies a further one between the tropological and the dialogic analysis of texts, that is, between poetics and dialogics. To situate de Man's brief and dense comments, it would be useful to consider Bakhtin's contrast between the poetic and the novelistic (or dialogic) in "Discourse in the Novel."

Bakhtin uses the term "dialogue" in two distinct senses. In one, *all* of language is said to be necessarily dialogic: it orients itself toward a listener, whose active response shapes the utterance from the outset. "Outsideness" always lies within the utterance, not just without. In this sense of dialogue, there can be no nondialogic language. The second sense of "dialogue" does admit of both dialogic and nondialogic (or monologic) uses of language. Some utterances exploit the dialogic resources of language to the fullest, and derive their power and interest by dramatizing as complexly as possible the play of voices and contexts enabling speech or writing as social acts. In Bakhtin's view, the nineteenth-century novel, and especially the novels of Dostoevsky, are the prime exemplars of this kind of maximal dialogism. But other forms of speech and writing derive their interest and power from the attempt, so far as possible, to "forget" the multiple dialogizing qualifications beyond the utterance — to speak, as it were, from outside the historical and social realm in a "utopian" language. According to Bakhtin, this purifying impulse characterizes lyric poetry (or at least the ideal pole he posits for lyric poetry).

According to Bakhtin, "the poet is a poet insofar as he accepts the idea of a unitary and singular language and a unitary, mono-logically sealed-off utterance";[58] this view of language is given in the very conventions of lyrical genres. The creative work of the poet is to "strip away" the traces of daily, prosaic usage and contexts: "Everything that enters the [poetic] work must immerse itself in Lethe, and forget its previous life in any other contexts; language may remember only its life in poetic contexts (in such contexts, however, even concrete reminiscences are possible)" ("Discourse," 297). Bakhtin's point is *not* that poetic language is less rich than novelistic language; rather, he wants to say that its richness is of a different kind. The richness and interest of poetic language, its po-lysemy and complex ambiguity, are the wealth of the trope; but the novelist derives complexity from the dialogic word. The treasure house of language supplies the poet with his resources; the passing speech of a passing world supplies the novelist, whose language is still "warm" from its daily use. Most important, the complexities of poetry lie within a single voice; in prose, the complexity can only be found *among* voices. Bakhtin's preference for the novel derives not from a sense that novels are somehow intrinsically richer, but rather from his preference for the prosaic values it embodies.

Of course, even the attempt to transcend daily social life is itself a social gesture, and therefore poetry is, in that sense, social. But "poetic forms reflect lengthier social processes . . . requiring centuries to unfold," whereas novelistic discourse "registers with extreme subtlety the tiniest shifts and oscillations of the social atmosphere" ("Discourse," 300). Similarly, the poet encounters the dialogism of language in the very act of transcending it; but in poetry, the "trajectory" of transcendence is left "in the slag heap of the creative process which is then cleared away (as scaffolding is cleared away once construction is finished), so that the finished work may rise as unitary speech, one co-extensive with its object, as if it were speech about an 'Edenic' world" ("Discourse," 331). At times, we may sense this process of attempted transcendence, which can never be *fully* achieved, and thus we may "experience a profound and conscious tension through which the unitary and

poetic language of a work rises from the heteroglot and language-
diverse chaos of the literary language contemporary to it" ("Discourse," 298). The numerous qualifications and many tropes that
Bakhtin must invoke to explain his idea allow de Man to ask whether
the distinction between dialogue and trope is itself a trope. If it is,
then "dialogue" may itself be a trope, which would mean there are
no significant differences between dialogic and tropic relations. And
that in turn would mean that dialogue cannot take us "beyond form
by way of formal analysis"; it must remain just another set of
reading practices.

Mathew Roberts's "Poetics Hermeneutics Dialogics: Bakhtin
and Paul de Man" situates the debate between these two thinkers
within their respective intellectual careers. Where de Man at one
moment of his life engages with one text of Bakhtin, Roberts describes the evolution of each thinker's recurring concerns of self and
other, text and reader, language and knowledge, and locates these
problems within a broader context of debate, including Heidegger
and modern poststructuralism generally. The wider debate he outlines by "drawing dotted lines" (Bakhtin's phrase) between de Man's
and Bakhtin's works of different periods is immensely complex.
Indeed, Roberts observes that "if the preceding exposition has been
of any value, it has been in demonstrating that the 'confrontation'
of these two theorists cannot occur around a problematic or conceptual opposition immanent to either."

Roberts's contribution is perhaps the most thoughtful study we
have to date of the relation of Bakhtin's texts of the 1930s with his
earliest (and latest) writings. His discussion of "outsideness" (he
prefers the rendition "extralocality" as de Man prefers "exotopy")
leads to the striking conclusion that the "novelocentricity" of "Discourse in the Novel" is in fact aberrant within the context of Bakhtin's thought as a whole. As he discusses the relation of "poetics"
and "hermeneutics," "trope" and "dialogue" in de Man and Bakhtin, he indicates that the "rather extreme emphasis on 'novelization'
as the source of all linguistic and literary creativity" was "a position
quite absent from Bakhtin's first textual models, and from which
he appears to retreat in his work of the 1970s." Indeed, he concludes, "Discourse in the Novel," when read in the broader context
of Bakhtin's development, becomes quite a different text, and not
the privileged summation of all his work. "If Bakhtin later retrieves

poetic discourse from its exile in this monologic realm," Roberts observes, "it is due to his belated re-cognition that *no* aesthetically creative discourse can do without the 'other logic' of extralocality [outsideness]."

The second half of the present volume begins with a pair of essays on Bakhtin's analyses of Tolstoy. Bakhtin's analyses are interesting for reasons other than profundity; it seems to be generally agreed that Bakhtin was at his least persuasive in discussing Tolstoy. We emphasize this point, because in presenting the first English translation of these prefaces to Tolstoy, we do *not* mean to suggest that these texts represent some provocative, "undiscovered" Bakhtin. On the contrary, the interest of these two essays on Tolstoy lies primarily in what is weak and wrong with them.

In these essays, Bakhtin characterizes Tolstoy's earliest dramatic works as completely unsuccessful, but claims that the nature of their failure is important for understanding Tolstoy's attitudes and cast of mind. We may say the same thing about these very prefaces. One may ask, indeed, why Bakhtin should have been so poor a reader of Tolstoy, and what that poverty indicates about his style of thought and the fundamental concerns of his intellectual life.

Ann Shukman's essay raises a number of important questions about Bakhtin's views. She begins by examining contrasting formulations, in the Tolstoy prefaces and in the contemporaneous Dostoevsky book, about the relation of a work of art to the society in which it arose. To set her comments in a broader framework, it would be useful to consider in more detail the arguments of the Dostoevsky book.

Chapter 1 of the 1929 Dostoevsky book consistently rejects Marxist (and Hegelian) interpretations of Dostoevsky's work as hopelessly reductive and distorting. Bakhtin argues at length against attempts to see Dostoevskian polyphony as some sort of dialectic arising out of the contradictions of capitalism.[59] To begin with, dialectics takes diversity and turns it into singular contradictions, which then may generate a synthesis; but Dostoevsky sensed keenly the multiplicity of forces and voices, some contradictory to each other (in diverse ways), others largely unrelated to each other, and described this multiplicity in "the cross section of a single moment" (PTD, 44). Dostoevsky's world (the world he described and the world in which he actually lived) was not "contradictory" in the Hegelian or Marxist sense, but was "profoundly *pluralistic*" (PTD, 41–42; italics Bakhtin's).[60]

Even worse, according to Bakhtin, the Marxist approach misconceives the ways in which society does influence a work. In his Tolstoy prefaces, Bakhtin provides a sample of the very kind of Marxist criticism the Dostoevsky book rejects. At one point in those prefaces, Bakhtin writes: "Tolstoy's creative output, like that of any other artist, was entirely determined, of course, by his epoch and by the historical arrangement of social and class forces in his epoch."

In the second edition of the Dostoevsky book, Bakhtin responded to a review of his first edition by Anatoly Lunacharsky, who served as People's Commissar of Education from 1917 to 1929 and who interpreted Bakhtin's views in Marxist terms. Bakhtin's reply to Lunacharsky is, in effect, also a reply to the position taken in his own Tolstoy prefaces. Bakhtin insists that epochs make artistic works possible, but in no sense is a work wholly determined by epoch and class. The contradictions of Dostoevsky's society were the "optimal conditions" (PDP, 35) for the creation of polyphony, just as Dostoevsky's personality was also an optimal condition. But further than that Bakhtin will not go. "New forms of artistic visualization prepare themselves over centuries; a given epoch can do no more than create optimal conditions for the final ripening and realization of this form. . . . A poetics cannot, of course, be divorced from social and historical analyses, but neither can it be dissolved in them" (PDP, 36).

If one does dissolve poetics into sociology, then one is likely to misperceive the value of great artworks. One may make them into mere documents of their times or reduce them to the class origin or social values that putatively gave them birth, both of which would be impoverishments. Bakhtin here approaches a problem that has perplexed sociological treatments of art from Marx to the present. Both Dostoevsky's epoch and his personality have long since faded into the past, Bakhtin observes, "but the new structural principle, *discovered* under these conditions, retains and will continue to retain its artistic significance under the completely different conditions of subsequent epochs" (PDP, 35). Italicizing the word "*discovered*," Bakhtin indicates a relation of work to social conditions that is far weaker than "determination." Emphasizing the future life of a discovery, however and whenever made, Bakhtin alludes to his favorite concept of potential.

Shukman's essay triangulates Bakhtin's views in the Dostoevsky book, in the Tolstoy prefaces, and in his religious activities to raise perplexing questions about evident contradictions. Those questions are hard to resolve, especially because the works in question were written or published very close together. What are we to say about Bakhtin's reference in the Tolstoy prefaces to "kulak-bloodsuckers," a term that Bakhtin applies anachronistically to Tolstoy's time, and which was beginning to accumulate the ominous resonance of agricultural collectivization, during which millions of peasants were to be starved, shot, or exiled? Was the anachronistic usage possibly part of a broader irony on Bakhtin's part? At times, Shukman argues, Bakhtin's Tolstoy prefaces seem to be self-parodies, and his comments on Tolstoy's themes double-voiced words "on the great social experiment that he saw sliding into violence and repression." Or is this reading too clever?

Caryl Emerson's essay explores the ramifications of Bakhtin's response to Tolstoy in the broader context of Bakhtin's career, during which he returned to the "Tolstoy problem" several times. In establishing the opposition of Dostoevsky and Tolstoy, Bakhtin produced examples of a favorite genre of Russian criticism, the description of these two writers as representative of radically opposed visions of the world. Just as thinkers may be classed as either Platonists or Aristotelians, so Russian critics (and foreign critics of Russian literature) have divided them into Dostoevskians and Tolstoyans.

Bakhtin clearly favored Dostoevsky, and used Tolstoy as a sort of foil. For this reason, Emerson observes, "Bakhtin is not a particularly good reader of Tolstoy." He was concerned not with interpreting Tolstoy's works, but with constructing an image of a specific authorial position. This concern was in keeping with Bakhtin's tendency to discuss less the literary work as a whole than "the creative force, the generic impulse that a novelist or a novel embodies."

For Bakhtin, Tolstoy is the distilled essence of monologism, of the "authoritative word" that cannot be engaged in dialogue. He is the poet of death, not of unfinalized life; the teacher rather than the interlocutor; the ideologue of loneliness and empathy but not of "live entering." By contrast, it was Dostoevsky who embodied one of Bakhtin's most cherished and most challenging insights: the image of "a unified truth that requires a multiplicity of consciousness, one that could not in principle be fitted within the boundaries of a single consciousness." Tolstoyan truth is a proposition, sufficient to itself; Dostoevsky's is an endless and endlessly enriching exchange.

At the close of her essay, Emerson suggests that Bakhtin passed up the chance to investigate Tolstoy on his own terms, and thus was not open to the possibility that Tolstoy, rather than Dostoevsky, was closer to Bakhtin's own views. After all, it was Dostoevsky, not Tolstoy, who wrote utopian and apocalyptic tracts predicting and advocating the imminent end of all contradictions and therefore of all unfinalizability. By contrast, Tolstoy always insisted that neither personalities nor history can ever be wholes of any kind, that the world will ever be open, and that contingency and individual agency always play a role.

The last two essays represent the most radical challenges to Bakhtin, although they still operate within an essentially Bakhtinian framework. In his study of Joseph Conrad, Aaron Fogel takes seriously Bakhtin's description of language as dialogic and of the novel as a maximally dialogic form, but he challenges Bakhtin's implicit image of dialogue itself. What if the defining instance of dialogue is not the free exchange of ideas in a mutually enriching and unpredictable interaction, but a sadistic "coercion to speak" under interrogation? In the beginning was the Inquisition. Perhaps "the ideal speech situation" involves not benevolent, voluntary exchange, but punishment, the *extraction* of answers; every time we speak, perhaps, the torture chamber haunts our discourse. Coercion to speak "seems the desublimated norm of human dialogue, the worst example of a general condition . . . the pattern of most (if not all) dialogic relations — including some that could be regarded as partly good." One might contrast this picture of dialogue with the ones Emerson discusses.

With Conrad's novels as his examples, Fogel explores the unexpected ramification of a seemingly obvious fact, that most speech is defined by a structure of *in*equalities inimical to dialogue as Bakhtin idealizes it. In Conrad, Fogel writes, "communication itself is by nature more coercive and disproportionate than we think when we sentimentalize terms like *dialogue* and *communication*." One may even develop a typology of coerced discursive forms. Fogel offers the category of Oedipal discourse — in the Sophoclean, rather than Freudian sense — which dares to *risk* dialogue, and which can destroy the interrogator rather than the interrogated. Perhaps, he suggests, the relation of author to hero in a literary work (which Bakhtin described in his early essay "Author and Hero" and in the Dostoevsky book) should be imagined in terms of the coercive typology. "When we think of 'dialogue' in general terms," Fogel concludes, "we must not sentimentally ignore force and danger." The "Oedipus dialogue complex" in literature and in reality has been underestimated.[61]

Fogel is probably right that Bakhtin did not address with sufficient care the problem of coercive and unequal dialogues, but Bakhtin did not entirely overlook it. In his "Notes of 1970–71," he asks us to remember the kind of "questions . . . that change the consciousness of the individual being questioned" (SG, 136), a phrase with an ominous ring in the Soviet context. He observes as well that the sphere of true (which is to say truly open) dialogue is easy to destroy; that all sorts of speech genres (threats, commands, prohibitions) hostile to dialogue fill our lives; and that the whole realm of rhetoric is inherently antagonistic to dialogue.[62] "[The dialogic] sphere is very fragile and easily destroyed (the slightest violence is sufficient, references to authority, and so forth)" ("Notes," SG, 150).

Michael André Bernstein's essay begins where Fogel's leaves off, in effect constituting a dialogic extension of it. Acknowledging the strength of Fogel's objections to Bakhtin, Bernstein contends that they do not go far enough. Proofs that most dialogue is not (properly) dialogic "might be sufficient to restrain some of the more exuberant affirmations of Bakhtinian dialogism, but they do not touch the future-directed longing we feel for a time when genuine, unconstrained dialogues will constitute the norm of our relationships." Fogel recharacterizes reality, but does not appear to challenge the ideal. But what if, as Bernstein argues, dialogue even at its best has a dark side and "is not always just clement and life-enhancing"; what if "the resonance of multiple voices may be as much a threat as a sustaining chorale"? What if the shadow of polyphonic dialogue extends across the cacophonous rantings of the madhouse, or the underground?

Bernstein turns Bakhtin's favorite texts, the novels of Dostoevsky, against him. Exploring the complex genealogy of *ressentiment* and the characteristically modern "crisis of citation," Bernstein interrogates Bakhtin's unquestioned valuation of the new, the original, the authentic. What the logic of the underground really demonstrates is the futility of those values. "As long as one desires an original, authentic consciousness and voice, as long, that is, as the fact of living a belated and already scripted existence is seen as the ultimate wound, making any claim to personal dignity derisory, *ressentiment* must remain consciousness's dominant emotion, structuring the narratives one lives, the narratives one tells, and ultimately, the narratives in which one figures as one more increasingly sorry character." Bakhtin himself describes all utterances as responding to "an already spoken about" world with already inhabited words; does not his theory of language implicitly challenge his values?

A deeply if unconventionally moral perspective informs Bernstein's intricate argument, as indicated, first of all, by his choice of literary texts—Céline, the underground man, the Devil in *Karamazov*—and in the reasons for his wariness of "originality." The more it becomes evident that the world is a tissue of citations, the more likely it is that the cult of originality will lead to a cult of the monstrous. He cites Céline's novels, and Nazi collaborationism, "as a reminder of how terrifying the power of an individual's *ressentiment* can be when it encounters a historical force based upon and dedicated to the unleashing of that emotion." To be sure, he concludes, Bakhtinian dialogue "offers part of the solution to the crisis of reminiscence, iteration, and hysteria," but "it is equally, as novels like Dostoevsky's or Céline's make only too clear, part of the problem as well."

Bakhtin has provoked, and continues to provoke, responses that enrich his most cherished concepts while still challenging them. The drawing of "dotted lines," the development of potential, has only just begun. Or, as Bakhtin himself observed in his notes for reworking the Dostoevsky book, "The person has departed, having spoken his word, but the word itself remains in the open-ended dialogue" (PDP, 300).

Extensions

A ·

THEORY OF PARODY

Gary Saul Morson

Parody, History, and Metaparody

PART ONE: WHAT IS PARODY?

Parody and Intertextuality

The functions of parody as a literary phenomenon are illuminated by the fact that parody is not only a literary phenomenon. There are pictorial as well as verbal parodies, and various social or institutional aspects of the artistic "environment"[1] may also become parodic targets. The dadaists and the Russian Serapion Brothers, for instance, parodied not only artistic works but also artistic movements, their mock manifestos and self-conscious exhibitions focusing irony on both the pretension of artists and the conventional responses of audiences. Moreover, parody is not limited to the arts, but can be found—under the names of "mimicry," "mockery," "spoofing," "doing a takeoff," and so forth—in the most diverse forms and most various contexts of everyday life. Indeed, it appears that any symbolic act, whether artistic or nonartistic, verbal or nonverbal, can become the object of parody. The converse is also true: when we parody someone's behavior, we are attributing symbolic significance to it. Thus, an important social function of mimicry (which may be regarded as a form of nonverbal parody) is to reveal the covert semiotic value of apparently unmotivated actions. That is, in mimicry we make the usually subliminal and peripheral world of gestures and mannerisms the center of our attention, and so render a usually unacknowledged channel of communication available for scrutiny. Literary parody is, in short, a special form of a more general communicative possibility, and many aspects of its nature and function are revealed when we begin to ask certain questions suggested by its more general communicative status: Under what circumstances do we engage (or refrain from engaging) in parody, and when do we respond (or fail to respond) to others' parodies? What functions does parody serve for the parodist, and what relation is implicitly set up between the parodist and his or her audience? How does parody resemble and differ from other types of utterances directed at the utterance or utterances of another speaker?

The work of Bakhtin and his close associate V. N. Voloshinov on intertextuality (or, to use Bakhtin's term, 'metalinguistics') offers a good starting point for answering these questions.[2] I should therefore like to summarize their approach to intertextuality before (1) identifying the class of texts that I shall call parodies and (2) describing those texts' essential methodology, by which I mean the ways in which a parody subverts its target and the relationship it establishes between the parodist and his or her audience.

Concerned with developing a sociology of language and literature, Bakhtin and Voloshinov considered the relation of utterances to their "extraverbal and verbal (i.e., made up of other utterances) milieu" and, especially, the "*active relation* of one message to another" (*Marxism*, 96, 116). Unlike some of their Formalist predecessors, they were interested not so much in how utterances are interpreted with reference to the transcontextual "system" of the language, but in how they function as components of the ongoing stream of communication. In their view, interpretation is not a matter of passive "decoding," but rather of an active and complicated process of orientation of a potential speaker to a previous speaker. That process involves selection, evaluation, the supplying of unstated premises, the invocation of social rules signaled by contextual cues, and, finally, the formulation, at least in inner speech, of a reply — a reply which is, in turn, constructed in anticipation of a similar process of active reception. For Voloshinov, the forms of reported speech (direct discourse, indirect discourse, and "quasi-direct discourse") and, for Bakhtin, parody and stylization, were, in effect, documents of that process of active reception, documents that could be used to formulate a typology of how utterances interact. Rather than viewing parody as a particular literary genre, or as a form of satire, or a special type of comedy, therefore, Bakhtin describes it in terms of the relation of any utterance, whether literary or nonliterary, to the context of its origin and reception.

For Bakhtin, parody and stylization are types of what he calls "double-voiced words," or utterances that are designed to be interpreted as the expression of two speakers. The author of a double-voiced word appropriates the utterance of another *as* the utterance of another and uses it "for his own purposes by inserting a new semantic orientation into a word which already has — and retains — its own orientation" (*PDP*, 156). The audience of a double-voiced word is therefore meant to hear both a version of the original utterance as the embodiment of its speaker's point of view (or "semantic position") *and* the second speaker's evaluation of that utterance from a different point of view. I find it helpful to picture a double-voiced word as a special sort of palimpsest in which the uppermost inscription is a commentary on the one beneath it, which the reader (or audience) can know only by reading through the commentary that obscures in the very process of evaluating. The distinction between double-voiced words, such as parody and stylization, and their closest single-voiced relatives, such as imitation (in the narrowest sense), is, according to Bakhtin, that in imitation the two voices are intended to merge completely so that only one is heard. Unfortunately, Bakhtin does not consider a range of intertextual utterances that his model would be well equipped to describe. For instance, imitation in the broader sense of a free adaptation of another text (e.g., Dr. Johnson's "Vanity of Human Wishes" as an imitation of the tenth satire of Juvenal) could be classed as a special type of double-voiced word, probably lying between parody and stylization.[3] Bakhtin's model might also be extended to utterances in which the audience is deliberately misled about the text's voicing. Plagiarism, for instance, denies the fact of an original speaker by attributing the utterance entirely to the second speaker; forgery misrepresents a doubleness as a singularity by denying the second speaker and attributing the utterance falsely to the "first." A consideration of plagiarism and forgery is helpful for stressing an important point about all intertextual utterances: namely, that they are best described not simply as an interaction of two speech acts, but as *an interaction designed to be heard and interpreted by a third person* (or second "second person"), whose own process of active reception is anticipated and directed. For this reason, successful forgers do not imitate an original as *they* perceive it, but rather the way such an original is likely to appear *to their intended victims,* perhaps subtly exaggerating what the latter are likely to regard as the original's most characteristic features and hence as the marks of its authenticity. Considered purely in terms of formal features, therefore, a forgery may sometimes resemble a parody, the difference lying in their anticipated reception or intended effect. One man's forgery may be another man's parody (and vice versa). Because both parody and forgery are constructed to foreground aspects of the original regarded as most characteristic, they may, indeed, serve as valuable documents for a history of perception and interpretation. That is, critics of one period may wonder how critics of another could have been deceived by an "obvious" forgery; and historians of art may take the earlier critics' *de*ception as evidence for their *per*ception of the original. The success of Ossian may be indicative of how Macpherson's contemporaries read Homer.

In Bakhtin's formulation, the difference between stylization and parody is to be found in the different relation that obtains in each between the first utterance and the second. In parody, the two utterances are antithetical, in stylization corroborative. "Stylization stylizes another style in the direction of that style's own tasks" (*PDP,* 160), Bakhtin observes. "The body of devices of another person's speech is important to the stylizer precisely as the expression of a particular point of view" (*PDP,* 157) with which the stylizer, though maintaining independence from the predecessor, largely agrees. Nevertheless, the very fact that the original utterance is subject to evaluation at all makes it inevitable that "a slight shadow of objectivization" (*PDP,* 157) is cast over it. In becoming characteristic of someone's particular point of view, it becomes conditional; instead of being simply asserted, it is defended and hence implicitly in need of defense. It is perhaps for this reason that cultures often protect their sacred texts from stylization — and from all other forms of dialogue — by recording them in an alien script or a dead language: there are some utterances with which we do not have the right to agree.

A parodic utterance is one of open disagreement. The second utterance represents the first in order to discredit it, and so introduces a "semantic direction" which subverts that of the original. In this way the parodied utterance "becomes the arena of conflict between two voices. . . . the voices here are not only detached and distanced, they are hostilely counterposed" (*PDP*, 160) — counterposed, moreover, with the second voice clearly representing a higher "semantic authority" than the first. The audience of the conflict knows for sure with whom it is expected to agree.

Criteria

We may now identify the class of texts to be called parodies. To be what I refer to as a parody, a text or utterance must satisfy *each* of the following three criteria: (1) It must evoke or indicate another utterance, which I will allude to henceforth as its "target," "object," or the "original utterance"; (2) it must be, in some respect, antithetical to its target; and (3) the fact that it is intended by its author to have higher semantic authority than the original must be clear.[4]

1) If the first criterion is not satisfied (i.e., if the audience sees no indication of a second utterance), the text will be taken as "single-voiced" and hence not as a parody. Sometimes this means mistaking an intended parody for its object, a misidentification that is especially likely to occur when the audience is remote from, and so unaware of, the original utterance. The parodies of alien cultures are particularly likely to go unrecognized, or, when they are recognized by a few who are well acquainted with that culture, to be difficult to translate or present to a broader audience. It is possible, indeed, that some of our evidence of past or remote cultures consists of parodies of what we take it to be.

If the authors of parodies anticipate the passing of interest in, or knowledge of, their dialogue with their targets, they may design their texts to be of interest on other grounds as well. In this case, the identification of the text as single-voiced will not be a misidentification of the author's intentions, but simply a partial appreciation of them. For most Western readers, *Notes from Underground,* which was understood by its original readers as a parody of Chernyshevsky's utopian narrative *What Is to Be Done?,* functions, as it was probably designed to function, apart from its unfamiliar target. It is also possible for a parodied text to survive and function primarily as the object of a parody that was itself designed or discovered to be meaningful in other ways: for example, *Amadis of Gaul,* the life of which has been prolonged by *Don Quixote*. When this happens, an ironic consequence may be that the parody helps in the revival of its object at a time when readers react against the parodist's point of view and identify the target as their forerunner: for example, the romantic revival of medieval literature, a process that often involved "amadisizing" the *Quixote* itself.

Furthermore, some texts that were originally designed to be single-voiced may later be "discovered" (or "re-authored") to be double-voiced—to be, in effect, parodies of themselves. This process is especially likely to occur with the inferior productions of great writers. Critics perplexed by what they regard as a platitudinous Shakespearean sonnet (say, 116) may reinterpret it as a parody of what it had previously appeared to be—and are likely to be faulted for doing so by others who either do not find it platitudinous or think the author should be allowed occasional platitudes. Conversely, a major work designated as a parody may not be taken as one when the culture of its origin "needs" to take it as a "serious" work: for example, nineteenth-century Russian readings of their first great novel, *Eugene Onegin*, as a romantic allegory of Russian cultural history or a mythic expression of national identity (as in Dostoevsky's Pushkin speech). Both kinds of reinterpretation may be regarded as part of the more general process that keeps a heritage vital through continual revision and reassessment of its canon.

2) The parodist must be seen to be in some way disagreeing with or disapproving of the target. Because there are an indefinitely large number of grounds for disagreement with any utterance, the parodist must indicate the grounds in any of a number of ways (for example, by exaggerating key passages in the original).

3) When the third criterion is not satisfied—that is, when readers do not know with which utterance they are expected to agree, or suspect that the second utterance may be no more authoritative than the first—then we do not have parody, but another dialogical relation, metaparody, which I shall discuss below.

The main thesis of this chapter can now be anticipated: there exist two classes of texts that enter into dialogical relation with utopias, namely *anti-utopias*, which parody utopias, and *meta-utopias*, in which utopia and anti-utopia themselves enter into an ultimately inconclusive dialogue.

It is instructive at this point to consider a number of criteria *not* included in this identification of parody. Parody is often described as a comic literary work that imitates another literary work by means of exaggeration.[5] By contrast, the class I have described requires neither the parody nor its target to be a literary work; nor does it require the target to be a single work. Some literary parodies, for instance, are designed to discredit a writer's total oeuvre, or a literary movement (e.g., romanticism), or a genre (e.g., romance, pastoral, epic, folktale, utopia — or, in principle, any other genre).

As I shall use the term, moveover, parody is not always comic. Parody recontextualizes its object so as to make it serve tasks contrary to its original tasks, but this functional shift need not be in the direction of humor. As negation can be on an indefinitely large number of grounds, parody can, in principle, adopt an indefinitely large number of tones. The direction and tone of the parody will depend on the nature of the parodist's disagreement with or disapproval of the original and the point of view from which he disagrees or disapproves. As Tynyanov observed, "if a parody of a tragedy results in a comedy, a comedy parodied may turn out to be a tragedy."[6] For instance, in parodying romantic novels for their frivolity and lack of serious ideological commitment, *What Is to Be Done?* is positively solemn; and *Notes from Underground*, which parodies the naive optimism of *What Is to Be Done?*, retells key incidents from the original in a context of dark psychological complexity. One might also recall the Renaissance tradition of "sacred parody," in which the devices and language of love poetry were used, with critical intent, for religious purposes (e.g., Herbert's lyric "A Parodie"). "Poets by abusing their talent, and making the follies and faygnings of love the customarie subject of their base endeavours," wrote Southwell of the objects of his sacred parodies,

have so discredited this facultie, that a Poet, a Lover, and a Lyer, are by many reckoned but three words of one signification. . . . For in lieu of solemne and devout matter, to which in duety they owe their abilities, they now busie themselves in expressing such passions, as onely serve for testimonies to how unworthy affections they have wedded their wills. And because the best course to let them see the errour of their works, is to weave a new webbe in their own loome, I have heere laid a few course threds together, to invite some skillfuller wits to goe forward in the same, or begin some finer peece; wherein it may be seene how well, verse and vertue sute together.[7]

"To weave a new webbe in their own loome" and so to induce them, or others, to "see the errour of their works" — this, not comedy, is the essence of parody.

Exaggeration, moreover, is not essential to parody. Exaggeration is, rather, simply one of several techniques parodists use (1) to inform readers that the text is a parody, which is to say that it refers to another, antithetical, text, and (2) to indicate what is objectionable in the original. Both of these goals can, however, be achieved without exaggeration. Parodists may, for instance, use the opposite technique, understatement, to deflate exaggeration itself (e.g., in the *New Yorker*'s brief replies to advertisements and announcements in other publications); or they may exploit the double meaning of a pun to double-voice a text. An especially common technique is the introduction of an element — an incident in the plot, let us say, or an unexpected choice of words — that is incongruous with the tone or generic conventions of the original. In this case, readers are implicitly invited to discover the new point of view from which the incursion was made, and a new structure that would resolve the incongruity. If this new structure is designed and adapted to survive after the parodic reference to an earlier work is no longer of interest, then it could prove exemplary for works to come. For example, *Joseph Andrews,* which was designed not only as a parody of *Pamela* but also, according to its preface, as a "species of writing . . . hitherto unattempted in our language,"[8] was to prove exemplary for the realistic novel. By creating a new kind of structure that incorporates elements from an old structure (or structures), parody can thus serve as an important laboratory — or perhaps, as Tynyanov argues, the most important laboratory — for emerging forms and new genres.

Indeed, it is possible to "weave a new webbe" without even changing the old web at all. That is, a parody can be *verbally identical* to its original if the parodist uses contextual, rather than textual, change to indicate the fact and grounds of double-voicing. He could, for instance, repeat the original in a significantly inappropriate social or literary setting. In everyday speech, inappropriate (and ironic) intonation are frequently used to discredit another's utterance, a technique that can be particularly effective precisely because the parody is "identical" to its target. Authors of literary parodies can exploit the implicit directive to read their text as a coherent whole in order to suggest a discrediting counterinterpretation of any "exact" citation or reproduced document. It is likely, for instance, that we would read any document that Sterne should have chosen to include in *Tristram Shandy* — as we read a number of documents that he did include, such as the Latin decree on baptism of the unborn — as parodically double-voiced, because the alternative — that is, to interpret the novel so that the document was not the object of parody — would defy plausibility or strain ingenuity. Moreover, not even *that* alternative is available when the original is reproduced "straight" in an anthology of explicitly designated "parodic works," a strategy Dwight Macdonald used in his anthology to discredit one of Eisenhower's political speeches.[9] A brief introduction and an ironic footnote indicate the two things Macdonald finds most objectionable in the original, namely the president's faulty logic, as reflected in his chaotic syntax, and his claim to be speaking impartially when he praises his own party. "As a bipartisan," Macdonald's footnote mimics the speech, "I must point out that, although [in this sentence] the syntax seems to put the Republican Party on record against freedom and liberty, the speaker almost certainly intended to say the opposite" (450n).

The Etiology of Utterance

The function and techniques of parody can now be described. Parody aims to discredit an act of speech by redirecting attention from its text to a compromising context. That is, while the parodist's ironic quotation marks frame the linguistic form of the original utterance, they also direct attention to the *occasion* (more accurately, the parodist's version of the occasion) *of its uttering*. The parodist thereby aims to reveal the otherwise covert aspects of that occasion, including the unstated motives and assumptions of both the speaker and the assumed and presumably sympathetic audience. Unlike that audience, the audience of the parody is asked to consider why someone might make, and someone else entertain, the original utterance. By pointing to the unexamined presuppositions and unstated interests that conditioned the original exchange, the parodist accomplishes what Fielding calls "the discovery of affectation" (preface to *Joseph Andrews,* 11) — the divergence between professed and unacknowledged intentions — or the discovery of naiveté, the difference between belief and disconfirming evidence. He or she does not, therefore, quote "out of context," as the targets often respond, but rather in "too much" context — in a context the targets would rather have overlooked. Parody is the etiology of utterance.

Parodies are usually described and identified as being of (or "after") a particular *author* or *work,* but the parodist's principal target may, in fact, be a particular *audience* or *class of readers.* The etiology of utterance includes the pathology of reception. For example, from *Don Quixote* to *Madame Bovary,* parodies have frequently been aimed at readers naive enough to mistake fiction for fact and romanticism for realism. Parodies have also been aimed at the complacency and hypocrisy, as well as the naiveté, of audiences. Tolstoy's parodies of opera in *War and Peace* and *What Is Art?,* for instance, are primarily concerned with why "rich, idle people" should enjoy such immoral artifice.[10] After describing the behavior of spectators during the entr'acte, Tolstoy concludes that their sanctimonious tributes to "great art" are an obvious cover for their cultivation of "refined and vicious feelings flowing from sexlove" (*What Is Art?,* 157). It may also be suggested that Fielding's *Shamela* was aimed primarily at the sanctimonious relationship that *Pamela* established with its readers, a relationship in which a moral lesson served as an excuse for titillation. Like many parodists, Fielding implies that readers must not be too ready to accept the invitations authors extend, and that reading is an action which, like any action, can be performed responsibly or irresponsibly.

This analysis suggests that the distinction drawn between "material" parodies and purely "formal" parodies, or, as it is sometimes put, between parodies of content and parodies of style, is oversimplified and in need of reformulation.[11] For in addition to its reliance on vague or questionable assumptions regarding the relation of form to content, this distinction also contributes to the misunderstanding of parody's basic nature and function. *We cannot parody words, syntax, or any other element, whether "formal" or "material," out of which utterances are made, but only utterances themselves — that is, speech acts as discourse in a context.* To the parodist, form and style are of interest because they betray, or can be shown to betray, the values, motives, and assumptions of those who would use or respond to that style on that occasion. The parodist recognizes language as dialect or idiolect, as *characteristic* of some group or speaker. Taking speech as an index of its speaker or listener, he or she selects and draws attention to whatever most clearly uncovers their affectation or folly.

The distinction of formal from material parodies is probably made in order to take account of comic imitations that neither discredit very much nor seem especially hostile to the original. In approaching such texts, we might note, first, that not all comic imitations are parodies (there are, for example, comic imitations of comedies) and, second, that parodies can be, as Bakhtin observes, "shallow" as well as "deep" (*PDP*, 160), which is to say, directed at superficial as well as fundamental faults of the original. As well as being more accurate, the distinction between shallow and deep, rather than formal and material, parodies is also more helpful in understanding the complex ways in which parodies are used. For instance, shallow parody is sometimes used to pay an author an indirect compliment. The opposite of damning with faint praise, this parody with faint criticism may be designed to show that no more fundamental criticism *could* be made. We have here an instance of a semiotic universal which I have often had occasion to describe in this study: every convention that can be used can be abused, any set of rules carries the possibility of its strategic violation. Those texts might best be called *false parodies*, for, under *cover* of parody, they do not function as parodies at all.

Even a true parody cannot help paying one compliment to its original, namely, that the original is important enough to be worth discrediting. One only discredits what others might credit, one only reveals as counterfeit what others might take for true coin. Parody implies currency. For this reason, works of remote times and cultures are rarely parodied; because parody locates a text in its compromising context, we tend not to engage in parody when that context is either unfamiliar or uninteresting. We speak ill of the dead, and parody their works, only to the extent they remain vital and present to *someone;* we discredit foreigners only when they are, or are becoming, influential among "us." To be precise, then, on those occasions when a work of a remote culture is parodied, the target is usually its circulators or readers in *our* culture. The parody may, for instance, be directed at inadequate translations, as in A. E. Housman's "Fragment of a Greek Tragedy," or at an enthusiastic group of imitators, as in many Russian verse parodies of the early nineteenth century. These "readdressed parodies," as Tynyanov calls them, are particularly common in works that belong to an anti-genre, like anti-utopia or mock epic. Mock epic allusions to Homer and Virgil are usually allusions to contemporary epic allusions to Homer and Virgil; not More and Plato but their latter-day imitators and followers are the targets of anti-utopian references to the *Utopia* and the *Republic*.

PART TWO: ANTI-UTOPIA AS A PARODIC GENRE

"Fortunately, the antediluvian time of those Shakespeares and Dostoevskys (or what were their names?) is past," I said in a voice deliberately loud.

— Eugene Zamyatin, *We*

Anti-genres

Anti-utopia is an anti-genre. Before turning to an examination of anti-utopia, we may consider briefly the nature of anti-genres in general. As a special type of literary genre, an anti-genre (or, as we shall sometimes call it, a parodic genre) may be identified, as are all other genres in this study, by (1) the membership of its works in a tradition of similar works and (2) the existence (or readers' assumption of the existence) of a set of conventions governing the interpretation of those works. The distinctiveness of anti-genres lies in the fact that those conventions establish a *parodic* relation between the anti-generic work and the works and traditions of another genre, the target genre.[12]

1. As I shall identify the class, anti-generic works are written in the tradition of previous works of the anti-genre. Like other genres, anti-genres have their classic texts and exemplars (e.g., for mock epic, *The Dunciad* and the Homeric *Battle of the Frogs and Mice*, respectively). Anti-genres do not, however, necessarily have exemplars — that is, acknowledged originating works — because the broader tradition of literary parody may provide models. An anti-genre may therefore develop a tradition of allusion to a parodic text

that does not belong to that anti-genre. *Don Quixote* has been, in this sense, exemplary for anti-utopia.

If the anti-genre has more than one type, its subgenres will have their own classic texts and may also have an exemplar or exemplars. Thus, Zamyatin's *We* has been made by its successors into an exemplar of the modern "dystopia," a type of anti-utopia that discredits utopias by portraying the likely effects of their realization, in contrast to other anti-utopias which discredit the possibility of their realization or expose the folly and inadequacy of their proponents' assumptions or logic. As in other genres, the tradition of an anti-genre creates the possibility of networks of allusions and references among its works. As *1984* and *A Clockwork Orange* develop motifs that occurred in *We, We* itself develops those of *Notes from Underground* and the legend of the Grand Inquisitor; and *Notes* and the legend allude, in turn, to *Candide*. Tradition may thus make, and frequently remakes, early works interesting as the source of motifs in later ones. Anti-generic motifs may also be drawn from a body of nonliterary texts, a knowledge of which is part of the competence the anti-genre presumes and encourages in its readers. Thus, just as utopias may require and reward familiarity with a tradition of nonliterary utopian ideology, anti-utopias often allude to a tradition of counterideology.

2. An anti-generic work must parody a target genre. That is, it must discredit not a single work in the target genre, but the genre as a whole. When a particular work is singled out for discrediting, it must be discredited, so to speak, synecdochically — that is, as representative of the genre. So *Notes from Underground* parodies *What Is to Be Done?* as a contemporary, and especially dangerous, example of a kind of literature and thinking extending back to the *Republic*. I shall not class a work as a member of an anti-genre when broader parody of the tradition is not intended (or presumed to be intended). For example, the class I identify as anti-utopias does not include a number of works that parody the specific utopian program inferable from *Looking Backward* (or any other utopia) without taking exception to utopianism per se. Rival utopias are not anti-utopias.

Because they allude to another generic tradition, works of an anti-genre may have two kinds of exemplars, namely, the positive models of its own tradition *and* the negative models of the target

genre. The *Republic* and *Utopia* served not only as positive models
for utopia, but also as negative models for anti-utopia. Grounded
in two traditions, a passage in an anti-genre is often designed to be
understood in terms of both the motifs of the target genre and the
countermotifs of the anti-genre. In *1984,* for instance, the essay on
Newspeak alludes both to utopian plans for a universal, unambiguous language and to anti-utopian parodies of utopian languages,
such as the projectors' replacement of words by sacks of things
("an universal language to be understood in all civilized nations")[13]
in *Gulliver's Travels* and by mathematical symbols in *We.* When
Winston Smith discovers Shakespeare, and the hero of *Fahrenheit
451* discovers the Bible, readers may discover not only positive
allusions to *Brave New World* and *We* but also negative ones to
Plato's suspicion of poetry and William Morris's rejection of novels
in *News from Nowhere.*

It will be recalled that my concern in this study is *not* to regulate
or account for the use of *terms,* but rather to identify and characterize classes of texts. We may note in this regard that not all works
which have been *called* anti-utopias or mock epics necessarily belong to the classes to which those terms will be applied in the
present study. For example, some works which have been called
mock epics use the divergence between epic virtues and contemporary vices not to parody epic but to satirize those vices; and
insofar as those works do not discredit epic (or its contemporary
readers or imitators), they will not be classed as mock epics, nor as
members of an anti-genre, *as those terms are used in the present
study* — though, to be sure, they might so be classed in another
generic system. A similar point could be made with regard to certain
"mock encomia" which, rather than discrediting encomia, reveal
the inadequacies of the person "praised"; and with regard to some
"anti-utopias" which are aimed not at utopias but at contemporary
social evils (e.g., *Erewhon*). Of course, it is difficult to avoid some
generic parody even when it is not the primary point of the work,
and it is common for authors to have, and for readers to take them
as having, both targets in mind. That is, such a work may be offered
and taken as both social satire and generic parody.

Anti-utopian, mock-epic, and other anti-generic works are, in
fact, frequently offered or taken as members of two generic traditions — that is, as related not only to the works of the anti-genre,

but also to works of another genre or anti-genre. For example, *The Praise of Folly* may be regarded as both a parodic sermon and a mock encomium, and *Joseph Andrews* as both a mock epic and a novel. The novel has been especially hospitable to anti-utopia (cf. *Notes from Underground*, *The Possessed*, *Under Western Eyes*, and some of Turgenev's works), probably because the novel's presuppositions are antithetical to those of utopia and because utopias have characteristically disapproved of traditional novels. For both reasons, an important theme of some anti-utopian novels is their own "novelness":[14] implicitly answering utopian criticisms of the genre of the novel, a particular work may self-consciously affirm what other novels simply assume, specifically, the existence of personality, the complexity of psychology, and the value of aesthetic experience. Responding to Chernyshevsky's attacks on these novelistic assumptions in *What Is to Be Done?*, *Notes from Underground* is just such a self-conscious novel—which is to say, it is, as an anti-utopia, an *anti*-anti-novel. More recently, many anti-utopias, such as Sinyavsky's *Lyubimov*, Bradbury's *Fahrenheit 451*, and Bulgakov's *Heart of a Dog*, have easily combined with and appropriated some of the conventions of science fiction, which, like anti-utopia, functions as a genre of fictional "thought experiments" examining present social trends, technological possibilities, or philosophical beliefs by taking them to an extreme.

Although an anti-generic work may be related to the tradition of a second genre, it need not, for that reason, constitute an example of what I have called threshold literature. For instance, in the cases just cited, the hermeneutic principles of the combined genres are not in principle incompatible or discontinuous. It is quite possible to read *Notes from Underground* as both a novel and an anti-utopia, *Joseph Andrews* as both a novel and a mock epic, *Fahrenheit 451* as both science fiction and anti-utopia, *The Dunciad* as both social satire and mock epic, and *The Praise of Folly* as both parodic sermon and mock encomium without confronting mutually exclusive interpretive directives. In other words, while such generic doubling does not necessarily lead to what I have called "hermeneutic perplexity," it may permit and encourage different readers, or the same reader at different times, to emphasize different aspects of the work. Depending on the tradition in which the reader chooses to locate the work, different allusions or generic *topoi* will become visible or predominant.

Parody and History

I have suggested that parody works by etiology. The parodist uncovers for each target an "irony of origins," which is to say, he or she reveals the relation of the text to the compromising and conditionalizing context of its utterance. A text or genre will be vulnerable to parody, therefore, to the extent that it ignores or claims to transcend its own originating context: parody is most readily invited by an utterance that claims transhistorical authority or implies that its source does not lie in any interests or circumstances of its speaker. The parodist typically reveals the historical or personal circumstances that led someone to make or entertain a claim of transhistoricity. Parody historicizes, and in so doing, it exposes the conditions that engendered claims of unconditionality.

In his study of *Gargantua and Pantagruel* as a composition of parodic genres, Bahktin described medieval parodies of liturgies, prayers, wills, epitaphs, and grammars as expressions, in the face of official claims to eternal truth and unchangeable social norms, of a sense of the "joyful relativity" of all things and the historical character of all rules.[15] We may add that the conventional semantic positions of these forms, in which truths and rules are handed down from an anonymous or impersonal source, must have invited parodic identification of the social or personal interests these forms often served. Modern dictionaries, grammars, and encyclopedias are also easy targets: the parodist returns the codification to the codifier, dates each attempt to arrest history. The well-known definitions in which Dr. Johnson expressed his personal opinion regarding what a word denotes (e.g., Whig, the name of a faction) or characterized the circumstances in which it is often used (patriotism, the last refuge of a scoundrel) were probably intended as what we might call *preemptive self-parody* — preemptive, that is, of such works as Ambrose Bierce's *Devil's Dictionary*. Like Bierce, who defined a lexicographer as "a pestilential fellow who, under the pretense of recording some particular stage in the development of a language, does what he can to arrest its growth" and who claimed for a chronicle the authority of a statute,[16] Dr. Johnson saw his own efforts and hopes as yet another example of the vanity of human wishes. He had begun his dictionary, its preface states, with the hope that it would check the history—he said decay—of English, which had been "suffered to spread, under the direction of chance, into wild exuberance; resigned to the tyranny of time and fashion; and exposed to the corruptions of ignorance, and caprices of the imagination." He had wished, he wrote, "that the instrument of language might be less apt to decay, and that signs might be permanent, like the things which they denote."[17] He knew, however, that such a wish was utopian, and in other places the preface anticipates those wry definitions that point away from words and toward their codifier. "To enchain syllables, and to lash the wind, are equally the undertakings of pride," Johnson wrote of lexicographers and academies.

Those who have been persuaded to think well of my design, will require that it should fix our language, and put a stop to those alterations which time and chance have hitherto been suffered to make in it without opposition. With this consequence I will confess that I flattered myself for a while; but now begin to fear that I have indulged expectation which neither reason nor experience can justify. When we see men grow old and die at a certain time one after another, from century to century, we laugh at the elixir that promises to prolong life to a thousand years; and with equal justice may the lexicographer be derided, who being able to produce no example of a nation that has preserved their words and phrases from mutability, shall imagine that his dictionary can embalm his language, and secure it from corruption and decay, that it is in his power to change sublunary nature, and clear the world at once from folly, vanity, and affectation.[18]

In short, *denial of history is invitation to parody.* More particularly, parodies are often directed at narrative genres in which the action unfolds in a time radically different from everyday time or discontinuous with the time of reading (e.g., epic, romance, and pastoral). Parodies of these genres typically renarrate their characteristic incidents in everyday time, and so use double narration as a means of double voicing. Thus, the *Quixote,* which parodies all three genres, answers each of its hero's generically orthodox descriptions of his adventures with a counterdescription by Sancho or the narrator. As he tells of giants and they of windmills, the text becomes a dialogue of simultaneous times. So do *Candide* and *Rus-*

lan and Lyudmila, both of which call attention to the kind of time in which the action of the romance unfolds. As Bakhtin has observed, time in romance bears no relation to biological chronology.

At the novel's outset the heroes meet each other at a marriageable age, and at the same marriageable age, no less fresh and handsome, they consummate the marriage at the novel's end. Such a form of time, in which they experience a most improbable number of adventures, is not measured off in the novel and does not add up; it is simply days, nights, hours, moments clocked in a technical sense within the limits of each separate adventure. This time — adventure-time, highly intensified, but undifferentiated — is not registered in the slightest way in the age of the heroes.[19]

But that time *is* counted in Voltaire's and Pushkin's parodies. Candide marries Cunegonde and Pushkin's wizard finally wins the love of his proud maiden when they are already hags. Has it been long since I left you? the wizard asks. "Rovno sorok let/ Byl devy rokovoj otvet" (Exactly forty years/ Was the maiden's fateful answer).[20] Here the wizard encounters not only time, but also his genre, and the reader is returned to the world of mutability in which he or she reads — and lives. In *Ruslan and Lyudmila,* and in his numerous other generic parodies (e.g., *Gabrieliad, Tsar Nikita, Count Nulin,* and that encyclopedia of parodies, *Eugene Onegin*), Pushkin also resembles his favorite models, Cervantes, Voltaire, and Sterne, in taking the stylized *language* of his target genres as an emblem of their distance from biographical time and historical flux. Juxtaposing their language of "remote allusions and obscure opinions" (to quote Dr. Johnson's well-known description of pastoral in *Rasselas*) — to a language that is clearly marked as characteristic of a particular group at a particular time, these parodists answer implicit claims to permanence and historical transcendence with the passing speech of a passing world.

PART THREE: META-UTOPIA

Some readers will probably want to know what I think of Pechorin's character. My reply may be found in the title of this book. "But that is a bitter irony!" they will say. I do not know. — Mikhail Lermontov, *A Hero of Our Time*[21]

Why does N. lose interest in Borges
— why is such a strange text?
? Ada

Metaparody

The books written by Borges's inhabitants of Tlön "invariably include both the thesis and the antithesis, the rigorous pro and con of a doctrine. A book which does not contain its counterbook is considered incomplete."[22] We reserved the term "parody" for those double-voiced texts or utterances that clearly indicate which of their conflicting voices is to be regarded as authoritative. The audience of a parody — that is, the readers who identify a text as a parody — knows for sure with which voice they are expected to agree. We may now consider a class of texts that are designed so that readers do *not* know. In texts of this type, each voice may be taken to be parodic of the other; readers are invited to entertain each of the resulting contradictory interpretations in potentially endless succession. In this sense, such texts remain fundamentally open, and if readers should choose either interpretation as definitive, they are likely to discover that this choice has been anticipated and is itself the target of parody. Caught between contradictory hermeneutic directives — between "this is a parody" and "this is a parody of a parody" — readers may witness the alternation of statement and counterstatement, interpretation and antithetical interpretation, up to a conclusion which fails, often ostentatiously, to resolve their hermeneutic perplexity. We shall refer to texts that are designed to exploit this dialogue between parody and counterparody (or, as we shall see, between genre and anti-genre) as *metaparodies.* Inasmuch as they create resonance between contradictory hermeneutic directives, metaparodies constitute a special type of threshold art. Readers of metaparody are expected to comprehend the work not as the compromise between book and counterbook, but as their ultimately inconclusive dialogue.

Metaparodies frequently work by first parodying an original, then parodying the parody of the original. Readers of the *Quixote,* for instance, may be reasonably sure that the first book is a parody directed at naive readers of romances and tales of knight errantry. But they may be less sure about the second book, which seems to be directed at readers of the first book as well — readers who, we recall, appear as characters in the second book and are portrayed as growing increasingly trivial in their complacent and sterile mockery. If Don Quixote is foolish, then so are they who think him

*too
→ Deep*

foolish — a paradox that corresponds to the essentially ambiguous vision of the work. Generally speaking, metaparodies anticipate readers of varying degrees of sophistication and appreciation of ambiguity, and are constructed to sort out, and so to define implicitly a typology of, their own readers. Ambiguities similar to those of the *Quixote* are also developed in Pushkin's metaparodic "novel in verse," *Eugene Onegin,* which has been interpreted both as a romantic novel and (as Shklovsky argued in his essay on "Pushkin and Sterne")[23] as a parody directed at readers of romantic novels. (Its prefatory verses, which describe the work as "a collection of motley chapters/ Half-humorous and half-sad," seem to invite both readings.) We may add that *Onegin* is also a parody directed at readers of parodies, and the readings it seems to anticipate and "parody in advance" include Formalist ones. Not simply a work in the tradition of Sterne and Byron, *Onegin* is also a parody of that tradition. *Onegin,* in effect, includes its own parody, and its essentially open dialogue is designed to exemplify a deep suspicion of all "statements" about the world — including its own. This openness of vision may be taken by the reader as the point of its nonending, which seems to be poised between the elegiac and yet another parody of the elegiac — an uncertainty that the poet deliberately leaves unresolved. "Blessed is he," he writes in his self-referential closing lines, "who left life's feast early,/ Not having drunk to the dregs/ Its beaker full of wine;/ Who did not read its novel to the end,/ And knew how to part with it suddenly,/ As I part with my Onegin."

Ambiguity of this sort may be a characteristic of a *genre* as well as of particular works. As there are genres and parodic genres, there are also metaparodic genres — that is, genres of works that are designed to be interpreted as a dialogue of parody and counterparody. When readers identify a work as belonging to a genre of this type, they will, in appreciating the conventions of the generic tradition, expect the work to exhibit this kind of hermeneutic resonance. One such genre is the rhetorical paradox, the praise of something regarded as essentially unpraisable.[24] Beginning in antiquity and including encomia to flies and fleas, to gnats and nuts, to baldness and incontinence, and to bastardy and the codpiece, this genre reaches a peak of complexity in Erasmus's *Praise of Folly* — which may also be taken as a metaparodic sermon (i.e., as both a parodic sermon and a parody of a parodic sermon). As many have noted, one cannot adequately comprehend the complexity of Erasmus's work by simply negating each of Folly's statements—or even by negating each of these negations. For as Folly herself points out, wisdom cannot be the unambiguous opposite of folly, because folly is necessary for wisdom—or, we may ask, is that simply Folly's foolish self-justification? Does she err when she argues that error leads to truth? Erasmus's work sharpens the paradoxes of self-reference and infinite regress traditional in praises of the unpraisable by allowing Folly herself to be the author of a rhetorical paradox in praise of Folly (she cites several generic precedents). It is, she argues, appropriate (and a wise choice) to have Folly praise folly—and praise self-praise as well. Repeatedly making statements which she subsequently calls foolish, she leaves no statement exempt from contradictory meta-statement, no meta-statement exempt from a potential meta-meta-statement. Everything she says implies (folds in upon) itself and includes (closes in upon) its opposite.

Folly's essentially unfinalizable dialogue of opposites ends (in much the same way that *Onegin* ends) with her refusal to resolve her contradictions with a summary—a refusal that is itself, paradoxically, an appropriate summary. No less appropriate and self-implicative is the work's prefatory dedication to Thomas More, in which Erasmus—whom Folly includes in her list of fools—treats his readers in much the same way that Folly treats her audience. "A satirist who spares none of mankind (himself included)," Erasmus writes, "is obviously concerned with human failings in general. . . . It follows that if anyone feels aggrieved by this book, he is discovering his guilt, or at least is afraid of having to do so."[25] Erasmus discovers his own folly when he observes, "Nothing can be a worse waste of time than a serious subject trifled with, nothing better worth while than nonsense turned to good account. It is for others to judge: still, unless the nymph *Self-Love* beguiles me, though I praise folly, I do not do so altogether foolishly" (5).

The rhetorical paradox plays an important role in More's *Utopia* and in the arguments of "the paradoxicalist" in Dostoevsky's *Diary of a Writer*. We may also observe that a number of Dostoevsky's characters are masters of its self-cancelling strategies. In *The Brothers Karamazov*, for instance, when Smerdyakov praises apostasy, he uses the biblical citations and jesuitical precision traditional for this mock-scholarly genre. And in that novel's best-known chapter, "The Grand Inquisitor," Ivan praises the devil and an antichrist (if not *the* antichrist) — praises them, moreover, for their Christianity. Ivan is the devil's advocate in the literal sense of the phrase — but also in the idiomatic sense, which is to say, he plays the role of the devil's advocate, rigorously defending a position so that it can be triumphantly refuted. His paradoxes are sharpened still more when his double, the paradoxically petty Satan, himself *plays* the devil's advocate. In the novel, only Father Zossima understands the equivocation in Ivan's professions of atheism: "you don't believe your own arguments, and with an aching heart mock at them inwardly," the elder observes. "That question you have not answered, and it is your great grief, for it clamors for an answer." Ivan's perplexed listener, Alyosha, seems almost to arrive at a similar understanding of his brother's contradictions when he declares that the legend is "in praise of Jesus not in blame of Him — as you meant it to be." Zossima would have understood that it is both. Ivan is, in fact, first introduced as the author of other paradoxes, such as the article on a controversial subject received favorably by both sides until "finally some sagacious persons opined that the article was nothing but an impudent satirical burlesque" — or, more accurately, a rhetorical paradox. And Zossima's interpretation of Ivan's contradictory meanings occurs right after Miusov reports that once, "in a gathering principally of ladies," Ivan defended the assertion that crime, even to cannibalism, is the only "honorable" course of action for an atheist. "From this paradox, gentlemen, you can judge of the rest of our eccentric and paradoxical friend Ivan Fyodorovitch's theories."[26]

The first part of *Notes from Underground* is an excellent example of the genre. The underground man — called a "paradoxicalist" by the editor of his notes — argues the self-interest of self-spite, the unhappiness of happiness, and the advantage of disadvantage — to the point where it is not clear what the words "advantage" and "disadvantage" mean. A descendant of that Cretan who swore that all Cretans are liars, he exhibits as well the genre's characteristic logical paradoxes of self-reference, especially through variations on the sentence "This sentence is false." "I was lying," he explains, "when I said just now that I was a spiteful official. I was lying out of spite." The passage in which he declares (to whom?) that he will have no readers exemplifies a closely related type of self-contradiction, the sentence "You are not reading this sentence." And like Folly, the underground man leaves no statement exempt from a contrary meta-statement and presents no position as his final position. His self-cancelling self-cancellations reach a dizzying apogee at the beginning of the last chapter of part 1:

The long and short of it is, gentlemen, that it is better to do nothing! Better conscious inertia! And so hurrah for underground!

Though I have said that I envy the normal man to the point of exasperation, yet I would not care to be in his place as he is now (though I will not stop envying him. No, no; anyway, the underground life is more advantageous!) There, at any rate, one can—Bah! But after all, even now I am lying! I am lying because I know myself as surely as two times two makes four, that it is not at all underground that is better, but something different, quite different, for which I long but which I cannot find! Damn underground!

I will tell you another thing that would be better, and that is, if I myself believed even an iota of what I have just written. I swear to you, gentlemen, that I do not really believe one thing, not even one word, of what I have just written. That is, I believe it, perhaps, but at the same time, without knowing why, I feel and suspect that I am lying myself blue in the face.

"Then why have you written all this?" you will say to me. . . . "You long for life and try to settle the problems of life by a logical tangle. . . . You talk nonsense and are pleased with it; you say impudent things and are constantly afraid of them and apologizing for them. . . . Lies, lies, lies!"

Of course I myself have made up just now all the things you say. That, too, is from underground.

Beginning on a paradox that he has examined before ("to do nothing"—as opposed to not doing anything) and proceeding through a maze of negations and negations of negations, this passage anticipates the *Notes'* own paradoxically appropriate non-ending.

Like the rhetorical paradox, *meta-utopia*—the subject of this chapter—is a metaparodic genre. A type of threshold literature, meta-utopias are designed to be interpreted as dialogues between utopia and the parody of utopia. One side of the dialogue—usually utopia—may seem to predominate, but that predominance is inconclusive and never free from the possibility of reversal. In some works, large sections may exhibit the *topoi* of utopian literature so well that, when considered separately or excerpted for anthologies, they appear to be utopian without qualification. Read in the context of the complete work, however, these sections are framed by others that do qualify them and may even make them seem to tend toward self-parody. Meta-utopias are perhaps best comprehended as examinations, rather than either endorsements or rejections, of the presuppositions of utopian thinking and literature — or, to cite the self-description of Wells's *A Modern Utopia*, as the dramatization of "the adventure of his [narrator's] soul among Utopian inquiries." The author of a meta-utopia allows himself to entertain utopian or anti-utopian arguments, but does not ultimately commit himself to them. However uncompromising in tone or scornful of indecision, his pronouncements are both compromised and indecisive. Poised between statements and performance, they are tentative and "neither cold nor hot."

Linda Hutcheon

Modern Parody and Bakhtin

What I am calling parody here is not just that ridiculing imitation mentioned in the standard dictionary definitions. The challenge to this limitation of its original meaning, as suggested (as we shall see) by the etymology and history of the term, is one of the lessons of modern art that must be heeded in any attempt to work out a theory of parody that is adequate to it. Joyce's *Ulysses* provides the most blatant example of the difference in both scope and intent of what I shall label as parody in the twentieth century. There are extended parallels with the Homeric model on the level of character and plot, but these are parallels with an ironic difference: Molly/Penelope, waiting in her insular room for her husband, has remained anything but chaste in his absence. Like Eliot's ironic echoes of Dante and many others in his poetry, this is not just a structural inversion; it also signals a change in what used to be called the "target" of parody. While the *Odyssey* is clearly the formally back-grounded or parodied text here, it is not one to be mocked or ridiculed; if anything, it is to be seen, as in the mock epic, as an ideal or at least as a norm from which the modern departs. This is not to say that there have not been modern heirs to Calverley and Squire, writers of what is more traditionally seen as parody. We need only recall the work of Max Beerbohm or even Pound's "Winter is icummen in." In fact, what is remarkable in modern parody is its range of intent — from the ironic and playful to the scornful and ridiculing.

Parody, therefore, is a form of imitation, but imitation characterized by ironic inversion, not always at the expense of the par-

odied text. Max Ernst's *Pietà* is an Oedipal inversion of
Michelangelo's sculpture: a petrified father holds a living son in his
arms, replacing the living mother and her dead son, Christ. Parody
is, in another formulation, repetition with critical distance, which
marks difference rather than similarity. In this it goes beyond mere
allusive variation such as in the *honkadori* technique in Japanese
court poetry, which echoes past works in order to borrow a context
and to evoke an atmosphere.[1] The ironic inversion of Dante's *Com-
media* by Pound's *Hugh Selwyn Mauberley* is more to the point.
Here the parody lies in the differences between the personal, aesthetic, and moral journeys of two exiles. Dante's dignity is replaced
by Mauberley's self-pity; his involvement with the political reality
of Florence is contrasted to the aesthete's self-willed alienation. Instead of inheriting a long tradition of classical, Italian, and Provencal
poetry, Mauberley has only the nineties' decadence. The concrete
materiality of Dante's descriptions even of things supernatural is
replaced by the "obscure reveries / of the inward gaze." As Dante
moves out of himself to beauty and finally to God in an act of
spiritual fulfillment, the modern journey leads only to the inner
ego, to the failure of love, to "subjective hosannah," and to the
inadequacies of the flesh. In Pound's poem, the imagery (of eyes,
mouth, and so on) is the same as in Dante's, but the context is
inverted. The same characters are mentioned and the same moral
stance suggested, but the relations to them are ironically different.
Instead of an acceptance and use of the past for new creation, Mauberley seeks to deny the social and aesthetic tradition that would give
his life and work meaning.[2]

Ironic inversion is a characteristic of all parody: think of Byron's
Don Juan's reversal of the legend (the women here chase after him)
and of the conventions of the epic. Similarly, criticism need not be
present in the form of ridiculing laughter for this to be called parody. Euripides was considered to have parodied Aeschylus and
Sophocles when, in his *Medea,* he replaced the traditional male
protagonist with a woman, and a woman who was an outsider
rather than a member of a Greek family of renown. The female
Corinthian chorus replaced the elders of state and the suppliants,
yet, with added irony, they also support Medea in her hatred of
Corinth. The male hero turns out to be base—hypocritical and
shallow. Although bloodied by four murders, Medea is saved by

the gods. This is the same kind of inversion we find in Pound or in a contemporary film such as Peter Greenaway's *The Draughtsman's Contract.*

In its attention to visual and verbal detail, this film is a loving parody of eighteenth-century painting and Restoration comedy. It is a parody and not an imitation because of what Greenaway does to the conventions of the form. First of all, they are superimposed upon the seemingly very different conventions of the murder mystery, and then both are inserted into a metadiscursive context focused on the representation of reality. As the "hero" sketches a country house, its owner is murdered, and clues (in the form of items of his clothing) are integrated into the accurate, realistic drawings. The framing device which the artist, Mr. Neville, employs in his drawing is frequently both used and mirrored by the camera, which composes scenes like paintings. The black and white of the drawings contrasts with the lush color of the film, but this contrast serves only to signal a second function of the color opposition, one that coincides with the conventions, not to say clichés, of all moral drama wherein black signifies evil and white denotes innocence. In this film, the traditional male sexual supremacy of Restoration comedy with which the plot begins is inverted in the second half, as the women take control of his sexual activities for their own purposes. It is totally *sub*verted at the end when the female plotters are replaced by the males who put the artist to death. The arrogant and manipulative Mr. Neville is portrayed at the beginning dressed in black, making black marks on his white sheets of paper; his innocent female victims are clothed in white. The irony of this coding becomes clear by the end as we realize the superior manipulation of the women in white, and indeed as the film progresses the colors are reversed, ostensibly because the women are now in mourning. In reality, their true colors, so to speak, finally show, and the truly innocent Neville is dressed in white, a lamb ready for the slaughter. This ironic playing with multiple conventions, this extended repetition with critical difference, is what I mean by modern parody.

When Eliot gives Marvell's poetry a new context (or "transcontextualizes" it), or when Stockhausen quotes but alters the melodies of many different national anthems in his *Hymnen,* parody becomes what one critic calls a productive-creative approach to tradition.[3] In Stockhausen's words, his intent was "to hear familiar, old, preformed musical material with new ears, to penetrate and transform it with a musical consciousness of today."[4] Similarly, the Brotherhood of Ruralists, whose very name suggests their admiration for the Pre-Raphaelite Brotherhood, overtly borrows and recontextualizes compositional elements from earlier English landscape artists like Samuel Palmer. Graham Arnold's parodically entitled series *Harmonies poétiques et religieuses* is a homage to Ruskin, Jefferies, and T. S. Eliot that combines painting with a collage of photos, bits of musical scores, and actual physical parts of the English countryside (an ear of corn, for instance). Quotation or borrowing like this is not meant to signal only similarity.[5] It is not a matter of nostalgic imitation of past models; it is a stylistic confrontation, a modern recoding which establishes difference at the heart of similarity. No integration into a new context can avoid altering meaning, and perhaps even value.[6] George Rochberg's Third String Quartet appropriates the conventions of an earlier period and gives them a new meaning. The third movement sounds like a set of variations by Beethoven, but we cannot analyze it as such. Its real significance lies in how it does *not* sound like Beethoven, because we know it was written in the 1970s: "Tonality simply cannot mean today what it did 150 years ago; it has a totally different relationship not only to the composer and listener but to the entire musical culture within whose context the piece exists and is experienced."[7] In his famous essay, "The Literature of Exhaustion," John Barth remarked that, if Beethoven's Sixth Symphony were composed today, it would be an embarrassment—unless it were done ironically to show that the composer was aware of where music both is and has been.[8]

The fact that I have been using examples from different art forms should make clear my belief that parody in non-literary works is not just a transfer from the practice of literature, as Bakhtin, however, claimed it was.[9] Its frequency, prominence, and sophistication in the visual arts, for example, are striking. It is part of a move away from the tendency, within a Romantic ideology, to mask any sources by cunning cannibalization, and toward a frank acknowledgment (by incorporation) that permits ironic commentary. This is a version of what Leo Steinberg calls "inter-art traffic."[10] The most parodied paintings are, not surprisingly, the most familiar ones: the *Mona Lisa,* the *Last Supper,* the works of Picasso, and those of Vermeer (by George Deem, Malcolm Morley, James McGarrell, Carole Caroompas, and others). Parodic "trans-contextualization" can take the form of a literal incorporation of reproductions into the new work (by Joseph Cornell, Audrey Flack, Josef Levi, Sante Graziani) or of a reworking of the formal elements: for instance, Arakawa's parody of da Vinci's *Last Supper* is entitled *Next to the Last,* referring to the last preparatory drawing before the painting, as well as to the work itself. The composition is squared out, the figures are silhouetted, as in a sketch, and some elements are labeled rather than drawn in (hand, cup). Such parody intends no disrespect, while it does signal ironic difference. It is one of the forms of what the 1978 exhibit at the Whitney Museum of American Art in New York called "Art about Art."[11] Such art could almost be considered self-parodic in that it calls into question not only its relation to other art but its own identity. Self-parody in this sense is not just an artist's way of disowning earlier mannerisms by externalizations (as with Coleridge's "On a Ruined Cottage in a Romantic Country" or Swinburne's "Nephelidia"). It is a way of creating a form out of the questioning of the very act of aesthetic production.[12]

In my focus on twentieth-century art forms, I hope to suggest that there are probably no transhistorical definitions of parody possible. Nevertheless, I shall constantly be using examples from other periods to show that there are common denominators to all definitions of parody in all ages — although they are *not* the ones usually cited. It is modern parodic usage that is forcing us to decide what it is that we shall call parody today. In fact the closest model to present practice was not called parody at all, but imitation. I am thinking of the central and pervasive force of Renaissance imitation as what Thomas Greene calls a percept and an activity which "embraced not only literature but pedagogy, grammar, rhetoric, aesthetics, the visual arts, music, historiography, politics and philosophy."[13] I am not claiming that modern parody is only Renaissance imitation: it would require the addition of an ironic and critical dimension of distanciation for it to be an accurate reflection of the art of today. But, like parody, imitation offered a workable and effective stance toward the past in its paradoxical strategy of repetition as a source of freedom. Its incorporation of another work as a deliberate and acknowledged construct is structurally similar to parody's formal organization. But the ironic distance of modern parody might well come from a loss of that earlier humanist faith in cultural continuity and stability that ensured the sharing of codes necessary to the comprehension of such doubly coded works. Imitation, however, offers a striking parallel to parody in terms of intent. In Greene's words: "Every creative imitation mingles filial rejection with respect, just as every parody pays its own oblique homage."[14]

With the eighteenth-century valorizing of wit and irony came a move away from this idea of respect, except in the mock epic (which did not, in fact, mock the epic).[15] The function of parody was often to be the malicious, denigrating vehicle of satire, a role it continues to play to this day in some forms of parody. Yet into the nineteenth century we find other persistent and extensive uses of parody, such as Jane Austen's,[16] which challenge the definition of parody as the conservative ridiculing of artistic fashion's extremes. Certainly the equivalent of the parodies of the Smith Brothers today would be the short, often satirical, parodies in *Punch* and other such magazines, but the more extended structural use of parody by Dickens in *Pickwick Papers* and Chesterton in *The Man That Was Thursday* is a closer model for the practice of novelists like Joyce and Mann, not to mention Barth and Banville. This is not to say that Christopher Ward's "The Dry Land," Samuel Hoffenstein's "The Moist Land," and Louis Untermeyer's "Einstein among the Coffee Cups" are not parodies of Eliot's poetry. What I do want to suggest is that we must broaden the concept of parody to fit the needs of the art of our century—an art that implies another and somewhat different concept of textual appropriation. Certainly new directors like Robert Benton and Brian De Palma are not attempting to ridicule Hitchcock in films such as *Still of the Night* and *Blowout*. Often the works of the past become aesthetic models whose recasting in a modern work is frequently aimed at a satirical ridicule of contemporary customs or practices.[17] The best historical model for this is the mock epic, as in *The Rape of the Lock* or the *Dunciad* with its use of Virgil's eclogues.[18] Some critics have argued that the subplots in Elizabethan drama function in the same parodic fashion.[19]

Like all of these forms, and in contrast to those short, occasional parodies that were gathered into anthologies with such regularity in the late nineteenth and early twentieth centuries, the kind of parody upon which I wish to focus is an integrated structural modeling process of revising, replaying, inverting, and "trans-contextualizing" previous works of art. Perhaps the archetypal manifestation of this process is what is now called Post-Modern architecture. Since 1960, architects such as Paolo Portoghesi, Robert Venturi, Charles Moore, and others have self-consciously restored the idea of architecture as a dialogue with the past, as being doubly coded (Modern plus something else) or parodic. Eschewing the hermeticism and denial of function and relevance of High Modernism, these architects critically display an interest in historical memory and in codes of communication.[20] This is not very different in either intent or structure from Iris Murdoch's modern inversions of earlier texts, her reworking (in the light of the Sartrean image of petrification by the "regard" of the Other) of the tales of both the Medusa and John the Baptist in her *A Severed Head,* for instance. In his novel, *The Name of the Rose,* Umberto Eco "trans-contextualizes" characters, plot details, and even verbal quotations from Conan Doyle's "The Hound of the Baskervilles" into a medieval world of monks and (literally) textual intrigue. His Sherlock Holmes is William of Baskerville; his narrating Watson is Adso, the scribe who frequently does not know what he recollects and records. In the context of medieval and modern semiotics, Eco's hero's first example of reasoning à la Holmes — in a situation out of Voltaire's *Zadig* — takes on new meaning; the work of the detective becomes an analogue for textual interpretation: both are active, constructive, and indeed more creative than true to fact. The deadly struggle over what turns out to be Aristotle's lost poetics of the comic provides the context for the attack, by the monk, Jorge of Borgos, on the propriety of laughter; Eco's other extended parodic context here is, of course, the work of Jorge Luis Borges. This complex novel also contains extended parodies of the *Coena cipriani,* of other art works (those of Breughel and Buñuel, to cite two that will give an idea of Eco's range), as well as many other literary works.

In music, what is commonly called quotation or borrowing has become a significant, self-conscious aesthetic device only in this century, though it existed before.[21] Just as Rochberg used Mozart

and Mahler in his *Music for the Magic Theatre,* so Foss uses the
Prelude of Bach's Violin Partita in E in his "Phorion" (*Baroque
Variations*), but his quotation is in fragmented form, offering an
ironic, nightmarish world through distortion. This is not the same
as Liszt's *Réminiscences de Don Juan,* which develops certain themes
of *Don Giovanni.* Ironic "transcontextualization" is what distinguishes parody from pastiche or imitation. Modern jazz, for instance, is therefore probably not in itself parodic, though there do
exist some parodies even in this, an art form that tends to take itself
very seriously. It is interesting that it is often women (a rarity in
the jazz scene) who are willing or able to create the necessary ironic
distance: Carla Bley's amusing "Reactionary Tango" is one such
example.

In the visual arts, parody can manifest itself in relation to either
particular works or general iconic conventions. René Payant's semiotic studies of what he calls quotation in painting reveal the complexity of the intersection of, in his terms, intertextuality and
intersubjectivity — that is, the complexity of the meeting of two
texts combined with the meeting of a painter and a viewer.[22] The
work of Magritte provides a clear example of a parodic transgression
of many levels of iconic norms that moves beyond mere quotation.
His simplest and most overt parodies are those based on specific
paintings: David's portrait of Madame Récamier becomes a portrait
of a coffin. It is clear from Magritte's letters that the work of Manet
and David represented to him the ultimate achievements of objective
representation in art and, as such, could not be ignored.[23] Indeed,
they must, for him, be superseded. But Magritte's parodies also
operate on other than direct iconic models. Paintings like the different versions of *The Human Condition* parody conventions of
both art (the function of framing) and visual perception. Magritte's
parody of the general conventions of reference as well as the specific
ones of the emblem form that we investigated earlier inspired more
than just Michel Foucault. David Hlynsky recently produced a hol-
ograph called *These are not the Pipes* which models itself — albeit
ironically — on Magritte's (the work is indeed a representation of
not one smoking pipe but of a number of plumbing pipes), but the
visual illusion of holography (of three-dimensional space) ironically
increases the intensity of the power of art's conventions of representation. A similar complexity is achieved in a different way by

Peter Blake's parodic *On the Balcony.* The four children on the bench hold a postcard or reproduction of Manet's *Le balcon,* a picture from *Romeo and Juliet,* implying the famous balcony scene (there is also a pennant from Verona elsewhere), and two photos of the royal family. The cliché of the lovers on the balcony is reechoed in the two doves outside the dovecote. This kind of complexity makes parody into a variation on what Gary Saul Morson calls a "boundary work" or doubly decodable text,[24] though these works are perhaps more accurately described as having multiple coding, especially since conventions as well as particular texts are often involved.

Sometimes, in fact, it is conventions *as well as* individual works that are parodied. For example, the New York artist Vito Acconci's 1973 *Runoff* is a parody of two different sets of conventions as well as one specific text. It challenges the bases of most performance art, but also aims particularly at Yves Klein's double and simultaneous performance of his *Monotone Symphone* (a string quartet played one note for the duration) and *Anthropometry,* in which the male artist directed nude female models to cover their bodies in paint and roll about on or against blank canvas. Acconci, instead, rubs his own, unpainted, male body against a freshly painted wall. He not only thereby ironically inverts Klein's sexist control but also reverses the standard conventions of instrumentality of brush to canvas. Here the body is the canvas; the wall is the applicator (as he moves against it). In this way, Acconci also manages to parody what abstract expressionists like Jackson Pollock felt was the correct "investiture of the self."[25]

The work of Tom Stoppard would provide another example of the complexity of the modern phenomenon that I want to call parody. In *Rosencrantz and Guildenstern Are Dead,* there is a tension between the text we know (*Hamlet*) and what Stoppard does to it. Whenever an event is directly taken from the Shakespearian model, Stoppard uses the original words. But he "trans-contextualizes" them through his addition of scenes that the Bard never conceived. This is not like Ionesco's total inversion of the diction and moral value of characters in his *Macbett;* Stoppard's intention is not as satiric as Ionesco's. The same is true in *Travesties,* but there is yet another level of complexity because, as its plural title suggests, not only is there more than one parody, but those texts parodied are themselves often parodies, especially *Ulysses* and *The Importance of Being Earnest*. Wilde's play parodies the literature of romance and the comedy of manners. What one critic has called its "queer double consciousness"[26] is really only its parodic double coding. In Stoppard's play, *The Importance of Being Earnest* is foregrounded both as a formal model and as a source of parodic play by the plot, which involves Joyce's production of it in Zürich. The baby switch in Wilde's play becomes appropriately and significantly inverted when Joyce's own parodic "Oxen of the Sun" text is switched for Lenin's plan for the revolution. We might also recall that in that section of *Ulysses,* in addition to the various famous stylistic parodies, Stephen ironically inverts the language and actions of the Last Supper and the mass,[27] in a manner similar to his usurpation of the language of the Creator to describe his induction into the priesthood of the eternal imagination in *A Portrait of the Artist as a Young Man.* In both cases he uses parody as much to resacralize as to desacralize, to signal the change in the locus of his allegiance. In some of the stories of *Dubliners,* Joyce uses the superimposing structure of parody to organize his plot (as in "Grace," with its echoes of the *Divine Comedy* and of Job)[28] to comment ironically on implications of certain literary forms (as in "Clay," where the Dickensian optimistic style of *A Christmas Carol* contrasts ironically with the reality described).[29]

Similarly, Magritte's coffin studies are more than just parodic play with single earlier paintings. His *Perspective* has a long and complex history that includes not just Manet's *Le balcon* but Matisse's *Porte-fenêtre à Collioure* (which voided Manet's scene of its people in another way, leaving only the door's form), and also Goya's *Majas on a Balcony* — a model of Manet's. I would not want to argue that such complex parodic echoing is unique to the twentieth century. Clearly works such as Petronius's *Satyricon libri* parodied not only the Greek novel form in its frame and episodes but other diverse specific works as well.[30] Nevertheless, the number of modern works of art in many media that partake of this mode does make it important, if not unique, to this century. The music of Peter Maxwell Davies provides another good example. His *Antechrist* was inspired, he claimed, by fifteenth-century woodcut blocks on the subject and by his own opera, *Taverner,* but its form begins with a straight rendering of "Deo confitemini-Domino," a thirteenth-century motet, which is then broken down and superimposed on related plainsong fragments — which the new context turns ironically inside out. For Davies, this inversion is related to the late medieval techniques of transformation processes (canon, etc.). He began his *Missa super L'Homme Armé* as an exercise to complete an anonymous fifteenth-century mass on the popular song "*L'Homme Armé*," but, inspired by the structure of Joyce's "Cyclops" episode in *Ulysses* (with its interrupted tavern conversation and parodic stylistic changes), he chose instead to rework the material to reveal more unorthodox relationships between foregrounded and backgrounded material. On the cover of the Decca L'Oiseau-Lyre recording, he calls the finished product a "progressive splintering of what is extant of the fifteenth-century original, with magnification and distortion of each splinter through many varied stylistic 'mirrors,' finishing with a 'dissolution' of it in the last automatic piano section."

I want to argue for calling such complex forms of "trans-contextualization" and inversion by the name of parody. It is indeed a form of "artistic recycling,"[31] but a very particular form with very complex textual intentionality. Robbe-Grillet's *The Erasers* is a parody of both *Oedipus Rex* and Bely's *Petersburg* in its structure, but the functions of the two parodic strains are more difficult to specify. What seems certain is that they are not the same. I want to retain the term parody for this structural and functional relationship of critical revision, partly because I feel that a word like quotation is too weak and carries (etymologically and historically) none of those parodic resonances of distance and difference that we have found to be present in modern art's reference to its past. Quotation might do, in a very general way, if we were dealing only with the adoption of another work as a guiding structural principle,[32] but even then its usefulness is limited. We need a term that will allow us to deal with the structural and functional complexity of the artistic works themselves. According to their teachings, parody can obviously be a whole range of things. It can be a serious criticism, not necessarily of the parodied text; it can be a playful, genial mockery of codifiable forms. Its range of intent is from respectful admiration to biting ridicule. Nietzsche, in fact, wondered what was Diderot's relation to Sterne's text in *Jacques le fataliste:* was it imitation, admiration, mockery?

While we need to expand the concept of parody to include the extended "refunctioning" (as the Russian Formalists called it) that is characteristic of the art of our time, we also need to restrict its focus in the sense that parody's "target" text is always another work of art or, more generally, another form of coded discourse. I stress this basic fact because even the best works on parody tend to confuse it with satire,[33] which, unlike parody, is both moral and social in its focus and ameliorative in its intention. This is not to say, as we shall see, that parody does not have ideological or even social implications. Parody can, of course, be used to satirize the reception or even the creation of certain kinds of art. (I am aware that this separation would break down in a deconstructionist perspective where there is no *hors-texte*, but such a view of textuality is not my immediate context in this study.)

What, then, can be parodied? Any codified form can, theoretically, be treated in terms of repetition with critical distance,[34] and not necessarily even in the same medium or genre. Literature is famous for parodying nonliterary discourse. *Pale Fire* plays with editorial commentary; *Tom Jones, Tristram Shandy,* and even *Finnegans Wake* undermine the conventions of scholarly annotation and footnotes.[35] Borges's "Pierre Menard, Author of the Quixote" parodies, among other things, the genre of the bibliobio-critical note on a writer. This cross-genre play is not only the province of literature: Woody Allen's *Zelig* is, among other things, a cinematic parody of the television documentary and movie newsreel. If there is no parodiable code, as might be the case in nonsense or extreme hermetic works, imitation may be possible, but not parody.[36] To say, quite simply, that any codified discourse is open to parody is more methodologically cautious and more true to fact than to assert, as some do, that only mediocre works of art can be parodied.[37] Twentieth-century art forms would not comply with such an observation, even if certain nineteenth-century ones would. It would seem that popular works of art are always parodied, whatever their quality.

* * *

An ironic reversal of Bakhtin's confident perspective, which often becomes negativized today, should act as a warning to us in our attempts to apply Bakhtin's theories to contemporary culture. We must remind ourselves that his own concepts are always rooted in history, in the specificity of time and place. Nevertheless, in discussing the particular case of the medieval carnival, Bakhtin seems to have uncovered what I believe to be another underlying principle of all parodic discourse: the paradox of its authorized transgression of norms. Bakhtin describes the subversive carnival as actually being "consecrated by tradition," both social and ecclesiastical.[38] Therefore, although this popular festival and its manifest forms exist apart from "serious official, ecclesiastical, feudal, and political cult forms and ceremonials" (5), in so being, they in fact also posit those very norms. The recognition of the inverted world still requires a knowledge of the order of the world which it inverts and, in a sense, incorporates. The motivation and the form of the carnivalesque are both derived from authority: the second life of the carnival has meaning only in relation to the official first life. However, Bakhtin writes: "While carnival lasts, there is not other life outside it" (7). True, perhaps; but that "while" is significant. The medieval church may have tolerated, legalized, perhaps even preserved or created, the carnivalesque forms, but it did so only for a permitted length of time. In Bakhtin's terms: "As opposed to the official feast, one might say that carnival celebrated temporary liberation from the prevailing truth and from the established order; it marked the suspension of all hierarchical rank, privileges, norms, and prohibitions" (10). Note that he said "temporary" "suspension" and not permanent destruction of "prevailing" norms. The social inversions (such as the crowning of fools) and the parodic literary ones were both temporary transgressions, and the laughter at their expense "was absolutely unofficial but nevertheless legalized" (89). Parodic disguise was used to hide, not destroy, the sacred Word:[39] Bakhtin cites a fifteenth-century theological statement which admits that "we permit folly on certain days so that we may later return with greater zeal to the service of God" (*Rabelais*, 75). Centuries later, William Hone was acquitted on blasphemy charges (against his parody of the Scriptures in a political satire) on the grounds that he had not, in fact, ridiculed the Bible at all. His transgression, in other words, was authorized in yet another sense.[40]

This paradox of legalized though unofficial subversion is characteristic of all parodic discourse insofar as parody posits, as a prerequisite to its acknowledgment of recognizable, stable forms and conventions. These function as norms or as rules which can — and therefore, of course, shall — be broken. The parodic text is granted a special license to transgress the limits of convention, but, as in the carnival, it can do so only temporarily and only within the controlled confines authorized by the text parodied — that is, quite simply, within the confines dictated by "recognizability." While Roland Barthes[41] argued that any textual multivalence was in effect a transgression of propriety, it was this particularly legitimized quality of parodic multivalence that caused him to denigrate parody as a "classic" discourse, his version of Kristeva's (1969) "consolidation de la loi." (In Bakhtin's name, Kristeva has sought to denigrate parody. She contrasts what she sees as Bakhtin's theory of *"transgression giving itself a law"* to parodic literature's principle of *"law anticipating its own transgression."*)[42] (That latter phrase, however, is as descriptive of Bakhtin's work as the former.)

Parody can also be seen, however, to be a threatening, even anarchic force, one that puts into question the legitimacy of other texts. It "disrealizes and dethrones literary norms."[43] On another level, appropriation (borrowing or pirating) of the property of others questions art's accepted status as individualized commodity.[44] Nevertheless, parody's transgressions ultimately remain authorized — authorized by the very norm it seeks to subvert. Even in mocking, parody reinforces; in formal terms, it inscribes the mocked conventions onto itself, thereby guaranteeing their continued existence. It is in this sense that parody is the custodian of the artistic legacy, defining not only where art is, but where it has come from. To be a custodian, however, as Post-Modernist architecture has revealed, can be a revolutionary position; the point is that it *need* not be.

The best historical model of this paradoxical process of authorized transgression in parody might be the Greek satyr play. This was performed after a trilogy of tragedies, and essentially it reworked, in comic form, the serious material of the three plays preceding it. This satyr play was thus legitimized and made as canonical as the tragedies themselves (Bakhtin 1978, 412). Likewise, in the Christian context, the authority behind the early *parodia sacra* had a particular force, since the authority was the Word of God or of His representatives on earth. Parody is, therefore, not only repetition; its imitation always entails differentiation,[45] and its legitimizing authority depends on its anteriority for its status. It is this conjunction of repetition and priority that has led to those psychoanalytic illuminations of parody and imitation.[46] Clearly the nature of the legitimizing authority in parody is a complicated issue.

Sometimes the work parodied is a laughable, pretentious one that begs deflating; but even more often it is very successful works that inspire parodies. Often the number of parodies attests to a pervasive influence.[47] Fifteen different parodies of Zola's *L'Assommoir* appeared on stage in the first eight months of 1879, including one by Zola himself.[48] In the eighteenth and nineteenth centuries, parodies of the most popular operas often appeared on stage contemporaneously with the original. Weber's *Der Freischütz* (1821) was parodied in 1824 by *Samiel, oder die Wunderpille*. This German parody was translated into Danish and Swedish — an obvious sign of its popularity. In the same year, an English parody was staged at Edinburgh called *"Der Freischütz," a new muse-sick-all and see-nick performance from the new German uproar.* The popular operas of Wagner seemed especially prone to parody: *Tannhäuser* (1845) was taken on by the French in the not very subtly named *Ya-Mein-Herr, Cacophonie de l'Avenir, en 3 actes entr'acte mêlée de chants, de harpes et de chiens savants.* His *Tristan und Isolde* was parodied by *Tristanderl und Süssholde* before it was even staged.[49] To some critics, parody makes the original lose in power, appear less commanding; to others the parody is the superior form because it does everything the original does — and more. There is no doubt that this latter kind of audience or reader would revel in nineteenth-century opera or in the literature of turn-of-the-century France or contemporary America, while others find all such overcoded discourse to be a sign of decadence.

This contradictory reaction is not, however, just a matter of personal taste. Its roots lie in the bi-directionality of the legitimacy of parody itself. The presupposition of both a law and its transgression bifurcates the impulse of parody: it can be normative and conservative, or it can be provocative and revolutionary. Its potentially conservative impulse can be seen in both extremes of the range of ethos, reverence and mockery: parody can suggest a "complicity with high culture . . . which is merely a deceptively off-hand way of showing a profound respect for classical-national values,"[50] or it can appear as a parasitical form, mocking novelty in the hope of precipitating its destruction (and, by implication, its own). Yet parody can, like the carnival, also challenge norms in order to renovate, to renew. In Bakhtin's terminology, parody can be centripetal — that is, a homogenizing, hierarchicizing influence. But it can also be a centrifugal, denormatizing one. And I think it is the paradox of its authorized transgression that is at the root of this apparent contradiction. Parody is normative in its identification with the Other, but it is contesting in its Oedipal need to distinguish itself from the prior Other.

*   *   *

There are many highly conventionalized forms that become either overt or covert models within metafictional works, models that act as narrative clichés which signal to the reader the presence of textual autorepresentation. While parody clearly asserts this kind of aesthetic self-reflexivity, it is not the only mechanism of auto-referentiality today. There is a danger of using parody as the paradigm of self-reflexiveness. For example, Margaret Rose's *Parody/ Metafiction* (1979) has obviously been influenced by Bakhtin, who saw the novel's polyphonic form as differing from the monologic epic in its overt rejection of any claim to authority or absoluteness of meaning or language. It is true that the self-conscious novel today does what parody has always had the potential to do: that is, in one novelist's words, "to displace, energize, and re-embody its criticism — to literally reunite it with our experience of the text."[51] Modern metafiction is both dialogic and truly parodic to a greater and more explicit degree than Bakhtin could have recognized. As with his prized *Don Quixote,* today's self-referential fiction has the potential to be an "auto-critique" of discourse in its relation to reality. In saying this, we must remind ourselves once again, however, that there is no necessary correlation between self-criticism and radical ideological change.

However, like the sixteenth century, the postmodern period has witnessed a proliferation of parody as one of the modes of positive aesthetic self-reference as well as conservative mockery. Perhaps parody can flourish today because we live in a technological world

in which culture has replaced nature as the subject of art.[52] One of
the things that these two widely separated periods have in common,
I suggested earlier, is the sense of ideological instability, of a challenging of norms. But parody today can be both progressive and
regressive.[53] Bakhtin felt that early parody prepared the way for the
novel by distancing language from reality, by making overt the
artifice that in fact defines all art. What we are reading today in the
works of those obsessively parodic and encyclopedic metafiction-
ists—from Jorge Luis Borges to Italo Calvino, from John Fowles
to Umberto Eco—is the logical result of this view of the novel's
engendering. But all of their parodic transgressions remain legitimized, authorized by their very act of inscribing the backgrounded
parodied text, albeit with critical distancing of various degrees.

What happens when an *un*authorized transgression occurs? I
suspect it would have to go beyond even the interlingual and intertextual play of Nabokov's *Ada.* Perhaps it would begin something like this: "riverrun, past Eve and Adam's, from swerve to
shore to bend of bay, brings us by a commodius vicus of recircu-
lation back to Howth Castle and Environs." Joyce's *Finnegans
Wake* is more than just an extreme of parody or self-reflexivity. It
is not just a distortion. Here, I think, we come the closest to total
subversion that is possible within the elastic confines of comprehension. This is not temporary legitimate *inversion;* it is closer to
permanent *perversion* —which aims at *conversion.* Joyce's "last word
in stolen telling," then, might sound like this: "A way a lone a last
a loved a long the" . . . "riverrun past Eve and Adam's . . ."

B·

DIALOGISM AND ABSENCE

Paul de Man

Dialogue and Dialogism

The set of problems that surrounds the relationship between fiction and reality in the novel recurs in many forms to organize contemporary theories of narration as well as of the relationship between narrative, discursive, and poetic language. Much is at stake, stylistically, philosophically, and historically, in these discussions whose importance, not only in the realm of theory but also in the practical sphere of ethics and politics, is superseded only by their difficulty. The higher the stakes the harder the game. Such situations, conducive to obsession and to fatigue, are prone to generate legitimate admiration with regard to predecessors who have somehow managed to sustain the ordeal of these difficulties and to bequeath to us some of the skills and strategies gained in the course of this experience. Literary theory, and especially theory of narrative, a rather barren area of endeavor constantly threatened by the tedium of its techniques as well as by the magnitude of the issues, offers poor soil for the heroes and the hero worship that it rather desperately needs. So when a possible candidate for such a status comes along, he is likely to be very well received, especially if he is safely and posthumously out of reach. Such belated "receptions," for being rare, are all the more intense in the field of literary theory. A fairly recent example is, of course, the case of Walter Benjamin. More recent, and more intense still, is that of Mikhail Bakhtin, who was recently heralded, by his highly competent and clear-eyed introducers, as "le plus important penseur soviètique dans le domaine des sciences humaines et le plus grand théoricien de la littérature au 20ᵐᵉ siècle" ("the most important Soviet thinker in the area of the human sciences and the greatest literary theorist of the twentieth century") and "as one of the leading thinkers of the 20th century."[1] In both cases, this entirely justified admiration is focused on Bakhtin's contribution to the theory of the novel, not only in the relatively well-known books on Rabelais and Dostoevsky but in more theoretical studies such as the essay entitled "Discourse in the Novel" which dates from 1934–35. This essay is singled out by both Todorov and Holquist as the major theoretical statement. And, within the theory of the novel, it is the concept of dialogism, rather than related but other Bakhtinian terms such as chronotopes, refraction, heteroglossia, or the carnivalesque, that receives major attention, as is apparent from the titles of the two books: *Le principe dialogique* (1981) and *The Dialogic Imagination* (1981).

The last thing I wish to do here is to dispute or dispel this enthusiasm. There is no merit whatever to the facile and always cheaply available gesture that protects mediocrity by exposing the blindness that is part of any dedication and of the admiration it inspires. The attentive and critical reading of Bakhtin's work has barely begun, at least in the West, and since I ignore the Russian language, it is not an enterprise in which I can responsibly hope to take part. My question therefore does not address the significance of Bakhtin, or of Voloshinov/Bakhtin or of Medvedev/Bakhtin, as a theoretician or as a thinker, but the much more narrow question of why the notion of dialogism can be so enthusiastically received by theoreticians of very diverse persuasion and made to appear as a valid way out of many of the quandaries that have plagued us for so long. Or, to put it in the terms of this issue: how does dialogism, as developed in Bakhtin and his group, cope with and indeed seem to overcome the ever-recurring question of the status of fact, meaning, and fiction in the novel?

Dialogism can mean, and indeed has meant, many things to many critics, sometimes without reference to Bakhtin. Its more or less submerged presence is noticeable in the papers presented in this issue [*Poetics Today* 4:1 (1983)], as when Hilary Putnam invites us to see criticism as "a conversation with many voices rather than as a contest with winners and losers" ["Is There a Fact of the Matter about Fiction?" p. 81]. It can, first of all, simply mean double-talk, the necessary obliqueness of any persecuted speech that cannot, at the risk of survival, openly say what it means to say: there is ample evidence, from what is known of Bakhtin's biography, that this meaning is entirely relevant in his case. The readers of oppressed thinkers, in the words of a major theoretician of the discourse of persecution, "are to be led step by step from the popular view [. . .] to the truth which is merely and purely theoretical, guided by certain obtrusively enigmatic features in the presentation of the popular teaching—obscurity of the plan, contradictions, pseudonyms, inexact repetitions of earlier statements, strange expressions, etc."[2] This quotation from Leo Strauss's *Persecution and the Art of Writing* fits the case of Bakhtin very well. Strauss could have added another salient feature: the circulation of more or less clandestine class or seminar notes by initiated disciples or, even more symptomatic, the rumored (and often confirmed) existence of unpublished manuscripts made available only to an enterprising or privileged researcher and which will decisively seal one mode of interpretation at the expense of all rival modes—at least until one of the rivals will, in his turn, discover the real or imaginary countermanuscript on which to base his counterclaim. What in the context of our topic interests us primarily in this situation is that it is bound to engender a community tied together by the common task of decrypting the repressed message hidden in the public utterance. As the sole detainers of an esoteric knowledge, this community is bound to be small, self-selective, and likely to consider itself as a chosen elite. To the extent, however, that the process of understanding becomes constitutively linked to the elaboration and the life of a society, fact and fiction are brought together by the mediation of shared communal labor. The possibility of this mediation is built within the production of the text itself: since it does not mean to say what it actually says, it is a fiction, but a fiction that, in the hands of the right community of readers, will become fact.

For Leo Strauss, the model of persecution applies predominantly to philosophical rather than to literary texts; Bakhtin's stress on the novel adds a potentially libertarian and revolutionary dimension. "Im Sklaven fängt die Prosa an": it is in the slave, says Hegel, that prose begins and he says this in the section of the *Aesthetics* that deal precisely with fables as the ancestors of the novel. Like Strauss's philosopher, Bakhtin's novelist is persecuted per definition and carries within himself the image of his liberation. But this image exists not, as is still the case in Lukács, in the form of a nostalgia for the presumably unified world of the epic; the novelist does not set out to take the place of his master, the epic poet, but to set him free from the restricting coercions of his single-minded, monological vision. Bakhtin's novel definitely belongs to what Northrop Frye calls the low-mimetic modes: it is ideologically prosaic, anti-romance, anti-epical, and anti-mythical; its multivoicedness or heteroglossia postulates distinct and antagonistic class structures as well as the celebratory crossing of social barriers. The dialogism of a revolutionary community reconciles fact and fiction in a manner that is not essentially distinct from the persecutory model, except for the introduction of a temporal dimension: the freedom that is being celebrated is not utopian, yet it is not actualized in the immediacy of the textual invention. It is projected in a metatextual future as the prolepsis of a no longer fictional freedom. The scheme is bound to exercize a powerful attraction on a type of literary criticism that stems from a rebellion against the constraints of transcendental and monological systems such as institutional religions. An author and a concept — dialogism — that can be made to accommodate the textual model of Leo Strauss as well as of some disciples of Gilles Deleuze shows, to say the least, remarkable scope.

In Bakhtin's writings, the notion of dialogism is also systematically developed, not only, as in "Discourse in the Novel" or in the Rabelais book, in dialectical exchange with the persecutory power of monistic discourses, but in a prolonged and complex discussion of formalism. As is well known, the topic figures prominently in the pseudonymous books *Marxism and the Philosophy of Language* (Voloshinov) and *The Formal Method in Literary Scholarship* (Medvedev). Very summarily put, it is possible to think of dialogism as a still formal method by which to conquer or to sublate formalism itself. Dialogism is here still a descriptive and metalinguistic term that says something about language rather than about the world. Bakhtin is consistent in his assertion that the dialogical relationship is intra-linguistic, between what he calls two heterogeneous "voices," as in a musical score. It is, in his terms, the image of a *language* (rather than the *image* of a language) and not of a society or of an interpersonal relationship.[3] Therefore, as becomes evident in examples taken from Dickens and Turgenev, it is possible to analyze descriptively dialogical structures in actual texts, in a manner that is by no means unusual to "formalist" practitioners of an American style of close reading. On the other hand, dialogism also functions, throughout the work and especially in the Dostoevsky book, as a principle of radical otherness or, to use again Bakhtin's own terminology, as a principle of *exotopy:* far from aspiring to the *telos* of a synthesis or a resolution, as could be said to be the case in dialectical systems, the function of dialogism is to sustain and think through the radical exteriority or heterogeneity of one voice with regard to any other, including that of the novelist himself. She or he is not, in this regard, in any privileged situation with respect to his characters. The self-reflexive, autotelic, or, if you wish, narcissistic structure of form, as a definitional description enclosed within specific borderlines, is hereby replaced by an *assertion* of the otherness of the other, preliminary to even the possibility of a *recognition* of his otherness. Rather than having to do with class structures, as in the societal models of "Discourse in the Novel," exotopy has to do with relationships between distinct cultural and ideological units. It would apply to conflicts between nations or religions rather than between classes. In this perspective, dialogism is no longer a formal and descriptive principle, nor does it pertain particularly to language: heteroglossia (multivariedness between discourses) is a special case of exotopy (otherness as such) and the formal study of literary texts becomes important because it leads from intralinguistic to intracultural relationships. At that point, the binary opposition between fiction and fact is no longer relevant: in any differential system, it is the assertion of the space *between* the entities that matters. Binaries, to the extent that they allow and invite synthesis, are therefore the most misleading of differential structures. Novelists like Dostoevsky or, one might surmise, Balzac reveal their exotopy when they simply ignore such strongly suggestive oppositions as those between author and character: Dostoevsky's or Balzac's characters are not voices of authorial identity or identification (not: *Madame Bovary, c'est moi*) but voices of radical alterity, not because they are fictions and the author isn't, but because their otherness *is* their reality. The reality principle coincides with the principle of otherness. Bakhtin at times conveys the impression that one can accede from dialogism as a metalinguistic (i.e., formal) structure to dialogism as a recognition of exotopy. The itinerary beyond form by ways of formal analysis is particularly attractive to someone skilled in the formal analysis of structural semiotics or structural stylistics but grown impatient with the inability to break out of the formal shell and to address, at long last, questions that appear no longer to be merely linguistic. Todorov is, of course, himself a case in point.

It is also by ways of exotopy that, finally, a larger philosophical claim can be made for Bakhtin not just as a technician of literary discourse but as a thinker or metaphysician whose name can be considered next to those of Husserl, Heidegger, or, as Todorov aptly suggests, Levinas. The radical experience of voiced otherness as a way to a regained proximity can indeed be found as a dominant theme in Levinas and to have at least a submerged existence in Heidegger. One can think of the lines in Hölderlin's poem *Mnemosyne,* "*Seit ein Gespräch wir sind / Und hören können von einander*" as a common ground. Whether the passage from otherness to the recognition of the other—the passage, in other words, from dialogism to dialogue—can be said to take place in Bakhtin as more than a desire, remains a question for Bakhtin interpretation to consider in the proper critical spirit. This renders premature any more specific consideration of how this recognition is to occur: as a religious transcendentalism which would allow one to read "God" wherever Bakhtin says "society," as a Heideggerian disclosure of ontological truth in the otherness of language or as a secular but messianic ideologism that would bear a superficial, and perhaps misleading, resemblance to the position attributed to Walter Benjamin. To adjudicate hastily between these various options would be unthinkable; what can be observed is that, in each case, dialogism appears as a provisional stage under way toward a more absolute claim, a claim that is not necessarily monological but that points, at any rate, well beyond the limited confines of literary theory. Whether such an extension of Bakhtin's range is sound and legitimate also remains to be established. But that it is a possibility is made clear by the tone, even more than by the substance, of what is being written about him in Western Europe and in the United States.

One sees that it would be possible to line up an impressive list of contemporary theorists of very diverse persuasion, all of which would have a legitimate claim on Bakhtin's dialogism as congenial or even essential to their enterprise: the list could include analytical

philosophers, formalist semioticians grown weary with their science, narratologists, technicians of reader reception, religious phen-
omenologists, Heideggerian critical ontologists, defenders of
permanent revolution, disciples of Leo Strauss — and one could easily play the game of extending still further this list of unlikely bed-
fellows. If one then would be curious to know what they have in
common, at least negatively, one should perhaps ask who, if anyone, would have reason to find it difficult or even impossible to
enlist Bakhtin's version of dialogism among his methodological tools
or skills. Such as, for example, a literary theoretician or critic concerned with tropological displacements of logic, with a rhetoric of
cognition as well as of persuasion. Bakhtin has very astute things
to say about tropes but, if one is willing to suspend for a moment
the potential dialogical otherness of these statements, he seems, on
the whole, to consider that the discourse of tropes is not dialogical,
does not account for dialogism, and remains, by and large, on the
near side of the theories of narrative that dialogism allows one to
elaborate. Bakhtin frequently asserts the separation of trope from
dialogism, for instance in the passage on the distinction between
discourse in poetry and in prose, as stated in terms of refraction,
in "Discourse" or in the later, even more dogmatically explicit passage in the same text, on the distinction between the tropological
polysemy of poetry and the dialogism of prose. Here Bakhtin unambiguously asserts that "no matter how one understands the in-
terrelationship of meanings in a poetic symbol (or trope), this
relationship is never of the dialogical sort; it is impossible under
any conditions or at any time to imagine a trope (say, a metaphor)
being unfolded into the two exchanges of a dialogue, that is, two
meanings parceled out between two separate voices."[4] These passages are among the richest in the canon of Bakhtin's works, but
this implies that they are also among the most contradictory and,
for that reason, monologically aberrant. More than any other, they
reveal the metaphysical *impensé* of Bakhtin's thought, the dogmatic
foundations that make the dialogical ideology so attractive and so
diverse. This is not the time and the place for a detailed analysis of
the passages in question. But lest you suspect me of being evasive,
let me state the direction that such a reading would take — while
adding, as a matter of course, that at the moment when I appropriate these passages as the ground of my own admiration for the

revealingly aberrant character of Bakhtin's writings, I have included myself in the odd list of Bakhtin admirers from which I first pretended to be excluded; this, however, in no way disposes of the negative thrust of the proposed argument. One would have to point out (1) that, for Bakhtin, the trope is an intentional structure directed toward an object and, as such, a pure *episteme* and not a fact of language; this in fact excludes tropes from literary discourse, poetic as well as prosaic, and locates them, perhaps surprisingly, in the field of epistemology; (2) that the opposition between trope as object-directed and dialogism as social-oriented discourse sets up a binary opposition between object and society that is itself tropological in the worst possible sense, namely as a reification; (3) and more revealing for us, that as the analysis of dialogical refraction develops, Bakhtin has to reintroduce the categorical foundations of a precritical phenomenalism in which there is no room for exotopy, for otherness, in any shape or degree. When it is said, for example, that "the heteroglot voices [. . .] create the background necessary for [the author's] own voice," we recognize the foreground-background model derived from Husserl's theories of perception and here uncritically assimilating the structure of language to the structure of a secure perception: from that moment on, the figure of refraction and of the light ray becomes coercive as the only possible trope for trope, and we are within a reflective system of *mise en abŷme* that is anything but dialogical. It is therefore not at all surprising that, still in the same passage, Bakhtin modulates irrevocably from dialogism to a conception of dialogue as question and answer of which it can then be said that "the speaker breaks through the alien conceptual horizon of the listener, constructs his own utterance on alien territory against his, the listener's, apperceptive background."[5] Again, there is no trace of dialogism left in such a gesture of dialectical imperialism that is an inevitable part of any hermeneutic system of question and answer. The ideologies of otherness and of hermeneutic understanding are not compatible, and therefore their relationship is not a dialogical but simply a contradictory one. It is not a foregone conclusion whether Bakhtin's discourse is itself dialogical or simply contradictory.

Let me turn, in conclusion, to a text which can, I think, be said to be dialogical, which also happens to be a dialogue and a dialogue about the novel at that. Rousseau's prefatory post-face to *La Nou-*

velle Héloïse, sometimes entitled *Dialogue on the Novel,* combines two modes of dialogue. First a hermeneutic mode in which author and reader are engaged in a sequence of questions and answers, a set of who's and what's for the purpose of determining whether the contents of the novel are fact or fiction: Who is Julie? Did she exist? The outcome of this hermeneutic quest is utterly inconclusive: the hermeneutics of reference are undecidable. But, in case you worry about the legitimacy of the present performance, the decision of undecidability is itself entirely rational and legitimate: although another session on fact and fiction within the novel in next year's MLA is not going to get any further than we got today, such a continuation is entirely legitimate and, in fact, inevitable. The formal expression of this certainty is manifest in the symmetry of the question and answer patterns which would allow one, within the orbit of such a question, to substitute author for reader without any loss of consistency: the unreadability of the referent is just as challenging, and for the same reasons, for the one as for the other, and their complicity in the hermeneutic quest is manifest.

On the other hand, the text also stages something very different: a battle of wits between author and reader in which they try to outdo each other, parrying, feinting, and setting traps in a sequence of attacks and defenses somewhat like a fencing match, or like the seduction which is being carried on in the exchange of letters that make up the first part of Rousseau's novel. In this exchange, the question is no longer a question of who or what: it would be naive to ask who wins the match since in this model, Rousseau, as author, controls the moves of each of the antagonists. And it would be equally naive to ask over what one is fighting: one fights over whether or not there is a question, which means that one is at least twice removed from any possibility of an answer as to what, in this fight, is at stake. All the interest focuses on *how* one fights (or seduces), on the how, the *poetics* of writing and of reading rather than the hermeneutics. The author wants to know what all authors always want to know: Did you read my book? Did you read it to the end? Do you think people will want to buy it? Will it sell in Paris? All of which amounts to wondering if he put it together right—questions all belonging to the realm of empirical poetics (how to write a book that will achieve fame) rather than hermeneutics (what is the truth of the text). This puts him at an obvious disadvantage in the ensuing battle in which the urbane reader can constantly play on the vulnerability of his position and make him look foolish: the smart reader always outwits an author who depends on him from the moment he has opened a dialogue that is never entirely gratuitous, that is always a battle for mastery. Yet, at the end of Rousseau's text, the character designated by *R,* and who is the author, refuses the substitution offered to him:

"N. . . . I advise you, however, to switch parts. Pretend that I am the one who urges you on to publish this collection of letters and that you are the one who resists. You give yourself the objections and I'll rebut them. It will sound more humble and make a better impression.

R. Will it also be in conformity with what you find to be praiseworthy in my character?

N. No, I was setting you a trap. Leave things as they are."

One of the ways in which this tricky passage has to be read is as the refusal, in terms of poetics, to grant the substitutive symmetry implied in a hermeneutics. Rousseau does not have the least intention to relinquish to his reader the benefit in fame or money of the 70,000 copies which, at the time of writing the so-called preface, he knew his novel had already sold, in Paris as well as in the provinces. *Rira bien qui rira le dernier.* This success of his poetics is in no way compatible, however, with the rules of his hermeneutics. The relationship between poetics and hermeneutics, like that between R the author and N the reader, is dialogical to the precise extent that the one cannot be substituted for the other, despite the fact that the nondialogical discourse of question and answer fully justifies the substitution. What one has to admire Bakhtin for (that is, want to be in his place in having written what he wrote), as all his present readers, including myself, do, is his hope that, by starting out, as he does, in a poetics of novelistic discourse one may gain access to the power of a hermeneutics. The apparent question of the relationship between fact and fiction in the novel hides the more fundamental question of the compatibility between the descriptive discourse of poetics and the normative discourse of hermeneutics. Such compatibility can only be achieved at the expense of dialogism. To imitate or to apply Bakhtin, to read him by engaging him in a dialogue, betrays what is most valid in his work.

Mathew Roberts

Poetics Hermeneutics Dialogics:
Bakhtin and Paul de Man

Among the more interesting phenomena of Bakhtin studies in recent years have been the attempts by both Marxists and poststructuralists to appropriate this Slavic thinker as their own — more often than not, to enlist his models of culture and textuality in the ongoing polemic with their own (structuralist, poststructuralist, and Marxist) opponents.[1] One result of this frankly partisan engagement has been to continue the tradition, established two decades ago by Soviet and French semioticians, of a laudatory appropriation rather than a critical analysis of Bakhtin's texts; poststructuralists in particular have shown little interest in *differentiating* their project from Bakhtin's. It is for this reason that Paul de Man's brief essay, "Dialogue and Dialogism," provides so valuable a starting point for such a differentiation.

I propose to continue from this starting point, although not quite along the lines suggested by de Man's deconstructive critique. That deconstruction begins in the space between the "monologic" trope of poetry and the "dialogic" discourse of the novel, as this distinction is set forth in "Discourse in the Novel." Ultimately I shall suggest that this opposition of trope and dialogism is itself highly emblematic of the confrontation between deManian and Bakhtinian textual models. There are several reasons, however, why it might be fruitful initially to bracket this opposition as it functions in de Man's critique. First, the essay which de Man takes as "the major theoretical statement" of the Bakhtin canon, while probably the best known to an English-speaking audience, is nevertheless only one such statement among many over fifty years of highly diverse, even heterogeneous theorizing. In several respects (including the crucial opposition of novel and poetry) the essay represents a rather extreme "novelocentricity" in relation to Bakhtin's earlier and later texts. As such, it may be a somewhat problematic vehicle for interrogating Bakhtin's underlying epistemology.

At the same time, the whole issue of trope versus dialogism is for de Man a preparatory move on the way to his major claim: that Bakhtinian dialogism attempts a movement from "formal" analysis, or poetics, to "ideological" analysis, or hermeneutics — a movement between incompatible discourses which "can only be achieved at the expense of dialogism." What is at stake for de Man in such a claim? Is this critique intelligible on Bakhtin's own terms? These two questions will orient my own approach to a Bakhtin/de Man confrontation. In pursuing them I want to consider a somewhat wider Bakhtin corpus than is discussed in "Dialogue and Dialogism," as well as some key texts in de Man's own theoretical development. Central to my discussion will be the notions of "understanding," of the subject, and of the role of temporality as these conceptions are developed by both theorists.

Bakhtin, de Man, Heidegger: Self and Understanding

Some of the most fundamental differences between Bakhtin and de Man lie in their respective conceptions of the self or subject. If the Bakhtinian self is dynamic but inalienable, continually constituted in the dialogic armature of "I" and a world of Others, the deManian subject is a radically suspect entity, a linguistic or theoretical construct continually *de*constituted or deconstructed in confronting the literary text. This issue is worth considering in some depth, for in both cases the concept of the self will profoundly influence the nature and possibilities of textual meaning.

In his introduction to *Blindness and Insight,* Wlad Godzich characterizes de Man's critical position as a form of "ascesis" which entails "a progressive renunciation of the representational."[2] With equal validity he could have insisted on the literal meaning of the term — a renunciation of the 'worldly self' in favor of some higher truth — for this is precisely how de Man speaks of his project in a

1966 essay on Ludwig Binswanger: "Because it implies a forgetting of a personal self for a transcendent type of self that speaks in the work, an act of criticism can acquire exemplary value. Although it is an asceticism of the mind rather than a plenitude or a harmony, it is an asceticism that can lead to logical insight" (*BI*, 49– 50).

The type of "criticism" for which de Man makes this not inconsiderable claim is phenomenology — specifically, the phenomenological hermeneutics inaugurated by Martin Heidegger in *Sein und Zeit*, which first established the "crucial distinction between an empirical and an ontological self" (*BI*, 50). As de Man develops it here, Heidegger's importance lies in his posing "the question of the self" not in terms of a conception of consciousness derived from empirical experience — as in a Kantian philosophical anthropology — but rather exclusively "in terms of [the self's] relationship to the constitutive categories of being" (*BI*, 38). Only through such a rigorous ontological quest for the ground of human Being can we approach any "philosophical understanding of existence" — an understanding which de Man clearly seeks to further in his own literary-critical project.

In its literary-critical transposition, however, this Heideggerian task requires a particular effort of "interpretive vigilance," for in literature "the problem of the self is particularly delicate"; one must continually struggle with "an almost irresistible tendency to relapse unwittingly into the concerns of the self as they exist in the empirical world" (*BI*, 38). The essay goes on to demonstrate how Binswanger's work succumbs to just this tendency; yet with reference to de Man's own work, a more general claim can be made. In assuming Heidegger's phenomenological project, de Man has committed his own critical efforts to the vigilant task for which Binswanger was found wanting: the ongoing and ever more radical discovering of the "ontological self" in the interpretation of literary texts.

In "Criticism and Crisis," for example, de Man suggests that the Structuralist "suppression of the subject" — implicit both in Lévi-Strauss's model of the self as "virtual focus" and in the structural linguists' concept of a metalanguage without a speaker — has direct and ominous implications for "the larger question of the ontological status of the self" (*BI*, 19). In "The Rhetoric of Temporality," de Man finds in Romantic irony a mechanism which "splits the subject into an empirical self that exists in a state of inauthenticity and a self that exists only in the form of a language that asserts the knowledge of this inauthenticity" (*BI*, 214). Perhaps the most extreme statement of this "renunciation of the self" appears in the 1979 *Allegories of Reading*, where de Man's reading of Rousseau yields a radically antisubjective model of language: "Far from seeing language as an instrument in the service of a psychic energy, the possibility now arises that the entire construction of drives, substitutions, repressions and representations is the aberrant, metaphorical correlative of the absolute randomness of language, prior to any figuration or meaning."[3]

We shall return in greater detail to the deconstructive project which has produced de Man's "ontological insights." For now we might simply note the consequences of these insights for the nature of literary meaning. Rather than serving as a privileged, stabilizing source of intentional or cognitive meaning, the deManian subject is itself radically destabilized or deconstructed in the process of reading a literary text. Indeed, if this deconstructed, 'ontological' self is precisely what "speaks in the work," then literature exists at least in part to *enact the inauthenticity* of the intending subject — to enact, as de Man writes in "Criticism and Crisis," the "presence of a nothingness": "Poetic language names this void with ever-renewed understanding and . . . it never tires of naming it again. This persistent naming is what we call literature" (*BI*, 18).

In his development of Heideggerian phenomenology, then, de Man answers the 'question of the self' by locating its negative truth in the "void" which constitutes literary meaning. The answer provided by Mikhail Bakhtin could hardly be more dissimilar, and yet, paradoxically, his own approach to the problem of the self is in some ways highly analogous to that of the young Martin Heidegger.

Among the various texts which survive from Bakhtin's early "neo-Kantian" period, there is a fragment of some seventy pages in which the author spells out his moral/aesthetic "philosophy of the act."[4] Bakhtin's *filosofia postupka* is an attempt to grapple with the ethical consequences of the Kantian "spirit"/"matter" dichotomy, which he sees manifested in the opposition of two 'worlds': the "world of culture," in which all phenomena take on "meaning" in the unity of abstract-theoretical systems, and the "world of life, the singular world in which we create, become aware, observe, in which we have lived and in which we die" (*KFP*, 82). The basic problem with all moral philosophy (including the neo-Kantian tradition out of which Bakhtin is operating) is that it attempts to generate norms and values for our real-life actions *from within* the abstract-theoretical realm of culture, without reference to the concrete, historical context in which those acts arise. Such attempts, for Bakhtin, are quite "hopeless": the "theoretical world" can say nothing to *me* of practical value, while my own concrete-historical existence is irrelevant to it. My life is "a responsive, risk-taking, open act-of-becoming *[stanovlenie-postupok]*"; I cannot and do not live in the predetermined, "completed" world of abstract cognition. "If this world were [truly] everything, then I would not exist" (*KFP*, 88). Only from within my act itself, and not from some abstract "transcription" of that act, is there any access to the "event of existence."

Some five years before Bakhtin wrote these lines, Martin Heidegger had engaged in a similar struggle with neo-Kantian philosophy and the problems of being and value—and had come to some very similar conclusions: valid knowledge of the self could not be derived from an abstract "theoretical subject," but must instead be grounded in the dynamic, concrete-historical context of personal human experience, in *one's own experience* as a being "in the world."[5] Here, both men were following the lead of Wilhelm Dilthey in his insistence on the dynamic and historical nature of human experience and cultural understanding. In particular, Dilthey's repudiation of "objective" knowledge in the human sciences in favor of a subjective, interested, and self-modifying *verstehen* would become central to both Bakhtin's and Heidegger's conception of the self.

Yet precisely *how* this process of "understanding" is fundamental to the self and its 'becoming' was conceived in very different ways by the two young thinkers. For Heidegger, the most pressing issue was ontological: to establish the basic conditions and categories of "Being as such," prior to the investigation of any specific 'being' or mode of existence. Through the phenomenological teachings of his mentor Husserl, Heidegger came to see Being as "being-manifest"—not an essence or property but the *event* of 'un-concealment.' Heidegger's own central contribution was to see human Being (*Dasein*) as the "temporal clearing" in which this being-manifest takes place. All human subjects constitute this clearing or "openness," which is the prerequisite for any specific cognition; yet most live "inauthentically," perceiving themselves as a timeless and self-adequate 'ego,' manipulating the objects of the factic world. To renounce this "fallen" state for an authentic self-awareness is to gain access to the true, ontological nature of one's own self—a process which must begin with the concrete experience of "facticity," but which must go beyond this to a dis-closing of the primordial relationship between Being, time, and human openness. Here, then, is the genesis of that vigilant task which lies at the base of de Man's deconstructive poetics: the rigorous, unending effort to dis-close and distinguish an ontological self from its fallen, empirical state in facticity.

Yet it is precisely this distinction that Bakhtin just as rigorously refuses to make in his own account of "authentic" human existence. For Bakhtin, the act of "understanding" the phenomenal world does not lead inward to a glimpse of one's own ontological structure but rather resolutely *outward,* for in the "responsive" act of cognition "I join myself to existence": "To understand an object is to understand my obligation with respect to that object (my obligatory orientation), to understand its relationship to me in the unity of event-existence *[bytie-sobytie]*" (*KFP*, 95). Cognition carries with it an immediate ethical imperative, for I "find myself" not only "in the world"—as for Heidegger—but at a radically singular point in that world in which, by definition, no one else may exist. "And around that singular point is arrayed the whole of existence in a singular and irrepeatable perspective. That which can be accomplished by me now, will never be accomplished by anyone else" (*KFP*, 112). This is my "obligation-laden singularity," my existential status "without an alibi in existence." It is only by *acknowledging* that obligation, through my "responsive act," that I participate in and thus gain access to the "ontological roots of authentic existence" (*KFP*, 115).

"Primary philosophy," then, can be nothing other than "a description, a phenomenology of this world of the act"—hence Bakhtin's critique of traditional philosophical categories. In ethical terms, 'necessity' [*dolzhestvovanie:* obligation, oughtness—eds.] becomes a category not merely of consciousness (as with Kant) but of the conscious *act* precisely in its singularity, its concrete-historical specificity. In epistemological terms, this focus on the responsive act affords a new possibility for mediating the gap between "mind" and "matter," and thus—to recall the inaugural concern of Bakhtin's essay—to bring together the two 'worlds' of theoretical cognition and historical existence. Brute matter for Bakhtin is something simply "given" (*dan*), ready-made, self-identical, and indifferent. As we have seen, however, the very act of cognition establishes a relationship of "answerability" (*otvetstvennost'*) with this object— that is, the object acquires axiological value with relation to the "becoming-event" of my own existence, an event which is always "posited" (*zadan*) or essentially conceptual. The totality of such relationships I chart (and continually rechart) with the world constitutes my singular "architectonics": "For my participatory consciousness it [the world] is an architectonic whole, and is arrayed around me as around the singular center from which issue my acts: it locates itself with respect to me to the extent that I go out of myself *[iskhozhu iz sebia]* in my visualization-act, thought-act and deed-act" (*KFP*, 124).

Everything which becomes part of this 'architectonic whole' is transformed from mere *dannost'* into *zadannost'*: this for Bakhtin is the dynamic/synthetic relationship of 'mind' and 'matter.' As with his conception of ethical necessity, Bakhtin goes beyond Kant here in grounding the unity, coherence, and ultimately meaning of the experienced world precisely in the *singularity* of the "participatory consciousness": only in correlation with the singular point defined by my responsive act—and not from the interrelations of any generalized, theoretical system—does a phenomenon of experience acquire an "evaluative center." Thus Bakhtin distinguishes between the abstract or "potential" meaning of the theoretical world and the axiologically "affirmed," "emotional-volitional" meaning that is generated "from within" the responsive act. In this sense abstract thought itself—indeed, the whole transcendent edifice of philosophical Truth—is only so much *dannost'* until it is appropriated, 'affirmed' by the participatory consciousness as part of its "project" (*zadanie*) of becoming.

For both Bakhtin and Heidegger, then, traditional ontology and epistemology are radically inadequate to the authentic nature of the self (as "event") and empirical experience (as concrete-historical). For Bakhtin, however, the essential Heideggerian project of "(self) dis-closure" is not only lacking in ontological significance — its very possibility is explicitly precluded by a fundamental aspect of his epistemology. This is the notion of "extralocality" or out-sideness (*vnenakhodimost'*) — what Julia Kristeva has referred to as Bakhtin's "other logic." Since "truth" for Heidegger consists in dis-covering or 'being-uncovered,' understanding is an aggressive and essentially *privative* process: "Truth is something that must always first be *wrested* from entities."[6] In contrast, Bakhtinian understand-ing respects and rigorously maintains the 'otherness' of the object, since meaning is not wrested away but rather *conferred* in a rela-tionship of answerability with the self. I "go out" to explore the object (thing, person, cultural artifact) in its own singular context, but then I must return to my own place, preserve my "extralocal-ity" vis-à-vis the object if it is to acquire meaning-for-me.[7]

In the case of another 'acting consciousness,' the self/other dis-tinction is categorically irreducible: "Between my singularity and the singularity of any other person, between my own concrete ex-perience and the experience of another . . . herein lies a profound ontological-event difference" (*KFP*, 136–37). In principle, then, "I" cannot become an object of my own understanding the way an Other can; certainly I cannot 'disclose' myself as an ontologically significant event *prior* to any specific act of cognition, for my very ontological significance lies solely in my responsive act of recogniz-ing *an other*. There is a basic incompatibility between the Bakhti-nian and Heideggerian epistemologies; for the former, the concept of extralocality explicitly denies what de Man will take as an "im-portant truth" of the phenomenological tradition: "the fact that philosophical knowledge can only come into being when it is turned back upon itself" (*BI*, 16).

This brief discussion is hardly meant to exhaust the possibilities of a Bakhtin-Heidegger comparison; there are, as Clark and Hol-quist have suggested, a number of "striking similarities" between the models of selfhood presented in *Sein und Zeit* and in the early Bakhtin texts. Our primary interest lies rather in de Man's appro-priation of the Heideggerian project — an appropriation which rad-ically transforms the notion of "authentic selfhood" in the service of hermeneutic understanding. We have already seen something of this transfigured "ontological self"; here we might consider one early instance of its derivation from the act of reading. For it is in

this scene of textual interpretation that the differences with respect
to Bakhtin, rather than the similarities, will become truly decisive.

Extralocality and Difference

For de Man as well as Bakhtin, the activity of understanding
a "text" (in the widest sense) is necessarily intersubjective, as opposed to the assumed "objectivity" of the natural sciences. Yet for
de Man this interpretive relationship is not one "in which two subjects engage in a self-clarifying dialogue." Rather, "the two subjec-
tivities involved, that of the author and that of the reader, co-operate
in making each other forget their distinctive identity and destroy
each other as subjects" (*BI*, 64). In "Criticism and Crisis" de Man
elaborates on this mutual de(con)struction that is inevitable in any
act of intersubjective interpretation:

> The observing subject is no more constant than the observed, and each
> time the observer actually succeeds in interpreting his subject he changes
> it, and changes it all the more as his interpretive process comes closer to
> the truth. But every change in the observed subject requires a subsequent
> change in the observer, and the oscillating process seems to be endless.
> (*BI*, 10)

As this dialectic of mutual dis-closure "gains in intensity and
truth," it tends ultimately toward the effacement of any difference:
"Both parties tend to fuse into a single subject as the original difference between them disappears" (*BI*, 10). In fact, suggests de Man,
it was precisely to avoid the "dangerous *vertige*" of such an encounter that Lévi-Strauss and other structuralists adopted their model
of "radical relativism," or "subject-free" cognition—a move with
its own sinister implications for both selfhood and textual meaning.

Yet it is exactly this vertiginous 'fusion,' or loss of self, that is
excluded from Bakhtinian understanding by the principle of extralocality. We have seen this principle enunciated in the context of
Bakhtin's ethical-philosophical project of the early 1920s; from this
point on, the irreducible categories of 'self' and 'other' would decisively structure his conceptions of language, of social and psychological processes, of generic interactions, and in particular the
great antigeneric force of "novelization." When Bakhtin returns
near the end of his life to the more general philosophical issues of

his youth, we find him once again inveighing against "the false tendency toward reducing everything to a single consciousness, toward dissolving in it the other's consciousness."[8] To be sure, the interpreting subject "must not reject the possibility of changing or even abandoning his already prepared viewpoints and positions" — for "in the act of understanding, a struggle occurs that results in mutual change and enrichment" (SG, 142). But this struggle is precisely *enriching,* not privative; secured by the epistemological armature of 'outsideness,' the interpretive situation is not de Man's destructive dialectic but rather a dialogic interaction of two singular and ineffacible architectonic positions — or, as Bakhtin here formulates it, a dialogue of two "contexts," the original context of the textual 'utterance' and the new context of its reader/addressee. "The event of the life of the text" — its "true essence" as a meaningful artifact — "always develops *on the boundary between two consciousnesses*" (SG, 106). Here, of course, Bakhtin is only restating the familiar theme of the Dostoevsky book and "Discourse in the Novel": the phenomenon of meaning is born, renewed, and augmented in dialogue.

In considering the role of "architectonics" and "extralocality" in forestalling de Man's interpretive *vertige,* we must not at the same time overlook the radical moments such concepts introduce into Bakhtin's own epistemology. Although he takes up Dilthey's methodological distinction between the natural sciences and the 'sciences of man,' Bakhtin's model of meaning as architectonically rather than structurally embodied threatens the "objectivity" of *any* knowledge that would be textually transmitted. "No thought, no issue, no theme can lie at the base of an architectonics," he writes in *K filosofii postupka,* for "they themselves require a concrete architectonic whole before they can be even partially finalized" (KFP, 140). Thus, "even the discursive prose explication of a scientific work is not conditioned by its essential idea, but rather by aspects completely arbitrary to this 'essence' — first and foremost, by the author's consciously or unconsciously limited field of vision."

Bakhtin goes on to suggest such an 'architectonic' reading of Kant's *Critique of Pure Reason;* at another point he speaks of the architectonically finalized or "aestheticized" nature of geographical, astronomical, and historical texts (KFP, 138). Of course, the insight that no verbal meaning can escape the provisionality (or determining effects) of its author's singular context is hardly original to Bakhtin; it was central to Dilthey's own *Geisteswissenschaft* and has been reiterated throughout the twentieth century. Yet Bakhtin goes far beyond most "contextualist" models of meaning in his insistence on the radical irrepeatability of any concrete-historical context. In *K filosofii postupka* Bakhtin attacks the rationalist doctrine that "the truth of a proposition is precisely what is repeatable and constant in it." This self-identical aspect, he argues, is only the abstract-semantic "potential" of the utterance; taken as a responsive *act*, however, its axiologically affirmed meaning is predicated upon its very singularity, which is to say its irreducible *otherness* with respect to our own semantic-ideological perspective (*KFP*, 110).

This argument will resurface in Bakhtin's ongoing critique of structural linguistic and literary models; in "The Problem of the Text," it appears as the "two poles" which he sees as constituting any text. On the one hand, "every text presupposes a generally understood (that is, conventional within a given collective) system of signs, a language" (*SG*, 105). On the other hand, "each text (as an utterance) is individual, unique and unrepeatable, and herein lies its entire significance." This second pole "is linked not with repeatable elements in the system of language (signs) but with other, unrepeatable texts by special dialogic . . . relations" (*SG*, 105). The distinction is crucial, for any language, as a sign system, "can always in principle be deciphered, that is, translated into other sign systems"; there is thus a "common logic" of sign systems, the "language of languages" that is semiotics (*SG*, 106). But the text, as an utterance, "can never be completely translated, for there is no potential single text of texts." Concrete textual meaning must always be "other" for Bakhtin — not through any inadequacy of language as a means of signification, but simply because extralocality inscribes an irreducible difference within the structure of understanding itself.

These epistemological strictures, it might be noted, are too often effaced in both semiotic and sociological appropriations of Bakhtin. Indeed — and here we return to our opening problematic — Bakhtin's "other logic" of *vnenakhodimost'* (outsideness) may be cited with some validity as evidence of an affinity with poststructuralist thinking. Yet as de Man correctly sees in "Dialogue and Dialogism," the epistemology of otherness is quite irreconcilable with his own textual model — for which the fundamental fissure lies between language and phenomenal experience as such. To grasp the nature of this fissure we must return to de Man's critical project in a more systematic way, and consider in particular the role of temporality in "demystifying" the referentiality of language.

De Man: Understanding (against) the Self

De Man's first statement of the "temporal problematic" of understanding appears in the 1967 essay, "Form and Intent in the American New Criticism." Written shortly after "Criticism and Crisis"[9] and the essay on Binswanger, this text pursues the ontology of literary understanding by focusing on two aspects of Heidegger's "hermeneutic circle." The first deals with "the epistemological nature of all interpretation" — specifically the interpretation of an 'intentional structure' such as a literary work. "To interpret an intent can only mean to understand it" (*BI*, 29), yet "we can only understand that which is in a sense already given to us and already known, albeit in a fragmentary, inauthentic way" (*BI*, 29–30). For Heidegger, hermeneutic understanding can only operate from a pre-existing "foreknowledge," established by Dasein's "primordial interpretation" or initial act of projecting itself within a world of phenomena it cares to know. Understanding of any object is therefore circular: complete only when the object has fully "become itself" through its dis-closure for Dasein. "For the interpreter of a poetic text," argues de Man, "the foreknowledge is the text itself. . . . Only when understanding has been achieved does the circle seem to close and only then is the foreknowing structure . . . fully revealed" (*BI*, 30–31).

But the circle only *seems* to close; in fact "the implicit foreknowledge is always temporally ahead of the explicit interpretive statement that tries to catch up with it." For the intentional structure of a literary work is not an 'object' but an event, constituted in the very act of interpretation: what we call literary "form" is "never anything but a process on the way to its completion" (*BI*, 31). Thus, form can never "become itself" as a synchronic totalization, but must remain a temporal phenomenon. "The act of understanding is a temporal act which has its own history, but this history forever eludes totalization" (*BI*, 32). This is the "temporal predicament" of understanding: the realization that the only horizon within which interpretive totalization may occur is time itself.

"Form and Intent" offers a specific critique of New Criticism and its 'organic' conception of poetic form; only at the end does de Man allude to a similar critique of French structuralism and its claims to "objective" interpretation. Yet it is precisely a structuralist model of meaning that is most gravely threatened by the confrontation of temporal experience and synchronic representation. Three years later, in "The Rhetoric of Blindness," one of de Man's many theoretical targets is the structural poetics of Tzvetan Todorov, which aspires to a "scientific," metalinguistic description of the literary text. Such a project, for de Man, sees interpretation as the 'duplication' of literary meaning; but in fact interpretation can only be "the narration of an understanding" — not so much a duplication as a *repetition*, "a temporal process that assumes difference as well as resemblance" (*BI*, 108). And in his reading of Rousseau which constitutes the bulk of this essay, de Man finds a model of language itself that embodies this very insight: "like music, language is a diachronic system of relationships, the successive sequence of a *narrative*" (*BI*, 131). Rather than employing the traditional metaphors of visual perception to describe linguistic meaning, Rousseau eschews such "misleading synchronism" for the figure of music: "a succession of discontinuous moments that create the fiction of a repetitive temporality" (*BI*, 131–32).

This critique of "synchronism" finds its most elaborate statement in "The Rhetoric of Temporality," where the 'temporal predicament' of understanding is brought to bear directly on the problematic of the self. De Man begins by questioning the traditional view that Romanticism privileges symbol over allegory; in fact, he suggests, this hierarchy is reversed when one considers the relative awareness each figure embodies of "authentic temporality." Romantic symbol posits an essential, 'organic' unity of sign and object or experience and representation; its relationship is one of spatial contiguity and thus of *simultaneity*. The allegorical sign, in contrast, primarily refers not to its conventional referent but to "another sign" — a relationship necessarily predicated on temporal distance: "Whereas the symbol postulates the possibility of an identity or identification, allegory designates primarily a distance in relation to its own origin, and, renouncing the nostalgia and the desire to coincide, it establishes its language in the void of this temporal difference" (*BI*, 207). But this epistemological "void," as we have seen before, is precisely the nonexistence of the self—here, the nonexistence of a stable or totalized identity between the "I" of pure experience and the aggregate "I's" of an unreachable anteriority. Romantic allegory, for de Man, is thus the diachronic narrative of "a conception of the self seen in its authentically temporal predicament" (*BI*, 208).

Yet the Romantics tell this story in another way as well, through the figure of irony. De Man defines this trope as a *dedoublement* or division of the self through a reflective act of consciousness— such as results from the abrupt demystification of the subject's assumed superiority over the natural world. This "reflective disjunction . . . transfers the self out of the empirical world into a world constituted out of, and in, language" (*BI*, 213)—inasmuch as language is the only available medium of "self-consciousness." "Language thus conceived divides the subject into an empirical self, immersed in the world, and a self that becomes like a sign in its attempt at differentiation and self-definition" (*BI*, 213). In this 'ironic self' we recognize the model derived from Heidegger—the quest for an essential, ontological relationship between the self, understanding, and temporality. Yet a crucial change has come about since de Man outlined this quest in the essay on Ludwig Binswanger: the ontological self is now explicitly *linguistic*, "like a sign," and we have already seen the fatal effect on linguistic integrity of 'authentic' temporal experience. Since the ironic self arises "at the expense" of the mystified empirical self, and must forever struggle to maintain this distinction, the ironic act of *dedoublement* "divides the flow of temporal experience into a past of pure mystification and a future that remains harassed forever by a relapse within the inauthentic" (*BI*, 222). The ironic self exists as the very understanding of the empirical self's inauthenticity, "but it remains endlessly caught in the impossibility of making this knowledge applicable to the empirical world. It dissolves in the narrowing spiral of a linguistic sign that becomes more and more remote from its meaning, and it can find no escape from this spiral . . ."

For de Man—and, he argues, for the Romantics as well—the figures of allegory and irony designate a common awareness of the "temporal void," at once the disjunction of sign and referent and the "nothingness" or fictionality of a self which is really no more than "a succession of discontinuous moments." This account represents a decisive stage in de Man's ongoing pursuit of the 'ontological self': unlike the "observing subject" which disappeared in the *vertige* of intersubjective interpretation, it is no longer even possible to situate this deManian self in relation to the Bakhtinian around any single opposition, such as hermeneutic versus transgradient understanding. Indeed, it is clear by this point that de Man is no longer operating (if indeed he ever was) with a recognizably Heideggerian conception of selfhood. While the notions of self, understanding, and temporality remain inextricably bound, the 'ontological self' has become a radically evacuated entity whose sole positive quality is its very instability, its very *fictionality* as enacted by the discourse of literature.

At the same time, it is evident from this essay that de Man has drastically reinflected the concept of "temporality" as well. Once the sole horizon for a possible totalized understanding, the very dimensionality of authentic self-becoming, temporality is now experienced by consciousness as an inexorable, mechanical repetition which denies both totality and authenticity to the subject. But since authentic temporality is "spoken" in the text by this very same "linguistic" self, the deconstruction of a totalized subject is at the same time the deconstruction of time itself as genuine duration, event, or becoming. Both temporality and self are now seen as fictitious, "authentic" only as tropes or rhetorical figures.

With this, "The Rhetoric of Temporality" both culminates the phenomenological critique of synchronic or totalized meaning and moves decisively beyond the conceptual space of Heidegger's project into the new realm of rhetorical textuality.[10] In the decade to follow, de Man will pursue his deconstruction of both temporality and the subject; we have already seen one extreme version of the latter in the 1979 *Allegories of Reading*. Yet these radically attenuated concepts have now become largely irrelevant in determining the fate of textual meaning for de Man — and thus irrelevant as well to the confrontation with a Bakhtinian textual model. Before returning to the site of that confrontation, however, it remains for us to trace a bit further the transfigured project of hermeneutic "understanding" itself.

In an essay dating from 1973, de Man reformulates his critique of literary structuralism in terms of an opposition between "semiology" and "rhetoric": the former studying the relations among "signs as signifiers," the latter being "the study of tropes and of figures." Semiology sees literary meaning in terms of "grammatical structures" which it seeks to elucidate and codify—a project de Man would appear to condone, were it not for the recurrent attempts by semioticians to extend this codification to rhetorical figures. As it turns out, however, he is not simply protesting this "reduction of figure to grammar" as a defense of rhetoric's autonomous domain against the hegemony of semiotics. As the essay goes on to enact first a "rhetorization of grammar" and then a "grammatization of rhetoric," de Man demonstrates that the two terms designate radically incompatible modes of understanding which are nevertheless coextensive in the operation of all discourse. Literature foregrounds the figurative or tropological potential of language and thus thematizes this tension between the "cognitive" (grammatical/referential) and "performative" (rhetorical) dimensions of discourse; but this thematization is itself an act of "reference" whose cognitive value is strictly undecidable. "We end up therefore, in the case of the rhetorical grammatization of Semiology, just as in the grammatical rhetorization of illocutionary phrases, in the same state of suspended ignorance."[11]

From this point, de Man's critical project will focus on the tropological dimension of language as that force, uncontrolled by any "subject," which perpetually dislocates grammatical cognition. The "negative knowledge" of this dislocation is the privilege and defining characteristic of literature—a knowledge that can be solicited only through a rigorous 'rhetorical' reading of the literary text. In critiquing semiotic theories of literature, which would replace "interpretation by decoding," de Man is accusing its practitioners of abdicating this task of critical hermeneutics for approaches less unsettling but ultimately unproductive of authentic "understanding." Behind the opposition of semiology and rhetoric, then, there lies the more fundamental confrontation of "poetics" and "hermeneutics"—the ultimate basis for de Man's polemic with structuralist models of textuality. It is also the central issue in de Man's critique of Bakhtinian dialogism—not because Bakhtin takes his stand among the semioticians, the "decoders" of literature, but rather because his dialogic methodology attempts an even more aberrant *violation* of the poetics/hermeneutics opposition itself.

Rhetoric and Dialogism

Returning at last to "Dialogue and Dialogism," we are perhaps in a better position to evaluate the force of de Man's critique — or rather, to situate it within the larger conceptual field which has been delineated. For if the preceding exposition has been of any value, it has been in demonstrating that the "confrontation" of these two theorists cannot occur around a problematic or conceptual opposition immanent to either. Thus the issue of poetics versus hermeneutics, with regard to Bakhtin, cannot hinge on the possibility of dialogism's somehow healing the rupture of grammar and figurality which de Man's project has elucidated. Rather, this question must bring into focus the fundamentally different attitudes of the dialogic and hermeneutic epistemologies toward semiotics and its Rationalist heritage. Unlike the author of *Sein und Zeit*, Bakhtin had never sought to de(con)struct the philosophical tradition he inherited — to wrench away its hidden 'truth' from the covering of *Vorhandenheit* — but merely to demonstrate the *inadequacy* of the 'theoretical world' to govern or explain the specific acts of actual human beings. In *K filosofii postupka* Bakhtin is prepared to acknowledge the "achievements" of contemporary ethical philosophy "in the area of its own specific tasks" — that is, the immanent laws of the "cultural world' to govern or explain the specific acts of actual human beings. tize or make available this abstract body of knowledge in the realm of the singular, acting consciousness.

This attitude is preserved in Bakhtin's critique of Russian Formalism, Saussurean linguistics, and, later, structuralism and semiotics. Elements of language *can* be studied in their repeatable, systemic aspect, but such analysis alone will never account for the concrete, semantic-axiological meaning of specific utterances — for this we need a "metalinguistics" which analyzes precisely the irrepeatable aspects of the utterance in its living, dialogic context. Similarly, both literary and nonliterary texts will contain repeatable elements which may be systematized or 'codified,' but in any given text these elements are organized into architectonic structures which embody the singular perspective and generic goals of its author, and with respect to which "everything repeatable and reproduceable proves to be material, a means to an end" (*SG*, 105). From his first critique of Formalist poetics (1924) and the Dostoevsky book, through "Discourse in the Novel" (1934) and "Speech Genres" (1953), to the final essays of the 1970s, Bakhtin never ceases to inveigh against the one-sided focus on this "material," the *dan* of verbal creativity. And yet, as we have seen, he nevertheless allows for the conceptual necessity of both "poles" in the text, the abstract-"semiotic" and the concrete-dialogic. To be sure, the latter is the realm of authentic, responsive understanding and as such is radically privileged in Bakhtin's own analyses and textual models. Yet his own "project" (*zadanie*) of dialogic understanding must always presuppose a certain semiotic *dan*, a grammatically coded "potentiality" to be actualized as concrete-historical meaning.

For de Man, of course, the semiotic aspect of language can play no such role in authentic understanding. We have seen that hermeneutic phenomenology has an explicitly negative or privative relation to any epistemology of self-identity. In *Sein und Zeit,* one of Heidegger's specific targets for 'destruction' was the notion of *logos* as logical proposition, as well as the models of language and grammatical rules engendered by this "error."[12] But if Heidegger deconstructed the Rationalist epistemology to elaborate a new *logos* in the service of authentic selfhood, de Man turns this new hermeneutic discourse against the self in pursuing its own "negative knowledge" in literature. Here subjectivity, temporality, and authentic cognition disappear into a universe of rhetorical textuality — and in the course of this deconstructive trajectory, de Man's hermeneutic project finds itself operating *within* the very conception of language with which it is so radically incompatible. Thus arises that model of "reading" we see in "Semiology and Rhetoric" and later essays — a tortured, fissured counterpart to Bakhtin's 'bi-polar' model — where the grammatical code is not transformed and augmented in the process of understanding but instead "is undone, at all times, by its rhetorical displacement."[13]

The juxtaposition of these two models, then, will itself constitute one moment of a Bakhtin/de Man confrontation — one among a vast number of possibilities, given the array of conceptual levels and terminologies employed by each theorist and partially common to both. In taking over from de Man the opposition of "hermeneutic" and "dialogic" understanding as the focus of my own discussion, I have hardly done justice to these terms as they function in the argument of "Dialogue and Dialogism." Rather, I have sought to reinscribe them within a wider, if less rigorous, field of vision. The same can be done with another set of terms to which I promised to return: the opposition of trope and dialogue, from which de Man begins his deconstructive reading of "Discourse in the Novel."

As I suggested above, the absolute distinction this essay establishes between "poetic" and "novelistic" discourse represents a rather extreme emphasis on 'novelization' as the source of all linguistic and literary creativity, a position quite absent from Bakhtin's first textual models and one from which he appears to retreat in his work of the 1970s.[14] One result of this sharp novel/poetry dichotomy is the characterization of poetic discourse as an (artistically) naive "monologism," which carefully suppresses all dialogic, intersubjective aspects of discourse in constructing its own tropic polysemy. Thus "in the poetic image narrowly conceived (in the image-as-trope), all activity . . . is completely exhausted in the play between the word (in all its aspects) and the object (in all its aspects)."[15] For de Man, this model creates an "opposition between trope as object-oriented and dialogism as social-oriented," an opposition which makes of trope "a pure *episteme* and not a fact of language"; which in fact "excludes tropes from literary discourse, poetic as well as prosaic, and locates them . . . in the field of epistemology."[16]

Yet where is this "field of epistemology" itself located? Or, more precisely, whose epistemology is it? Immediately following the 'trope vs. dialogism' passage quoted by de Man, Bakhtin explicitly discusses the epistemological dimensions of tropic or symbolic polysemy: "It is possible to interpret the interrelationships of different meanings in a symbol logically . . .; one may grasp this relationship philosophically and ontologically, as a special kind of representational relationship, or as a relationship between essence and appearance and so forth" (*DI,* 328). Yet his whole point here is that such monoreferential (author-word-referent) relationships belong to the realm of "monologic consciousness," to the "utopian philosopheme" of a unitary, singular language which is presupposed not only by poetry but even more essentially by "linguistics, stylistics and the philosophy of language" (*DI,* 274). Thus the "epistemology" de Man sees here is *not Bakhtin's;* it belongs rather to that 'theoretical world' of abstract unity, where a "common logic" would ensure complete decodability of texts. If Bakhtin later re-trieves poetic discourse from its exile in this monologic realm, it is due to his belated re-cognition that *no* aesthetically creative dis-course can do without the 'other logic' of extralocality.

Such an objection cannot of course 'refute' de Man's critique of Bakhtin. It can only demonstrate, once again, the mutual unintel-ligibility of their perspectives on meaning. Whereas de Man sees the classical *trivium* of grammar, rhetoric, and logic as riven within by the middle term, and thus disarticulated from "the knowledge of the world in general,"[17] Bakhtin sees "the world in general" obtruding on this classical epistemology from without, as an open totality of singular event-contexts, at once concretizing its abstract potentiality and radically denying its abstract unity.

Challenges

C.

AUTHORITY AND THE
TOLSTOY CONNECTION

Ann Shukman

Bakhtin's Tolstoy Prefaces

The explicit purpose of Bakhtin's two Tolstoy prefaces is to show how Tolstoy's dramatic works[1] and the novel *Resurrection*[2] relate to the social background of the period with its class struggles, and how they express Tolstoy's own ideological position at those moments in time when they were written. Of all Bakhtin's "own name" writings these prefaces are the most apparently Marxist in conception and vocabulary. In the preface to Tolstoy's dramas, for instance, we read, "And indeed, Tolstoy's writings, like those of any other writer, were wholly determined [*vsetselo opredelialos'*], of course [*konechno*], by his period and by the historical disposition of the social-class forces in that period."[3] (Note the "wholly" and the "of course," to be discussed below.)

The plays are treated as reflections of Tolstoy's current concerns and of those ideological strands that prevented him from perceiving the "genuine motivating forces of peasant life" (*podlinnye dvizhushchie sily krest'ianskoi zhizni*).[4] The ideology of Akim, Tolstoy's mouthpiece in the play *The Power of Darkness*, Bakhtin describes as that of a "declassed person . . . who has left the real stream of contradictory class formation" (*deklassiruiushchegosia . . . vyshedshego iz real'nogo potoka protivorechivogo klassovogo stanovleniia cheloveka*).[5]

In similar vein, in the preface to *Resurrection*, Bakhtin deals with Tolstoy's crisis of the 1880s, not in personal terms of the writer's inner development, but as an "inevitable response to the changing conditions of the time," as "prepared and stimulated by those complex social-economic and ideological processes which were taking place in Russian life."[6] In an aside on *War and Peace* Bakhtin comments that the patriarchal social order that Tolstoy so vividly portrayed in that novel was not the actually existing social-economic form, not the "stagnant world of the real serf-owning landlord," but a "semi-real, semi-symbolic canvas on to which the epoch, by means of the hand of the artist, itself wove the threads of other social worlds, other relationships."[7] (Note the passive role of the artist!) And even Tolstoy's "overflowing love of life," which is felt in all his writings up to the crisis, was, according to Bakhtin, "to a large extent the expression of those new social forces and relationships which in those years were bursting onto the arena of history."[8] Bakhtin quotes approvingly from Lenin on Tolstoy as the mirror of the contradictions of the society of his time[9] (though he also, a few pages later, perhaps somewhat contradictorily, quotes Plekhanov on Tolstoy's inability "to replace the exploiters with the exploited in his field of vision"[10]). What does this inability do to his mirror-like qualities, one may wonder?

Turning to the novel *Resurrection* itself, Bakhtin comments that Tolstoy's criticism of social institutions in the novel is "deprived of a genuine sense of history" (*lishena podlinnoi istorichnosti*),[11] and that his thesis likewise is "deprived of any historical dialectic" (*lishen vsyakoi istoricheskoi dialektiki*).[12] Bakhtin summarizes, "The ideology of the novel *Resurrection* is addressed to the exploiters. It emerges wholly from those tasks which faced the repentant representatives of the class of the nobility, now in the grip of decay and expiry. These tasks were deprived of any historical perspective."[13]

One would be hard pressed to find such *sustained*, such *explicit*, such *monologic* Marxist writing, with references to the historical dialectic, to the "genuine" understanding of history, to the class struggle, to exploiters and exploited in any other of Bakhtin's writings, or indeed, those published under the names of his associates. True, in the 1929 book on Dostoevsky we find remarks such as:

At the basis of our analysis lies the conviction that every literary work is internally and immanently sociological. Within it living social forces intersect; each element of its form is permeated with living social evaluations. For this reason even a purely formal analysis must take each element of the artistic structure as a point of refraction of living social forces, as a synthetic crystal whose facets are structured and ground in such a way that they refract rays of social evaluations, and refract them at a specific angle.[14]

And it is true too that Bakhtin remarks that an immanent sociological analysis of style should lead on to the question of "the historical social-economic conditions for the birth of that style."[15] But a consideration of the "refractions" of social forces in a work, and of the "immanent social evaluations" with which it is "permeated," is quite a long haul from declaring, as Bakhtin does in the first Tolstoy preface, cited above, that "of course" every work of literature is "wholly determined by [the writer's] period and by the historical disposition of the social-class forces in the period." And, indeed, the Tolstoy prefaces are not just immanent stylistic analyses: they are far more concerned with Tolstoy's writings as reactions to current events and current ideas than is, for instance, Bakhtin's nearly contemporary book on Dostoevsky.

In both Medvedev/Bakhtin's *The Formal Method in Literary Scholarship* of 1928 and Voloshinov/Bakhtin's *Marxism and the Philosophy of Language* of 1929 (also near contemporaries to the Tolstoy prefaces), the thrust of the argument is to establish, in the case of the former, a sociological poetics which takes cognizance of the refractory nature of all ideological constructions, and in the case of the latter, a theory of language usage that takes cognizance of the actual matter of living speech. In both books, quite explicitly, assumptions of mechanical causality between base and superstructure are refuted.[16]

If we turn further back to Bakhtin's writings of the first half of the 1920s, then the contrast is even more striking: in none of the essays so far available to us[17] is there any consideration of either history or society, still less of economic conditions. These are philosophical writings: an existentialist account of human responsibility, a philosophical quasi meditation on the nature of man and of literary creation and an attempt at an aesthetic philosophy of the literary text, written as a polemic against the Formalists. Admittedly, the keynotes of all Bakhtin's thinking are already announced and explored: "Author and Hero" is the first of Bakhtin's works to consider the essential nature of the "other" both in the constitution of consciousness (the "I") and in artistic creation. "The Problem of Content" discusses the inclusive nature of the work of art which as an aesthetic event (*sobytie*) brings together elements from many different spheres and subsumes them through the action of the artist into the aesthetic creation.

It is worth at this point recalling what Bakhtin had to say in much later years about the sociological approach to literature. When in 1963 the study of Dostoevsky was republished in revised form and under a new title,[18] Bakhtin added a section commenting on the reviews of the book's first edition. Referring to Lunacharsky's review of 1929, Bakhtin took the opportunity to summarize his attitude to the historical-genetic approach and clearly to set out his view on the limits of historical determinism, taking as his example the polyphonic novel:

The exceptionally acute contradictions of early Russian capitalism, and the duality of Dostoevsky as a social personality, his personal inability to take a definite ideological decision, are, if taken by themselves, something negative and historically transitory, but they proved to be the optimal conditions for creating the polyphonic novel. . . . Both Dostoevsky's epoch, with its concrete contradictions, and Dostoevsky's biological and social personality, with its epilepsy and ideological duality, have long since faded into the past—but the new structural principle of polyphony, *discovered* under these conditions, retains and will continue to retain its artistic significance under the completely different conditions of subsequent epochs. Great discoveries of human genius are made possible by the specific conditions of specific epochs, but they never die or lose their value along with the epochs that gave them birth. . . . Dostoevsky's discovery of the polyphonic novel, will outlive capitalism.[19]

Art, in other words, is historically and socially conditioned but is also timeless (or, as Bakhtin would express it later, it exists in "great time"). It follows that the study of art, or poetics, "cannot, of course, be divorced from social and historical analyses, but neither can it be dissolved in them."[20]

A great watershed, of course, divides the essays and philosophical works of the early 1920s, written in the pre-Leningrad years, and the writings of the later 1920s (including the Voloshinov and Medvedev works). And that watershed is surely to a great extent associated with Bakhtin's discovery of modern linguistics and the consequent shift of his focus of interest from consciousness and the inner world to speech, dialogue, and social intercourse. The Bakhtin of the later twenties is altogether more extroverted: language, lit-

erature, man himself are all now conceived of as set in a real world
of social interaction, which impinges on and shapes consciousness
and art as consciousness and art refracts and responds to it.

But another, smaller watershed divides the Tolstoy prefaces from
all that Bakhtin (with or without his associates) had written hitherto: for in the prefaces the notion of the mediating, refracting role
of language and form are set aside; his analysis focuses on Tolstoy's
ideology and the ideology of the characters. There is no consideration of language as such and apart from a brief final reference to
the "social-ideological novel," of which *Resurrection* is a superb
example, no reference to form. But by their treatment of the historical context, the prefaces may be counted as a foretaste of Bakhtin's historical poetics of the 1930s, of the great writings on the
history of the novel and on Rabelais that were to come.

Let us now look more closely at the Tolstoy prefaces, works
which Tzvetan Todorov referred to as "the most Marxist" of all
Bakhtin's writings.

The preface to Tolstoy's dramatic works deals first with the
early, "pre-crisis" plays. Why, Bakhtin wonders, were they so unsuccessful as literary works? His answer is on the level of Tolstoy's
personal predilections: first, Tolstoy all through his literary career
was opposed to convention, and drama, as he was later to make
explicit, was the most conventional of all literary genres and therefore the one in which Tolstoy was least likely to succeed. Second,
says Bakhtin, Tolstoy in the first part of his career was above all
concerned with the freedom and independence of the authorial
voice — which is, of course, excluded from drama. The early dramas, *The Infected Family* and to some extent *The Nihilist,* express
Tolstoy's attitude toward some of the ideas of the sixties — the
"women's question," nihilism, the peasant problem. Since these
works were written at the time (1863) when Tolstoy was beginning
to plan *War and Peace,* their significance in Tolstoy's development
as a writer must be to have made him seek values not in contemporary life but in the patriarchal way of life of an earlier generation.

The second part of the preface is concerned with the later plays
and in particular with *The Power of Darkness.* This work, says
Bakhtin, is Tolstoy's dramatic presentation of his personal belief
that evil is a universal and timeless problem, but it is also a hidden
polemic with the Populists who gave primacy to the social-ethical

over the individual-ethical, and to the ideas of land and commune over the notions of God and conscience. In this play, says Bakhtin, Tolstoy portrays the social background as a fixed, unchangeable backdrop, while "the real moving forces of peasant life, which determine peasant ideology, are neutralized, excluded from the action of the drama."[21] The play depicts the peasants and peasant life in the light of Tolstoy's own ideological seekings, and the "power of darkness" of the title is least of all "the power of ignorance engendered by the economic and political yoke," but "the eternal power of evil over the individual soul who has once sinned."[22] In other words, Bakhtin is arguing, the play is Tolstoy's attempt to turn the problem of social evil into a problem of personal evil.

This is explicitly the main point that Bakhtin makes about *Resurrection* in the second of the two prefaces. The nub of the ideology of the novel, says Bakhtin, is that no one may judge or punish another person, for the solution to the problem of evil lies within the individual. Bakhtin comments on Tolstoy's ideology (Bakhtin's emphasis):

This question of personal participation in evil overshadows actually objectively existing evil, makes it somehow subordinate, somehow secondary in comparison with the tasks of personal repentance and personal perfection. . . . From the very outset there was a fateful substitution: instead of the question of objective evil the question of personal participation in it was posed.[23]

The "fateful substitution," says Bakhtin, set the focus of the novel on the guilt feelings of the exploiting classes, and the novel is thus a typical expression of the ideology of the repentant nobleman. Tolstoy's error, in Bakhtin's view, was to have been too condemning of all social institutions, to have ignored history and the constant process of renewal in social life:

Tolstoy's nihilism, which extends its negation over the whole of human culture . . . is the result of that same failure to understand the historical dialectic which buries the dead only because the living have come to take their place. Tolstoy sees only the dead. . . . He sees only the exploiting relationships and the social forms they engender. But he fails to see, or to sense, or to believe in the positive forms which are maturing among the exploited . . .[24]

We do not know, as yet, the precise moment when Bakhtin wrote these prefaces, nor do we know the circumstances in which

Eikhenbaum and Khalabaev, the editors of that edition of Tolstoy's literary works, invited him to contribute, nor do we know how he was allotted, or chose to write on, what are some of Tolstoy's most outspokenly Christian works (Christian, of course, in Tolstoy's anti-ecclesiastical spirit).[25]

Though the subject of Bakhtin's involvement, or possible involvement, in various church groups has been discussed at some length by Clark and Holquist,[26] we do not yet clearly know what was in Bakhtin's mind at that period when he wrote the Tolstoy prefaces and when, it seemed, arrest was imminent, or what was his attitude toward the Christian faith and its possible survival under the increasingly hostile Soviet policy toward the Church. It is worth summarizing what documentary evidence we have for Bakhtin's beliefs:

1. In November 1918 a public debate was held in the Karl Marx People's House in Nevel', the subject being "God and Socialism." Bakhtin and Pumpyansky spoke in favor of religion, the speeches of all participants being reported in the local newspaper *Molot* ("The Hammer") of 3 December 1918.[27]

2. In 1926 Pumpyansky in a letter to Matvey Kagan reports that he, Bakhtin, M. V. Yudina, and M. I. Tubyansky are "concentrating on theology."[28]

3. Then there is the evidence from Bakhtin's own writings, mostly from the essay entitled "Author and Hero in Aesthetic Activity":

Bakhtin comments on the human need for God:

Without God, without faith in the absolute otherness, self-awareness and self-expression are impossible, and this is not, of course, because they would have no meaning in practice, but because trust in God is the immanent constructive factor of pure self-consciousness and self-expression. (At that point where valuational self-sufficiency of being in the here and now is overcome in myself, then what was concealing God is overcome; there where I absolutely do not coincide with myself, a space is opened to God.)[29]

On faith: "Life (and consciousness) within oneself is nothing other than the coming into being of faith; pure self-consciousness of life is awareness of faith (that is the awareness of need and of hope, of one's lack of self-sufficiency, and of possibility). The life that does not know the air it breathes is naive."[30]

These remarks are followed by three references to episodes from the Gospels: the parable of the Pharisee and the tax collector (Luke 18:10–14), Christ's encounter with the Canaanite (Syro-Phoenician) woman (Matt. 15:21–28) and Christ's healing of the epileptic boy (Mark 9:17–27). These episodes, comments Bakhtin, are, in "an ideally compressed form," models of human faith, models of human recognition of need, of hope, and of lack of self-sufficiency. The point of the parable is that the Pharisee demonstrates in his praying the ultimate in human self-sufficiency, whereas the tax collector, "standing far off," says merely: "God, be merciful to me a sinner."[31] The point of the story of the Canaanite woman is that she calls insistently on Christ to heal her daughter until he answers her and says: "O woman great is your faith! Be it done for you as you desire." In the story of the healing of the epileptic it is the boy's father who cries out: "I believe; help my unbelief!" These models, comments Bakhtin, "do not come to an end, they can be eternally repeated, within themselves they are not completed, this is movement itself (the repetition of prayers)."[32] They show human beings calling out to God, or to Christ, from the very depths of the self, those depths in which, as Bakhtin wrote in the same essay, we sense our incompleteness and long for the miracle of new birth.[33]

We should also particularly note that the three Gospel episodes to which Bakhtin refers also have to do with evil: the Canaanite woman and the father of the epileptic boy call to Christ to save their children from demonic possession, while the tax collector calls out to God who alone can relieve him of the burden of his sin and personal guilt. Each are personal appeals for help to overcome evil.

If we now return to look again at the Tolstoy prefaces we may perhaps read them in a rather different light. We may now be struck by the fact that the preface on the dramatic works concludes with two pages devoted exclusively to Tolstoy's religious outlook. Bakhtin sees Tolstoy as torn between two kinds of sectarianism. One is the Protestant (Calvinist) strand which stresses productive labor and approves of property owning, and which is exemplified by the *kulak* type in the Russian peasantry. (This is illustrated in the play *The Fruits of Enlightenment*.) The other is the radical sectarianism of Eastern religions and of the Russian *stranniki*, the wandering pilgrims of old Russia, who reject all property and deny the use of any action in combating evil, but stand for nonparticipation and for escape. In Tolstoy's plays this strand is illustrated by Peter the Tax Collector (in the play of that name), Fedya Protasov (in *The Living Corpse*), and Nikolai Saryntsov (in *The Light Shines in the Darkness*). All these characters, says Bakhtin in conclusion, "are facing the problem of individual escape from evil, of personal non-participation in it." They are individuals "who have broken away from their class."

One might well expect the preface to end at that point, but Bakhtin adds another sentence: "And that road, on which they wanted to enter and which might absolve them personally from participation in social evil—that was the great road of the Eastern ascetic wanderer."[34] Why end a sociologically Marxist account of Tolstoy's dramas with that image? Why indeed devote the last two pages of the preface to Tolstoy's *religious* outlook? (The whole preface is only nine-and-one-half pages long.)

A closer look at the preface to *Resurrection* reveals some similar incongruities. We may note the long (disproportionately long?) passage that summarizes Tolstoy's main religious message and Nekhliudov's discovery of it. The passage starts, however, with a disclaimer: "What then is the content of this [Tolstoy's] thesis? This is not the place to go into Tolstoy's social-ethical and religious outlook. So we will touch on the content of this thesis in just a few words."[35] Bakhtin then continues as follows:

The novel opens with the Gospel texts (the epigraphs)[36] and closes with them (Nekhliudov's reading of the Gospel).[37] All these texts are intended to emphasize one fundamental idea: that it is inadmissible for one man to judge another and also that any activity intended to correct existing evil is inadmissible. People, sent into the world by the will of God, the master of life, must like the workers, do the will of their master. This will is expressed in the commandments which forbid any violence against one's neighbors. Man may act only on himself, on his inner "I" (seeking the kingdom of God which is *within* us) and all these things will be yours as well.[38]

There are several curious features about this passage:

1. It is first of all not any exact summary of Nekhliudov's (Tolstoy's) new realization of the need not to resist evil because it omits Nekhliudov's main point about the necessity of realizing our guilt and the need to forgive.[39]

2. The third sentence ("people sent into the world by the will of God, the master of life, must like the workers do the will of their master") is a reference to the parable of the vineyard which Nekhliudov is turning over in his mind on the very last page of the novel,[40] but whereas Nekhliudov, thinking aloud, says: "For if we are sent here, then it is by someone's will and for some purpose. . . . The master's will is expressed in these commandments. If only people would obey these comandments, then the kingdom of God would come on earth," Bakhtin summarizes in the far more definitive and unconditional form: "people sent into the world by the will of God . . . must like the workers do the will of their master." And he adds a phrase "the master of life" to describe God, which is not found in Tolstoy's text at that point.

3. Most curious of all is Bakhtin's final sentence, for in Tolstoy's text there is no reference to the "inner 'I,' " nor to the Lucan phrase "the kingdom of God which is within us" which Bakhtin particularly emphasizes. Nekhliudov at the very end of the novel quotes Matt. 6:33: "But seek ye first his kingdom and his righteousness and all these things shall be yours as well."[41] Bakhtin preserves the latter part of the quotation from the Gospel of Matthew, but precedes it with a phrase based on a saying which is to be found only in the Gospel of Luke: "For the kingdom of God is within you."[42]

Bakhtin's commentary is then followed by a long direct quotation from the novel itself about Nekhliudov's awakening.[43] The quotation includes the words: "The only way to save oneself from that terrible evil from which people suffer was for people to admit always that they are guilty before God. . . . Now it was clear to him that all that terrible evil which he had seen in the prisons and gaols . . . arose only from the fact that people wanted to do the impossible: being evil to cure evil."

Although the remaining three or so pages of the preface to *Resurrection* return to the generally detached Marxist tenor of the rest of the text, one is irresistibly drawn to the conclusion that in the passages quoted, and because of the points noted, Bakhtin was using Tolstoy's thesis to present his own personal position. For Bakhtin's idiosyncratic summary of the Tolstoyan thesis, as well as his lengthy quotation concerning Nekhliudov's awakening, seem like the sudden intrusion of "another voice" into the sustained sociological-Marxist tenor of the preface as a whole. One cannot but be reminded of Bakhtin's own writings on self-realization through faith, on the need to seek God's help in confronting evil.

There is some poignancy, too, if we remember that prisons and jails were already by the time of the writing of the prefaces becoming a reality of Soviet life. Pumpyansky was arrested in December 1928 and Bakhtin himself in January 1929.[44] Bakhtin's sentence to imprisonment on the Solovki islands was commuted to exile to Kustanai, whither he and his wife departed early in 1930. Bakhtin was perhaps lucky, for the Gulag was to claim several of his associates. "Being evil to cure evil": is this phrase not Bakhtin's own two-voiced comment on the great social experiment that he saw sliding into violence and repression?

There is poignancy, too, if we recall that by the late twenties the Church was hardly able to function, and the unofficial religious organizations with which Bakhtin was associated were repressed in 1928 – 29.[45] Was not then Bakhtin using the opportunity afforded by the prefaces, and using Tolstoy's religious outlook as cloak, to express his own prognosis for the future of the life of the faithful? Is there not something prophetic, or at least apprehensive, of Bakhtin's own destiny in the image of the homeless ascetic wanderer which so strikingly (and unmotivatedly) closes the preface to the dramas? Is not Bakhtin's choice of the Lucan saying about the kingdom of God being *within* a reference to the solitary fate of the Christian believer when all church structures have been removed?

Then should we not now reread that declarative remark in the preface to the dramas that Tolstoy's writings, "like those of any other writer, were wholly determined, of course, by his period and by the historical disposition of the social-class forces in that period"? Is not the dismissive "of course" a signal that here we have an example of two-voice discourse? And that the adverb "wholly" could be taken with some degree of detachment, if not irony?

But then was Bakhtin really writing one thing and trying to say another? Was he condemning Tolstoy for his limited class ideology, and yet presenting him as the mouthpiece for a message of vital importance and universal validity? Perhaps the answer lies in Bakhtin's clear sense of that inalienable inner freedom that is the human endowment for as long as consciousness lasts. Ideas on this score are to be found in his writings of all periods. In "Author and Hero," he wrote: "This essential inner self stands apart from the world . . .

within me there is always something essential which I can oppose
to the world, namely my inner activity, my subjectivity . . . I always have an exit along the line of inner experience . . . there is a
loophole through which I can save myself from being wholly a fact
of nature."[46] Compare this statement from the "Notes of 1970–71":
"The better a person understands his determinism (his thingness),
the closer he is to understanding and realizing his true freedom."[47]
Bakhtin fell under the necessity of writing about Tolstoy at that
particular period in a particular way, but he kept his inner freedom
and used it in order to proclaim the essential Gospel message for
that moment in time, namely, that the kingdom of God is within
us, a kingdom just as inalienable and indestructible as consciousness
itself.

Caryl Emerson

The Tolstoy Connection in Bakhtin

About polyphonic music. A voice ought to say something, but in this case there are many voices, and each one says nothing. —Leo Tolstoy, diary entry for 18 December 1899

The juxtaposition of Tolstoy and Dostoevsky is one of the most familiar and time-honored practices in Russian literary criticism. It is hardly surprising, therefore, that Mikhail Bakhtin contributed to the great debate over these two novelists; he was a master at exploiting the polemical frameworks of his time, the better to speak his own unconventional word. To be sure, he left no monograph on Tolstoy comparable to the masterwork *Problems of Dostoevsky's Poetics.* [1] There are only numerous scattered references, prefaces to two volumes of Tolstoy's collected fiction, and several ideological constructs in which Tolstoy plays a crucial part. Despite this low profile, the Tolstoy-versus-Dostoevsky opposition was exceptionally congenial to Bakhtin. In fact, his presentation of the dialogue, explicit and implicit, between these two great nineteenth-century writers can provide a fruitful organizing principle for understanding his work as a whole, both its power and its limitations. It tells us much about the two novelists as well.

First, however, a cautionary note on the general purpose to which Bakhtin puts artists of the word. He is fond of explaining the "spirit of a time" through a single writer: Rabelais for the Renaissance, Dostoevsky for the polyphonic second half of the nineteenth century. [2] But Bakhtin is not primarily interested in the individual novelist as such or in the individual novel as an artistic whole. He does not do the traditional "close readings" of the novels he so admires. Rather, he analyzes small chunks, scenes, patterns, always seeking an artistic imperative more fundamental than the particular structure of any single finished work. In his book on Dostoevsky, indeed, the longer and more complex the work the more fragmentary and synchronic is his use of it. After a lengthy discussion of the early short novels *Poor Folk* and *The Double* and an exhaustive analysis of the brief late pieces "Dream of a Ridiculous Man" and tiny "Bobok," Bakhtin mines the big novels for "new structural elements" — admitting, however, that "we shall spend less time on them" (*Problems*, 237). In his opening remarks to the revised version, Bakhtin acknowledges this aspect of his critical method. "Of course even in this new edition," he writes, "the book cannot pretend to a complete analysis of the questions it raises, especially questions as complex as that of *the whole* in a polyphonic novel" (4).

Bakhtin, in short, is not after specific interpretations of specific novels. He is after the creative force, the generic impulse that a novelist or a novel embodies. He then uses that force as a prism through which to focus a philosophy of language, a hypothesis about authorial intention, or an understanding of a particular cultural period.

What, then, does the "Tolstoyan force" mean for Bakhtin? We should first recall where Tolstoy stood in the Russian tradition — a position that by the 1920s was already almost a cliché.[3] In that tradition, Dostoevsky is a mystic, the apocalyptic poet of the underground, the celebrator of the trap of human consciousness. His characters live on the edge of perpetual crisis, and his plots rely heavily on madness, murder, and suicide. Tolstoy, in contrast, is the teacher of life. His is the realm of *zhivaia zhizn'* ("living life"),[4] an aboveground and exuberant immersion in nature, physicality, and organic process. Bakhtin, in fact, acknowledges this tradition in his theoretical articles of the thirties and forties. There he identifies Dostoevsky with "crisis time" and "threshold space" while defining the Tolstoyan "chronotope" (or time-space matrix) as quite the opposite — as "biological time, flowing smoothly in the interior spaces of townhouses and noble estates."[5] These contrasts are also present in his book on Dostoevsky. But there Bakhtin assigns Tolstoy a harsher and more polemical role. Within Bakhtin's decidedly binary universe, the two great Russian novelists emerge as two rallying points, two poles for opposing tendencies in literature and language.

At the Dostoevsky pole, consciousness is individualized, disunified, made concrete. At the Tolstoy pole, consciousness is generalized, unified, made abstract. When Bakhtin refers to Tolstoy, then, it is not so much to the world of the novelist's writing as to the striving of that world, its outer limit, its fascination with the possibility of "absolute language."[6] Through Bakhtin's lens, Tolstoy is far from being the poet of "living life." He becomes, in fact, the poet of death.

Bakhtin's inversion of received literary canon is characteristically eccentric. But it is more. His Tolstoy-Dostoevsky polemic is, as we shall see, a remarkably selective construct. It emerges as a binary model that can accommodate three of his most insistently recurring concerns: monologism versus dialogism, the relationships of authors to their characters, and the concept of the self.

Bakhtin makes his first detailed case against monologism in the 1929 edition of his book on Dostoevsky. Whereas Dostoevsky, we are told, seeks maximally free words for his heroes, Tolstoy seeks objectified images fixed in words. Dostoevsky's heroes create themselves out of their discourse, but in Tolstoy's characters consciousness and speech are merely two components among many — no more important, say, than a raised upper lip or a plodding step:

In [Tolstoy's] world a second autonomous voice never appears alongside the author's voice. Therefore the problem of voice linkage never arises, nor does the problem of a special positioning for the author's point of view. Tolstoy's word and his monologically naive point of view penetrate everywhere, into the smallest corners of the world and the soul, subjugating everything to its unity. (*Problemy*, 68)

What matters here is not so much Tolstoy the artist as Tolstoy's "monologically naive point of view." In chapter 3 of this edition ("The Hero in Dostoevsky") Bakhtin develops his concept of monologism, and although he does so at a suitably abstract level, one can easily grasp the real issue he is addressing under cover of Tolstoy, master monologist. Bakhtin's argument is roughly this. Monologism is a brand of idealism that insists on the unity of a single consciousness. It has been the guiding principle in a variety of modern movements, including European rationalism, the Enlightenment, and utopianism. Wherever monologic perception dominates, everything is seen in false unity—as the spirit of a nation, of a people, of history. This unity is false because it is only an apparent oneness; in fact, monologism demarcates, abstracts, excludes, and it is only from within this closed and lopped-off system that everything can be seen as one. Dialogism alone allows for the restoration of a larger, inclusive unity in diversity, through the sort of comprehension of opposites that Bakhtin would later extol in Rabelais. In a dialogic universe, inclusive unity is celebrated by the fact that truth about the world is linked with specific position, with truth for the individual personality.[7]

In a monologic world, truth is impersonal. It is placed in a character's mouth by the author. Characters are not creators of ideas but merely carriers. The ideas belong to no one. In such a world, an independent idea cannot be acknowledged on its own terms: it is either affirmed (that is, absorbed) or repudiated. Only one individualizing principle is recognized, and that is error. Without any genuine interaction among consciousnesses, dialogue can never be more than "pedagogical."

This question of "pedagogical dialogue" might serve as a useful focus. Pedagogy is crucial to Bakhtin, as it is to Tolstoy; both are fascinated with the image of the ideal teacher. But for Bakhtin, true learning is dialogic and therefore horizontal, an interpenetration of points of view. Interactions become "pedagogical" when dialogue is debased, when the teacher turns out to have known all the answers all along—as happened, Bakhtin claims, in the later Socratic dialogues (*Problems,* 110). For Tolstoy, on the contrary, learning is always and ideally vertical. The revealing document here is Tolstoy's tract on peasant schools: "Who Should Teach Whom to Write, We the Peasant Children or the Peasant Children Us?"[8] That the hierarchy is flipped and Count Tolstoy is now at the feet of his peasants is not significant. The axis has not changed. It is still the omnipresent, monologic *kto kogo* ("who does what to whom")— either I know and teach you, or you know and teach me. Tolstoy's essay might advocate abolition of hierarchy, but it is still cast in what Bakhtin would call a "pedagogical dialogue": "Someone who knows and possesses the truth instructs someone who is ignorant of it and in error, that is, it is the mutual relationship of teacher and pupil" (*Problemy*, 78). For Bakhtin, this mode is inevitable in a monologic world.

Under monologic conditions, Bakhtin concludes, ideas are not represented. They are merely distributed by some higher power or expressed directly, with no distance at all. Distance, of course, is what guarantees voice autonomy in a work: a world where others' ideas cease to be represented is ultimately a world where others' ideas cease to exist. But this insistence on many autonomous voices does not mean the absence of unified truth. And here we glimpse Bakhtin's powerful, veiled, ultimately spiritual relationship with the genuinely authoritative word. The search for a unified truth, Bakhtin insists, need not be carried out under repressive monologic conditions:

It is quite possible to imagine a unified truth that requires a multiplicity of consciousnesses, one that could not in principle be fitted within the boundaries of a single consciousness, one that is, so to speak, social by its very nature and full of event-potential, one that is born at a point of contact among various consciousnesses. . . . (*Problemy*, 78)

Indeed, this seems to be Bakhtin's ultimate task: to make a unified truth compatible with multiple consciousnesses. It is the triumphant accomplishment of this task that in 1929 he ascribes to Dostoevsky, a fellow believer; and it is this achievement he denies to Tolstoy, monologic rationalist.

This fundamental distinction between monologic and dialogic conditions is crucial for another aspect of Bakhtin's image of Tolstoy: the complex relationships Bakhtin charts between authors and their heroes. We must begin with the magisterial protoessay on authors and protagonists that Bakhtin wrote in the early 1920s, a work that permeates (and that was probably composed alongside) the early drafts of the book on Dostoevsky.[9] In this early essay, Bakhtin stresses the fragility of the author-hero relationship and the degree of discipline required to sustain a responsible "outsideness." At this point, Bakhtin has not yet opposed Tolstoy to Dostoevsky; he illustrates his typologies with heroes drawn from the work of both writers, often placing them in the same category. That opposition was to happen only in the late 1920s, when Bakhtin began to see finalization not as a necessary step to art but as a threat to human freedom. The more he came to prefer "unfinalizability" to finalization, the more he exalted Dostoevsky over Tolstoy.

What strikes us in this early essay is the remarkable ease with which Bakhtin crosses the boundaries between art and life. The relationship of author to created character is treated essentially like the relationship of any "I" to any "other." But there is this one distinction: in life we author fragments, "we are not interested in the whole of a person but only in his separate acts," whereas art requires that we assume "a unified reaction to the whole of the hero" ("Avtor," 7–8). Getting the whole of a hero right is an arduous task, Bakhtin admits; how many "grimaces, random masks, false gestures" can result from the whims or caprice of an author (8). But the task is necessary, for only as a conceptualized whole can a hero be released to develop freely within the logic of his *own* reality.

At its most elevated level, of course, authorship is theological — a reenactment, writ small, of supreme authority creating humanity. But here Bakhtin brings the scenario maximally close to our everyday, and continuously creative, experience. To stress the continuity in function between formally aesthetic authorship and its "everyday" real-life counterpart, Bakhtin frequently employs the terms *avtor-sozertsatel'* ("author-perceiver") and *avtor-zritel'* ("author-spectator") ("Avtor," 63–65). Authorship is the problem of one consciousness perceiving another consciousness. "How the other looks from my position," then, is the starting point both for aesthetic perception and for an ethical act ("Avtor," 23).

Two individuals are confronting each other, looking into each other's eyes. One can always see something that the other cannot, if only what is behind the other's head (22), if only the other's act of looking. Each is in the process of "authoring" the other, and this is possible because each enjoys a "surplus" (*izbytok*) of vision vis-à-vis the other. Only from the other's perspective can each appear whole; to oneself, there is always an inner loophole, an open-ended potential for change. Whatever stable definitions the "I" possesses are inevitably acquired from the other.

Thus one cannot author oneself: the very fact of expression, aesthetic and otherwise, requires a second consciousness to supply boundaries and impose external integrity. In the visual and literary arts and in real life as well, it is impossible to construct a self out of a single consciousness. Painting one's self-portrait, looking in the mirror or at a photograph of oneself, is always somehow false, the results untrue. "In this sense," Bakhtin writes, "one can speak of the absolute aesthetic need of one person for another, for the seeing, remembering, gathering, and unifying activity of the other, which alone can create his externally completed personality; this personality will not exist if the other does not create it" (34). However abounding or lacking in love, this activity is always beneficial because it always "formally enriches" the object, fixing it in time and space from a point of view fundamentally inaccessible to the object itself. "What would I have to gain," Bakhtin asks, "if another were to *fuse* with me? He would see and know only what I already see and know, he would only repeat in himself the inescapable closed circle of my own life; let him rather remain outside me" (78).

Bakhtin is not suggesting here that we must reject who we are, or that the normal relationship to self is one of self-abasement. But he does claim that we cannot form authoritative images of ourselves from within. An important aspect of our freedom is the fact that inside we are all restlessness, change, movement; whatever temporary stabilizations we enjoy — rest, pleasure, joy, triumph, even the secure sense that something is our own — are gifts bestowed on us by the other ("Avtor," 101, 119–20). To be the other for another is a privilege; "only by being outside another's potential consciousness can we feel its gift-giving, resolving, and consummating potential" ("Avtor," 175).

In *Problems of Dostoevsky's Poetics* this indispensability of otherness emerges with special clarity during discussions of "the word with a loophole" (*slovo s lazeikoi*). In speaking one's idea, Bakhtin claims, one always retains a loophole "in case the other person does not make use of his *privilege* as the other." In *The Idiot*, Nastasya Filippovna, in the wildness of her contradictions, condemns herself and "at the same time insists that the other person, precisely as the other, is obliged to vindicate her" (234). We should not be misled, Bakhtin seems to suggest, by the surface texture of scandal, madness, and eccentricity in Dostoevsky. Underneath them all is a profoundly pluralistic and healing impulse: a faith that the function of the other is not to alienate but to resist our negating ideas of self, to contradict our helplessness by providing new options for the self. Dostoevsky always privileges the other, because it alone can protect individual personality from the awful trap of the final word.

How, then, does the Tolstoy-Dostoevsky dichotomy express itself in the issue of the other's responsibility? In Tolstoy, Bakhtin would maintain, characters exist so that the author can address them, and ultimately the readers, with a truth that transcends them all. Characters have a responsibility toward this truth, and the text as a whole reflects their search. In Dostoevsky, in contrast, a character exists to address an idea to someone else. This other person has a responsibility to challenge (not merely to reinforce) that idea or that concept of self.

Bakhtin's insistence on the validity of a second (and usually dissenting) opinion might explain in part his curious reluctance to engage, in any serious way, the carriers of authoritative discourse. There were, of course, ready political reasons why a literary critic — or any intellectual — might refrain from analyzing "figures of authority" in the increasingly monologic and hero-worshipping climate of the Soviet 1930s.[10] But Bakhtin's reluctance goes deeper than a dialogue with his own time, and deeper than a debate between these two authors. He dismisses the authoritative word in novels wherever he finds it, in Dostoevsky as well as in Tolstoy. "Images of official-authoritative truth, images of virtue, have never been successful in the novel," Bakhtin writes. "It suffices to mention the hopeless attempts of Gogol and Dostoevsky in this regard . . . [as well as] the evangelical texts in Tolstoy at the end of *Resurrection.*"[11] Prince Myshkin, Alyosha Karamazov, and the Elder Zosima can hardly be considered "hopeless attempts" in Dostoevsky's fictional universe. How in fact do characters properly use the authoritative word? What role does Tolstoyan comprehensive truth play for Dostoevsky, and how does Dostoevsky approach and embody such truth?

In a discussion of *The Idiot* Bakhtin briefly suggests one possible mediator, the "penetrated word" (*proniknovennoe slovo*) (*Problems*, 241–42, 249). The penetrated word, a term Bakhtin adopts from the Dostoevsky criticism of Vyacheslav Ivanov,[12] is linked with hagiographic discourse (although unlike hagiography it need not be stylized) and is informed by authority: it is, Bakhtin tells us, a word without a loophole, without a reservation, confident in its power to mean. Its task is to interfere actively in the interior dialogue of another person and "help that person find his own voice" (242). But unlike the authoritative and authorial discourse that Tolstoy directs toward this end, the penetrated word does not stand above or outside the discourse of the characters. It does not come down but *across* — we recall Bakhtin's distinction between authentic and pedagogical dialogue — and therefore its resolutions are highly context-specific within a given pool of personalities. Bakhtin uses the example of Prince Myshkin. What makes the prince a Dostoevskian and not a Tolstoyan carrier of truth? The prince can, and often does, appeal to one of the voices warring inside another person, and if he reaches an "authentic voice" he can trigger a major moral reversal. But the penetrated word does not last. It can only enter at a specific time and place to work a temporary realization. It is only possible in dialogue, in a specific dialogue with another person; it never accumulates authority and therefore lacks ultimate sovereignty (242). Myshkin's inner dialogue, Bakhtin assures us, is just as active and anxiety-ridden as that of any other character in the novel. The penetrated word makes authority real, but only for the moment; it remains personal, historical, and conditional.

Authority, then, resides only in specific situations. For Bakhtin, and for Dostoevsky in Bakhtin's reading of him, the ideal relationship between personality and authority is embodied in Christ. He is the ideal other, the supreme demonstration of the fact that the one who creates us also saves us — and this fact should be understood on a plane quite separate from questions of religious belief. Christ is a symbol of the necessity for enfleshment. Abstract cognition and pretensions to an ultimate, singular authority cannot embody values; only a view made concrete in time and space, Bakhtin argues, can create a soul within the other and participate in an active relationship. "Even God had to be enfleshed in order to pardon, to suffer, and to forgive" ("Avtor," 113). Resurrection in the flesh is a powerful image, not because it allays our fears of physical extinction but because it emphasizes the inseparability of soul and body ("Avtor," 89), the need for soul to be enacted through a particular and delimited body.[13]

Thus Bakhtin reverses the traditional idea underlying the wonder of resurrection. He stresses the inseparability of body and soul not because the body has a soul but because souls must have bodies; his is a religion not so much of resurrection as of incarnation. Bakhtin therefore does not take kindly to all those Tolstoyan gestures that would abstract Christ's words, fuse these words with personal conviction, or erect them into moral systems. Proper unity with authority is achieved not through fusion but by asking a question of the ideal authoritative image:

[For Dostoevsky] the image of the ideal human being or the image of Christ represents the resolution of ideological quests. . . . Precisely the image of a human being and his voice, a voice not the author's own, was the ultimate artistic criterion for Dostoevsky: not fidelity to his own convictions and not fidelity to convictions themselves taken abstractly, but precisely a fidelity to the authoritative image of a human being. (*Problems*, 97)

One does not fuse with an ideal image but chooses, from another integral position, to follow it. Its separateness and unfinishedness — as well as our own — are always paramount. Near the end of his life Bakhtin jotted down this provocative sequence of thoughts: "Dostoevsky's search. . . . The word as something personal. Christ as truth. I put the question to him . . ." ("Iz zapisei," 353). Dostoevsky sees ideal authority present only as relationship. It is an "image-discourse" that is listened to, interrogated, freely followed by the whole person. Tolstoy, in contrast, would not "put the question" to truth, for to do so would too bluntly emphasize the specific time, space, and mortality of the questioner — and of the answerer as well. Tolstoy's impersonal word lies in the realm beyond dialogue; his convictions have become truth as proposition.

In Bakhtin's view, then, the status of authority has close parallels with the status of language. As Tolstoyan discourse strives to rise above specific times and places, it inevitably dehistoricizes language — that is, makes it possible to value a word regardless of when it was spoken and by whom. Bakhtin charges Tolstoy with ignoring, or naively presuming to transcend, the problematic status of language. For Tolstoy, language is not a problem; it is merely a means. His characters all partake of "openly pathetic discourse": either Tolstoy allows a speaker to assume directly the didactic role of teacher, judge, or preacher, or he presents discourse itself as something more solid and impersonal than it is — as a direct impression from life, or as something untainted by ideological preconceptions.[14] In Dostoevsky, on the contrary, it is precisely the ideological preconception that is valued in language:

It is characteristic that in Dostoevsky's works there are absolutely no *separate* thoughts, propositions or formulations such as maxims, sayings, aphorisms which, when removed from their context and detached from their voice, would retain their semantic meaning in an impersonal form. But how many such separate and true thoughts can be isolated (and in fact commonly are isolated) from the novels of Leo Tolstoy, Turgenev, Balzac . . . separated from a voice, they still retain their full power to mean as impersonal aphorisms. (*Problems*, 95–96)

Impersonal truth is, in Bakhtin's view, a central element in Tolstoy's monologic world. And it is markedly absent in Dostoevsky, where we find only "integral and indivisible voice-ideas, voice viewpoints" (*Problems*, 96).

At the end of his early study on authors and their heroes, Bakhtin asks: What is the author's task? It does not lie, Russian Formalism to the contrary, in a response to other literary schools and languages or in a manipulation of devices. The author's task, which Bakhtin calls "godlike," is "to find a fundamental approach to life from without" ("Avtor," 166), to define and shape others in a way in which they cannot define and shape themselves. Crises in authorship come about, Bakhtin suggests, when authors begin to despair of "the right to be outside a life and to give it final form," when the conviction takes hold that life is understandable only when lived in the category of "I-for-myself" rather than "I-for-another," when, in short, there is a fear of drawing boundaries (176). Omniscient narrator-authors, who admit of no barriers between themselves and their created characters, cannot be enfleshed or delimited. Far from strengthening a moral or evaluative position and making it more authoritative, such narrators, in Bakhtin's universe, merely discredit and devaluate that position.

Nowhere does Bakhtin directly confront Tolstoy's theory of art. But his early writings do offer a potential challenge to the idea of art as "infection." In the opening pages of "Author and Hero" Bakhtin discusses the proper way to empathize with another's suffering:

My projection of myself into the suffering person must be followed by a *return* to myself, to my own place outside the sufferer; only from this place can the material of empathy be rendered meaningful ethically, cognitively, or aesthetically. If this return did not take place, we would have an instance of the pathological phenomenon of experiencing another's suffering as one's own, an infection by the other's suffering and nothing more. ("Avtor," 25)

Later in the essay (55–81), Bakhtin criticizes Romantic "expressive aesthetics" for much the same failing. Expressive theories of art know only the doubling act of *co*-experience; they strive to make aesthetic value real in a way "immanent to a single consciousness; [such theories] do not permit the counterpositioning of *I* to *other*" (58).

One might contrast Bakhtin's views with Tolstoy's argument in *What Is Art?*:

A real work of art destroys, in the consciousness of the receiver, the separation between himself and the artist—not that alone, but also between himself and all whose minds receive this work of art. In this freeing of our personality from its separation and isolation, in this uniting of it with others, is the chief characteristic and the great attractive force of art.[15]

The "communication imperative" in Tolstoy's treatise would have appealed to Bakhtin; the implication of fusion, however, would have been rejected. According to Bakhtin, the aesthetic experience should strive not to duplicate another's emotions but, rather, to assume an attitude toward them, to respond to them in a different and supplementary way. It could be argued that in the Tolstoy-Dostoevsky polemic Bakhtin is dealing less with individual authors than with categories of authoring—and, ultimately, with the nature of aesthetic experience.

This observation leads to a final area in which the Tolstoy connection can help focus a major conceptual node in Bakhtin's thought. How much "other" is necessary for the formation of a self? How is an open concept of selfhood compatible with the act of literary authoring, and with the harshly bounded realities of our individual birth and death? Here it is instructive to compare the 1929 and 1963 versions of Bakhtin's book on Dostoevsky. The publication dates of these two editions loosely bracket the years of Stalinism. One might expect a trace of this period in the second edition, some subtext of death and survival that would address Bakhtin's own fate and the general fate of "multiple consciousness" in that troubled and monologic time. One such trace can in fact be found in the expanded polemic with Tolstoy. At issue is the hegemony of the hero's consciousness, and Bakhtin examines it through the severe prism of death.

In the 1963 edition, chapter 2 ("The Hero in Dostoevsky") is greatly expanded. Among the new material is a discussion of Tolstoy's short story "Three Deaths" (69 – 72) — a model, Bakhtin says, of monologic thinking. In this story, we recall, the three deaths (of a noblewoman, a coachman, and a tree) are connected solely in an external and mechanical way. This externality is not the sort that communes with or interrogates the other. Since the three heroes are not conscious of one another, they can be made meaningful to one another only in the authorial, and authoritative, field of vision that encompasses them all. Noblewoman, coachman, and (of course) tree do not think and talk but rather have their thinking and talking done for them by someone who sees more than they could ever see. There are no true dialogic relationships among the characters, and none at all between the characters and Tolstoy, their creator. Whereas "Three Deaths" is a rather primitive example, Bakhtin claims that Tolstoy's longer stories and novels also reflect this basic structure (72).

Bakhtin asks whimsically how those three deaths would have looked if Dostoevsky had written them. But, he quickly remarks, Dostoevsky would never have chosen three *deaths*. His characters could not function if created from that point of view. "Death in the Tolstoyan interpretation of it," Bakhtin concludes, "is totally absent from Dostoevsky's world" (73).

Bakhtin planned more for the Tolstoy-Dostoevsky confrontation than ever got into the final revision of the book. In some posthumously published notes for the second edition ("Toward a Reworking of the Dostoevsky Book") Bakhtin raised this debate on death to a metaphysical level. There the philosophical underpinnings of the Tolstoy-Dostoevsky polemic are, as it were, laid bare:

> In Dostoevsky there are considerably fewer deaths than in Tolstoy — and in most cases Dostoevsky's deaths are murders and suicides. In Tolstoy there are a great many deaths. One could even speak of his passion for depicting death. . . . Tolstoy depicts death not only from the outside looking in but also from the inside looking out, that is, from the very consciousness of the dying person, *almost* as a fact of that consciousness. Tolstoy is interested in death *for the person's own sake*, that is, for the dying person himself, and not for others, not for those who remain

behind. He is in fact profoundly indifferent to one's own death as it exists for others. . . .

Dostoevsky *never* depicts death from within. Final agony and death are observed by others. Death cannot be a fact of consciousness itself. . . . Death from within, that is, one's own death consciously perceived, does not exist for anyone: not for the dying person, nor for others; it does not exist at all. . . . Death in Dostoevsky's world is always an objective fact for other consciousnesses; what Dostoevsky foregrounds are the privileges of the other. (*Problems*, 289 – 90)

These remarks on death invite some expansion. First, Bakhtin suggests that depictions of death can be classified according to a larger literary category, point of view. Because of the brute role played by consciousness, crossing the boundary between life and death is *the* most transparent fictional act, the one event certain to reveal authorial position and the whereabouts of the author's voice. We recall that Bakhtin places Dostoevsky and Tolstoy prominently at opposite ends of a spectrum with regard to authorial position. Dostoevsky, at one extreme, tends to distribute his knowledge among the personalities of his fictional world; what he knows about his characters they know too, or at least have access to — often to their horror. Conversely, what they do not know, Dostoevsky does not pretend to know either. In this respect, Bakhtin claims, Dostoevsky is quite different from Tolstoy, who tends to exploit his privileged position as creator. His totalizing vision reduces the independence of his characters, whose words can be separated from their personalities. Tolstoy's special vantage point permits him to understand a course of events that is still unclear to its participants. In the event of death, he can be on both sides of the boundary.

This spectrum suggests a second and related issue. How the two authors use death is a function of what they expect death to resolve. For Tolstoy, death can be a central event because it accomplishes something; the dying process is bathed in external and internal light, and the great scenes (Ivan Ilych's final agony, Brekhunov's freezing to death in "Master and Man," Andrei Bolkonsky's slow dying after the Battle of Borodino) resolve a question for the victim. This is not to say that all questions are resolved for the reader. But we do sense that the dying person has experienced a necessary resolution, whether or not we can partake of it, and that this resolution closes down and harmonizes the narrative.

The situation is different in Dostoevsky. There, in Bakhtin's words, "death finalizes nothing:"

Personality does not die. Death is a departure. The person *himself* departs. Only such death-departure can become an object (a fact) of fundamental artistic visualization in Dostoevsky's world. The person has departed, having spoken his word, but the word itself remains in the open-ended dialogue. (*Problems*, 300)

Death resolves nothing because, in Dostoevsky's world, consciousness cannot be present on both sides of the border to appreciate the resolution. The word is immortal, and its carrier has merely "departed." Bodily death as an act can itself be a word—as it is, say, for Kirillov—or it can simply be irrelevant to the word, as in the case of Zosima. But never does it resolve the word or give it finality.

Why is death of no significance to Dostoevsky as an event for consummating personality, whereas for Tolstoy it is of such paramount importance? Again the beginning of Bakhtin's answer can be found in his early essay on authors and protagonists, specifically in his discussion of the connection between genuine otherness and death. My birth and my death, he argues, are events only for others, not for me ("Avtor," 92). Therefore death is the ultimate aesthetic act, a gesture that turns the whole of my life over to the other person, who is then free to begin an aesthetic shaping of my personality (94–95). Only after death, Bakhtin claims, can plot, form, and rhythm begin (103, 115). Death is what makes the other available; it is a gift. But the "gift" is not, of course, free: personal loss is the price we pay for this gift of wholeness from the other. Bakhtin (contrary to some easy readings of him) has great respect for the finished life. But—and this is the crucial point—only the other can bestow this completion on us. We cannot do it ourselves. Thus all the luminescent death scenes in Tolstoy, in which the dying see an inner light, withdraw into themselves and grasp a mystery available to them alone, irritate Bakhtin and strike him as false. In all those instances, the process of dying is marked by an increasing self-sufficiency, by a proud solitude and an indifference to outer context. The dying are completing themselves, and this is not their privilege.

Bakhtin ultimately charges Tolstoy with faulty perspective. No self, not even our own, can be controlled or created from within; we can only be completed from without. In Bakhtin's view, Tolstoy too quickly dispenses with the other. Bakhtin sees this danger already potentially present in the quasi-fictional phenomenon of Tolstoy's diaries, one of Bakhtin's examples of the aesthetic dead end of the confessional form ("Avtor," 124). Confession tries to eliminate the need for the other, to take all the blame on the self. But the other will inevitably appear, either as God (prayer, repentance) or as judge (condemnation). Under such conditions, any positive assessment of self is seen as a further impurity, as a further falling away from the procedures of honest self-analysis. This is the desperate realization of the Underground Man. Solitary confession, Bakhtin argues, is not really open to new birth because it is not open to the purifying effects of the other. Although it can be an ethical act in the world, it resists authentic aestheticization.

In Dostoevsky, the need of the other is absolute. Like any other author he must complete his characters. But he uses his authorial "surplus"—his extra vision—to juxtapose their inner lives, and he submits the whole to a very uncertain ideological resolution. Dostoevsky's "other" comes to represent a relationship among characters, with the author using his surplus to coordinate. Tolstoy's "other," in contrast, represents a relationship between author and character, in which character is infected with author and reader is infected with character. Inevitably, in such situations the authorial surplus is used to instruct.

It is now time to put Bakhtin's vision of Tolstoy versus Dostoevsky into some perspective. It should be admitted at the outset that Bakhtin is not a particularly good reader of Tolstoy. This should not surprise us, however, for Bakhtin does not design his world to accommodate writers like Tolstoy. In it Tolstoy is a loser, the negative example. Bakhtin does make some intoxicating generalizations and insightful comments on certain short pieces. But the longer and more complex the work—that is, the closer he comes to the novelistic masterpieces—the less distinguished his commentary becomes.

Bakhtin is very selective in his sources. He does not, for example, engage Tolstoy's complex and highly self-conscious critique of history, free will, and necessity in the epilogues or draft prefaces to *War and Peace*. Nor does he confront the many uses to which Tolstoy puts his authorial discourse: Tolstoy's frequent, deliberate undermining of illusions of authority, for instance, or his varied techniques for evading closure. Most telling, Bakhtin shies away from what is certainly the crucial aspect of Tolstoyan discourse: the interaction between the worlds of the characters and the "rhetorical" passages that come, or so it seems, direct from the author's mouth. According to Bakhtin, there is no real interaction. Such authorial insertions simply dry up whatever novelistic contexts they enter and "fall out of the work" — like the evangelical texts at the end of *Resurrection* and the philosophy of history at the end of *War and Peace*.[16]

Bakhtin does deal with one Tolstoyan novel in a sustained way, and his treatment is suggestive. In 1929, the year the book on Dostoevsky appeared, Bakhtin also published on Tolstoy. A new edition of Tolstoy's collected literary works was then in production, and for two of the volumes (vol. 11, on the plays, and vol. 13, on *Resurrection*) Bakhtin wrote the prefaces. In the second of these prefaces, Bakhtin distinguishes between the multiplicity of the earlier great novels and the single-mindedness of *Resurrection*.[17] Tolstoy's final novel, Bakhtin claims, is in fact a masterpiece of a new genre, the "socioideological novel" — a genre built on a utopian thesis and thus tendentious by definition. Absolutely no element in such a work is neutral; "every word, every epithet, every comparison emphatically demonstrates the ideological thesis" (13: xv – xvi). The preface ends on a reference to Soviet reality:

> In recent times our Soviet literature has been tenaciously laboring over the creation of new forms for the socioideological novel. This is perhaps the most pressing and important genre on today's literary scene. The socioideological novel — ultimately the socially tendentious novel — is a completely legitimate artistic form. Not to recognize its purely artistic legitimacy is a naive prejudice of superficial aestheticism, which we should have long ago outgrown. But actually this is one of the most difficult and risk-laden forms of the novel. . . . To organize the entire artistic material from top to bottom on the basis of a well-defined socioideological thesis, without stifling it or drying up the living concrete life within it, is a very difficult task.
>
> Tolstoy handled this task with consummate mastery. As a model of the socioideological novel, *Resurrection* can be of great use to the literary aspirations of the present day. (xx)

Resurrection becomes the model for the didactic socialist-realist novel; the late Tolstoy becomes a model for early Soviet monologism.[18]

Thus the plea Bakhtin makes for Dostoevsky in the first chapter of *Problems of Dostoevsky's Poetics* — that the novelist should be read for his formal innovations and technical artistry, not for any particular ideology — is inverted for Tolstoy. Tolstoy's artistry is seen precisely as an ally of ideology, and of a singularly tendentious ideology at that. In Bakhtin's world, Tolstoy has only one function: he stands for a single voice coincident with a completed self. Tolstoy is "monologic," Bakhtin would say, because the necessity that rules his novels is of a fundamentally lonely sort; personality, shaped and hemmed in by its unique environment, strives to break through to the author's truth. Dostoevsky, in contrast, stands for selfhood in process. He is "dialogic" because there is no "author's truth" — there is authorial position but no truth outside the context of a specific dialogue among other selves.

Bakhtin's recasting of the Tolstoy-Dostoevsky polemic contains much that is original and evocative. But it does not interrogate Tolstoy on his own terms. Bakhtin closes Tolstoy down, makes his contradictions less provocative, and never satisfactorily confronts the complex issue of personality in the Tolstoyan novel. This issue is worth pursuing, for here, one suspects, an authentic dialogue between Tolstoy and Bakhtin is waiting to be spoken.

In Bakhtin's view, Dostoevsky and Tolstoy demonstrate quite different understandings of the role of the idea vis-à-vis the individual personality. Dostoevsky's method, simply stated, is to use the idea as his basic structural unit and to create plots by passing one idea through many characters. They may commit murder, go mad, hang themselves, create improbable scandals, live always on the unstable edge of society, but the idea each represents is remarkably stable. It is the very durability and inviolability of these ideas, which interact and coexist on a number of planes at once, that produce conflict in society and madness in the individual. The exemplary case here is Raskolnikov, whose great interior monologues are battlegrounds between coexisting personified ideas (*Problems*, 73–75). His interior voice moves quickly from individual biographies to the life positions they represent: "Oh, the Luzhins, the Sonechkas of the world!" (*Problems*, 238). These life positions address themselves dialogically to the unfinished inner core of Raskolnikov's personality (86). Ideas, in short, *use* personality, enriching

it, tormenting it, even discarding it once the ideas have been established in circulation. A major character — say, Stavrogin — who generates ideas but then passes through them coldly, unable or unwilling
to invest his personality in them, is marked for a meaningless death.

In Tolstoy this relation of idea to personality is reversed. There
the dominant and stable force, the major structural unit, is the
individual personality itself — perceived not as an ideological position but as an accumulation of life experience. It survives by its
flexibility and its capacity to adjust. Instead of passing one idea
through many characters — Dostoevsky's route — Tolstoy tends to
create his plots by passing many ideas through one personality. The
ability to assume and shed ideas, to pass through and remain open
to as many life situations as possible, is precisely what defines a
major Tolstoyan hero. Tolstoy himself stressed this characteristic in
one of his draft prefaces to *War and Peace*:

> It is not a novel because I cannot and do not know how to confine the
> characters I have created within given limits. . . . I cannot call my work
> a tale because I am unable to force my characters to act only with the
> aim of proving or clarifying some kind of idea or series of ideas.[19]

One cannot imagine in Tolstoy an interior dialogue such as Raskolnikov's, one in which a hero refers to "the Bezukhovs, Andrei
Bolkonskys, and Konstantin Levins" of this world. Those lives
stand for too many things, and Tolstoyan characters are related to
one another in a different way. Each identity is "secure" to the
extent that it is *not* fastened down to a single idea.

Consider two famous conclusions that focus this difference between Dostoevsky and Tolstoy. The first, also singled out by Bakhtin (*Problems*, 239), is the ending of *The Double:* "Our hero shrieked
and clutched at his head. Alas! This is what he had known for a
long time would happen!" The second, which brings *Anna Karenina* to a close, describes Levin's spiritual regeneration:

> I shall still get angry . . . I shall still express my thoughts inopportunely;
> there will still be a wall between the holy of holies in my soul and other
> people . . . I shall still be unable to understand with my reason why I
> am praying and I shall continue to pray — but my life, my whole life —
> every moment of it, is no longer meaningless as it was before, but has
> an incontestable meaning of good, *with which I have the power to invest
> it.*

The Kingdom of God, Tolstoy tells us, is Within You.

Both Dostoevsky's hero and Tolstoy's hero realize a truth. But for Golyadkin, the hero of *The Double,* the realization is that nothing has changed, that the idea has won out over all his attempts to mask or evade it. He is at last forced to confront what has been, for him, always true. For Levin, in contrast, the realization (which, we are told, saves him from suicide) is that his personality can win out over any individual idea that may seek dominance over him — that his personality is in fact validated by the richness and multiplicity of ideas it can accommodate. "Confrontation with the truth," in Levin's sense, means not a face-to-face showdown between carriers and the ideas they represent, but precisely the inability of any single idea at any given moment to be forever decisive or binding on the personality.

This comparison raises some interesting questions about Bakhtin's famous, and far too facile, categorization of Dostoevsky as a "polyphonic" thinker and of Tolstoy as a "monologic" one. Both, it is clear, exhibit a genius for multiplicity. But each writer has a different way of connecting multiplicity with language and with the formation of a self. For Dostoevsky, multiplicity is spatial, coexistent, and — for want of a better word — immortal. Voices are refracted, juxtaposed, but never assimilated or eliminated. Death can be an act in this world, but conflict cannot be resolved through it. Once death occurs, the word that had been embodied returns to the pool of ideas out of which selves are born. The Kingdom of God is located not within you but among you.

For Tolstoy, multiplicity is located elsewhere. It is more linear and temporal than spatial and coexistent. Life is a matter not of seeking external confrontation with other equally and eternally valid ideas, but of processing an idea or a situation at the proper time to guarantee the survival of the organism. For all his robust fullness of setting, Tolstoy is a master at mapping the ways in which people are *not* free. The choices a person can make depend on a very specific and restricted immediate context. Thus Tolstoy's obsession with timing: Vronsky breaking the back of his mare, Varenka and Koznyshev out mushroom picking, the awful last-minute sense of accident in Anna's death, and the horrible casualness with which Petya Rostov is killed in battle. Bakhtin is right, Tolstoy *is* a poet of death — but not because of any special morbidity on Tolstoy's part. This emphasis is, rather, the natural result of a fictive world in which ideological systems exist to serve individual personality, and not the other way around. When the personality is cut off by death, there is an absolute cutoff of one person's unique, unrepeatable accumulation of ideas and interactions. No one but the author is left to step in and fill the gap, with his absolute language and extrapersonal perspective.

The Bakhtinian model, in sum, does not really allow for any investigation of the Tolstoyan sense of self.[20] Bakhtin to the contrary, that self is not consummated through the activity of an unfairly privileged author, sitting above and apart from his characters and completing them from within rather than from without. The Tolstoyan self is simply consummated in another way. Not even the other has power to complete it. Because the self has no single internal point of crystallization, no ideational center, the best it can do is focus, for a while only and at considerable mental effort, on a select sequence of events. These events do not penetrate a given mind "logically." They must confront a highly individualized, contradictory complex of habits, reflexes, and accumulated experience — a complex that is, at the same time, enormously vulnerable to the accidents of the outside world. Just as history, in Tolstoy's construct, has no ultimate coherence, so the *I* does not cohere; thus it can be profoundly and irreversibly moved by random environmental factors. Tolstoy is deadly serious about chance. This fact has led Gary Saul Morson to suggest that *War and Peace*, that unclassifiable work, is closer to satire than to any other genre. Its target, he proposes, "is all forms of thinking that would explain away the randomness, the asystematicity and 'unstorylike' character of history and psychology."[21] Tolstoy's greatest works all explore this ruthless radical contingency, and his successful heroes learn how to build a life within it. In each of these protagonists the absence of an ultimate coherence to the self, along with Tolstoy's failure to endorse a strategy of explanation, constitutes a sort of freedom and terror that Dostoevsky could not have envisioned for his characters.

Dostoevsky, of course, also shows us a world where not everything is known and where incompatible truths are carried around in individual selves. But for Dostoevsky, the unknownness of the world is a matter of mystery, not of contingency. The accidents and "coincidences" that saturate his work eventually add up to a revelation. To be sure, the revelations may be multiple; in this sense Dostoevsky is truly polyphonic. But such polyphony can increase as well as decrease the authority of the author. As one critic has ably noted, under polyphonic conditions characters

are neither equally significant nor equally evaluated, but to the extent that it is possible each is confirmed by the writer in his own special truth. . . . What is called "polyphonism" in Pushkin and Dostoevsky imparts a loftiness not only to the heroes, but to the authors as well. It makes the author's view on things maximally broad, objective — the view not only of an artist, but of a wise man, a prophet, as well.[22]

In Dostoevsky, a character cannot explore this prophecy alone; individuals need one another in their pursuit of the mystery. Tolstoy's world is by far the lonelier place. There is no mystery there, only the brute facts of everyday experience. Such a vision was understandably alien to Dostoevsky, and, for other reasons, to Bakhtin as well. In his lectures on Tolstoy to high school students in Vitebsk (1922 – 23) Bakhtin stressed just this loneliness of the Tolstoyan hero: "Ivan Ilych understood that he lived alone, that all that is most essential took place in solitude. Life as reflected in the consciousness of others was a fiction, a mirage, a falsehood."[23]

It was, in fact, this loneliness that Bakhtin addressed in his 1961 notes toward the new edition of his book on Dostoevsky. "Separation, dissociation, and enclosure within the self as the main reason for the loss of one's self. . . . No nirvana is possible for a *single* consciousness."[24] Bakhtin saw the Tolstoyan self, at its most intense moments, vainly seeking that nirvana, which to Bakhtin was nonexistence.

D.

THE DANGERS OF DIALOGUE

Aaron Fogel

Coerced Speech and the
Oedipus Dialogue Complex

For reasons particular to each, no theorist of the novel has been centrally interested in recurrent dialogue form. Bakhtin, who steers outside the usual dilemmas (formalism vs. antiformalism, invention vs. representation, structuralism vs. historicism) for a socially vital definition of the novel, though he points to Lucianic dialogue as a major source of the novel and implies that the "dialogic" of true novelistic prose subverts the hierarchical "dialectic" of philosophy, is out to emphasize the unresolvable wildness of ideological and marketplace speech, the interference of plural consciousness and plural glossaries. It would not be in accord with this stance to spend too much time on the contractuality of dialogue in great novels like *Don Quixote* or *Moll Flanders.* Lukács, of course, would find this feature of dialogical recurrence, even where there is a "progress of dialogue" as in Bunyan or Austen, too static, marginal — perhaps a symptom of the bourgeois will to static constitution and resistance to dialectical change. In *The Rise of the Novel,* Ian Watt, discussing Richardson's epistolary form, describes just such a resistance in a class fixation on one kind of discourse, but does not in his account of the novel as "formal realism" discuss dialogue form itself as repetition. He also alludes only briefly and dismissively to the connection between the novel and the Platonic dialogue.[1] James, though he called "the question of our speech" central, and filled his late novels with a dictated, spoken syntax that returns to the American tradition of spontaneous Protestant witness bearing — the talk show — referred to real speech as "deluge" and as first chaos. The essence of the world's actual dialogue is for him an almost terrifying lack of form, which the novelist works to direct, moving over the face of the waters. (Stevenson, recall, when citing the "key" of dialogue, called it invention, as *against* representation.)[2] Mark Lambert, in an excellent book on dialogue technique in Dickens, also associates dialogue emphatically with the "fun" and "free" part of the novel, indulgence, white space.[3] Such readers as Stanley Rosen in *The Symposium*, Kenneth Burke in *A Rhetoric of Motives*, and Gilbert Ryle in *Plato's Progress* probably come closest to meditation on recurring dialogue form as the shape of a work, but they deal with what are generally considered philosophical dialogues.[4] Strong critics and theorists of the novel, then, whether antiformalist or formalist in final perspective, have generally associated "speech" and "dialogue" as they occur in the world with freedom: the spontaneous, uncontrolled, plastic, idiomatic, digressive part of life that, to the formalists, has to be reined in, made part of the action, and to a genius of pluralism like Bakhtin represents the ultimate potential of the novel as an open genre.

Of course in practice not all dialogue is free, natural, spontaneous, informal, or lively. On the contrary, it may be true that most real dialogue is variously constrained and forced. But for some reason we usually say that the best novelistic dialogue has those qualities: the unforced movement of common, popular, or natural talk; vivid displays of low (dialect, idiolect, oaths) and high (mutually liberating) free speech. It would be shabby to dismiss all images of free dialogue as nothing but ideology, or I-Thou philosophy as just a utopian myth. But revelatory and intimate I-Thou conversation, of the kind that the greatest characters in Austen, Eliot, Lawrence, and Forster reach toward, does usually occur between those who belong to a high, even an ideal, spiritual class, who can master difficult rules; the conversational idealism of the "great tradition," with its images of autonomous but energetic intellectual intimacy, describes heroes and heroines who transcend dialogical constraints that they are alert, witty, and sensitive enough to understand. They are the "winners" in the conversational scene: an elite of sympathetic imagination, who can even overcome the flaws and limits in conventional ideas of "sympathy"; slightly below them in this world picture is a class of common people whose talk is "natural." Novelistic dialogue, however, obviously doesn't begin and end with free, natural lower-class speech and freely achieved upper-class mutual sympathy. Most real speech between classes is probably not conversational. And there is a set of great nineteenth-century *anti*-conversational, yet extremely dialogical, novels which fix on a more coercive and authoritarian dialogue regime to return it incessantly upon the reader. Scott's meditation on the varieties of dramatic forced speaking in *The Heart of Mid-Lothian* is probably the first great example. Alice's recurrent encounters with illogical, self-absorbed, and insane pedagogues is another. Melville's *The Confidence-Man* may be the most furious. Its barrage of scenes of forced selling amounts not only to a formal burden but to an attempted ethnography of American dialogue.[5] In this American Menippean satire, dialogue formalism and cultural representation meet: extreme dialogue repetition represents the scene of selling. Possibly dialogue between the classes, as opposed to "conversation" which takes place within a class, will involve more "drama," more actions like coercive inquiry, detection, selling, negotiating, blackmailing, and so on. If we can define Leavis's unstated principle in choosing most of the works of the "great tradition" as a high-conversational bias, in which moral insight and the worth of life appear through developing conversational struggle, it may be a kind of contrary, somber, critical realism, rather than an obsessive formal impulse alone, that overformalizes and even stagnates dialogue in the novel, to indicate, with necessary repetition, the rule-governed, hierarchical, fatal fixation of social and political dialogue, as Conrad oppositionally does. Here, "form" and "key" in dialogue are not just compositional or aesthetic requirements, as for Stevenson; they are, on the contrary, at the heart of the novel's critical realism.

The Conradian novel, then, as defined here—along with a small group of novels since Scott to which it belongs—has a very strong will to objectify and contemplate dialogue as constrained form, and the plurality of such dialogue forms in their social distribution. In this light, consider "Heart of Darkness" as a story about the progressive objectification of its own disproportionate and forced dialogue forms. It is, of course, easy to take Conrad's most famous story as an instance of freespoken "oral literature," in which Marlow is the *skaz*, yarn spinner, or ancient mariner. But the story itself has to be seen as having for one of its main actions the increasing objectification of the speaking narrator himself, so that as it proceeds, the reader has an increasingly uncanny—partly comic, partly disappointed—feeling that Marlow's longwinded yarn is proportionally and therefore somehow morally linked to the more obviously imperial and abject forms of excessive talk like Kurtz's. That is, Marlow and Kurtz, as speakers, are progressively identified with each other through a covert appeal to the reader's sense of "normal" prose masses and of the ordinary length of a talk. We increasingly see that each does "almost all" the talking in his own dialogical context: Marlow to his audience, Kurtz to the natives and to his clownish Russian disciple.

Here is a typical short passage from "Heart of Darkness" which in its onrush might go unnoticed but which is meant to make us contemplate and "equate" three or four dialogue scenes formally. Marlow has come ashore and is listening to the young Russian, exploding with a need to talk, tell about Kurtz:

> In the next breath he advised me to keep enough steam on the boiler to blow the whistle in case of any trouble. "One good screech will do more for you than all your rifles. They are simple people," he repeated. He rattled away at such a rate he quite overwhelmed me. He seemed to be trying to make up for lots of silence, and actually hinted, laughing, that such was the case. "Don't you talk with Mr. Kurtz?" I said. "You don't talk with that man—you listen to him," he exclaimed with severe exaltation.

These sentences set up a hierarchy of dialogue scenes—which the reader is invited to tear down. Lowest, apparently, are the simple natives, overwhelmed by a boat's whistle. On the next level, the Russian's talk itself, a kind of social chatter, here ironically overwhelms Marlow. At the presumed highest level is philosophical discourse like Kurtz's, awing disciples into pious silence. Implicitly, on the fourth level, framing all this, and making its own claim to truth, is Marlow's narration to his audience, who object and grunt a few times. We might, that is, easily organize these scenes of forceful speech and disproportionate dialogue, combined so rapidly and formally that they seem to make a "dialogue fugue," into a self-congratulatory hierarchy similar to the Russian's, but with the last—ours—fiction or art, at the top, as transcendent consciousness: Marlow's ironic contemplative art, the truest frame. But just as clearly, Conrad stands behind the analogous disproportionate dialogues to suggest that all the scenes, including Marlow's art, and his writing to us, are alike: imperial assertions of "overwhelming" force.

In each scene, the speaker impresses the listener by the force of sound. If the jungle's "darkness" and civilization's "light" will nearly be "wielded together without a joint" by the story, the same fusion applies to our preconceived images of some dialogues as civilized and some as uncivilized. The natives overwhelmed by the ship's whistle resemble the Russian himself (their narrator and explainer) being overwhelmed by the force of Kurtz's altruistic oratory. Less clear, but most important, Marlow's silent audience (representing ourselves) falls — at least potentially — into this field. But whether we accept or refuse this last irony, this passage shows *how* Conrad asks the reader to think about dialogue as formal and proportional rather than simply expressive: by seeing and hearing the parallel ratios so as to find startling affinities among apparently discrete dialogue scenes.

Note, in terms of the history of readings of "Heart of Darkness," that Marlow's portentous, forceful repetition of adjectives can be understood somewhat differently. Leavis's conversational idealism rejects some of Marlow's incessant rhetoric as hot air — which of course it is. But in this reading, Marlow's relentless insistences, his own excess of verbal steam (even the mist that pervades the landscape is an image of rhetoric), is part of the conscious imagery of the story, and of the dialogical mood of imperialism, of "overwhelming the other" by misty imperial words. The scene of "overwhelming" noise is the common denominator of the story's main theme — imperialism — and what Conrad called its "secondary" theme, Marlow's obsession with the image of Kurtz speaking. The "dialogic" here welds together the two themes "without a joint." The proportional resemblance of all dialogue scenes is both tragic and comic, even oddly hilarious, and appears as an irrationally temporal, rather than simply atemporal, simultaneity: Marlow the young man, we could say — if we break with rational time sequence — became obsessed with his image of Kurtz talking "because" Kurtz talks to his disciples in the same disproportion which Marlow the older man and narrator *now* has vis-à-vis his audience. Young Marlow was obsessed by the image of Kurtz speaking, which was itself the metaphoric and predictive image of older Marlow narrating. The "cause" of Marlow's inexplicable obsession with Kurtz's talk is his own "later" identity with its proportions during the time of the story's actual telling. From a perspective of speech production, of course, this is all rational, because the older Marlow's production of the story for his audience *is* the "origin" of the story. There is, then, a simple repetition of dialogue form in time (Kurtz's overwhelming verbosity generates Marlow's overwhelming verbosity about him), but also a simultaneity or "knot" of dialogue scenes, which has to do with the production of the story itself. Marlow's original obsession with Kurtz — which Conrad has to impose on the reader partly by fiat or pure force of insistence — has its strongest but most irrational explanation in his predestined identity with Kurtz as the current talkative narrator before us (almost in the way that Oedipus's rational power to conduct judicial inquiries and force speech from his witnesses is inherited from the Sphinx's earlier grosser power — which he dissolved and inherited — to demand the answer to the riddle, to force replies).

The fusion of categories such as "psychological" and "political" in and by dialogue form can be seen clearly here. While Marlow's resemblance to Kurtz can be read psychologically, so that each is the other's son and father in speech disproportion, and the two are "insanely" identified as willful speakers (Marlow of course trying but failing to eradicate this will to power in himself), there should be no question that this resemblance presents itself to us first as a historical and political idea. Disproportion and coercion in the speech scene become the constants because, as Conrad writes in one essay, "man is a conquering animal,"[6] and history is imperialist. The famous "horror" at the end of the story is partly a joke, said twice, narcissistically, by self-echoing Kurtz, and partly a non-answer, punch line, or "detonation" coming at the close of what we could call a "shaggy dog story" (the entire action of "Heart of Darkness" is more defiantly funny than most critics have argued); but it is lastly the identification of art and politics as imperial speech. The first sentence of the story describes how the ship "swings to" (describes a forced circle about) its anchor until it rests. The secondary action of the story is the "swing to" that Marlow's own freer telling makes toward Kurtz's compulsive talk, becoming slowly and inevitably linked to it in moral and political status. In this gradual parallelism, a universal "dialogic" is being contemplated and objectified: by the end of the story the "swing to" has implicitly united philosophical dialogue (Kurtz as mock Socrates), fictive narration (or the dialogue between writer and audience), and imperialist cant into

a single scene of dialogue, and Conrad has assigned himself and the
reader to the same unavoidable intention of conquest and the same
imperial scene. Artistic force, the desire to make the reader see,
hear, or feel, is a sublimation at most of the other desires to conquer.
It "must" participate in the general dialogue form.

In *Don Quixote* the repeated dialogue, in addition to its comedy, mimicked a typical debate of the age, between biblical authority and sense experience; it was then also used in the second
part for baroque paradoxes, in which the *Quixote* became a new
profane Bible, a book determining reality. Conrad constructs "Heart
of Darkness" on similar lines, to make a baroque "knot," a "mirror" of dialogues reflecting each other out onto the audience, so as
to define the typical dialogue scene of his time. As *Quixote* mimics
a typical dialogue of the age, Conrad brings contemporary imperialism home in his forced dialogues. The point is that the proportions of imperialism are everywhere in an imperial age—even in
stories told on yawls on the Thames, or in our reading of the nov-
ella. What bothered Leavis—Marlow's incessant, insistent, domi-
neering, adjectival style—was meant to bother. The story could not
exist without an excess of fiat. The disproportions in Kurtz's speech,
in Marlow's telling, and in Conrad's representation of Marlow's
telling resemble each other; from different angles each could be said
to come first and "cause" the others. Conrad "repeats" the scene
of dialogue abstractly, not merely in the story of the characters but
from level to level of the story's production, until we finally see
Conrad, or the author, in a dialogical relation to us that resembles,
in its desire for conquest, all the others. What Conrad called the
"secondary" plot of "Heart of Darkness," in this reading, is this
gradual identification of all dialogue relations as disproportionate
and imperial.[7]

Parenthetically, it is worth adding that this process is not primarily "deconstructive" despite some apparent resemblances. "Deconstruction," from the standpoint being developed here, is another
philosophical sublimation of the Oedipal drama of forced inquiry:
text, language, writing oversees its own intentional disintegration.
The "text" plays the role of Oedipus, undoing itself for a general
sacrificial peace; though it can be argued in reverse that Oedipus's
inquisitorial self-eradication is a dramatic version of what in fact
writing does. But in any case all deconstructions, as Derrida writing

about force half-indicates, have eristic elements, and, though "play-ful," are shaded by inquisition. To "make" the other's text decenter by a reading of disjunctive metaphors reenacts Socrates' forcing of the other into logical self-contradiction — elenchus. But when Kurtz scribbles "exterminate the brutes" at the bottom of his enlightening canticle, or when Marlow closes with the evasive lie "your name," or when Conrad himself uses various methods to call attention to the forced conditions of his own writing, there is certainly a drama *like* that of deconstruction, a change of intonation violent enough to be a "detonation," but the stress falls not on self-contradiction, or on endless linguistic difference and reinterpretation, but on the idea that all dialogue, even dialogue with the self, involves coercive disproportion. Kurtz's relation to himself, when he repudiates him-self, remains imperial. Implicitly, nobody quarrels even with himself as an equal. Conrad is not as interested, then, in the tropes and actions we call deconstruction — which make the text itself the sub-lime Oedipal actor — as in outlining the inescapably disproportion-ate forces at work in any dialogue, including storytelling, lyrical quarrel with the self, and philosophical critique.

The power to abstract and objectify dialogue forms, then, gives fiction the force of "comparative dialogic." The novel can make startling juxtapositions of dialogues in broadly different scenes. Comparative dialogic makes it possible to move among discrete institutions of dialogue — social, religious, literary, pedagogical — to compare them formally. For example, let us isolate a dialogue pat-tern found in the *Oedipus Tyrannus,* that of the punishment of the speech-forcer, the discovery of the guilt of the coercive interrogator himself. We might then put aside, at least temporarily, distinctions between literary genres, between psychology and politics, or be-tween literature and reality, and ask if we find this dialogue form anywhere else. It could be posited that this form is inscribed in the unconscious as "Oedipal" — in a sense of the term which combines Sophoclean and Freudian insights to supplement each other. It is the scene in which the father figure initiates a coercive dialogue and is surprisingly and "thrillingly" annihilated by the answers he forces from those he interrogates. In this scene the father is punished by the examination or catechism he appears to institute, but of which he is in fact the predestined victim. This dream of vengeance upon the father by the surprising but inevitable "boomerang" of catechism could be regarded either psychoanalytically or politically. And it would not be surprising to find variants of this scene both in literature and in ongoing public ritual: in the opening of *Lear*, in Dostoevsky's "Grand Inquisitor," in the resolution of the McCarthy hearings, in a popular television show of journalistic inquisition like *60 Minutes*, or in Foucault's vision (an unconsciously Oedipal vision by this account) of the world as all examination without real subjects. Wherever the democratic punishment of the speech-forcer, or the idea that inquiring power might be undone, or undo itself, by its own inquiry, is attended by feelings of fear and gratification, we might see an Oedipal dialogue process.

Likewise, a simpler idea of dialogue, the notion of necessary disproportion between speakers which I have been exploring here — the picture of one speaking a great deal and one very little — can itself be applied expressively to diverse worldviews. For Leopardi, dissymmetry is the expression of a pessimistic psychology; for Valéry, dissymmetry is the essence of all dialogue, an aesthetic-mathematical universal;[8] for Richard Ohmann, disproportion is a sign of class domination in sociological interviews.[9] My thesis is that Conrad was, if anything, a dialogist conscious of these plural possibilities, and that he used the stark universal of dialogue disproportion, sometimes adding to it the more complex Oedipal dynamic of the punishment of the speech-forcer, to "fuse" categories like the psychological, the poetic, and the political. Teaching this idea to a class, one might draw a long line and a short line on the blackboard, representing the speaker who speaks a great deal and the speaker who speaks very little, and then show how this simple, radical disproportion ironically covers diverse dialogue scenes in Conrad's works (marriage, inquisition, storytelling, selling, hiring, courtship, séance) and might incidentally be applied to other well-known scenes such as psychoanalytic dialogue. In each case the one doing most of the speaking, or the one doing very little, may be the forcer, and there are many other specific variables. The power of this formal objectification is precisely that it allows him to cut across conventional categories, putting aside any one rational standpoint — psychology, aesthetics, politics — to merge all of these into a deeply disturbing dialogical constant. Just as the interrogation of Joan of Arc in Carl Dreyer's film can't be said to be singly political, religious, or sexual but all of these fused, so strategies of reading Conrad which make him out as primarily a psychologist, a metaphysician, or a political thinker have tended to ignore his dialogical understanding. He is the novelist who most consciously understands the classical action of coercion to speak as a sometimes explicit and sometimes sublimated unifying motif. The implicit ground of poetics itself becomes the scene of coercion to speak, and genre and tone become responses to this ground.

Theories about dialogue are relatively common, but theories about the historical development and change of dialogue forms are scarce. There have been many practical comments on the uses of philosophical dialogue for pluralistic exposition by Hume, Herder, Diderot, Landor, and others; and many theories, for instance in Plato criticism from Schleiermacher to Gadamer, or in the modern line of dialogical polemics that runs from Buber to Bakhtin, give the term *dialogue* a very high place. Rudolf Hirzel's *Der Dialog* is the one major scholarly study of the development of the dialogue as a genre; but it does not really apply to the novel. It is Gilbert Ryle who has in a searching and jovial way written the one modern study of Plato, skeptical and formal, which takes changes in dialogue form not as the transcendental sign of the interpersonal as the true but as an indication of someone's actual changing social milieu. It is of course daring and ironic to apply this strategy to Plato. Looking at changes in the dialogue forms, Ryle argues — iconoclastically, entertainingly, not very believably — that Plato in the end was moving away from the theory of Ideas toward a sort of Aristotelian naturalism. He hints at an ironic novel — the book is called *Plato's Progress*[10] — in which the hero finally forsakes Ideal Forms. Plato is (by the present definition) novelized — that is, made into a dialogical progress in a historical setting. We see him first practicing eristic dialogue forms in Athens, then moving toward his Forms when politically cut off from real educational encounter, and then finally coming back to a different, less transcendental notion of form itself. Recognizing Ryle's joking allusion to Bunyan in the title word *progress* (Ryle seems to see the connection between English Protestantism and the search for new liturgical dialogue forms), we might take Ryle's hint, and for a moment, before going on to some specific examples of forced dialogue, consider Conrad's own early "progress" in dialogue.

There is no question that Conrad before the middle period which will be the main concern of this study was already a conscious formalist in dialogue. Each of the major early works has its own dialogue craft, partly distinct from that of the others, and selectively matched to its themes. There is time here only to sketch the development. In *An Outcast of the Islands,* Willems, allegorically named, is a crude early version of the parallel talkatives Kurtz and Marlow; Willems bullies his wife by making her the audience of his egotistical monologues. The Malays, by contrast, have a capacity for inexhaustible and free *collective* speech. They are viewed, romantically enough, as a primitive people "to whom talk is poetry and painting and music, all art, all history; their only accomplishment, their only superiority, their only amusement." In this early novel there is a stark contrast between the civilized man's egocentric, one-sided, disproportional talk and the native's unforced, communal, totally "immersed" collective talk, never exhausted or decayed, and beyond representation. The phrase "their only superiority" seems purposely duplicit — this talk with its continuity and force (it is not represented as dialogue, because the Greek word now implies formal division of the speakers) gives them their only superiority to animals, or nature, but likewise their only superiority to civilization. The idea of a purely continuous and generative speech is probably high romantic, as expressed most convincingly in Wordsworth or Hölderlin.[11] With *The Nigger of the "Narcissus,"* certainly a technical breakthrough for Conrad in many ways, this idea undergoes plastic revision and modernization. Perhaps taking a hint from Stephen Crane,[12] Conrad amasses forecastle talk into paragraphs containing many short speeches, many of which are oaths, more "force of sound" than "meaning." He abandons the convention of speeches individuated into separate paragraphs (rejecting the image of talk as an individual act, or "dialogue") in order to suggest that forecastle "we" speech is immersed in its collectivity. The talk clusters, partly because he doesn't discard quotation marks, look radically different from the earlier idealized image of Malay talk as pure collective genius: pointillistic, lonely, isolated, the forecastle's amassed speeches are at once orchestral and anomic. This conscious break with the conventions of dialogue paragraphing to represent forecastle speech as pointillistic solidarity is one of the clearest instances in early Conrad of the association of speech and labor; it could be seen as patronizing. In a very different formal mode, *Lord Jim* collects a sort of international symposium of responses or commentaries — French, German, English — around the hero. The philosophical symposium, with its verdict of uncertainty, is reemployed here, with strong traces of Menippean satire, or attack on the presumptions of intellectual understanding.

After this, we have the highly conscious temporal arrangement of dialogue forms in "Heart of Darkness," just discussed. It criticizes the romantic ideal of a historically prophetic speech that itself has continuity and force but is innocent of evil. Tentatively, the story decides that the modern storyteller cannot get back to Malay ideal talk but rather has to be only another imperial speaker, conscious at best, "immersed" in coercion to speak rather than in a community of free speakers. The story's closure, the dialogue with the Intended, predicts Conrad's increasing turn toward dialogues of force: the turn away from romantic ideas of lyrical speech toward an objectification of tragic forced dialogue. The heart of darkness reached at the end of the story is partly the realization that fiction cannot be lyrically and narratively produced as an "only superiority," a pure lyrical freedom outside historical force, but is itself the product of coercion. The fact is that the Intended, however "horrible" and grotesquely melodramatic the scene, rescues Marlow from the idea of a sublime internal compulsion to speak out by showing him external compulsion. Partly liberated by this scene from the romantic idea that his own writing should be inner compulsion, Conrad himself can go on to become a more "objective" dramatist (whether it is a loss or gain is not the point), who makes the scene of forced speech take place between the characters rather than inside a character. This is precisely what "The End of the Tether" begins to study. In that story there is a rich distribution of dialogue forms, intended to be seen and compared by the reader, but the forced dialogue now occupies the central place, rather than the place of ironic closure. That is, with "The End of the Tether" we come to the middle period of Conrad's work, in which the forced dialogue now gives the central organization to Conrad's dialogues; and this will remain the case until the completion of *Under Western Eyes* in 1912, the book in which Conrad raises to its highest pitch, analyzes, and perhaps also has done with his interest in coercion to speak, after which he will go on to write a series of romances of "interference," *Chance, Victory,* and *The Rescue.*

Since one of the main powers of the forced dialogue comes from its provocative reuse in the political novels to compare and equate what seem to be different relations and institutions (marriage, selling, inquisition, and so on), the scene chosen here as a first example of the form will have to bias us temporarily toward the clearly political use of the scene for the extortion of information. Nevertheless Sotillo's interrogation of Hirsch, with its highly "striped" counterpoints between speech and silence, dialogue and narration, made obvious on the page, and its nearly unanalyzable tension between force and farce, makes the best starting place. Placed near the end of *Nostromo,* it is the novel's most detailed, foregrounded, physical description of the interrogatory torture which is in the background of every character's consciousness—not only Monygham's—as *the* definitive scene in the culture. Hirsch suffers the "estrapade"—his arms are tied behind his back and then lifted, so that his shoulders dislocate, and he hangs by a rope (as do some other main characters in the novel, more figuratively). The attempted speech-extortion here takes the form of a primary distortion of the body, or torture. The body of the prose, the stark alternation of narrative and dialogue, is also clearly "striped," sadistic, dislocating.

Sotillo looked at him in silence. "Will you depart from your obstinacy, you rogue?" he asked. Already a rope, whose one end was fastened to Señor Hirsch's wrists, had been thrown over a beam, and three soldiers held the other end, waiting. He made no answer. His heavy lower lip hung stupidly. Sotillo made a sign. Hirsch was jerked up off his feet, and a yell of despair and agony burst out in the room, filled the passage of the great buildings, rent the air outside, caused every soldier of the camp along the shore to look up at the windows, started some of the officers in the hall babbling excitedly, with shining eyes; others, setting their lips, looked gloomily at the floor . . .

The sun had set when he went in once more. A soldier carried in two lighted candles and slunk out, shutting the door without noise.

"Speak, thou Jewish child of the devil! The silver! The silver, I say! Where is it? Where have you foreign rogues hidden it? Confess or—"

A slight quiver passed up the taut rope from the racked limbs, but the body of Señor Hirsch, enterprising businessman from Esmeralda, hung under the heavy beam perpendicular and silent, facing the colonel awfully. The inflow of the night air, cooled by the snows of the Sierra, spread gradually a delicious freshness through the close heat of the room.

"Speak — thief — scoundrel — picaro — or — "

Sotilla had seized the riding-whip, and stood with his arm lifted up. For a word, for one little word, he felt he would have knelt, cringed, grovelled on the floor before the drowsy, conscious stare of those fixed eyeballs starting out of the grimy, dishevelled head that drooped very still with his mouth closed askew. The colonel ground his teeth with rage and struck. The rope vibrated leisurely to the blow, like the long string of a pendulum starting from a rest. But no swinging motion was imparted to the body of Señor Hirsch, the well-known hide merchant on the coast. With a convulsive effort of the twisted arms it leaped up a few inches, curling upon itself like a fish on the end of a line. Señor Hirsch's head was flung back on his straining throat; his chin trembled. For a moment the rattle of his chattering teeth pervaded the vast, shadowy room, where the candles made a patch of light around the two flames burning side by side. And as Sotillo, staying his raised hand, waited for him to speak, with the sudden flash of a grin and a straining forward of the wrenched shoulders, he spat violently into his face.

The uplifted whip fell, and the colonel sprang back with a low cry of dismay, as if aspersed by a jet of deadly venom. Quick as thought he snatched up his revolver, and fired twice. The report and the concussion seemed to throw him at once from ungovernable rage into idiotic stupor. He stood with drooping jaw and stony eyes.(447 – 49)

This scene is one of Conrad's dialogue "sonnets," or formal meditations on the nature of dialogue. It has the characteristic rhythm, in which demanding speeches alternate liturgically with silences until a final explosion which is a "detonation" or loud silence. Scenes with this rhythm, though less violent, appear in many places throughout Conrad's work, and, in a large sense, the lives of Stevie, Winnie, and Verloc, of Razumov, of Whalley, of Nostromo, of Heyst have this rhythm: they are cornered people who finally "detonate," resolving themselves atonally. The physical triad rest, unrest, arrest, which governs much of Conrad's sense of motion, is at work here: the tension between rest (silence) and unrest (demand for speech) culminates in an arrest. Specific to this passage is the equation of speaking and spitting: Sotillo's demand, "Speak," retroactively sounds like the spitting it provokes. It is a spitter's duet. But if we try to get past this kind of observation about rhythms to deal with themes, we immediately confront a large field of possibilities open to facile commentary but in fact extremely resistant to any conclusions. Some major themes seem to be: the stupidity of Jew-baiting and anti-Semitism, without, as others have noted, its being clear where Conrad stands; formal sadism, easily psychoanalyzed; the picaresque and the "low" novel; motion and immobility; crude desublimation of Spinoza's "of human bondage"; and the violent integration of narrative to dialogue. Each of these could lead to lengthy commentary. But note only two small, strange, and related gestures in the above dialogue poem. Sotillo identifies Hirsch as picaro (the word appears in Spanish and italicized as *pícaro* in some later editions), and so calls up the whole relation between the picaresque and Spanish Jewry, suggesting that Conrad knew the social history of the genre accurately enough to allow him to revive it in a serious historical picture of the formality of persecution. From another angle, however, the word *pícaro* seems to appear here itself only as a kind of acoustic point in the series of spat words: *picar* means "to puncture," "to pick at," "to sting," "to stab." Sotillo, the inquirer wrong about everything, does not realize that Hirsch is no picaro, but a terrified decoy who like himself knows nothing; the picaresque as a genre knows nothing, and seems to have been turned inside out in a scene of absolutely ignorant inquiry. A second anomalous but intentional detail is the weather report. In bizarre contrast to Sotillo's speech-forcing ignorance (he tries to get the details from Hirsch), the "omniscient" narrator — not simply Conrad — has a peculiar and punctilious sadism, which appears as the desire to inform the reader about all details. This desire seems most clearly ridiculous in information about the "delicious" cool air drifting into the room from the mountain peaks. The sentence seems ludicrously misplaced, since neither character can enjoy the weather. The narrator, by this reading, has a tone decadently transcendent, seeing fit to notice an irrelevant "appreciated" natural deliciousness, as if nature were cuisine. It seems one of the many startling parodies of omniscient information in *Nostromo*. Yet, significantly, the mountain air may also be one of Conrad's many parodies of romantic "inspiration," or the *cause* of speech: it is what revives Hirsch enough to spit. And the term *delicious,* in its inappropriateness to nature, which is not culinary, has an oblique sadistic reference to the scene of coercion to speak itself as a kind of cooking. Some slang metaphors for coercion to speak imply that it is acculturation as cooking, in a Lévi-Straussian way (to grill, to roast); others are theatrical (the heat, the spotlight). Conrad's usual early metaphor had been mechanical and ejaculatory: to "pump" someone. The scene of coercion to speak — as violent acculturation — has many optional metaphors, low and high, which can be employed at will for various desublimating ironies.

But put aside these details to consider this scene in the light of the tradition of such scenes. Mikhail Bakhtin tried to revive the New Testament Greek term *anacrisis* for the scene of making the other speak.[13] For him it referred to the whole field of devices, mostly *subtle,* for getting the other to talk. Socrates is the archetypal high master of subtle, ironic anacrisis. But Oedipus and Lear — Bakhtin does not say this — are examples of a more blunt coercion. Bakhtin necessarily, in studying Dostoevsky, used the term to mean the ingenious strategies of verbal pressure to speak, but the dictionaries remind us that in its origins it refers more often to examination by extreme physical torture. Whatever Bakhtin's reasons for tacitly underplaying the physical violence of anacrisis, and emphasizing instead what he calls "the provocation of the word by the word," Conrad's scene above is a deliberately regressive, historically acute, violent, low, physical anacrisis, strangely worked up into high formal shape. It is not Bakhtinian. Arguably, it is more radical and critical, and less innocent than Bakhtin. Taken as a whole field, anacrisis, verbal *and* violent, is a crux or foundation of dramatic imagination for many reasons. To mention only one: it amounts to a common ground between (1) being a dramatic author oneself (finding convincing ways to "make" one's characters speak the truth); (2) being a strong, directive, main character (who commands the action, stages plays within plays, or conducts inquiries); and (3) being one of the real social authorities entitled to force speech (judges, teachers, police, detectives). If, however, we look through the high English novel, and even the Russian, though we will of course necessarily find pressure to speak, we will not find direct and formal torture as in the Hirsch scene. Where then does this low and regressive dialogue poem come from? Conrad took it from his readings in history, and from adventure novels, perhaps. But even if we look to those other traditions of history, romance, and adventure, as Conrad knew them, we won't find much that is simultaneously brutal and formal in this way. There are many scenes of harsh legal examination in Scott; but Scott holds off from the reductive and insane brutality witnessed above, since his whole point is to defend the ultimate need for legal institutions. In Marryat's description of the Inquisition at Goa, which Stevenson admired, or even in Marryat's father-son coercions to speak in a boy's book called *The Little Savage,* there is nothing like this sadistic ritual of speech extortion;[14] and in the atmosphere of universal legalism in *Bleak House* or even in Kafka's *Trial* and *Amerika,* low violence and bizarrely stylized speech coercion are not combined. In Conrad's poetics above, not the skin of the victim but the prose itself becomes "striped." Unjust whippings abound in nautical protest literature, but not in connection with coercion to speak as a ritual of knowledge. As a result, Conrad's formal anacrisis here combines the supposedly "lowest" and most "popular" types of melodramatic fiction — to be anachronistic, scenes like those in Mickey Spillane[15] — with a classical, virtually epistemological sense of interrogation, to make a new kind of prose poem about the dramatic dialogue of inquiry.

Conrad's scene, then, manages to fuse the extremely low and the extremely formal in a study of anacrisis. The focus on the scene is the theme of making the other *speak* (as it is not, for example, in Sade). The result is a formal architecture which implies that this scene describes something essential to information and communication: that what we are seeing is something like the "primal scene" of inquiry. In *Nostromo,* the above is not just bizarre, idiotic cruelty, though it is that. Instead it seems the desublimated norm of human dialogue, the worst example of a general condition, in which coercion to speak, the will to make the other speak, which seems an even more general desire than that of "conquest," is the pattern of most (if not all) dialogue relations — including some that could be regarded as partly good.

A more sublimated, but equally formal and disturbing, variant of this dialogue poem appears in the balladic coda to chapter 3 of *The Secret Agent.* The entire marriage of the Verlocs is a set of contrapuntally alternating forced dialogues: sometimes she wants him to talk, sometimes he her. In the following scene, Verloc wants to tell Winnie about his forced mission to blow up Greenwich Observatory, but cannot, because she is too engrossed in lamenting

Stevie's exposure to anarchist rhetoric in their home. She sticks to her favorite subject, the victimization of her brother.

"He isn't fit to hear what's said here. He believes it's all true. He knows no better. He gets into his passions over it."

Mr. Verloc made no comment.

"He glared at me, as if he didn't know who I was, when I went downstairs. His heart was going like a hammer. He can't help being excitable. I woke mother up, and asked her to sit with him till he went to sleep. It isn't his fault. He's no trouble when he's left alone."

Mr. Verloc made no comment.

"I wish he had never been to school," Mrs. Verloc began again, brusquely. "He's always taking away those newspapers from the window to read. He gets a red face poring over them. We don't get rid of a dozen numbers in a month. They only take up room in the front window. And Mr. Ossipon brings every week a pile of these F.P. tracts to sell at a halfpenny each. I wouldn't give a halfpenny for the whole lot. It's silly reading — that's what it is. There's no sale for it. The other day Stevie got hold of one, and there was a story in it of a German soldier officer tearing half-off the ear of a recruit, and nothing was done to him for it. The brute! I couldn't do anything with Stevie that afternoon. The story was enough, too, to make one's blood boil. But what's the use of printing things like that? We aren't German slaves here, thank God. It's not our business — is it?"

Mr. Verloc made no reply.

"I had to take the carving knife from the boy," Mrs. Verloc continued, a little sleepily now. "He was shouting and stamping and sobbing. He can't stand the notion of any cruelty. He would have stuck that officer like a pig if he had seen him then. It's true, too. Some people don't deserve much mercy." Mrs. Verloc's voice ceased, and the expression of her motionless eyes became more and more contemplative and veiled during the long pause. "Comfortable, dear?" she asked in a faint, far-away voice. "Shall I put out the light now?"

The dreary conviction that there was no sleep for him held Mr. Verloc mute and hopelessly inert in his fear of darkness. He made a great effort.

"Yes. Put it out," he said at last in a hollow tone.

This grimly funny scene amounts to another attempt, like the interrogation of Hirsch, to picture the extreme formal antithesis of conversation. The repetition of the phrase "Mr. Verloc made no comment" makes the reader aware of an extreme and even ludicrous anticonversational formality on the page. Nevertheless it would be

misleading to say that because this is not conversation it is simply
"monologue." Mrs. Verloc makes her husband her listener, while
he in turn flatly beseeches her to hear about his forced mission.
Obliquely they answer each other, and are aware of each other as
mutual censors. Her implicit answer to him is that she does not
want to hear. She responds to his attempt to start a conversation
by becoming a masturbatory narrator; the entire drift of her reverie
answers his weak hint that he is in bad shape by telling him that
Stevie — who represents herself — cannot stand to hear of, to "ov-
erhear," any contingent violence. Information is too much for
them — it is *over*hearing in the sense of amplified forced listening —
and it overexcites. Winnie's speech describes a paradoxical crescendo
against crescendo, a steady raising of her voice in indignation against
raised voices. A voice against itself is Shakespearean, as is the bath-
etic joke about Othello ("put out the light"), predicting murder as
marital closure; but the most authentically Shakespearean touch in
the scene is the anecdote about the ear torn "*half*-off," which drives
her into a frenzy of indignation. Winnie's other comments show
that she wants deafness: to tear an ear only half off is to tease the
wish to be deaf at the core of her imagery. She hates the officer for
not causing complete deafness. The climax of the scene oddly gra-
tifies this wish, when Verloc, forced to answer her little question,
gives her his "detonation" — his "hollow tone" of putting out. He
is her husband. What Conrad tries to formalize here is not monologue or soliloquy, and not even double monologue, but subdued
"forced dialogue."

The use of the overall pattern of forced dialogue in this case —
and the murder scene will of course bring this constant relation
between them into open violence, with Verloc trying to get her to
talk until she kills him — has several other strong reverberations.
For one thing, the pattern emphasizes the political character of their
marriage. That Mr. and Mrs. Verloc talk together in the same
rhythmic form in which Sotillo and Hirsch engage in the earlier
novel may not seem a valid comparison, as it leaps from one novel
to another. But the rhythm always has some political component,
and here it recalls the more obviously political grillings in *The Secret
Agent* itself. The Verlocs have a "political" marriage: each has entered into it partly out of unstated politic motives, and till now has
profited from the other's predictably businesslike, silent habits.

Winnie's strategic silences governed their courtship. In the bedroom now, Verloc's "no comments," as the narrator indicates them, resemble the traditional silences of interrogated politicians. Strikingly, Winnie is a kind of reverse Emma Bovary or Quixote: she tries to reject the fantasy literature of romantic politics, the "rousing" anarchist tracts, and to connect only to what seems to be reality; but her life is destroyed by the hallucinated political world anyway. She must participate.

Most abstractly, the rhythm of this scene unfolds and deadens the structure of jokes because of the way in which the three statements followed by three non-answers are left unresolved in the detonating, deliberatley unfunny "punch line," "Put it out." The reader waits through three "no replies" to be finally given this hollow forced answer. The technique here is to "dialogize" the monological structure of jokes in an unsatisfying way. If usually one person tells and controls a joke up to its funny resolution, here two minimal characters are forced to participate unconsciously in a lifeless joke, so that the laughter and release of tension associated with punch lines is withdrawn. The punch line of a real joke or riddle liberates. This couple—there sometimes seems to have been a competition among English novelists to invent the worst marriage—seems to be "immersed" involuntarily together in a bad joke that doesn't work. All that they get, and all that we get at the end, is a "detonation," a willed defeat of the freeing effect of punch lines themselves. Bakhtin referred to a buried quality in ostensibly serious literature which he called *rire resorbé*, "reabsorbed laughter," the muffled presence in a serious work of its carnival, comic, popular origins—as tragedy has traces of the satyr plays or Dostoevsky of Menippean satire.[16] But in Conrad one often feels a strange, conscious desire to expose, prolong, and defeat the conventional structures of laughter, to take the formally condensed parts of the joke, decondense them, and redistribute them back among the characters for a grim anticomic effect. Here is the joke that it takes two to make, and that is no longer funny: history as forced form. Yet force *between* persons is not the evil at this moment. In this marriage-bed scene we see a fact of dialogue that is like a fact of life: for dialogue to happen, someone must initiate it. The Hirsch interrogation is all the lowest and stupidest form of coercion to speak; but if Verloc at this moment did act more aggressively to "make" her come out of her reverie to talk with him, Stevie wouldn't die; Winnie's lonely "sympathy," though in some ways admirable, destroys the family as much as his cowardice. The implication is that some more open force in any relation on both sides might sometimes make marriage possible. Obviously the scene is too static and ritualized, the people too minimal, or tragicomically puppetlike, for any such Lawrencian thesis. Conrad's point is, on the contrary, against the grain of the "great tradition": the extreme facts of dialogue, for certain people, are beyond repair, and beyond the sentimentality of saying that they lack "communication."

The gross rhythmic resemblance between the scene in the Costaguana torture room and the scene in the Verloc bedroom implies an unusual objectification of modern dialogue into one recurrent format. The repetition of this format in not one but many of Conrad's works leads to a feeling of the politically contractual—the same social contract, or formal dialogue relation, at work over a wide social horizon. In social practice, repeated dialogue rituals as diverse as the Quaker meeting, the talk show, and "playing the dozens" can be said to enact a symbolic constitution for the group: dialogue "liturgies," they enact how persons belonging to this group speak together: this is our dialogical symbol, our first idea of relation. In literature, whenever dialogue scenes appear with high and prolonged stylization, they also constitute a (conscious or unconscious) first scene of dialogue, a picture of the social covenant. Genesis 22, for example, with Abraham's dialogized repetition of the words "Here I am"—to God and then to Isaac—a concise repetition indicating the dilemma of absolute obligation to both— is the best-known formal scene of covenant, a dialogical crisis that finds a dialogical resolution. In Conrad, who sometimes formalizes dialogues with almost biblical intensity, the first idea of social covenant leads away from the dialogic of "sympathy" toward a critical, antiromantic idea of the necessity of some initiating force and action. If there is to be "dialogue," someone must make it happen. This idea does not lead to passive determinism, since it requires agency between persons; at the same time it rejects a definition of "dialogue" or "communication" as simple interpersonal freedom, or as something inherently "mutual," "sympathetic," or "good." We are on the verge of an idea of dialogue that is in fact unexpected and difficult to identify comfortably; on the one hand this idea seems potentially authoritarian and on the other intellectually freeing. This tension is itself part of the question being asked by the novels.

A hostile critic might argue that Conrad's shift to coercive dialogue was the result of a purely personal defect. This is a charge which he in fact addressed, quietly. In the prose meditation titled "A Familiar Preface," which begins his autobiographical *A Personal Record,* Conrad apologizes at one point for attempting there a "familiar" style: "I fear that in trying to be conversational I have only managed to be unduly discursive. I have never been very well acquainted with the art of conversation — that art which, I understand, is supposed to be lost now." Like many of his apparently simple sentences, these sentences gesture ironically, yet somehow manage to register a dislike of their own irony. Conrad writes first that he is not himself "well acquainted" with, or on close speaking terms with, conversation — the joke is like something in Beckett — and this dangerous admission for a novelist might lead us to become biographical critics who peck the wound, reviewing family memoirs and portraits of him for hints about his social ineptness. But the reports are too various for a single picture of his social self, or of the personal meanings he gave to speech and silence. We know, for example, that his father at least once remained silent under interrogation,[17] and that family and friends alternately represent him as an excellent conversationalist and as taciturn.[18] George Gissing's first, romantic response to Conrad's work was to see the "soul of the world" in Conrad's expressive silences[19] — that is, to find in the silences not withdrawal but contact. A reader of the family memoirs can find, if he wants to, a disturbing, teasing distance toward Conrad that sometimes seems nasty. They seem to have treated him not as a foreigner but as an individual eccentric. But perhaps this was a way of Anglicizing him, warmly enough: in their inability to understand his manners they sometimes made him out the old bird, the Victorian papa, whose authority was worn as ornate eccentricity. It's probably not useful to judge or summarize.

Conrad's foreignness itself, however, may be important if we want to speculate about experiences that might have shaped his sense of dialogue. A sailor and then an exile is perhaps not likely to develop a dialogical art like Austen's, Balzac's, or Tolstoy's, tracing very local signals of trust or power. No one comes away from

Conrad's dialogue remembering it for witty repartee, or for lyrical shading like Turgenev's. But in his context one is more likely to become alert to something else: the larger, governing shapes which make dialogue happen or not happen at all. For all his embarrassment about minor mistakes in diction or idiom or syntax, the foreigner may actually be particularly alert to major catastrophes: he may be positioned wrongly in space, or aware of the courage required to start talk at all. While from the letters it is clear that Conrad had a gift for criticism in flattery, for getting by with people if not exactly along with them, his fictional dialogues are often about a more stark near impossibility; and his real gift is for creating a remarkable variety of dialogues that happen on the brink of not happening at all, and which someone, as an agent, has to initiate or desperately cause. His dialogues do not, as in a comfortable society, simply or playfully happen; they have to be made to happen by someone, and this "making" is the main source of their variety.

But all this might sound too much like an assertion that his work is about "lack of communication," a bad contemporary cliché which, as later parts of this study will try to show, is not to the point. The theme in his work is not "lack of communication" but the recognition that communication itself is by nature more coercive and disproportionate than we think when we sentimentalize terms like *dialogue* and *communication.* In fact, there is in Conrad's work probably more communication — relay of information across a political fabric — than in most English novels. But he sees it as being effected by aggression, or conquering force, and as a result often sinister — as in international relations, for example, if communication is coercive and disproportionate in its installment, an increase in communication becomes an increase in domination and violence. The telegraph lines being built across the mountains in *Nostromo* are installed by force. When the state communicates into the family in *The Secret Agent,* it is no savior. At the same time, silence, as a reaction to communication as force, is not romanticized as always heroic, smart, or even decent; it is often mere withdrawal, and is not to be glamorized as Silence. Conrad's sense of these issues is extremely thoughtful, skeptical, complicated, and I hope that one effect of these studies will be to increase the sense of the plurality of meanings both of silences and of coercions to speak in Conrad, rather than to try to affix static values to them. Notably, in thinking this scene through, he manages in some extraordinary moments to trace the conflict between coercion to speak and silence back to the scene of tragic inquiry in which Oedipus coerces witnesses only to be destroyed by the answers: that is, he seems to grasp at some "Oedipal" — in Sophocles' sense — dialogue archetype. This gives the final sense that the "Oedipus complex," translated into politics, becomes the risk of inquiry; that when we think of "dialogue" in general terms we must not sentimentally ignore force and danger; and that there is such a thing as an "Oedipus dialogue complex" in literature and in reality which has been overlooked.

Michael André Bernstein

The Poetics of *Ressentiment*

"Die Romane sind die sokratischen Dialoge unserer Zeit" (Novels are the Socratic dialogues of our times.)   —[Friedrich Schlegel, "Kritische Fragmente"]

Today, it often seems as though we are about to lose any perspective from which to initiate a serious questioning of Bakhtin's "dialogic imagination," so thoroughly have his values and rhetoric penetrated our own reflections. For his American admirers, dialogism is nothing less than the "characteristic epistemological mode" of our world, and they can use terms like "this dialogic imperative" without unease because, with the exception of those "deluded" into a different view, dialogism must be recognized as "mandated" by the essential truth of the human condition.[1] Skepticism about the curiously monological exhortations cataloguing the claims of the dialogic is bound to appear simultaneously foolhardy and ungenerous: foolhardy since it finds itself condemned to charges of epistemological/linguistic "delusion" and ungenerous since what it hesitates to applaud is so manifestly both individually uplifting and communally responsible. To contest the hopes embodied in so fecund a principle casts the doubter in a role curiously analogous to the one occupied in the middle years of the nineteenth century by a few paltry and disgruntled malcontents, mostly underground grumblers or blind reactionaries, who remained unenthralled at the prospect of the coming era of universal harmony, an era whose imminence was already symbolized and, as it were, guaranteed, by Sir Joseph Paxton's Crystal Palace in London's Great Exhibition of 1851. Listen, for example, to Wayne Booth testify about how his encounter with Bakhtin made him rethink the arguments of his own earlier critical works, and, more important, how certain he is that reading Bakhtin is an experience crucial for us all:

... what is at stake, in reading Bakhtin, is far more than the question of how we read, or even how we evaluate, fiction. ... it is rather part of a lifetime inquiry into profound questions about the entire enterprise of thinking about what human life means. How are we to know and to say anything to each other about what our lives mean, without reduction to destructive or irrelevant simplicities? When novelists imagine characters, they imagine worlds that characters inhabit, worlds that are laden with values. Whenever they reduce those multiple worlds to one, the author's, they give a false report, an essentially egotistical distortion that tells lies about the way things are. Bakhtin's ultimate value—full acknowledgment of and participation in a Great Dialogue—is thus not to be addressed as just one more piece of "literary criticism"; ... It is a philosophical inquiry into our limited ways of mirroring—and improving—our lives.[2]

I use the term "testify" deliberately, because, although Booth makes an occasional gesture at pointing out possible limitations in Bakhtin, much of his introduction reads more like a profession of faith or account of a conversion experience than a sustained critical argument. Like all such professions it asks to be accepted and seconded for reasons that leave little ground for doubts or qualifications. Against so insistently moralizing a critical rhetoric it is hard entirely to silence within oneself the uncharitable countermurmur of a voice Poe called "The Spirit of Perverseness," to insist, in other words, precisely on the value of what Booth terms the monological author's "essentially egotistical distortions." Of course yielding to such a voice is hardly prudent, but as Poe has already explained: "Yet I am not more sure that my soul lives, than I am that perverseness is one of the primitive impulses of the human heart—one of the indivisible primary faculties, or sentiments, which give direction to the character of Man. Who has not, a hundred times, found himself committing a vile or silly action, for no other reason than because he knows he should *not?* Have we not a perpetual inclination, in the teeth of our best judgment, to violate that which is *Law*, merely because we understand it to be such?"[3] Or, to switch to the still more potent example of a novel which I have already invoked and with which this essay will be much concerned, how can we fail, when faced with the seamless progression of Booth's paragraphs as they celebrate dialogism's promise of "mirroring—and improving—our lives," to find companionship in the characteristic gesture that Dostoevsky's Underground Man used to salute the Crystal Palace?

... what would be the good of a crystal palace if there could be any doubt about it? . . . You believe in a crystal edifice that can never be destroyed; that is, an edifice at which one would neither be able to stick out one's tongue nor thumb one's nose on the sly. . . . [But] I have just rejected the crystal edifice for the sole reason that one cannot put out one's tongue at it.[4]

Admittedly, the Underground Man's reactions are quite futile (not to mention both foolhardy and ungenerous), and to acknowledge him here as an avatar of one's own temptations is hardly an edifying realization. Nonetheless, it is worth stressing that as a moral value, an epistemological axiom, or even as "just one more piece of 'literary criticism,' " dialogism must be tested, not merely lauded. It must, by its very definition, be brought into our contentions as a participant without any guarantee or privilege, rather than as a kind of ultimate Court of Assizes under whose jurisdiction the debate proceeds and according to whose criteria the worthiness of the enterprise will be determined. And by this I intend more than to stress that the very open-endedness of Bakhtin's notion of dialogue ought to have prevented, as a blatant contradiction in terms, the kinds of hypostatization of the dialogic principle so prevalent in current criticism. More important, I want to suggest that dialogism itself is not always just clement or life enhancing, and that the resonance of multiple voices may be a catastrophic threat as much as a sustaining chorale.

Some of Bakhtin's more searching critics have begun to notice the curious lacunae in his accounts of dialogism, and studies like Aaron Fogel's *Coercion to Speak: Conrad's Poetics of Dialogue* have done much to remind us of the pressures and constraints within which most human exchanges take place.[5] Instead of the generous mutual attentiveness that a dialogue is supposed to foster, what we find just as often are speakers stalking one another with the edgy wariness of fighters ready to erupt into lethal violence the moment one of them senses an opening. Substitute the word "interlocutor" for "boxer" in Joyce Carol Oates's brilliant account, and an image emerges of a dialogue very different from the usual Bakhtinian description:

> The boxer meets an opponent who is a dream-distortion of himself in the sense that his weaknesses, his capacity to fail and to be seriously hurt, his intellectual miscalculations — all can be interpreted as strengths belonging to the Other; the parameters of his private being are nothing less than boundless assertions of the Other's self. This is dream, or nightmare: my strengths are not fully my own, but my opponent's triumph. He is my shadow-self, not my (mere) shadow.[6]

Such images are especially powerful because they force us to confront how abstract and idealized Bakhtin's notion of a full dialogue really is, and how unlikely its chances are of ever being realized anywhere except — and even then rarely — in the specialized discourse of the work of art.[7] But of course dialogism's champions could still argue that the very coercion so nakedly evident in the public world only underlines the importance of the principle as a long-term goal, as, in fact, *the* central, grounding hope for any more tolerant and responsive *communitas*. Seen in this light, objections like Fogel's might be sufficient to restrain some of the more exuberant affirmations of Bakhtinian dialogism, but they do not touch the future-directed longing we feel for a time when genuine, unconstrained dialogues will constitute the norm of our relationships.[8]

But there is also a quite different contention to be registered, one that does not depend exclusively upon actual political and social practices, but which, instead, questions the whole impulse toward dialogism as a universal desideratum. The emotional logic of such a contention is starkly articulated in the following lines by Jorie Graham, lines it might be useful to weigh against the earlier quotation from Wayne Booth:

> . . . Without,
> we are able to listen to someone else's story, believe in
> another protagonist, but within,
> his presence would kill us.[9]

Or consider how fundamental a rejection of any universal dialogism is voiced in Emily Dickinson's poem:

The Soul selects her own Society —
Then — shuts the Door —
· · · · ·

I've known her — from an ample nation —
Choose One —
Then — close the Valves of her attention —
Like Stone — [10]

It is obviously not accidental that both Graham and Dickinson are
lyric poets, that is, artists in a genre notoriously inhospitable to
dialogue in Bakhtin's sense, but I think it may be equally pertinent
to emphasize that they, and Oates, are all women as well, and that
there may be something distinctly more gendered than is usually
granted in Bakhtin's dialogical principle. How can we be so certain,
Jorie Graham leads us to ask, of our capacity to endure so many
other stories if their very existence as internalized voices threatens
to rupture the fragile integument of our own identity and desires,
if our hold on the world is already too fugitive for it to be stretched
any further? Or what if, in a still darker vision, the dialogues do
not open onto a universe of stimulating, vibrant exchanges, but
rather deliver us to a vast madhouse whose loudest curse is our own
at being thus abandoned? Caliban's delight in the dialogic potency
of his new-found tongue ("You taught me language; and my profit
on't/ Is, I know how to curse . . .")[11] is, after all, considerably
more attenuated than that of his masters.

Finally, there is yet another direction from which to pursue our
questioning, a line that we might initiate by noting, if for the moment only in passing, that what Bakhtin understands by the "dialogical imagination" is uncomfortably similar to Nietzsche's account
of the slave's reactive, dependent, and fettered consciousness. Every
word the Nietzschean slave utters, every value he posits, is purely
reactive, impregnated by the words and values of others and formulated entirely in response to and as an anticipation of the responses he will elicit. Responsiveness, usually regarded as an entirely
laudable quality, is unmasked in *The Genealogy of Morals* as itself
inherently double: noble when it stems from an acknowledgment
of the Other grounded in a prior self-confidence about the validity
of one's own impulses and values, and base when it originates in
and remains completely saturated by doubts about the ways in
which one will be evaluated and judged:

While every noble morality develops from a triumphant affirmation of itself, slave morality from the outset says No to what is "outside," what is "different," what is "not itself"; and *this* No is its creative deed. This inversion of the value-positing eye—this *need* to direct one's view outward instead of back to oneself—is of the essence of *ressentiment:* in order to exist, slave morality always first needs a hostile external world; it needs, physiologically speaking, external stimuli in order to act at all—its action is fundamentally reaction.[12]

Now to be attacked by Nietzsche is hardly sufficient grounds for abandoning a principle that seems to promise so rich a harvest, and I am far from denying that we have much to learn from Bakhtin's dialogism, especially, perhaps, from its challenge to formalists of all persuasions, whether literary, political, or linguistic.[13] But the diversity in number and kind of the criticisms to which the dialogic principle is vulnerable—criticisms I have merely summarized thus far and thereby no doubt greatly simplified—ought to raise some discomfort among those with whom these pages are engaged in conversation. I doubt, however, that the minority voices out of whose murmurs I have spun this conversation will ever be incorporated into an unrigged dialogue about dialogism. Rather, I foresee two monologisms continuing to enact a small comedy of Wildean relationships: cutting one another dead while fascinated by the same questions and citing the same texts with unembarrassed earnestness.

Revealingly enough, though, the one link joining Nietzsche, the Underground Man, and Jorie Graham in their rejection of the dialogic principle is their obsession—although from radically different vantage points—with the continuing problem of pain, with the immediate, intractable, and existence-embittering suffering from which Bakhtin's theories (although certainly not his life) are so remarkably free. Perhaps, then, it makes the most sense to begin our own inquiry with the same issue, with the dilemma of pain and with the voices that speak to, of, and from within the solitary prison-house of their suffering.

*   *   *

"Ah! oui, c'est beau, l'éducation!" (Oh yes indeed, isn't education a wonderful thing!)
— Gustave Flaubert, *Bouvard et Pécuchet*

"Hysterics," so Freud thought at the outset of his career, "suffer mainly from reminiscences."[14] And in spite of the famous — and today bitterly contested — reversal signaled by the letter to Fliess of September 21, 1897, the change in the status of the painful reminiscences from scars left by objective events to the repression of inner impulses and phantasies did not fundamentally undermine the importance of memory as a privileged arena of psychoanalytic work. Although Freud confided in Fliess that "I no longer believe in my *neurotica*," and offered, as one of his grounds for such disbelief, "the certain insight that there are no indications of reality in the unconscious, so that one cannot distinguish between truth and fiction that has been cathected with affect,"[15] it nonetheless remained largely through its probing of the patient's reminiscences that psychoanalysis proceeded to demarcate both its theoretical axioms and clinical methodology. The abandonment of the "seduction theory" of neurosis undoubtedly announced a fundamental redirection of the therapeutic gaze from the search for a historical occurrence to the questioning of desire's own supreme fictions. Yet the power of those scenarios — whether memories of actual narratives or narratives of imagined memories — to proliferate their poisonous aftereffects throughout the life of their author remained equally compelling in either perspective. In a sense what Freud so eagerly rushed to announce to Fliess was the realization that to grasp the link between reminiscence and suffering demanded more than what the nineteenth-century historian prized as the technique for uncovering "wie es eigentlich gewesen war" (the way it really was [Leopold von Ranke]), that it required, instead, the kind of principled suspicion Nietzsche had called genealogy.

Genealogy, in Nietzsche's appropriation of the term, refuses to lend credence to the identity of any immutable, originary event, a sole cause that remains itself unmoved by the vicissitudes it unleashes; rather, it seeks "a continuous sign-chain of ever new interpretations and adaptations whose causes do not even have to be related to one another," an understanding of historical unfolding as "a succession of more or less profound, more or less mutually independent processes of subduing, plus the resistances they encounter, the attempts at transformation for the purpose of defense and reaction, and the results of successful counteractions."[16] What psychoanalysis would later call overdetermination, in other words, is itself overdetermined, and one of its chains of reinterpretations and rearrangements clearly leads back to the concepts first articulated in *The Genealogy of Morals*. Or, to phrase the issue in a still more deliberately polemical fashion: the Freud of 1892 to 1897 was, at best, pre-Nietzschean in his quest for a distinct inaugural trauma behind each memory, and only after the illumination of 1897 did psychoanalytic thinking begin to rival the radical comprehension of the link between reminiscences and suffering articulated in texts like *The Genealogy of Morals, Human, All Too Human,* and *Thus Spoke Zarathustra.*

Undoubtedly the parallels between crucial strands in Nietzsche's and Freud's thinking is of compelling interest to current debates in both philosophy and psychoanalytic history, but although my present concerns will necessarily engage some of these themes, they will do so only indirectly. Instead, I propose to examine the ways in which reminiscence-as-suffering operates as a kind of master trope in an entire series of nineteenth-century fictions, discernible like the ground bass upon which a surprisingly intricate and diverse set of variations were performed by narratives whose consanguinity criticism has chosen largely to ignore. My aim, then, is not merely to locate a rival tradition to those works exemplifying Bakhtin's dialogic imagination, but rather to show how the very dialogism he celebrates already contains a darker and more desperate strand than his account usually acknowledges. More generally, I hope to isolate, as accurately as possible, a number of interrelated problems whose pertinence is only the more compelling, in spite of, or perhaps even because of, the fact that they have yet to be thematized with sufficient rigor.

Still, the hysteric does continue to suffer mainly from reminiscences, and this remains true no matter how differently reminiscence itself is remembered in our genealogies. Reminiscence-as-suffering is the most succinct definition I can imagine for one of the central terms of Nietzsche's thinking, *ressentiment,* and it is upon this concept that the rest of this essay will seek its own unstable ground.

*   *   *

"Everyone, as it were, wishes to revenge himself upon someone for his [own] nullity." —Fyodor Dostoevsky, *Diary of a Writer*

"The defeat of one man is the triumph of the other: but we are apt to read this 'triumph' as merely temporary and provisional. Only the defeat is permanent." —Joyce Carol Oates, *On Boxing*

Nietzsche himself defines *ressentiment* as the chief characteristic of "natures that are denied the true reaction, that of deeds, and compensate themselves with an imaginary revenge."[17] It is marked by an inability to forget, to rise above, or to avenge an injury. Each slight, each abject compromise or moment of cowardice is lived through again and again, and since the sense of injured vanity can never be assuaged, existence itself is experienced as an endless recurrence of humiliations, fresh only in their infinite variety but dreadfully familiar in their affect and structure. A maddening sense of impotence is united to a daemonically obsessive total recall, until the sufferer's entire consciousness is like an open sore whose sight evokes only disgust in both the victim himself and those around him.[18] In fiction, no author has chronicled the inscape of *ressentiment* with more skill than Dostoevsky, whose *Notes from Underground* Nietzsche so praised.[19] Let us, for the moment, just listen to an early passage in which the Underground Man offers, in the process of his ironic self-description, what is virtually an itemization of *ressentiment's* major preoccupations:

There, in its nasty, stinking underground home, our insulted, crushed and ridiculed mouse promptly becomes absorbed in cold, malignant and, above all, everlasting spite. For forty years together it will remember its injury down to the smallest, most shameful detail and every time will add, of itself, details still more shameful, spitefully teasing and irritating itself with its own imagination. It will be ashamed of its own fancies, but yet it will recall everything, it will go over it again and again, it will invent lies against itself pretending that those things too might have happened, and will forgive nothing. Maybe it will begin to revenge itself, too, but, as it were, piecemeal, in trivial ways, from behind the stove, incognito, without believing either in its own right to vengeance, or in the success of its revenge, knowing beforehand that from all its efforts at revenge it will suffer a hundred times more than he on whom it revenges itself, while he, probably, will not even feel it. On its deathbed it will recall it all over again, with interest accumulated over all the years. (10–11)

The crushing sense of one's own insignificance, evoked here in the image of a mouse, was prefigured earlier in the assertion that

"I could not even [manage to] become an insect" (6) — a quest, by the way, that Kafka's Gregor Samsa unwittingly carried to a successful conclusion — but what is crucial about this passage is the thoroughness with which *ressentiment's* grievances are itemized. The spite is cold because it is denied any sudden and passionate purgation through action, it is venomous because it poisons both the sufferer and whatever he encounters, and it is everlasting because without forgetfulness, no release can be conceived. More important, though, is the admission that not only does the memory of an injury continue its torment forever, but that the passage of time only adds fresh details and new provocations to the reminiscences. *Ressentiment* does not merely recollect slights, it *creates* them from its own imaginings, establishing a psychological economy of abjection in which time breeds a quarterly dividend of new shame to swell the capital already deposited in the sufferer's emotional account. But, of course, the whole question of an original outrage is deliberately undermined, since the Underground Man freely confesses the fictional status of his sufferings, admits, that is, his own authorship of the very humiliations and reminiscences that victimize him. What "might have happened," the degrading images of his "own imagination," and the taunts actually encountered in society are all spun into a single narrative whose self-reflexivity heightens, rather than mitigates, the intensity of the hysteria. In Nietzsche's lapidary account, the cry of *ressentiment:* " 'Ich leide: daran muß irgend jemand schuld sein' " [I suffer: it must be somebody's fault][20] already reveals both the arbitrariness of any external agent in creating the sufferer's misery and the simultaneous necessity of blaming someone and everyone for his lacerations. Or, in the Underground Man's parallel formulation: "though you can't come up with an enemy, you do have pain."[21] *Ressentiment* is like an author in search of characters to populate the seedy dramas of its own spite, and like an author it creates scenarios to justify what is only — but also never less than — the narratives it will then remember and ceaselessly amplify. Like a Freudian case history, the narrative of memory and the memory of narrative are indistinguishable in their effects, and it makes no difference that *ressentiment* is as ready to blame itself as another, since the self is already experienced as radically multiple, constantly divided from itself in the exteriority of time experienced as pure repetition.

But if I have thus far tended to emphasize the instances of similarity among various attempts to theorize about the nature of reminiscences-as-suffering, it is only to highlight what I take to be the central difference for literary invention: the subject matter and motivation of the memories themselves. Freud liked to say that his discovery of the unconscious had delivered the third great injury to human narcissism, decentering the claims of a sovereign *cogito* much as Copernicus and Darwin had compelled a fundamental reevaluation of mankind's animal origin and place in the physical universe. But perhaps Freud himself was too cheerfully self-congratulatory in his description, since his patients at least suffered their own impulses, enjoyed, that is, the admittedly thin consolation of taking their traumas as unique burdens, irreducible marks, if nothing else, of their existence as distinct beings. How readily even misery can be converted into a sign of individual distinction is amply demonstrated by the Underground Man, who in some of his moods makes precisely such a claim, locating in his very unhappiness the evidence of a singular identity. But the Underground Man, unlike the Freudian analysand, also knows well how dubious such a claim really is and how vulnerable even one's anguish can prove to the charge of mere plagiarism.

Indeed, it seems to me that it is exactly his sense of being only an ambulatory incarnation of literary clichés that governs all of the Underground Man's other, more luridly visible grievances, and that a crisis of citation constitutes the central injury of all his reminiscences. The Underground Man is only the most extreme example of a problem that, beginning with Diderot's *Le Neveu de Rameau,* starts to dominate, with increasing ferocity, both the consciousness of major nineteenth-century fictional creations and the narrative structures of the texts in which they appear. One could summarize this predicament by emphasizing that we may not always find the Underground Man's speeches easy to read, but it is usually very easy to know just what he has been reading. There is a careful and increasingly detailed body of scholarship that has traced the literary echoes in works like *Notes from Underground,* but this research has been aimed primarily at documenting the novel's polemical relationship to its contemporary context, to showing Dostoevsky's fiercely partisan role in a moral-ideological debate in which works like Chernyshevsky's *What Is to Be Done?* and Henry Thomas

Buckle's *The History of Civilization in England,* or the sentimental romanticism of the Schillerian 1840s, represent the main antagonists. But invaluable as such scholarship clearly remains, it is curious how its concentration upon *Dostoevsky's* savage wit in exposing the intellectual clichés and moral bankruptcy of socialist reformism or sentimental idealism has come at the price of slighting the problematic nature of the Underground Man's own relationship to these positions. It is undoubtedly true, to return to the problem with which we began this discussion, that *Notes from Underground* is among the most profoundly dialogical works ever imagined, that its every utterance is, from the outset, already engaged in a torrent of other statements, its every word "is not only a word with a sideward glance; it is also . . . a word with a loophole,"[22] but it seems prudent to remind ourselves that this dialogism is not only a positive aspect of Dostoevsky's narrative practice but the very root of the Underground Man's whole dilemma.

The dialogic status of their words, ideas, and sentiments is experienced as pure entrapment, triggering only rage and *ressentiment* in the characters who must endure that endless chatter of already uttered utterances. In crisis after crisis, the Underground Man cries out for "a real regular quarrel — a more decent, a more *literary* one, so to speak" (43), and in the bitter narrations of his phantasies, what confirms the paltriness of his abjection, branding his most "personal" longings with the unmistakable sign of triviality, is the knowledge that even these wish fulfillment daydreams are only commonplace quotations from Rousseau, Byron, Pushkin, Lermontov, etc. etc.: "I was actually on the point of tears, though I knew perfectly well at that very moment that all this was out of Pushkin's *Silvio* and Lermontov's *Masquerade*" (74).

It is a truism of literary history that the nineteenth-century novel substitutes "the hero's evolution through time" for the earlier structuring of narratives as physical journeys.[23] In works as otherwise diverse as *Pilgrim's Progress* or *Jacques le Fataliste,* "change is envisaged spatially, as the picaresque character moves across the face of a varied but otherwise unchanging earth,"[24] as opposed to the temporal progression and diachronic development of nineteenth-century novelistic characters. What has been less often remarked, however, are the ways in which temporality and succession themselves become increasingly marked by anxiety and desperation, the ways, in other words, that time becomes not so much a novelistic resource as a crisis of originality in which all of the various stages can only repeat configurations and echo speeches already scripted by earlier narratives.

Imagine, as a momentary illustration, the following, perhaps familiar, situation: two men meet in a bar or train station and one begins to tell the other of his woes, introducing numerous details of his well-deserved failures in life, his despair, and so forth, always including, of course, instances of wild self-praise and congratulations. But the listener keeps interrupting, "You know, I've already read that in Diderot and Dostoevsky. Aren't you only imitating Jean-François Rameau and the Underground Man? Can't you find a more original problem or at least a new story?" And if, indeed, the first speaker is not only familiar with these authors but quite aware that no matter how he tries, his narrative can never emerge except as a variation on their literary paradigms, then, presumably, the last possible claim for his own dignity will have been proved derisive.

Faced with so helpless a predicament, the abject hero's most promising option is to attempt to pass himself off as a monster. The very reading that has helped blight his self-esteem has shown him the curious prestige habitually attached to the monster. If he were to succeed in embodying, both for himself and his interlocutor, the role of civilization's daemonic double, the madman who rages forth when all the compromises and repressions of socialization have been shattered, then the abject hero might indeed effect a sudden reversal in his wretched position. And so Rameau's Nephew, the Underground Man, or his most extreme modern descendant, the Célinian narrator, each keep trying to sound ever more monstrous. But for them, even that tone—one which ought to issue forth as an untamed natural force—is itself as mediated as all of their other attitudes and poses. To mimic the monstrous is still to be only a mimic, and to model one's speech after the mad is still to be dependent upon prior examples. But paradoxically, to desire such a voice for oneself *is* genuinely monstrous, and to attempt to convince others of its truth is, in its very fraudulence, a distinctly mad enterprise. So the abject hero is again doomed to a doubled existence: parodying a role that is, in reality, already his own and imitating a state that he already inhabits.

The logic of such a position is perhaps most fully articulated by Dostoevsky's most wretchedly abject and self-ironizing figure of evil: Ivan's Devil in *The Brothers Karamazov*. The satanic as an impoverished relative, not clothed in fire and brimstone but like a poor country cousin coming to sponge a loan, is so disturbing because he freely admits that he only exists by virtue of and in order to engage in just such conversations, in order, that is, to be given a palpable reality by the dialogic principle: "Here when I stay with you from time to time my life gains a kind of reality and that's what I like most of all."[25] Actually, what Satan wants most is to be able to fascinate his conversational partner with "such artistic visions, such complex and real actuality, such events, even a whole world of event, woven into such a plot, with such unexpected details from the most exalted matters to the last button on a cuff, as I swear Leo Tolstoy could not create."[26] But alas, the tone of helpless longing makes it clear that Dostoevsky's devil is no match for Tolstoy. Being unable to create aesthetically convincing narratives of his own, Satan will need to cite those of his betters, but it is not only, nor even primarily, Scripture that he quotes to his own ends, and certainly not the novels of Leo Tolstoy, but rather the words of such congenial fictional frauds as Ivan Aleksandrovich Khlestakov, Gogol's fake Inspector General.[27] This is an incarnation of evil who, in Gary Saul Morson's phrase, "is content to be, if not a real, then at least an imitation imposter."[28] Ivan then promptly accuses the Great Accuser of plagiarizing from his own adolescent anecdotes, but in a universe in which everything is pure citation such a charge is essentially tautological and carries little sting. In *The Brothers Karamazov*, the monstrous exists as pure mimic and as pure monstrosity at the same time, and in that simultaneity Dostoevsky has crystallized the most disturbingly modern metaphysics of evil that I know.

But it is necessary already to be haunted by religious questions for Ivan's devil to be able to initiate a dialogue. In *The Brothers Karamazov*, that is, these crucial exchanges remain framed entirely within a Christian metaphysics and derive much of their power from showing how the core of that metaphysics (the soul-destroying nature of evil) exists independently of its conventional narrative and iconographic props (the fire-and-brimstone, horns-and-tail imagery). For this investigation, however, it is probably more perti-

nent to remain on the secular side of Ivan's eternal questions, and
to consider the bitterness with which even the most worldly characters respond to a feeling of imprisonment in dialogues they know
consist only of citations from earlier dialogues. Once the dilemma
is formulated in this way, the kinship between works like *Le Neveu
de Rameau, Notes from Underground,* and, in this century, Céline's
World War II trilogy, *D'Un Château l'autre, Nord,* and *Rigodon,*
becomes easier to comprehend. In each of these texts dialogism is
not just a literary technique by whose means the narrative unfolds,
but rather the fundamental problem with which the characters
themselves consciously wrestle. The abject hero, whether Jean-
François Rameau, the Underground Man, or the Célinian narrator,
exists only in relationship to others, and the strategies of their in-
terlocutors are as crucial in determining their options as any inner
impulses.

Of course, the same dialogic principle and concomitant risk of
entrapment apply just as much to us as readers of such works as
they do to the fictional characters whose family resemblance I have
been tracing. For example, in the anecdote I recounted earlier, the
unwilling listener might as easily be telling himself, "Well, yes,
everything I'm hearing is just a garbled compendium of literary
citations. But how can I be sure he isn't suddenly going to reveal
something true that I've always been afraid to acknowledge? If I
dismiss him without a thought, aren't I exposing myself as just one
more smug coward? Even if he is just parroting Rameau and the
Underground Man, how does my repugnance distinguish me from
the *philosophe's* complacency or the obtuseness of Dostoevsky's
rationalist 'gentlemen'-readers?" And so the dialogue continues,
between the speakers and within each one as well, the voices doubled and then doubled again until it is closing time in the bar, or
the train finally arrives, taking each man in a different direction,
one home to his burrow in the Underground, the other to his
duplex in the company (or faculty) compound.

If only my two speakers had read their Bakhtin as carefully as
their Diderot or Dostoevsky, however, perhaps none of their problems need have occurred. As Caryl Emerson explains, "On the
issue of repetition, Bakhtin is his own best counsel. His entire
understanding of the word, and of the specificity of the utterance,
invalidates the very concept of repetition. Nothing 'recurs'; the

same word over again might accumulate, reinforce, perhaps parody what came before it, but it cannot be the same word if it is in a different place. Repetitiveness is not repetitiousness."[29] Strictly speaking, of course, there is considerable justice in such reasoning, but I suspect that ultimately it provides less comfort than it promises. The context may indeed change the emotional-intellectual valence of a given word, but as Emerson herself recognizes, it is as likely to turn it into parody as anything else. In fact, I would argue that the passage of time and the ensuing dissimilarity in context come close to ensuring that the second utterance will be experienced as either a banal echo of its earlier affirmation or, still worse, as a parodic falling-off of the energy once released by a forceful word. Certainly this is how the Underground Man feels about deriving his very desires from, and then only being able to articulate them through, images and situations borrowed from works like "Pushkin's *Silvo* and Lermontov's *Masquerade.*"

A similar fear of futility and degradation through repetition haunts the famous opening of Marx's *The Eighteenth Brumaire of Louis Bonaparte:* "Hegel remarks somewhere that all facts and personages of great importance in world history occur, as it were, twice. He forgot to add: the first time as tragedy, the second as farce."[30] To understand that our inevitable "repetitiveness is not repetitiousness," then, is actually a reason for dismay, not, as in Bakhtin, for comfort, since only the never-to-be-attained exact duplication (e.g., Nietzsche's realm of eternal recurrence) could guarantee the preservation of all the initial force crystallized in the utterance whereas the repetitiveness to which we are condemned merely assures that a kind of entropy principle insinuates itself into the operations of our consciousness.

It is not just the Bloomian strong poet who must endure "the anxiety of influence": even the characters of modern fiction are compelled to realize their *post festum* existence. Their development is permanently scarred by the rage against their belatedness. For them, self-consciousness is largely a question of recognizing the massive citations out of which their self is assembled. The Underground Man is not only "fictitious," in the words of Dostoevsky's curious footnote at the novel's outset, because he appears in a fictional text. Rather, he is fictitious because he himself is entirely composed of fictions, a being whose ideas, desires, and aspirations are only citations "gotten out of books" (40). But, so too, as he keeps insisting, are those of all the Underground Man's antagonists/interlocutors, including the editor, the gentlemen readers he ceaselessly addresses and whose attention he so fears losing, or his historical-ideological opponents like Buckle and Chernyshevsky, whose theories are only plausible to someone with a conception of human nature formed entirely by the naive abstractions of philosophical tracts. (And here it is interesting to note that it is precisely in *The Genealogy of Morals,* his principal treatise on *ressentiment,* that Nietzsche also rages against Buckle's intellectual vulgarity.) Both the Underground Man's own phantasies and those of his opponents are entirely derivative, and the only area of choice that remains seems to be what kinds of narratives to quote and imitate: "Leave us alone without books and we will be lost and in confusion at once — we will not know what to join, what to cling to, what to love and what to hate, what to respect and what to despise" (115).

It is against fiction itself, against the fictional status of his own consciousness, that the Underground Man's *ressentiment* explodes, and I want to suggest that it is the peculiar logic joining fiction, dialogism, and temporality as mutually linked sources of *ressentiment* that determines the narrative structure of exemplary texts like *Notes from Underground* and constitutes one of the central imaginative crises of nineteenth-century thought. Freudian neuroses may be specific and personal, but *ressentiment* is, by definition, a herd phenomenon: the state of mind, temperament, and imagination of a being who suffers most from the realization that even his worst grievances lack any trace of particularity. And here, the genealogical technique of examining a concept's etymology is especially fruitful, since if Nietzsche took over and extended the word *ressentiment* from the French moralists he so admired, a little time with the dictionary soon reveals how at one time the word carried no pejorative connotation. Philologically, the *re* in *ressentiment* once functioned purely as an intensifier rather than as a mark of repetition, and Littré offers several citations in which the word means no more than "sentiment de reconnaissance" (a feeling of gratitude).[31] It is only through a long temporal process, in other words, that *ressentiment* becomes linked to time itself as the "feeling-again" of something vile, something whose vileness, in fact, is a function of its repetitive nature. It is this meaning to which Nietzsche gave a new depth and resonance, and what is crucial for our purposes here is to grasp how intimately Nietzsche linked *ressentiment* to the experience of temporality.

Of all the emotions issuing out of the frustration of *ressentiment*, none, as we have seen, is more striking than the desire for revenge. Revenge and *ressentiment* are twin movements of the same malign emotional orchestration, and their deepest rage is aimed at time itself: " 'Es war': also heißt des Willens Zähneknirschen und einsamste Trübsal. Ohnmächtig gegen das, was getan ist—ist er allem Vergangenen ein böser Zuschauer . . . Dies, ja dies allein ist *Rache* selber: des Willens Widerwille gegen die Zeit und ihr 'Es war' " (" 'It was': that is what the will's teeth-gnashing and most lonely affliction is called. Powerless against that which has been done, the will is an angry spectator of all things past . . . This, yes, this alone is *revenge* itself: the will's antipathy towards time and time's 'It was' ").[32] This is how, in *Also Sprach Zarathustra*, Nietzsche defined the fundamental nature of revenge as a constant and nagging rage at the human experience of temporality. All the slights and humiliations which formed the scenarios of *ressentiment* now turn out to be only manifestations of a still deeper sense of injury, a layer of impotent fury that finds the very fact of being delivered over to succession and history intolerable.

If we now return to Dostoevsky's introductory footnote, we read that the Underground Man is "one of the characters of the recent past" (3). Undoubtedly, one sense of this phrase is the character's location as a man of the 1840s, a self-indulgent and nasty worshiper at the shrine of "all that is beautiful and sublime," unhappily surviving into the politically volatile atmosphere of the 1860s. But in a more radical interpretation, I think it is just to say that the Underground Man was always a personality of the past, that as a creature of *ressentiment*, haunted by memory and fashioned by citations, he can have no present except for his impotent misery at the process of time itself. To return for a moment to *The Eighteenth Brumaire of Louis Bonaparte*, when Marx writes, in what is surely one of the most Romantically Gothic and thus antimaterialist images of his entire *oeuvre*, that "the tradition of all the dead generations weighs like a nightmare on the brain of the living,"[33] he crystallizes a sense of time-as-oppression that can be heard again and again throughout the century, even, and perhaps especially, in thinkers like Dostoevsky and Nietzsche, who would seem furthest removed from his views.

What makes the Underground Man's misery so acute, is, as he himself confesses with something akin to a perverse pride, his self-consciousness, his awareness of precisely how degraded his condition really is. But the reason this self-consciousness only intensifies his pain — or, more accurately, actually creates it — is that it is *not* an awareness of unconscious (in the Freudian sense) impulses, but rather a too vivid recollection of the texts whose belated and trivial successor he is. Unlike, for example, the haunted figure in "The Dream of Reason Brings Forth Monsters," the most famous of Goya's "Los Caprichos" of 1799, by Dostoevsky's time it was the waking dream of the too-close reader that summoned forth life's monstrous aspects.[34] *Notes from Underground* is a pastiche of countless prior texts, in part because that is all the Underground Man himself really consists of, except for his additional burden of finding this existence-as-pastiche intolerable. The hysteric of *ressentiment* also suffers reminiscences, but his particular tragedy, a specifically modern and abject one, is that these reminiscences are always recognized as borrowed from others. And if his suffering is one of reminiscence/quotation, so too is the only vengeance open to him. Just because he is such a storehouse of literary clichés, he has the ability on occasion to wield those same tropes against someone with even less self-awareness, against, that is to say, a creature whose mind is equally formed by literary commonplaces but who is not as aware of her own dependence upon such narrative models. Here, off course, I am thinking of the Underground Man's relationship to the prostitute Liza, an episode that seems to me among the most carelessly interpreted of any in the novel.

It is impossible not to notice how the stories the Underground Man tells Liza are a cento of literary commonplaces about the unhappy fate awaiting the "fallen woman," and at first his narrative aggression is so obvious that Liza herself is moved to mock him for speaking "exactly like a book' " (86). But gradually he begins to find the right models and succeeds in moving both of them to tears, "the lump in my throat" (91) showing at once how vulnerable he is to his own sentimentality and the typical salesman's need to become his own first customer before being able to persuade anyone else to consider buying his obviously shabby goods. But Liza's reactions, down to tearfully showing him a letter written "to her from a medical student or someone of that sort — a very high-flown and flowery, but extremely respectful, declaration of love" (93) — are themselves straight out of typical nineteenth-century romances, and the Underground Man's emotional triumph over her in the brothel has less to do with her purity of soul than with a need to see her situation in precisely the terms laid down by such tales. All of this is clearly signaled by Dostoevsky himself in his ironic citation of Nekrasov's appalling verses at the outset of part 2 — verses, incidentally, that are themselves only a pastiche of other poets like Victor Hugo.[35]

The redeemed prostitute motif is the one trope common to both the types of fiction satirized in *Notes from Underground*, the sentimental novels of the 1840s and the socialist fiction of the 1860s, and in the Underground Man's relationship with Liza, Dostoevsky unerringly seized upon the one literary cliché that could expose the common ground of moral-emotional bankruptcy in two otherwise distinct types of narrative. But the curious thing, surely, is how Dostoevsky — and I am afraid the vast majority of his readers as well — seem to be quite willing to embrace just this very cliché in their desperation to find some kind of positive beacon in the shabby and sleet-filled grimness of the novel's atmosphere. In *Resurrection*, Tolstoy offers a direct critique of precisely this cliché. There, the prostitute Maslova initially spurns Prince Nekhliudov's marriage proposal because she realizes, in a way that both Dostoevsky's readers and his romanticized "fallen women" all too rarely do, that "you want to save yourself through me . . . You had your pleasure from me and now you want to get your salvation through me."[36] Indeed, the whole *topos* of the redeemed and redeeming prostitute was soon to be recognized as no longer suitable for anything but ironic treatment, and in tales like Chekhov's "An Attack of Nerves," there is a wonderfully comic itemization of the standard programs which sensitive young men draw upon to rescue a "fallen woman":

All these not very numerous attempts . . . can be divided into three groups. Some, after buying the woman out of the brothel, took a room for her, bought her a sewing-machine, and she became a seamstress. And whether he wanted to or not, after having bought her out he made her his mistress; . . . Others, after buying her out, took a lodging apart for her, bought the inevitable sewing-machine, and tried teaching her to read, preaching at her and giving her books. . . . Finally, those who were the most ardent and self-sacrificing took a bold, resolute step: they married the woman.[37]

When Liza visits the Underground Man in his tawdry flat and reacts to his tears and abject hysteria by rushing to him with a gesture of acceptance and love, I have no doubt that Dostoevsky, the Christian apologist, intended this moment to seem like an instance of genuine self-sacrifice and inspired comprehension, the revelation of a depth of heart unavailable to either the Westernizing rationalists or the tormented dwellers of the underground. And so too it has been regularly accepted, even by commentators otherwise as canny in their judgments as Joseph Frank, Tzvetan Todorov, and Michael Holquist.[38] But isn't Liza's gesture itself really just another quotation, an essentially bookish cliché, even if a "noble" one, repeated by a regatta of similar women in Balzac, Georges Sand, Victor Hugo, and, yes, Nekrasov's poetry itself? Isn't, in other words, her gesture as entirely prescribed as the Underground Man's own, and the whole episode less the one chance for redemption which he fails to seize than another proof of the terrible power of the Library to create even our most passionately inspired moments?

I am well aware that my reading of this episode, even in the schematic form the constraints of space have necessitated here, will evoke disbelief or outrage from many Dostoevsky scholars. But in fact, I am saying only that *Notes from Underground,* as a novel, is cleverer than the Dostoevsky of the letters, diaries, and polemical journalism; that as a novelist he was able to challenge the very ideas he valued most and that this ability is what most obviously characterizes his particular authority as a writer. Phrased in this manner, my observation is not only uncontroversial, but itself a deliberate echo of a favorite commonplace of Dostoevsky criticism, and thus scarecely likely to provoke dispute. What fascinates me, however, is how rapidly the difficulties accumulate when one tries to move from such a generalized critical banality to a specific instance, how committed we are to siding with Dostoevsky against his fiction as soon as the pressures of the split become too acute. Not only is Liza's very compassion, like her medical student's letter, a citation from her predecessors in the trade, but the ensuing episode reveals just how limited an emotional repertoire such citations offer.

The Underground Man, we remember, reacts to her outpouring of sympathy with what he—and most readers—agree in considering his vilest "atrocity." He turns her "rapturous embrace" (110) into a sexual provocation, then tries to dismiss her as quickly as possible with the added insult of thrusting a five-ruble note into her unwilling hand. But why are we so ready to see this "atrocity" as his *final* entrapment in the hell of the underground? After all, in what way is his behavior here worse than the vituperations with which he greeted Liza upon her arrival at his flat, or his earlier quest in the brothel for the right narrative to provoke her tears, his search for the most efficacious "cute little pictures, that's what will get you, these cute little pictures"?[39] Or conversely, why is this last gesture less a cry of pain than any of the earlier ones? Why, if Liza's intuitive wisdom and depth of soul enabled her to see through and forgive his suffering before, can she not do the same now? The answer, I think, is that in the narratives upon which her consciousness of behavior is based, such scenes only happen once—that in the world of sentimental novels, the instant the "fallen woman" has compassion upon the cruel man and recognizes that he, too, like her, is one of the "insulted and injured," he is released from his anguish and the two are mutually purified by their common ordeal. But when the Underground Man does not act according to her sentimental scenarios, but reverts back to the revenge-centered paradigms of *ressentiment,* Liza is wounded beyond endurance, beyond, that is, her repertoire's capacity to find a consolingly redemptive narrative model. The Underground Man at least knows that the "atrocity was so phony, so cerebral, so deliberately contrived, so *bookish,*"[40] but because he draws from a different, more savagely wounded and wounding text than any Liza has encountered before, she can have no response but flight, her powers of interpretation exhausted.[41]

Notes from Underground continuously satirizes the sentimental use of the prostitute figure in the tales of the 1840s, in Nekrasov's verses, and in Chernyshevsky's novel. Even though Dostoevsky finally intended Liza to function as just such a figure of redemptive suffering and love, the logic of his own narrative undercuts this solution at every turn. *Ressentiment* can never be healed by copying anyone, not even the sacred example of Mary Magdalene. This is true because every act of imitation—no matter how worthy, or even divine, the model—simply confirms the initial predicament, and even the most uplifting narratives are transformed, through the very fact of being copied, into merely fresh aspects of, rather than solutions to, the crisis of reminiscences. (How clearly Dostoevsky understood this bitter truth is evident from the end of *The Idiot*, whose Christ-like hero, Prince Myshkin, finishes his life back in a Swiss sanatorium, completely incapacitated by his mental and physical collapse.) As long as one desires an original, authentic consciousness and voice—as long, that is, as the fact of living a belated and already scripted existence is seen as the ultimate wound, making any claim to personal dignity derisory—*ressentiment* must remain consciousness's dominant emotion, structuring the narratives one lives, the narratives one tells, and ultimately the narratives in which one figures as one more increasingly sorry character.

At the beginning of this essay, I quoted Flaubert's mordant dictum on education, a sentence that speaks volumes about precisely the kind of crisis of reminiscences I have been discussing. To be trapped into living one's life as an *imitatio librorum* is, in Flaubert's narratives, the curse of modern existence, a trajectory that leads mostly to provincial adulteries and suicide or to the nostalgic tedium of late middle age that is only *ressentiment* in a minor key. And, as unlikely as a comparison between Flaubert and Dostoevsky might at first appear, it is worth considering that the only nineteenth-century novel to end on as thoroughly depressing an image of human futility as *The Idiot* is *L'Education sentimentale*. Our characteristic attempt to evade the thrust of Flaubert's not-all-that-stoic pessimism is to attribute the flailings of his characters to the *quality* of the books upon which their actions are modeled. If only the *exempla* were less shabby, so our hope runs, their effect would be enlightening rather than destructive. But if this claim is at least theoretically plausible in the case of Emma Bovary, the situation of Frédéric Moreau or Bouvard and Pécuchet cannot be recuperated quite so reassuringly.[42] Flaubert's clerks, for example, as the scholarship upon *Bouvard et Pécuchet* has demonstrated so abundantly, draw upon representative—and by no means always discredited—tomes from virtually the entire canon of Western speculative and practical thought. Their problem is not with the kinds of texts consulted, but with a certain entrapment in reading, with what we might call the theme of the Book as model, inspiration, and guide.[43]

Similarly, it is not the *content* of specific utterances that determines their suitability for being placed into the *Dictionnaire des idées reçues,* so much as the unavoidable nature of their iterability per se. I suspect, as well, that it is our own desire for some humanly attainable shelter from Flaubert's irony at the inevitable bathos of *ressentiment* that prompts the creation of a sentimentally heroicizing myth ("the hermit of Croisset," etc.). A clear index of this development is the manner in which Flaubert's letters have come to be valued as highly as his novels, in large part, I feel, because it is in the correspondence that the myth of the writer as proto-martyr and heroic victim is so seductively developed. It is, of course, just this motif that Flaubert sought, with increasing success, to keep entirely out of the fiction itself, and the novels make us uncomfortable to the precise degree to which they succeed in permitting no such avenues of escape.

But, at the end of *Bouvard et Pécuchet,* I think Flaubert finally found a literarily plausible solution, one that only the abjection of the dilemma and the desperate humor of the narrative authorize me to call optimistic. After all their efforts have failed, and failed grotesquely, the two clerks reach what I like to think of as the most exhilaratingly trivial *Aufhebung* in nineteenth-century literature: "Copier comme autrefois."[44] "Let us return to being copyists again," faithfully recording for the rest of our lives the models one no longer even tries to imitate. Here, at last, we do reach a kind of final subversion in which *ressentiment* is ultimately overcome — by the spirit, I only want to underline, of a glorious stupidity. The Lesson of the Master!

* * *

"Ohne Grausamkeit kein Fest: so lehrt es die älteste, längste Geschichte des Menschen . . ." (Without cruelty there is no festival: so the most ancient and longest part of human history teaches . . .) — Friedrich Nietzsche, *Zur Genealogie der Moral*

In his classic study, Max Scheler observed, "In present-day society, *ressentiment* is by no means most active in the industrial proletariat . . . but rather in the disappearing class of artisans, in the petty bourgeoisie and among small officials."[45] Though Scheler wrote these words well before the rise of fascism, his account seems uncannily pertinent to historians of Vichy France or readers of Louis-Ferdinand Céline's novels. But if considerations of space make it impossible here to extend my earlier questioning of dialogism and repetition into the world of books like *D'Un Château l'autre, Nord,* and *Rigodon,* it is worth at least mentioning them briefly as a reminder of how terrifying the power of an individual's *ressentiment* can be when it encounters a historical force based upon the dedicated to the unleashing of that emotion.[46]

Céline's trilogy is often mistakenly read as a monological outpouring of rage in which passages of pure scorn and vituperation are occasionally interrupted by brilliantly inventive grim humor or incendiary imagery. In reality, however, I know of no narratives that are less monological than Céline's, that depend more upon engaging — even if it is by evoking outrage — the counterwords and counteremotions of their readers. Like Dostoevsky's Underground Man, the Célinian narrator's very existence depends upon eliciting a reaction from his reader/antagonist, and like his Russian ancestor, he has learned, in part precisely from such earlier novels, that it is pointless even to pretend to a monological solipsism. But unlike Ivan Karamazov's dialogue with the devil, Céline's nightmare does not occur within the enclosed confines of a single, feverish, ex-student's rooms, but rather is acted out on a global scale. Earlier, I called Ivan's confrontations the most disturbingly dialogical metaphysics of evil in literature, and I now want to suggest that Céline has retained Dostoevsky's dialogism but shifted the arena of the clash from metaphysics to the cataclysmic events of twentieth-century history. He has, furthermore, adopted the Underground Man's strategy of trying to make *himself* the monster while leaving to his reader the tone of disgust, boredom, repulsion, and finally even appalled self-recognition. For our purpose here, however, what is so unsettling is that all the racism, rage, and hatred to which he confesses are seen as a means to shout down the intolerable babble of other voices both outside of and within his consciousness. He is abject, not monstrous, and his support for the genuinely monstrous is a pathetic attempt to silence the dialogism in which he feels entrapped. Raised in a culture that fetishizes originality and singularity, but living a life condemned to iteration and dialogue (the iteration of, among other commonplaces, exactly those texts in which the necessity for originality is emphasized), the Célinian

narrator would find a solution like Bouvard's and Pécuchet's intolerable. So, rather than returning to his copying, he offers the model
of a descent into the mire of Pétainist collaboration and the delirium
of racist phantasies, a descent, however, that is itself only a kind of
limit-case of the crisis of dialogism and iteration we have been tracing. The Célinian abject hero is a true child of both the Underground Man and Ivan's devil, and like them he has none of the
traditional recklessness or pride of the daemonic: he calculates the
cost of each repudiation with the obsessive accuracy of a bankrupt
accountant and feels himself constantly on the verge of exhaustion
or collapse. His rage is never far from a whine and his sarcasms
always contain a furtive supplication. Indeed, to be abject is never
to have experienced the monster's single-mindedness. Instead, there
is a cringing defiance deprived of any trust in one's own power and
vitiated by a self-contempt at least equivalent to one's loathing for
others. His whole being is, in essence, a helpless dialogue between
the urge to curse and attack without restraint and the anxiety immediately aroused by even the slightest danger. Where the monster
is monologic in his self-absorption, the abject hero is condemned
to dialogue, since his consciousness is an echo chamber of incompatible desires and prohibitions, a sound box in which the voices
of the monster, the successfully contented citizen, the desperately
hungry parasite, and the resigned failure exchange insults and advice
with bewildering inconsistency. The essence of abjection is to occupy, as it were, the logically impossible space created by the intersection of the satanic and the servile, a role that not only describes
the Célinian narrator's literary tone and *persona,* but also the fundamental logic and daily practice of Vichy collaboration with the
Nazi conquerors.

Hermann Göring is supposed to have enjoyed quoting Hanns
Johst's abysmal slogan: "Wenn ich Kultur höre . . . entsichere ich
meinen Browning." (When I hear the word Culture, I reach for my
pistol.)[47] Of course Göring did require a literary text, even if so
tawdry a one as Johst's *Schlageter,* to provide him with the appropriate aphorism against the potential threat of cultural objects like
literary texts. But if we remember that the realm of culture is preem-
inently the domain of memory, and then, in turn, remember that
"hysterics suffer mainly from reminiscences," we can, I think, begin

to understand both the hysterical violence with which fascism confronts the culture it sees as its antithesis and, more disturbingly, the ways in which that culture itself is implicated in the fascist's hysteria. What makes the whole issue of dialogism so vexed, though, is that if, as its champions like Wayne Booth no doubt rightly emphasize, it offers part of the solution to the crisis of reminiscence, iteration, and hysteria, then it is equally, as novels like Dostoevsky's or Céline's make only too clear, part of the problem as well. And if this account itself already seems too comfortably dialogic for its own polemical purposes, it is no doubt wiser to close with the Underground Man's formulation: "This is not literature any more, but corrective punishment."[48]

Bakhtin's Prefaces to Tolstoy (1929)

Mikhail M. Bakhtin

Preface to Volume 11: *The Dramas*

I

Tolstoy's dramatic works fall chronologically into two groups. The first group contains the plays "The Contaminated Family" and "The Nihilist." These plays were written by Tolstoy in the 1860s, soon after his marriage (September 1862), during a period of family happiness, at the very height of his economic activity on his estate and, finally, at a time when the basic plan for his greatest work, *War and Peace*, was coming together and already beginning to be realized. The year 1863 was something like a culmination point in Tolstoy's life before his crisis: Tolstoy the passionate and supremely competent landowner, Tolstoy the happy family man, Tolstoy the life-affirming artist.

To the second group belong all the remaining dramatic works of Tolstoy — from "The Power of Darkness" (1887) to "Everything Stems from It" (1910).[a] All these plays were written after the so-called crisis in Tolstoy's life, after he had renounced his landowning activity, acknowledged his previous artistic manner to be false, and withdrawn from his family.

All plays of the first group, to which one should also assign "Scenes about the Landlord Who Became a Beggar" (1886), have only recently become public property. In their own time they were not published. This is fully understandable. Their artistic value is insignificant in the extreme. They are carelessly constructed, not polished, and have a random, topical quality to them. What might be the reason for this artistic failure?

The fact is that the dramatic form was, at that time, profoundly incompatible with Tolstoy's fundamental artistic aspirations. From the very beginning of his literary career, Tolstoy, a follower of Rousseau and the early Sentimentalists, had declared himself an enemy and exposer of all conventionality and of artistic convention most of all—however it might be expressed. Dramatic form, which must satisfy the demands of stageability, is the most difficult form to free from convention. Tolstoy was later to provide a critique of basic dramatic devices in his article on Shakespeare, which is appended to the present volume (and in his "Article about Art" as well).[b] But Tolstoy had already provided a debunking picture of theatrical convention in *War and Peace*, in his famous depiction of the opera and how opera must look through the eyes of an uncomprehending spectator.

But apart from this renunciation of artistic convention, there was yet a deeper reason making dramatic form inadequate to Tolstoy's artistic aspirations. Here we have in mind the peculiar positioning and extremely important functions of the authorial word in the works of Tolstoy. Authorial discourse in his writings aspires to complete freedom and autonomy. It is not a stage direction to the hero's dialogues, something that creates no more than scene and background, nor is it a stylization of another's voice, the voice of the storyteller (*skaz*). This free and essential narrating word is important to Tolstoy for the realization of his own authorial point of view, his authorial evaluation, authorial analysis, authorial judgment, authorial sermon. And this epic word in Tolstoy's works felt itself to be confident and strong, it depicted lovingly, it penetrated with its analysis into the most remote little corners of the psyche and at the same time opposed to the hero's experiences a genuine, authorial reality. It did not yet doubt its right to do this, in all its objectivity. The authorial position was self-assured and firm.

Later, during the time Tolstoy was reorienting socially his entire life and work, the narrating word lost its confidence and became conscious of its own class-bound subjectivity: it was stripped of any epic depicting force, and all that was left for it was a purely negative prohibitive moral. This crisis of the narrating epic word also opened up for Tolstoy new and profound possibilities embedded in dramatic form, which now became adequate to his basic artistic tasks.

But precisely for this reason these plays of the 1860s, devoid of artistic significance, constitute to the highest degree a valuable document for understanding Tolstoy's attitudes toward the sixties and toward the ideological currents that agitated it.

Tolstoy's attitude toward the social and ideological life of the sixties is very complex and as yet insufficiently researched. If every novel by Turgenev was a clear and unambiguous response to some specific inquiry posed by contemporary life, then Tolstoy's works seem completely alien to any sort of topicality, deeply indifferent to all the social questions agitating his contemporaries.

In actual fact Tolstoy's creative output, like that of any other artist, was entirely determined, of course, by his epoch and by the historical arrangement of social and class forces in that epoch. Historians of literature are now bringing to light a profound bond between Tolstoy's works and the tasks of the epoch, even the most topical questions of the time — a bond that was for the most part polemical.[1] But this bond is, as it were, well encoded in Tolstoy's works, and for us, readers of the twentieth century, it can be clarified only by means of specialized literary-historical research.

Thus today's reader of *Family Happiness* (1859) can scarcely appreciate directly the fact that the work is a lively response to the "woman question" topical at that time, that it was aimed polemically against "George-Sandism" and those more extreme points of view on the subject that were being defended by representatives of the Russian radical intelligentsia. At the same time, *Family Happiness* echoes positively books by Proudhon and Michelet that were then causing a stir.

So here the plays of the sixties, namely, "The Contaminated Family" and to some extent "The Nihilist," reveal to us Tolstoy's actual subjective evaluation of fundamental social and ideological phenomena of the sixties. It is a pamphlet on the "men of the sixties." Here Tolstoy's real attitude toward the nihilists, toward the woman question, toward the emancipation of the peasants and free hired labor, toward exposé literature is expressed sharply and unambiguously. If we remember that these plays were being written during the period of first plans for *War and Peace,* then we will understand to what extent they can shed light on the actual connection between this "historical epic" and the social and ideological struggle of the sixties. In these comedies from 1863 we see how repelled Tolstoy is by his own present day, by its agitated social structure, by contemporary people and the contemporary posing of fundamental questions about world view, and how repelled he is by all these things on the threshold of creating his own historical epic. In this lies the historical and literary value of "The Contaminated Family."

The basic theme of this play is the woman question (in this respect it is a commentary on *Family Happiness*). But grouped around the woman question are all the other topical themes of the sixties. As a result we have before us a picture of the destruction of the patriarchal family and patriarchal relationships. New people and new ideas penetrate the home of the landowner Pribyshev and contaminate him and his family. Tolstoy portrays the social movement of the sixties as some sort of epidemic. Tolstoy's biographer Pavel Biryukov, fearing — as he himself writes — to make a mistake in the difficult task of assessing Tolstoy's attitude toward the sixties, put the question directly to Tolstoy himself. And he received the following answer:

"As regards my attitudes at that time toward the agitated condition of society as a whole, I must say (and whether this is a good or a bad trait of mine, it has always been peculiar to me) that I have always involuntarily resisted influences from without, epidemic influences, and if I was at that time aroused and joyful, then it was for my own personal inner motives, those that led me to the schools and to a communality with the common people."[2]

According to Tolstoy, life flows on and must flow on in its own eternal, innate patriarchal forms. "Convictions" and "ideas" are not capable of changing it: they are no more than a superficial, thin coating behind which elementary innate and moral inclinations are hidden. So-called convictions only screen real-life relationships from people. The hero of "The Contaminated Family," the landlord Pribyshev, an inveterate advocate of serfdom, tries to assimilate all the new ideas and be a "man of his times"; he deceives himself and tries, contrary to his own nature and to his own manifest economic interests, to convince himself that everything new is much better than the old.

It would be a great mistake, of course, to think that Tolstoy completely sympathizes with the serf-owner Pribyshev. But Tolstoy understands him, as an outspoken advocate of serfdom, just as he understands the peasants who do not wish to work for the landlord and who try to extract from him as much land and as many advantages as possible. What Tolstoy finds repugnant are only those so-called convictions which, in his opinion, only distort a healthy and sober practical understanding of things. Tolstoy was no advocate of serfdom: he understood the emancipation of the serfs as a necessity and even as a positive, progressive historical necessity. But he did not accept those new capitalist relations which inevitably had to replace the demolished feudal relations. It seemed to him that the peasant and the landowner would be able to work out, on the basis of their common labor and common economic interests, forms of interaction that would be, as before, patriarchal in character but at the same time economically productive.[3] Tolstoy wants to preserve the same patriarchal relationships in the family as well, and in this spirit he resolves the topical woman's question. But reality could not but contradict these views of Tolstoy. New capitalist relations came into force, dispersing all illusions, and to find adequate forms for the embodiment of his patriarchal ideals Tolstoy had to turn to the life of his fathers and grandfathers, to the family chronicle.

The portrayal of people and of the ideological movement of the sixties in "The Contaminated Family" is at the level of a crude pamphlet. This is not the place to enter upon a historical and literary analysis of that work. For us it is important only to point out the significance of this comedy for understanding the social impulses in Tolstoy's creative work. For the historian of literature, those social evaluations which permeate and organize the "eternal" images in *War and Peace* become clearer and more palpable.

"Scenes about the Landlord Who Became a Beggar" links, as it were, the dramatic output of the sixties with Tolstoy's artistic quests after his crisis. This is his first attempt to dramatize a parable. From an ideological point of view, it is, as it were, his first anticipation of the theme of withdrawal (in this instance, involuntary withdrawal). To be sure, there is no hint as yet of Tolstoy's later social and ethical radicalism. The impoverished nobleman again becomes a rich landlord, only a kinder and more humble one.

II

All the plays written by Tolstoy after his crisis fall, in their own turn, into two groups. "The Power of Darkness," "The Fruits of

Enlightenment," and "Everything Stems from It" can be called folk dramas. In their language as well as the fundamental ideological project they pursue, they directly join, on the one hand, Tolstoy's folk tales, and on the other his social, ethical, and religious preaching. "Peter the Publican," "The Living Corpse," and "A Light Shines in the Darkness" are united by the common theme of withdrawal, a theme deeply autobiographical.[c] In this group the peasant-hero is replaced by a hero belonging to the privileged classes, one who feels all the evil of his situation and his life and is trying to make a radical break with his surroundings. If the folk dramas aspire, at their outer limit, to the mystery play ("The Power of Darkness"), then the dramas of the latter group aspire to tragedy (especially "A Light Shines in the Darkness").

"The Power of Darkness" is usually considered an authentically peasant drama. Tolstoy himself even said that he wanted to write a drama for the folk theater, and he thought his play would be performed in the show-booths.[4] In fact Tolstoy's drama does in many respects deserve the epithet "peasant drama." However, it would be a mistake to think that the depiction of the peasants and their world was not permeated by elements of nonpeasant ideology. The depiction of the peasants and of peasant life is presented in the light of Tolstoy's own ideological quests, and these quests are far from being a pure and unalloyed ideological expression of the class aspirations of the peasantry itself (one or another group of the peasantry, that is).

In analyzing this drama one is struck first and foremost by the following peculiarity: the peasant world, its socioeconomic structure and everyday life, appear as something absolutely immobile and unchanging. In fact they are no more than an immobile background for the "spiritual cause" of the heroes. Peasant life serves Tolstoy only as a concretization of the "universally human" and "extra-temporal" struggle of good with evil, of light with darkness. The socioeconomic structure and peasant way of life are outside the action of the drama; they do not create conflicts, motion, struggle — like the constant pressure of the atmosphere, they do not need to be palpably felt. Evil, darkness are born in the individual soul and are resolved in the soul. A Syutaev-like "everything is within you" lies at the heart of the drama's construction.[d] The capitalist decay of the countryside, the struggle with the *kulak-miroyed* (kulakbloodsucker)[e] and with the petty bureaucrat, landlessness, the horrors of civil lawlessness — none of that is mentioned in Tolstoy's drama. But the countryside lived precisely by such things in the eighties. And it was precisely about those matters that the *narodnik* writers wrote in the seventies and eighties, idealizing and distorting in their own way, to be sure, these truly vital themes of peasant life, reinterpreting them in the spirit of their own *narodnik* ideology.[f] Perhaps Tolstoy even deliberately counterposed in his drama his own countryside to the countryside of *narodnik* literature, "The Power of Darkness" to "The Power of the Earth" (a sketch by Gleb Uspensky);[g] to the *narodnik* primacy of the *social*-ethical he counterposed his primacy of the *individual*-ethical, to their ideas of land and commune, his idea of God and individual conscience.

"The Power of Darkness" is, in Tolstoy's understanding, least of all the power of an ignorance born of economic and political oppression, a power historically constituted and which therefore is capable of being abolished historically. No, Tolstoy has in mind the eternal power of evil over the individual soul that has once sinned: one sin inevitably drags another sin after it — "One claw gets stuck, and the whole bird is lost."[h] And only the light of the individual conscience can triumph over this darkness. For this reason the drama is, in its basic concept, a mystery play; for this reason also the socioeconomic structure, the peasant way of life, the magnificent, deeply individualized peasant language is no more than an immobile, unchanging background and dramatically dead shell for the internal spiritual deed of the hero. The underlying moving forces of peasant life, which determine peasant ideology as well, are neutralized, excluded from the action of the drama.

For good reason the carrier of light in the drama is the old man Akim, who is almost a holy fool. This is the proletarianized peasant: his own household is in ruins, he feeds himself for the most part by seasonal work (he cleans latrines in the city); he has already almost broken with the interests of the land and the peasant community, and finds himself somewhere between the village and the city. He is a *declassé*, already almost a holy fool and wanderer, one of those who played a considerable role in Tolstoy's life and the sort that Tolstoy often met on the road near Yasnaya Polyana. These are all peasants who have broken with the real interests of the peasantry but have not attached themselves to any other class or group.

To be sure, they have still preserved a peasant leaven in their ideology, but deprived of actual dynamic soil this ideology degenerates
into an immobile and crooked religion of the inner deed, purely
negative and hostile to life. Precisely the figure of such a holy
fool – wanderer – although enserfed, like Alyosha the Pot, to someone else's household[i] – becomes more and more the center of Tolstoy's ideology. Thus the central ideological nucleus that organizes
"The Power of Darkness," and whose verbal carrier is Akim, is in
no sense a peasant nucleus. This is the ideology of a person in the
process of being declassed, a person who is breaking with his class,
who has left behind the real-life torrent of contradictory class evolution. There are nuances here of the ideology of the "repentant
nobleman" (Mikhailovsky's term),[j] and nuances of the ideology of
the rebellious urban intelligentsia, and there are, finally, nuances of
the ideology of the peasant becoming proletarianized, all profoundly captured by Tolstoy. Such is the ideology that lay at the
base of "The Power of Darkness."

Here it is essential to note the following. In Tolstoy's religious
world view we must take into account a struggle between two principles. In its ideological content and class nature, one principle is
close to European Protestant (Calvinist) sectarianism, with its bless-
ing on the gifts of the earth, with its elucidation of productive labor,
welfare and economic growth. The other principle is deeply akin
to Eastern sectarianism, especially to various Buddhist sects, with
their holy wandering, with their hostility to all property and any
sort of external activity. If the first principle brings Tolstoy close
to the powerful peasant household-builder in Europe and especially
to the farmer-colonizers of America, then the second principle brings
him close to China and India. These principles struggle with each
other in Tolstoy's world view, but the latter, Eastern, "homeless"
principle triumphs. If in the seventies the peasant around whom
Tolstoy oriented himself was the powerful proprietor and home-
builder, if in 1870 Tolstoy was intending to write a novel about a
contemporary Ilya Muromets,[k] if later in 1877 he projected a peasant novel about resettled families colonizing the wide-open lands
to the east and wanted to depict in them the "idea of the people"
in the sense of a force that possesses or conquers,[5] then we see that
in 1886 Tolstoy is constructing "folk drama" not at all based on this
"possessing force." Akim, if he were truly forced to break defini-

tively with his village, would never become a colonizer of new lands—he would become a homeless holy fool, a wanderer across the great roads of Russia.

One must not ignore these two principles and their struggle within Tolstoy's religious ideology. Because of them, Tolstoyanism is a complex phenomenon: it can have both a *kulak*-like and a "homeless" (one might even say a lumpenproletariat) nature. Some people assimilate from Tolstoy his active Protestant aspects but reject his eastern radicalism and nonactivity. Others, on the contrary, gravitate toward the eastern element in his teaching. And the latter group more correctly understands the later Tolstoy, who had withdrawn from life.

In "The Fruits of Enlightenment" we see, as it were anew, the victory of the Protestant, one would even say the Puritan principle in Tolstoy's ideology. A powerful peasant-proprietor with his yearning for the earth, a peasant of real earthly deeds is needed as a foil of the fictive, imagined life of the nobles. Not the internal deed of an individual conscience but questions of land and economic growth ("the possessing force") creates the contrastive parallel to the spiritualistic devil's sabbath of the enlightened urban nobles.[1] The peasant is necessary here precisely as a producer of material goods, as a contrast to the sterile parasitism of the masters.

Tolstoy's last three dramas are dedicated to the "theme of withdrawal." "Peter the Publican," selling his own self as a slave in order to give away everything that he has (his family does not permit him to give away all their property); the nobleman Fedya Protasov, who has seen the lie of the life surrounding him ("But to be a director, to sit in a bank—it's so shameful, shameful . . .")[m] and has become a "living corpse" in order not to hamper another person's life; and, finally, Nikolai Ivanovich Saryntsov ("A Light Shines in the Darkness"), living out the tragedy of an unrealizable withdrawal from his family and from his home—all these embody one and the same idea: the impossibility of any sort of adequate activity under existing social conditions and at the same time the rejection of any actual external struggle to change those social conditions. They all resolve the problem by individual withdrawal from evil, by nonparticipation in it. They, like Peter the Publican, would sooner be prepared to sell themselves as slaves than to enter an actual struggle for the abolition of all slavery. It is not the objective contradictions of reality itself that determine the drama here, but rather the contradictions in the personal, individual situation of that individual person who is breaking with his class. And the path upon which they wish to embark and which may rescue them personally from participation in social evil is that same great road of the eastern wanderer-ascetic.

TRANSLATED AND ANNOTATED BY CARYL EMERSON

Mikhail M. Bakhtin

Preface to Vol. 13: *Resurrection*

I

Ten years had already passed since the completion of *Anna Karenina* (1877) when Tolstoy began work on his last novel, *Resurrection* (1890). During that decade Tolstoy's so-called crisis occurred, a crisis of life, ideology, and artistic creativity. Tolstoy renounced his property (in favor of his family), declared his earlier convictions and views on life to be false, and rejected his own literary works.

This whole break in world view and life was perceived by the writer's contemporaries as something abrupt, precisely as "Tolstoy's crisis." But nowadays scholarship looks on the matter differently. Now we know that grounds for this revolution were already embedded in Tolstoy's early work, that in the 1850s and sixties tendencies were already clearly outlined which, in the eighties, found their expression in his "Confession," in folk tales, in religious and philosophical tracts, and in a radical break with his earlier pattern of life. But we also know that this rupture cannot be understood solely as an event in Leo Tolstoy's personal life: the rupture was prepared for and stimulated by complex socioeconomic and ideological processes being accomplished in Russian social life, processes demanding from an artist who had been formed in another epoch changes in his entire creative orientation. What took place in the 1880s was a *social reorientation* of Tolstoy's ideology and literary creativity. It was an inevitable response to the changed conditions of the epoch.

Tolstoy's world view, his artistic work, and the very style of his life had always been characterized—from his first literary efforts onward—by an opposition to the reigning tendencies of his own present day. He began as a "militant archaicizer," as the defender of the traditions and principles of the eighteenth century, of Rousseau and the early sentimentalists. He again advocated obsolete principles as a defender of the patriarchal-landlord system, with its serf base, and as an irreconcilable enemy of developing liberal-bourgeois relations. For the Tolstoy of the 1850s and sixties, even such a representative of gentry literature as Turgenev seemed excessively democratic. A patriarchically organized estate, the patriarchal family, and all the human relationships that developed within those forms—relationships half idealized and deprived of any ultimate historical concreteness—were at the center of Tolstoy's ideology and literary creativity.

As a real-life socioeconomic form, the patriarchal estate was off to the side of history's main road. But Tolstoy did not become a sentimental describer of the guttering everyday life of feudal gentry nests. Even if the romance of dying feudalism did enter into *War and Peace,* it did not, of course, lend its tone to the entire work. Patriarchal relations and the entire rich symphony of images, experiences, and feelings connected with such relations in Tolstoy's work, together with Tolstoy's special understanding of nature and its life in a human being, served from the very beginning in his art as no more than a half-real, half-symbolic canvas into which the epoch itself, through the hand of the artist, wove threads of other social worlds, other relationships. The Tolstoyan country estate is not the sluggish world of the real-life landlord-serfowner, a world hostilely closed off from new emerging life, blind and deaf to everything in that life. No, it is the position of an artist—a position not free of a certain conventionality—freely penetrated by other social voices of the sixties, the most multivoiced and tension-filled epoch of Russian ideological life. Only from such a semistylized feudal estate could Tolstoy's creative path lead unswervingly to the peasant hut. And for this reason, criticism of emerging capitalist relations and of everything that accompanies these relations in the human psyche and in obsequious ideological thought possessed, from the very beginning, a social basis in Tolstoy's work far broader than the serf-owner's estate. The other side of Tolstoy's artistic world—his positive depiction of the bodily and spiritual life of human beings, that turbulent joy of life which permeated Tolstoy's work before his crisis — was to a significant extent a reflection of those new social forces and relations that had stormily burst on to the arena of history during those years.[1]

Such was the epoch. An ideological world of new social forces, still weakly differentiated, stood opposed to the dying structure of serfdom. Capitalism was not yet able to relegate social forces to their proper places, their ideological voices were still confused and interwoven in variegated ways, especially in creative art. The artist at that time could indeed have a broad social base — to be sure, one that already concealed within itself inner contradictions, but contradictions that were still latent, not yet revealed, just as they were not yet completely revealed in the very economy of the epoch. The epoch heaped up contradictions, but its ideology, and in particular its artistic ideology, remained in many ways still naive — since the contradictions had not yet been brought to light, had not been fully realized in life.

On this broad, not yet differentiated, still covertly contradictory social base Tolstoy's monumental artistic works grew, full of those same internal contradictions — but naively so, not acknowledging them and therefore titanically rich, saturated with heterogeneous social images, forms, points of view, evaluations. Such is Tolstoy's epic *War and Peace,* such are his novellas and short stories, such also is *Anna Karenina.*

In the 1870s differentiation had already begun. Capitalism was consolidating, with cruel consistency relegating social forces to their proper places, disuniting ideological voices, making them more precise, drawing sharp boundaries. This process becomes more acute in the 1880s and nineties. During that time, the Russian socium differentiates once and for all. Inveterate preservers of the gentry-landowning class, bourgeois liberals of all shades, populists, Marxists mark themselves off from one another, work out their own ideology, which in the intensifying class struggle becomes more and more clear-cut. Creative personality must now orient itself in this social struggle in an unambiguous way if it is to remain creative.

Artistic forms were also subject to this same internal crisis of differentiation and realization of hidden contradictions. An epic, uniting in itself the world of Nikolai Rostov and of Platon Karataev, the world of Pierre Bezukhov and of the old Prince Bolkonsky under the even light of artistic reception, or a novel in which Levin, while remaining a landowner, finds respite from his inner troubles in a peasant God — by the 1890s this is no longer possible. All these contradictions, too, have been brought to light and intensified in artistic creativity itself, exploding its unity from within, just as they had been brought to light and intensified in objective socioeconomic reality.

During this internal crisis, a crisis both of Tolstoy's own ideology and of his artistic creativity, attempts begin to orient both of them toward the patriarchal peasant. If up to that time the position from which Tolstoy rejected capitalism and criticized the whole of urban culture had been the semiconventionalized position of the old-fashioned landowner, now it is the position of the old-fashioned peasant, who is also deprived of any ultimate historical concreteness. All those elements in Tolstoy's world view that from the very beginning had gravitated to this point, to this second pole of the feudal world, to the peasant, and that were radically and irreconcilably opposed to the entire surrounding sociopolitical and cultural reality, now completely dominate Tolstoy's thinking, forcing him mercilessly to reject everything incompatible with them. Tolstoy the ideologist, the moralist, the preacher was able to retune himself in a new social key, and he became, in Lenin's words, a mouthpiece for the multimillioned peasant element. "Tolstoy," Lenin says, "is great as a spokesman of those ideas and sentiments that coalesced among millions of Russian peasants during the onset of the bourgeois revolution in Russia. Tolstoy is original, for the sum total of his views, harmful when taken as a whole, expresses the peculiarities of our revolution as a *peasant* bourgeois revolution. The contradictions in Tolstoy's views, from this point of view, are a real mirror of those contradictory conditions into which the historical activity of the peasantry has been placed in our revolution."[2]

But if such a radical social reorientation toward the peasant could be realized in the abstract world view of Tolstoy as thinker and moralist, then in artistic creativity matters are considerably more complex and difficult. For good reason does artistic work begin to take a back place to moral and religious-philosophical tracts from the end of the 1870s on. Although Tolstoy had rejected his old artistic manner, he could not work out new artistic forms adequate to his own changed social tendencies. The 1880s and nineties in Tolstoy's artistic creativity are years of intense searching for peasant forms of literature.

The peasant hut, with its world and its point of view on the world, had been present from the very beginning in Tolstoy's work, but it had been an episode, it had turned up now and then in the field of vision of heroes from another social world, or else it had been advanced as the second member of an antithesis, as an artistic parallelism ("Three Deaths").[a] The peasant here existed in the field of vision of the landowner and in the light of his, the landowner's, quests. The peasant himself did not organize the artistic work. And what is more, the placement of the peasant in Tolstoy's works was such that he could not be the carrier of the plot or the action. Peasants were an object of interest, an object of the ideal aspirations of the artist and his heroes, but not the organizing center of the artwork. In October 1877, S. A. Tolstaia [Tolstoy's wife] noted down the following characteristic admission of Lev Nikolaevich: "The peasant way of life is especially difficult and interesting to me, but as soon as I describe my own way of life—suddenly I'm completely at home."[3]

The idea of a peasant novel had occupied Tolstoy for a long time. Even before *Anna Karenina*, in 1870, Tolstoy had planned to write a novel whose hero would be "Ilya Muromets," a man of peasant origins but with a university education; that is, Tolstoy wanted to create a type of peasant-hero in the spirit of folk epics.[4] In 1877, during the finishing up of *Anna Karenina*, S. A. Tolstaia records the following words of Lev Nikolaevich:

"How I'd like to finish up this novel (i.e. *Anna Karenina*) more quickly and begin something new. My idea is now very clear. In order for an artistic work to be good, one must love the main, basic idea in it. Thus in *Anna Karenina* I love the *family* idea, in *War and Peace* I loved the *national* idea, a result of the war of 1812; and now it is clear to me that in the new work I will love the idea of the Russian people in the sense of a *possessing force.*"[5]

What Tolstoy has in mind here is a new conceptualization of his novel about the Decembrists, which now had to become precisely a peasant novel. Konstantin Levin's idea—that the historical mission of the Russian peasantry lies in the colonization of the endless Asiatic lands[6]—most probably lay at the base of the new work. This historical task of the Russian peasant is realized exclusively in forms of agriculture and patriarchal household building. According to Tolstoy's plan, one of the Decembrists ends up in Siberia with the resettled peasants. In this plan there is no longer a place for the inactive image of a Platon Karataev in Pierre's field of vision; rather, Pierre appears in the field of vision of an authentic historical peasant and man of action. History is not the "14th of December" and does not take place on Senate Square;[b] history is in the resettlement movement of peasants ill-treated by their landlords. But this plan of Tolstoy's remained unrealized. Only a few fragments were written.[7]

Another approach to solving the same task of creating a peasant literature was realized by Tolstoy in his "folk stories," stories not so much about peasants as for peasants. Here Tolstoy was genuinely successful in feeling his way toward some new forms — forms, to be sure, connected with the tradition of a folklore genre (specifically the folk sermon), but deeply original in their stylistic embodiment. Such forms are possible, however, only in the minor genres. No path led from them to the peasant novel, nor to the peasant epic.[c]

For this reason Tolstoy withdrew more and more from literature and poured his world view into the forms of the treatise, journalistic article, anthology of wise sayings of various thinkers ("For Each Day"[d]), and so forth. All the artistic works of this period ("The Death of Ivan Ilych," "The Kreutzer Sonata," and others) were written in his old manner, but with a sharp predominance of the critical exposé element and with much abstract moralizing. Tolstoy's stubborn but hopeless battle for a new artistic form, which ends everywhere in the victory of the moralist over the artist, leaves its stamp on all these works.

During these years of intense struggle for a social reorientation of his artistic work, the plan for *Resurrection* is born — and slowly, with difficulty, with crises, work on his final novel drags on.

The structure of *Resurrection* differs sharply from the structure of Tolstoy's previous novels. We must assign this final novel to a special generic category. *War and Peace* is a family-historical novel (with a bias toward the epic). *Anna Karenina* is a family-psychological novel; *Resurrection* must be designated a *socioideological* novel. Judged by its generic traits it belongs to the same group as Chernyshevsky's novel *What Is to Be Done?* or Herzen's *Who Is to Blame?* and in Western European literature, the novels of George Sand. At the base of such novels lies an ideological thesis about a desired and obligatory social system. Fundamental criticism is offered, from the point of view of this thesis, of all existing social relations and forms. This criticism of reality is also accompanied by — or interrupted by — direct proofs of the thesis in the form of abstract arguments or sermonizing, and sometimes by attempts at depicting a utopian ideal.

Thus the organizing principle of the socioideological novel is not the everyday life of social groups as in the social-everyday novel, and not psychological conflicts generated by specific social relations as in the social-psychological novel, but rather a certain ideological thesis expressing a socioethical ideal, in the light of which a critical portrayal of reality is offered.

In keeping with these fundamental features of the genre, the novel *Resurrection* is composed of three aspects: (1) a radical criticism of all existing and available social relations; (2) a portrayal of the "spiritual cause" of the heroes, that is, the moral resurrection of Nekhlyudov and Katyusha Maslova; and (3) the abstract development of the sociomoral and religious views of the author.

All three of these aspects were also present in Tolstoy's earlier novels, but there they did not completely dominate the construction and receded into the background before other fundamental, organizing aspects: before the positive portrayal, under semi-idealized conditions, of spiritual and bodily life of the patriarchal landowner and family sort, and before the depiction of nature and the life of nature. Of such things there is no longer any mention in the new novel. We recall how critically Konstantin Levin perceived urban culture, bureaucratic institutions and social-minded activity, his spiritual crisis and his search for the meaning of life. How very small is the specific gravity of all that in the whole of *Anna Karenina*! Whereas precisely on that, and *only* on that, is the entire novel *Resurrection* constructed.

The composition of the novel can be related to this as well. It is extremely simple in comparison with the preceding works. In the earlier works there were several autonomous centers of narration, united among themselves by durable relationships essential to the pragmatics of the plot. Thus in *Anna Karenina:* the world of the Oblonskys, the world of Karenin, the world of Anna and Vronsky, the world of the Shcherbatskys and the world of Levin are portrayed, as it were, from within, with equal care and detail. And only the secondary characters are portrayed in the field of vision of other heroes — one in Levin's field of vision, others in Vronsky's or Anna's, and so on. But even such characters as Koznyshev sometimes concentrate around themselves an autonomous narration. All these worlds are connected and interwoven in the tightest possible way by family ties and by other essential pragmatic relationships. In *Resurrection* the narration is concentrated only around Nekhlyudov and in part around Katyusha Maslova; all the other characters and all of the remaining world are depicted in Nekhlyudov's field of vision.[e] Except for the hero and the heroine, none of the novel's characters are linked to one another by anything, and they are united only externally by the fact that they come into contact with Nekhlyudov, who visits them while soliciting on his own case.

The novel is one long row of images of social reality, illuminated by a sharply critical light, united by the thread of Nekhlyudov's outer and inner activity; what crowns the novel are the abstract theses of the author, reinforced by citations from the Gospels.

The first aspect of the novel — its critique of social reality — is indisputably the most important and meaningful. This aspect also has the most significance for the contemporary reader. The critical grasp of reality here is very broad, broader than in all of Tolstoy's other works: the Moscow prison (Butyrki), transit prisons of Russia and Siberia, the court, the Senate, the church and church service, high-society salons, bureaucratic spheres, middle and lower administration, criminals, sectarians, revolutionaries, liberal lawyers, liberal and conservative court personnel, bureaucrats and administrators of high, middling, and low calibre from ministers to prison wardens, ladies of high society and of the bourgeoisie, the urban petty bourgeoisie, and, finally, the peasants — all these are pulled in to Nekhlyudov's critical field of vision and into the author's. Certain social categories, for example the revolutionary intelligentsia and the worker-revolutionary, appear here for the first time in Tolstoy's artistic world.

The critique of reality in Tolstoy — just as in his great predecessor of the eighteenth century, Rousseau — is a critique of any and all *social conventionality* erected by man over nature, convention as such, and therefore this critique is denied any authentic historicity.

The novel opens on a broad generalizing picture of the city, which crushes external nature and crushes nature in a human being.

The construction of a city and of urban culture is portrayed as the attempt of several hundreds of thousands of people, gathered together in one place, to mutilate that land onto which they have crowded themselves, to pave it with stones so that nothing grows on it, to clean away any blade of grass that might force its way through, to smoke it up with coal and oil, to cut down trees, to drive out all the animals and birds. And the newly arrived spring, bringing to life a nature not yet completely driven out, is incapable of pushing its way through the thick mass of social lies and conventions which city people have themselves devised to rule over one another, to deceive and torment themselves and others.

In its breadth, lapidary force, and paradoxical boldness this broad and purely philosophical picture of an urban spring, of the struggle between a kind nature and an evil city culture, holds its own with the most powerful pages in Rousseau. This picture creates the tone for all the exposés of human invention that follow: the prison, the court, high society. As always in Tolstoy, from this broadest possible generalization the narrative immediately moves into the most minuscule details, registering with precision the smallest gesture, the most arbitrary thoughts, sensations, and words of people. This peculiarity — the abrupt and unmediated transition from the broadest generalizing to the most minuscule detailing — is a fundamental trait in all of Tolstoy's works. But perhaps this trait is manifested most abruptly of all in *Resurrection*, thanks to the fact that generalizations there are more abstract, more philosophical, and the detailing more minuscule and drier.

The most detailed and profoundly elaborated scene in the novel is the scene of the court; the pages devoted to it are the most powerful in the novel. Let us pause on that scene.

The citations from the Gospels chosen as an epigraph to the first part of the novel reveal Tolstoy's basic underlying thesis: the absolute impermissability of any person passing judgment on any other. This thesis is justified first of all by the basic plot situation of the novel: Nekhlyudov, who finds himself legally a juror at Maslova's trial, that is, Katyusha's judge, is in fact the person guilty for her downfall. According to Tolstoy's plan, the scene of the court must show the unattractiveness of all the other judges as well: the president of the court, with his biceps, his good digestion and his affair with the governess; and the very precise member of court, with his gold-rimmed spectacles and his bad mood on account of his quarrel with his wife — which influences the way he acts during the trial; and the good-natured member of court with his catarrh of the stomach; and the public prosecutor with all the obtuse ambition of a careerist, with his senseless and pretentious chatter. There are no attractive judges, nor can there be any, for a court in its very essence, no matter of what sort, is an evil and false invention of men. Senseless and false also is the entire procedure of the court, all its fetishism of formalities and conventions, beneath which the authentic nature of a human being is hopelessly buried.

Thus does Tolstoy the ideologue speak to us. But the artistically striking picture of the court created by him also speaks to us of something different.

What exactly is this scene, taken as a whole? It is a *judgment on the court* [*sud nad sudom*],[f] a judgment both persuasive and proper, a judgment of the nobleman Nekhlyudov, of the bureaucrat-judges, of the petty-bourgeois jurors, of the class structure and the false forms of "justice" generated by it! The entire scene created by Tolstoy is a profound and convincing social condemnation of the class-based court under the conditions of real Russian life in the 1880s. Such a *social judgment* is possible and not in the least false, and the very idea of judgment [a court] — not moral judgment over an abstract human being but social judgment over exploitative social relations and their carriers: the exploiters, bureaucrats, and others — becomes ever clearer and more persuasive against the background of the artistic scene Tolstoy offers us.

Tolstoy's works in general are profoundly saturated with the passion of social judgment, but his abstract ideology acknowledges only moral judgment over oneself, and social nonresistance. This is one of the deepest contradictions in Tolstoy, one which he was not able to overcome, and it is especially clearly revealed in this authentic *social judgment on the court* discussed by us above. History with its dialectic, with its relative historical negation that already contains an affirmation, is absolutely alien to Tolstoy's thinking. Thus his rejection of the court as such becomes absolute and therefore inescapable, non-dialectical, contradictory. His artistic vision and portrayal is wiser, and, rejecting the class-based bureaucratic court, Tolstoy affirms another: the social court, sober and not formal, the court that judges society itself and judges in the name of society.

This exposure of the underlying sense or, more accurately, the underlying senselessness of everything that takes place in court is accomplished by Tolstoy through specific artistic means — means, to be sure, that are not new in *Resurrection* but are also characteristic of all his preceding work. Tolstoy portrays one or another act as if from the point of view of a person seeing it for the first time, not knowing its purpose and therefore perceiving only the external side of the act, with all its material details. Describing an action, Tolstoy painstakingly avoids all those words and expressions by which we are accustomed to make sense out of a given act.[g]

Closely linked with this device of portrayal is another device which supplements it and is almost always combined with it: in portraying the external side of one or another socially conventional act — for example, taking the oath, the exit of the court, the pronouncement of the sentence, and so forth — Tolstoy shows us the experiences of the persons carrying out these acts. These experiences always turn out not to correspond at all to the act, lying as they do in a completely different sphere, in most instances in the sphere of crudely everyday concerns or of spiritual and bodily life. Thus one of the members of the court, importantly mounting the judge's platform as the hall respectfully stands, counts his steps with a concentrated air in hopes of divining whether or not a new remedy will help cure him of his catarrh of the stomach. Thanks to this device the act is, as it were, distanced from the person himself and from his inner life and becomes a sort of mechanical, senseless force independent of people.

Finally, these two devices are combined with a third: Tolstoy continually shows us how people begin to make use of this mechanized, senseless social form, a form alienated from the person, for their own personally avaricious or pettily ambitious goals. As a consequence people hold on to an internally dead form, they preserve and defend it, those, that is, to whom it is beneficial. Thus the members of the court, occupied with thoughts and sensations utterly unrelated to the solemn procedures of the court and to their own uniforms embroidered with gold, experience a vainglorious satisfaction from the awareness of their own impressiveness and, of course, value highly the benefits bestowed upon them by their position.

All other "exposé" scenes are constructed in a similar way, including the well-known scene of the prison church service.

Exposing the conventionality and internal senselessness of church rituals, high society ceremonies, administrative forms, Tolstoy arrives at an absolute rejection of all social convention of whatever sort. And here his ideological thesis is lacking any sense of the historical dialectic. In fact his artistic scenes unmask only foul convention, convention that has lost its social productivity and that is preserved by ruling groups in the interests of class oppression. But social convention can also be productive and can serve as an indispensable condition for communication. After all, the human word, which Tolstoy himself controls so masterfully, is ultimately a conventional social sign.

Tolstoyan nihilism, applying its negation to all of human culture as something conventional and invented by man, is a result of this same misunderstanding of the historical dialectic on Tolstoy's part, a dialectic that buries the dead only because the living have come to occupy their place. Tolstoy sees only the dead, and the field of history — so it seems to him — remains empty. Tolstoy's glance is riveted to that which is decomposing, to that which cannot and must not remain; he sees only exploitative relations and the social forms generated by them. Those positive forms which ripen in the camp of the exploited, which are in fact organized by that very same exploitation, he does not see, does not feel, and does not believe in. He addresses his sermon to the exploiters themselves. And thus his sermons inevitably must take on a purely negative character, they assume the form of categorical prohibitions and absolute, nondialectical negations.[8]

This likewise explains the portrayal — also critical and unmasking — that Tolstoy gives in his novel of the revolutionary intelligentsia and the representative of the workers' movement. In this world as well, he sees only a foul conventionality, human invention; he sees only the disparity between the external form and the internal world of its carriers, and also the avaricious and vainglorious use of this dead form.

Here is how Tolstoy describes the member of the People's Will[h] movement, Vera Bogodukhovskaia:

"Nekhlyudov began to ask her [Bogodukhovskaia] how she came to be in prison. In answer she began relating all about her case with great animation. Her speech was intermingled with foreign words such as propagandizing, disorganization, groups and sections and subsections, about which she seemed to think everybody knew, but which Nekhlyudov had never heard of.

"She told him all the secrets of the People's Will movement, evidently convinced that he was interested and pleased to hear them. Nekhlyudov looked at her miserable little neck, her thin, unkempt hair, and wondered why she had been doing all these strange things, and why she was now telling all this to him. He pitied her, but not as he had pitied Menshov, the peasant with his hands and face bleached white like potato sprouts, kept in this stinking prison for no fault of his own. She was pitiable because of the confusion that filled her mind. It was clear that she considered herself a heroine and was showing off in front of him, and for that reason she was especially pitiable to him."[9]

The nonconventional natural world of the peasant Menshov is opposed here to the conventional, invented, and vainglorious world of the revolutionary activist.

Even more negative is the depiction of the revolutionary leader Novodvorov, for whom revolutionary activity, the position as a leader in the party, and political ideas themselves are only material for the satisfaction of his own insatiable ambition.

The worker-revolutionary Markel Kondratiev, studying the first volume of *Das Kapital* and blindly believing in his teacher Novodvorov, is denied in Tolstoy's portrayal any mental independence, and fetishistically bows down before conventional scientific systems of human knowledge.

Thus does Tolstoy construct a critique and exposé of all conventional forms of human communication, created by people of urban culture "in order to torment one another." In Tolstoy's view, the preservers of these exploitative forms and the destroyers of these forms — the revolutionaries — are equally incapable of moving beyond the bounds of this endless circle of the socially conventional, the invented, the unnecessary. Any sort of activity in this world, whether conservative or revolutionary, is equally false and evil and alien to the true nature of a human being.

What, then, is counterposed in the novel to this entire rejected world of social and conventional forms and relations?

In Tolstoy's earlier works, what is counterposed to this world are nature, love, marriage, the family, childbirth, death, the growth of new generations, sturdy economic activity. In *Resurrection* there is none of that, not even death with its authentic grandeur. What stands opposed to the rejected world is the inner cause of the heroes, the cause of Nekhlyudov and Katyusha, their moral resurrection, and the purely negative prohibitory sermonizing of the author.

How is the spiritual cause of the heroes depicted by Tolstoy? In the final novel we will not find those striking pictures of spiritual life with its dark and spontaneous strivings, with its doubts, hesitations, rises and falls, with those finely tuned interruptions in feelings and moods that Tolstoy developed when depicting the inner life of Andrei Bolkonsky, Pierre Bezukhov, Nikolai Rostov, even Levin. In his relationship to Nekhlyudov Tolstoy displays an unusual restraint and dryness of tone. Only those pages about the young Nekhlyudov, about his first youthful love for Katyusha Maslova, are written in his earlier manner. The inner deed of resurrection is not, strictly speaking, depicted at all. In the place of living spiritual reality there is dry information about the moral meaning of Nekhlyudov's experiences. The author, as it were, hurries away from spiritual aspects of the empirical situation, which are now unnecessary and repellent to him, in order to pass all the more quickly over to moral conclusions, to formulas and to the texts of the Gospels. We recall Tolstoy's note in his diary, where he speaks about his disgust at Nekhlyudov's spiritual life, especially at his decision to marry Katyusha, and about his own attempt to depict the feelings and life of his hero "negatively and with a smirk."[i] Tolstoy did not succeed with his smirk; he was not able to separate himself from his hero; but his mind's disgust hindered him from devoting himself to a portrayal of his hero's spiritual life, forced him to dry up his words about his hero, to deprive those words of an authentic and loving descriptiveness. Everywhere the moral sum total of experiences, a sum total from the author, squeezes out their living pulse, which resists a moral formula.[j]

The inner life of Katyusha is also depicted in the same dry and restrained way, depicted in the words and tones of the author and not of Katyusha herself.

Nevertheless, the dominating role in the novel is assigned to the image of Katyusha Maslova. The image of a "repentant nobleman" of Nekhlyudov's sort was by this time already presenting itself to Tolstoy in an almost comical light. With good reason did he speak in the above-mentioned passage from his diary about the necessity of a "smirk" in his portrayal of him. The entire positive narration had to be concentrated around the image of Katyusha. She could and had to cast a shadow on Nekhlyudov's own inner cause, that is, on his repentance, as a "gentleman's cause."

"You want to save yourself through me," Katyusha says to Nekhlyudov, rejecting his marriage proposal. "You enjoyed yourself with me in this life, and you want to save yourself through me in the next."[k]

Here Katyusha defines, profoundly and truly, the egoism at the root of the "repentant nobleman," his exclusive concentration on his own "I." Ultimately, Nekhlyudov's entire inner cause has as its sole object this "I." This concentration on himself defines all his experiences, all his acts, all of his new ideology. The entire world, all of reality with its social evil, exists for him not in itself, but only as an object for his inner cause: he wants to save himself by means of it.

Katyusha is not repentant—and not only because, as a victim, she has nothing to repent of, but first and foremost because she both cannot and does not want to concentrate on her own inner "I." She looks not at herself, but around herself, at the world surrounding her.

In Tolstoy's diary there is the following note:

"[To Konevskaya.] Katyusha, after her resurrection, has periods during which she slyly and lazily smiles and, as it were, forgets everything that she had earlier considered to be the truth: she is simply cheerful, she feels like living."[10]

This motif, splendid in its psychological force and depth, unfortunately remained almost completely undeveloped in the work. But even in the novel [as we have it] Katyusha cannot blot out her own inner resurrection and concentrate herself on that purely negative truth that Tolstoy has forced her to find. She simply feels like living. It is completely understandable that Tolstoy could not fasten to Maslova's image either the ideology of the novel, or his own absolutely negative critique of reality. For after all, this very ideology and the critique's absolutely negative nature (quasi-independent of class considerations) grew precisely out of a concentration on one's own "I," the "I" of a "repentant nobleman." The organizing center of the novel had to be Nekhlyudov; the depiction of Katyusha is both skimpy and dry, and is constructed entirely in the light of Nekhlyudov's quests.

Let us move on to the third aspect, to the ideological thesis upon which the novel is constructed.

The organizing role of this thesis is clear from all that has come before. In the novel there is literally not a single image which is neutral as regards the ideological thesis. In his new novel Tolstoy does not allow himself simply to admire people and things and to portray them for their own sakes, as he was able to do in *War and Peace* and *Anna Karenina*. Every word, every epithet, every comparison emphatically demonstrates the ideological thesis. Tolstoy not only does not fear tendentiousness, but with extraordinary artistic boldness, even with a challenge, he emphasizes it in each detail, in each word of his work.

To be convinced of this it is enough to compare Nekhlyudov's waking-up rituals, his toilette, morning tea, etc. (chap. 3), with the scene, completely analogous as regards content, of Oblonsky's waking up, with which *Anna Karenina* opens.

In Oblonsky's waking-up scene, each detail, each epithet fulfilled a pure representing function: the author was simply showing us his hero and showing us things, losing himself thoughtlessly in his portrayal; both the strength and the succulence of this portrayal lie in the fact that the author is admiring his hero, his joie de vivre and freshness, and admiring as well the things that surround him.

In Nekhlyudov's waking-up scene, each word fulfils not a representing function but primarily an unmasking, reproaching, or repenting function. The entire representation is utterly subordinated to these functions.

Here is the beginning of that scene:

"When Maslova, accompanied by two soldiers, reached the building, wearied out by the long walk, the very nephew of her mistresses, Prince Dmitry Ivanich Nekhlyudov, who seduced her, was still lying on his high crumpled bed, with a feather-bed on top of the spring mattress, and, having unbuttoned the collar of his clean, linen nightshirt with its well-ironed pleats across the chest, smoked a cigarette."[1]

The "seducer's" waking up in a comfortable bedroom in a comfortable bed is directly counterposed here to Maslova's prison morning and her difficult route to the court. This immediately gives a tendentious orientation to the entire portrayal and determines the choice of every detail, every epithet: they must all serve to further this unmasking opposition. The epithets attached to the bed: high, a spring mattress, a feather-bed; to the shirt: linen, clean, with ironed pleats across the chest (so much of someone else's labor!) — all this is utterly subordinated to a nakedly emphasized socioideological function. Strictly speaking they do not portray, they unmask.

And the entire subsequent portrayal is constructed in the same way. For example: Nekhlyudov washes with cold water his "muscular white body, covered over with a layer of fat"; he puts on his "clean ironed underwear, his boots that had been cleaned like a mirror," and so on. What is everywhere emphasized is the huge amount of other people's labor that every trivial detail of this comfort swallows up, emphasized by the words — "it was prepared," "it was cleaned," "the shower was prepared," "his clothes brushed and lying ready for him on a chair," "the parquet floor which had been polished by three peasants the day before." It is almost as if Nekhlyudov gets dressed in people's labor spent for him; his entire setting is saturated with this alien labor.

Stylistic analysis thus everywhere reveals a deliberately emphasized tendentiousness of style. The style-shaping significance of the ideological thesis is clear. It determines as well the entire construction of the novel. We recall how the thesis of the inadmissability of one man judging another determined all the devices employed for portraying the court session. The scene of the court, the scene of the Church service, and other such scenes are constructed as artistic *proofs* of specific positions held by the author. Each detail in them is subordinated to the task of serving as proof of the thesis.

In spite of this extreme and provocatively naked tendentiousness, the novel did not in the least turn out tediously tendentious and lifeless. Tolstoy resolved his task to construct a socioideological novel with consummate mastery. One could say outright that *Resurrection* is the most consistent and perfect example of the socioideological novel not only in Russia but in the West as well.

Such is the formal artistic significance of the ideological thesis in the construction of the novel. What, then, is the content of this thesis?

This is not the place to consider Tolstoy's socioethical and religious world view. Thus we will touch upon the content of the thesis in a few words only.

The novel opens on Gospel texts (the epigraph) and closes with them (Nekhlyudov's reading of the Gospels). All these texts are meant to strengthen a single basic thought: the impermissability not only of one man's judgment over another, but also the impermissability of any sort of activity directed toward the correction of existing evil. People, sent into the world by the will of God—the Master of life—must, like the laborers, fulfill the will of their master.[m] This same will is expressed in the commandments forbidding any sort of violence against one's neighbors. A person can act only on himself, on his own inner "I" (the quests for a Kingdom of God which is within us);[n] all the rest is merely appended.

When this thought is revealed to Nekhlyudov on the final pages of the novel, it becomes clear to him how to conquer the evil reigning around him, the evil whose witness he has been throughout the entire action of the novel: it can be conquered only by *inactivity,* by *nonresistance* to it. "In this way the idea that the only certain means of salvation from the terrible evil from which men are suffering is that they should always acknowledge themselves to be guilty before God, and therefore unable to punish or reform others, became clear to him. It became clear to him that all the dreadful evil he had been witnessing in prisons and jails, and the quiet self-assurance of perpetrators of this evil, resulted from men wanting to do the impossible: to correct evil while being themselves evil. . . . 'But surely it cannot be so simple,' Nekhlyudov said to himself, and yet he saw with certainty, however strange it had seemed to him at first, being so accustomed to the opposite, that that was without doubt not only a theoretical but also a practical solution to the question. The usual objection—What is one to do with evil-doers? Can they really be left unpunished?—no longer confused him."

Such is Tolstoy's ideology organizing the novel.

Revealing this ideology not in the form of abstract moral and religious-philosophical tracts but under the conditions required by artistic portrayal, on the basis of concrete real-life material and in connection with Nekhlyudov's concrete and socially typical life's path, brings to light with extraordinary clarity the social class and psychological roots of this ideology.

How was the very question, answered by the ideology of the novel, posed through the life of Nekhlyudov?

After all, from the very beginning what had tormented Nekhlyudov and had posed for him a difficult question was not so much social evil in itself as his own *personal participation in that evil.* From the very beginning it is precisely to this question of personal participation in reigning evil that all of Nekhlyudov's experiences and quests are riveted: How to bring this participation to an end, how to free himself from comfort that swallows up so much of other people's labor, how to free himself from owning property, linked with the exploitation of the peasants, how to free himself from fulfilling his social obligations, which serve to intensify enslavement, but first and most important of all—how to atone for his shameful past, his guilt before Katyusha?

This question of personal participation in evil overshadows the existing evil itself, makes it something subordinated, something secondary in comparison with the tasks of personal repentance and personal self-perfection. Objective reality with its objective tasks is dissolved and swallowed up by the inner deed with its subjective tasks of repentance, purification, personal moral resurrection. From the very beginning a fateful substitution of question took place: instead of the question of objective evil, the question was posed about one's personal participation in it.

It is to this final question that the ideology of the novel provides an answer. For this reason the ideology must inevitably lie in the subjective plane of the internal deed: this is decided in advance by the very posing of the question. Ideology indicates a subjective way out for the repentant exploiter, it calls those who have not yet repented to repentance. The question of the exploited did not even arise. Things are good for them, they're not guilty of anything, one must look on them with envy.

During his work on *Resurrection,* right around the time when he was trying to reorient his novel toward Katytusha, Tolstoy jotted down in his diary: "Went for a walk today. Dropped in on Konstantin Bely. Very pitiable. Then took a walk through the village. It's good around them, and around us it's shameful."[11]

The peasants, sick or swollen with hunger, are pitiable, but things are good for them because they're not ashamed. The motif of envy toward those who have nothing to be ashamed of in the world of social evil runs like a red thread through Tolstoy's diaries and letters of this period.

The ideology of *Resurrection* is directed at the exploiters. It grows entirely out of those problems that rose up before the repentant representatives of the landowning class, riddled with decay and dying out. These tasks are deprived of any historical perspective. The representatives of the departing class have no objective foundation in the external world, no historical cause or aim, and therefore are concentrated on the inner cause of personality. In Tolstoy's abstract ideology there were crucial aspects, to be sure, that brought him close to the peasantry, but these sides of his ideology did not enter the novel and were not able to organize its material, concentrated as it was around the personality of the repentant landowner Nekhlyudov.

Thus at the basis of the novel lies Tolstoy's-Nekhlyudov's question: "How am I, an individual personality belonging to the ruling class, to free myself, working on my own, from participation in social evil?" And to that question this answer is given: "Become a nonparticipant in it externally and internally, and to this end fulfill purely negative commandments."

Plekhanov speaks absolutely correctly in characterizing Tolstoy's ideology:

"Not being in the position to substitute in his field of vision the exploited for the exploiters — or, put another way, not able to pass from the point of view of the exploiters to the point of view of the exploited — Tolstoy naturally had to direct his primary efforts toward morally correcting the oppressors, having prompted them to refuse to repeat their foul acts. This is why his moral preaching took on a negative character."[12]

The objective evil of the social class structure, depicted by Tolstoy with such striking force, is framed in the novel by the subjective field of vision of a representative of the departing class, a man who seeks a way out along the paths of the inner cause, that is, *objectively historical inaction.*

Several words about the significance of *Resurrection* for the contemporary reader.

We have seen that the critique element is dominant in the novel. We have also seen that the underlying form-shaping force of this critical portrayal of reality was a passionate judgment upon it, a judgment that is artistically effective and merciless. The artistic accents of this portrayal are considerably more energetic, forceful and revolutionary than those tones of repentance, forgiveness, nonresistance that adorn the inner cause of the heroes and the abstractly ideological theses of the novel. This artistically critical aspect constitutes the main value of the novel. The artistically critical devices of depiction worked out here by Tolstoy are models for us to this day, and have not been surpassed.

In recent times our Soviet literature has been tenaciously laboring over the creation of new forms for the socioideological novel. This is perhaps the most pressing and important genre on today's literary scene. The socioideological novel—ultimately the socially tendentious novel—is a completely legitimate artistic form. Not to recognize its purely artistic legitimacy is a naive prejudice of superficial aestheticism, which we should have long ago outgrown.[13] But actually this is one of the most difficult and risk-laden forms of the novel. It is too easy here to take the path of least resistance: to recoup one's losses in ideology, to transform reality into a poor illustration of ideology or, on the contrary, to render ideology in the form of stage directions to the portrayal which do not fuse internally with that portrayal, or in the form of abstract conclusions, and so on. To organize the entire material from top to bottom on the basis of a well-defined socioideological thesis, without stifling it or drying up the living concrete life within it, is a very difficult task.

Tolstoy handled this task with consummate mastery. As a model of the socioideological novel, *Resurrection* can be of great use to the literary aspirations of the present day.

TRANSLATED AND ANNOTATED BY CARYL EMERSON

Notes

Introduction

1. The idea of "ventriloquized" texts appears in Michael Holquist, "The Politics of Representation," in *Allegory and Representation: Selected Papers from the English Institute, 1979 – 80,* ed. Stephen J. Greenblatt (Baltimore: The Johns Hopkins University Press, 1981), 162 – 83.

2. Bakhtin discusses the concepts of "potential" and "great time" in "Response to a Question from the *Novy Mir* Editorial Staff," *Speech Genres and Other Late Essays,* trans. Vern W. McGee, ed. Caryl Emerson and Michael Holquist (Austin: University of Texas Press, 1986), 1 – 9. Further references to this volume are to SG.

3. We discuss Bakhtin's career—the extent to which his thought is unified, the genuine development of his ideas over time, and the stages of that development—in our forthcoming study, *Mikhail Bakhtin: Creation of a Prosaics* (Stanford University Press, in press). A companion volume, *Heteroglossary: Terms and Concepts of the Bakhtin Group,* is also in preparation.

We largely accept the periodization offered by Michael Holquist in his entry on Bakhtin for *Handbook of Russian Literature,* ed. Victor Terras (New Haven: Yale University Press, 1985), 34 – 36, but we differ with him regarding the precise content of those periods, the relations among them, and the authorship of the disputed texts.

4. "Toward a Reworking of the Dostoevsky Book" appears in English as Appendix II of Mikhail Bakhtin, *Problems of Dostoevsky's Poetics,* ed. and trans. Caryl Emerson (Minneapolis: University of Minnesota Press, 1984). Further references to this volume are to PDP.

The other essays from this last period are translated in *Speech Genres and Other Late Essays.*

5. A brief description (in Russian) of this unfinished essay is provided by its editor, Sergei Bocharov, and it is uncertain how much editorial reconstruction has gone into this edition. Bocharov tells us that the fragment, which occupies eighty printed pages and which Bakhtin himself never prepared for publication, consists of three parts. The first appears to be a section of the introduction to a major study of aesthetics and ethics. Its first eight pages are missing. A shorter fragment appears to be a section of part one of this projected study. The third part is a fragment on the relation of an author to his protagonists, which was apparently meant to preface another work of this period ("Author and Hero in Aesthetic Activity," published in Russian in 1979). The text contains numerous abbreviations and brackets indicating illegible words; in thanking his three transcribers, Bocharov refers to "the extremely difficult work of reading the manuscripts and preparing them for print." Perhaps as a result of its unfinished state, the printed text contains two versions of Bakhtin's analysis of Pushkin's poem "Parting." The title, "Toward a Philosophy of the Act," is Bocharov's, not Bakhtin's.

The first installment of these early manuscripts appeared in excerpted form in the Soviet periodical *Sotsiologicheskie issledovaniia*, no. 2 (1986), 157–69, under the title "Arkhitektonika postupka" (The Architectonics of the Act). The full text was published soon after as "K filosofii postupka" (Toward a Philosophy of the Act) in the 1984–85 issue of *Filosofiia i sotsiologiia nauki i tekhniki*, a yearbook (*ezhegodnik*) for the Soviet Academy of Sciences (Moscow: Nauka, 1986), 80–160. Our references are to the full text, which is henceforth referred to as "Act."

According to Bakhtin's Soviet editors, "Act" was written *before* "Author and Hero in Aesthetic Activity," the other major published segment of Bakhtin's early manuscripts (in *Estetika slovesnogo tvorchestva* [Moscow: Iskusstvo, 1979]: 7–180). We agree with this dating. "Act" is concerned with the primary ethical obligations of consciousness; "Author and Hero" recasts the problem of obligation on the aesthetic plane.

6. If one wishes to look for a source of Bakhtin's ethical concerns, a key one is doubtless the great tradition of nineteenth-century Russian literature. Bocharov notes correctly that "Dostoevsky was not only a subject but also a source" of Bakhtin's work ("Act," 158n1).

7. For a similar argument directed against contemporary literary theories that "absolutize the derivative," see W. Wolfgang Holdheim, "Idola Fori Academici," *Stanford Literature Review*, no. 4 (1988), 7–21.

8. The Russian word *dolzhestvovanie* means "obligation," as does its more common root word *dolg*. We prefer "oughtness," with its slightly

irregular sound, in this context, because the word is clearly meant to correspond to Bakhtin's equally odd coinage, *eventness (sobytiinost')*.

9. On this point, see Susan Stewart, "Shouts on the Street: Bakhtin's Anti-Linguistics" in *Bakhtin: Essays and Dialogues on His Work,* ed. Gary Saul Morson (Chicago: University of Chicago Press, 1986), 41–57.

10. Because his concern is with the individual agent's perspective, Bakhtin frequently switches without warning to the first person; we follow this practice in our paraphrases.

11. Compare this argument with the following passage in *Problems of Dostoevsky's Poetics*: "We see no special need to point out that the polyphonic approach has nothing in common with relativism (or with dogmatism). But it must be noted that both relativism and dogmatism equally exclude all argumentation, all authentic dialogue, by making it either unnecessary (relativism) or impossible (dogmatism)" (PDP, 69).

12. If this point seems obvious to Western readers, it is worth mentioning that Soviet history has had numerous episodes of rejecting theories of physics, chemistry, and biology—not to mention social sciences and humanities—on the Leninist principle that one need not examine arguments in terms of the discipline from which they derive in order to reject them; if the arguments are opposed to the interests of the Party, the laws of history themselves ensure that the theories must be wrong. At the time Bakhtin was writing this essay, the role of ideology and the Party as an arbiter of disciplinary disagreements was hotly debated.

13. In his book on Dostoevsky, Bakhtin dwells on Dostoevsky's remarkable observation that he was *not* a psychologist, but "a realist in the higher sense." In Bakhtin's terms, Dostoevsky understood how the mind works without recourse to "theoretism" and "transcription." Debates on the status of psychology and its relation to knowledge and ethics were commonplace in the latter part of the nineteenth century in Russia. See, for instance, part 1, chapter 7 of *Anna Karenina.* We are indebted to the manuscript of David Joravsky's forthcoming study, *Russian Psychology (And Ours).*

14. Bakhtin's argument here parallels points made in the opening to "Author and Hero," 22–26. The Russian text (still untranslated) is M. M. Bakhtin, "Avtor i geroi v esteticheskoi deiatel'nosti," *Estetika slovesnogo tvorchestva* (Moscow: Iskusstvo, 1979), 7–180.

15. Bakhtin appears to pun on the Russian phrase *sobytie bytiia* by interpreting the etymology of *sobytie* as "so-" (English "co-") plus *bytie* (being).

16. "Act," 94. This is the sole theological passage in this text as it has come down to us, although the manuscript appears to contain thirty-two "indecipherable" words at this point. (If the text is really indeci-

pherable, how can the editors be so sure there are precisely thirty-two words?)

17. Fyodor Dostoevsky, *Notes from Underground* in Dostoevsky, *"Notes from Underground" and "The Grand Inquisitor"*, ed. and trans. Ralph Matlaw (revision of the Garnett version) (New York: E. P. Dutton, 1960), 115. The underground man describes the "retort-made man" on p. 9.

18. This view, which we call "prosaics," is developed in our forthcoming study *Mikhail Bakhtin: Creation of a Prosaics*; in Morson, *Hidden in Plain View: Narrative and Creative Potentials in "War and Peace"* (Stanford: Stanford University Press, 1987), 128 – 29, 218 – 23, 269 – 71; in Morson, "Prosaics: An Approach to the Humanities," *The American Scholar* (Autumn 1988): 515 – 28; and in Emerson, "Problems with Baxtin's Poetics," *Slavic and East European Journal, 32* no. 4 (1988): 503 – 25.

For a recent defense of ethics as a matter of cases not reducible to rules, see Stephen Toulmin, "The Tyranny of Principles," *Hastings Center Report* 11, no. 6 (December 1981): 3 – 39; and Toulmin, "Equity and Principles" in *Osgoode Hall Law Journal* 20, no. 1 (March 1982): 1 – 17.

19. There are two other brief passages on language on pp. 107 and 156; see the discussion below.

20. As we argue in *Mikhail Bakhtin: Creation of a Prosaics*, this idea was to be the link between "prosaics" as a view of the world focusing on the everyday ("the prosaic") and prosaics as a theory of literature that privileges prose (prosaics as opposed to poetics).

21. That account takes us beyond our present purpose; but see our account of polyphony in *Mikhail Bakhtin: Creation of a Prosaics*.

22. These clusters are part of what Bakhtin means by *edinstvo*, "unity," a word that has caused his translators some difficulty. *Edinstvo* for Bakhtin is neither a fusion nor a system; in a sense, it is not a *unity* but a *unit-y*. It is the unit of inseparable, individual factors making up an event, none of which can be simplified or factored out if the event is to be correctly understood. See "Act," 110: "In this sense the very word *unity* must be abandoned as too theoretized; not unity but singularity of one's self, of the non-repeating whole and its reality . . ."

23. Sartre was to offers a similar critique of traditional Marxism in his *Search for a Method*.

24. Bakhtin may be alluding to the development of alternative, non-Euclidian geometries, as well as to relativity theory here. He was to invoke Einstein specifically in his essay on the "chronotope" (time-space) in the 1930s.

25. Bakhtin's reading of "Parting" is published in two variants at the end of the published version of "Act," 131 – 38 and 141 – 54. (Bakh-

tin's Soviet editors have assigned the text to the first chapter of Bakhtin's "Author and Hero in Aesthetic Activity," probably written after "Act.") The first reading analyzes the poem's voices largely dualistically (author/hero and heroine); the second reading (chronologically later, and assigned by the editors to "Author and Hero") stresses the role of the author as distinct from the persona. This move from dual to triangulated models is characteristic of Bakhtin's thought in the twenties.

26. "Indifference frees us from the multiplicity of existence," Bakhtin writes, "that is the function of forgetting" ("Act," 130).

27. Bakhtin's reading is remarkable, of course, for what it omits. In contrast to Tomashevsky's and Bely's studies of this period, Bakhtin does not deal at all with the quantifiable or statistical aspects of verse analysis. Neither does he investigate historical prototypes or tropes.

In the first chapter of her *Distant Pleasures: Alexander Pushkin and the Writing of Exile* (Stanford: Stanford University Press, forthcoming), Stephanie Sandler suggests that Bakhtin's analysis of "Parting" might be a response to the quasi-Formalist poetician V. M. Zhirmunsky, whose influential essay "Zadachi poetiki" (The Tasks of Poetics, 1921–23) used this poem to illustrate quite different techniques of poetic analysis.

28. The repetitiveness of the Rabelais book has especially troubled readers; portions of the chronotope essay are also astonishingly "inefficient."

29. SG, 130. We have corrected an error in the first printing of the published text of the translation, which mistakenly reads: "but it also has cognitive, creative significance." The second printing corrects the error.

30. Katerina Clark and Michael Holquist, *Mikhail Bakhtin* (Cambridge, Mass.: Harvard University Press, 1984); references in the text are henceforth to C&H. See especially the chapter on "The Disputed Texts," 146–70.

31. We note here that we do not bring to this reconsideration any new archival material or oral evidence. Our conclusions were reached through a rereading of Bakhtin's texts and those of other members of his Circle, and through an assessment of the major arguments and evidence about the authorship question currently in print.

32. The "Forum" appeared in *Slavic and East European Journal*, vol. 30, no. 1 (Spring 1986). It includes Morson's article "The Baxtin Industry," pp. 81–90; Titunik's "The Baxtin Problem: Concerning Katerina Clark and Michael Holquist's *Mikhail Bakhtin*," pp. 91–95; and Clark and Holquist, "A Continuing Dialogue," pp. 96–102.

33. In his essay "The Baxtin Industry," Morson characterized Clark and Holquist's case as unconvincing but did not himself take a stand on

the authorship question. In their reply, "A Continuing Dialogue" (considered below), Clark and Holquist concentrated on Titunik's objections.

34. See Nina Perlina, "Bakhtin-Medvedev-Voloshinov: An Apple of Discourse," *University of Ottawa Quarterly* 53 (1983): 35–47; and Edward J. Brown, "Soviet Structuralism, a Semiotic Approach" in *Russian Formalism: A Retrospective Glance, a Festschrift for Victor Erlich*, ed. Robert Louis Jackson and Stephen Rudy (New Haven: Yale Center for International and Area Studies, 1985), 118–20.

See also part 3 of David Carroll, "The Alterity of Discourse: Form, History, and the Question of the Political in M. M. Bakhtin," *Diacritics* 13, no. 2 (Summer 1983): 72–74. Carroll questions the inner logic of Holquist's idea of "ventriloquization," as well as the twin assumptions that Bakhtin's early manuscripts contain in embryo all his later ideas and that those ideas were primarily theological.

35. For an account of these debates, see Peter Seyffert, *Soviet Literary Structuralism: Background, Debate, Issues* (Columbus: Slavica, 1983). Caution is needed in reading this excellent study to allow for Seyffert's expressed preference for the semioticians, but Seyffert wisely includes numerous direct and lengthy quotations from influential articles so that readers can draw their own conclusions.

36. Recently there has been a call within the Soviet academic establishment for a thoroughly annotated Academy Edition of Bakhtin School writings, with the disputed texts provisionally attributed to Bakhtin. See Sergei Averintsev, review of *M. M. Bakhtin. Literaturno-kriticheskie stat'i* (1986) in *Druzhba narodov* 3 (1988): 256–59. In a footnote to a review of Boris Eichenbaum's *O literature*, A. Nemzer calls for a reprinting of Medvedev's critique of Formalism "so that the serious reader will be able to see the strength and weakness of this book and understand what in it is from Bakhtin, and what from the style of polemics at the end of the twenties" [*Novy mir* 4 (1988): 262]. The rehabilitation of Voloshinov and Medvedev, should it come, will be welcome for Bakhtin studies and for the history of Marxist thought.

37. The first American edition of the book originally published under Medvedev's name gives its author as "P. N. Medvedev/M. M. Bakhtin"; the Harvard University Press paperback reprint (1985) reverses the order and attributes the work to "M. M. Bakhtin/P. N. Medvedev." A Russian-language edition printed in New York attributes the book solely to "Mikhail Bakhtin." The introduction to this edition takes a high moral tone, as it claims to be restoring the book to its true author. It offers as proof that the Wehrle translation mentions a document Bakhtin signed for the Soviet copyright agency, in which Bakhtin allegedly claimed authorship (pp. 5–6). In fact, Wehrle's statement is not so categorical. He

claims only that Vadim Kozhinov informed him of the existence of such a document. As we mention below, Clark and Holquist indicate that Bakhtin *refused* to sign such a document.

On the other hand, Harvard University Press reprinted Voloshinov's *Marxism and the Philosophy of Language* and his *Freudianism: A Critical Sketch* without any attribution to Bakhtin, perhaps because I. R. Titunik, co-translator of *Marxism* and sole translator of *Freudianism*, has been the most consistent and long-standing opponent of "Bakhtin imperialism."

Clark and Holquist also mention translations of the disputed texts into other languages, with authorship attributed to Bakhtin. According to their biography, the Soviet copyright agency VAAP insists that credit be given to Bakhtin. See C&H, p. 147.

The editions are: P. N. Medvedev/M. M. Bakhtin, *The Formal Method in Literary Scholarship: A Critical Introduction to Sociological Poetics*, trans. Albert J. Wehrle (Baltimore: Johns Hopkins University Press, 1978); the reprint attributing authorship to "M. M. Bakhtin/P. N. Medvedev" was issued by Harvard University Press in 1985. The Russian language reprint is Mikhail Bakhtin, *Formal'nayi metod v literaturovedenii* (New York: Serebrianyi vek, 1982). Page references, henceforth in the text, are to the Harvard reprint.

38. Viach. Vs. Ivanov, "The Significance of M. M. Bakhtin's Ideas on Sign, Utterance, and Dialogue for Modern Semiotics" in Henryk Baran, ed., *Semiotics and Structuralism: Readings from the Soviet Union* (White Plains, N.Y.: International Arts and Sciences Press, 1974), 366. The original passage may be found in Viach. Vs. Ivanov, "Znachenie idei M. M. Bakhtina o znake, vyskazyvanii i dialoge dlia sovremennoi semiotiki," *Trudy po znakovym sistemam* (Tartu, 1973), 6:44.

Brown [fn. 34] comments on Ivanov's methodological assumptions in "Soviet Structuralism," 118–20.

[Item 5 in the bibliography is *Marxism and the Philosophy of Language*. Items 1–4 and 7 are: Voloshinov, "Discourse in Life and Discourse in Poetry" (1926); Voloshinov, *Freudianism* (1927); Medvedev, *The Formal Method in Literary Scholarship* (1928); Voloshinov, "New Currents of Linguistic Thought in the West" (1928); and Voloshinov, "The Construction of the Utterance" (1939).]

39. Elsewhere in the chapter, Clark and Holquist write: "The earliest 'Voloshinov' text that seems a candidate for Bakhtin's authorship is 'Beyond the Social,' which was published in *The Star* early in 1925. Many sections in this article are similar to sections in 'Voloshinov's' later *Freudianism*, published in the summer of 1927, which is also by Bakhtin" (162); "The next 'Voloshinov' publication, 'New Currents of Linguistic

Thought in the West,' was published in 1928. It was presented as a synopsis of three chapters of 'Voloshinov's' forthcoming book *Marxism and the Philosophy of Language*. Inasmuch as the book is Bakhtin's, the article is presumably his likewise, though Bakhtin could have assigned to Voloshinov the onerous task of preparing a synopsis. The authorship of *Marxism and the Philosophy of Language*, published in 1929, is clearly Bakhtin's" (166). Although toward the end of their chapter Clark and Holquist concede that the problem is "one about proportion and ratio rather than identity as such," this chapter and their book as a whole clearly limit Voloshinov and Medvedev to purely mechanical roles: preparing a synopsis or making a few minor insertions. All the creative energy, and everything from main specific points to overall argument, are said to belong to Bakhtin.

40. We discuss the probable influence of Voloshinov and Medvedev on Bakhtin, as well as the influence of Bakhtin on Voloshinov and Medvedev in our forthcoming study, *Mikhail Bakhtin: Creation of a Prosaics*.

41. In his article "The Politics of Representation," Holquist argues that Bakhtin deliberately published his books under the names of his friends to illustrate his theories: this is "the example provided by the relation he himself bears to certain texts that he authored [the disputed texts]" (p. 167; similar passages appear throughout the article).

42. These arguments are presented in Holquist, "The Politics of Representation," and criticized by Titunik in the *SEEJ* "Forum." Holquist writes: "At this point [in the latter half of the 1920s], the theoretical epicenter of his work —-how to reconcile modern linguisitics with the biblical assurance that the Word became flesh — overlapped with his own pressing practical needs: How was he to find an appropriate ideological flesh for the spirit of his own works so that he could sell his work before wasting away completely? . . . If the Christian word were to take on Soviet flesh it had to clothe itself in ideological disguise" (172 – 73). This theological comparison is not meant as a mere analogy: Holquist discusses Russian Orthodox theology to demonstrate the theological terms of Bakhtin's thought and action with regard to the authorship question.

43. I. R. Titunik, "Bakhtin &/or Vološinov &/or Medvedev: Dialogue &/or Doubletalk," *Language and Literary Theory*, ed. Benjamin A. Stolz et al., Papers in Slavic Philology, 5 (Ann Arbor: Department of Slavic Languages and Literatures, 1984), 8.

44. See Titunik, "The Baxtin Problem" in the *SEEJ* Forum, 93. Titunik observes: "Baxtin's interest in carnival (and associated topics such as Menippean satire) seems to have originated with his work on Rabelais. Yet, the authors identify Baxtin as 'carnival man' from the start, asserting that the very ambience of his life from the earliest period of his career

was 'carnivalesque.' " In their reply, Clark and Holquist note that Bakhtin had long been familiar with Menippean satire. But that does not mean, of course, that he had thought of analyzing Menippean satire in terms of carnival and "carnivalization."

45. Titunik, "The Baxtin Problem," 93–94. Titunik asks (93), "Perhaps it is just a matter of one's sense of humor?" Clark and Holquist reply (98) that Voloshinov did not finish his dissertation and no notes survived, so "a definitive answer simply does not exist."

46. On this point, see Wlad Godzich's "Foreword" to the paperback reprint of *The Formal Method* (1985).

47. Our own reading of this passage appears later in this introduction. See also Ann Shukman's paper in the present volume for a gloss.

48. For example, see Bakhtin's response to Engelhardt's theory of Dostoevsky's "dialectical evolution of the spirit" (PDP, 22–26). This critique occupied a proportionately even more prominent place in the first (1929) edition of the Dostoevsky book.

49. Katerina Clark and Michael Holquist, "A Continuing Dialogue," in the *SEEJ* "Forum," 96. Further references to this article are to "ACD."

50. Clark and Holquist write, "For Kanaev is, as we state very clearly, *still alive* (or, at least, was alive when we wrote our book), and is thus able to deny or validate claims that it was Baxtin who actually wrote the text [on vitalism] in question" (ACD, 97). To whom did Kanaev confirm Bakhtin's authorship? "As we make clear in the book, we did not personally interview him (not, as we hasten to add, for want of trying)" (ACD, 97).

51. Titunik writes:

The result of their efforts is not, in my opinion, a study, but something like an *apologia*, or even more than that: Clark and Holquist have produced what can be described . . . as *hagiography*, that is, an account both of a "saint" of ideas (like Einstein, to whom the authors compare Baxtin) and of a Christian, even—in the authors' view—a specifically Russian Orthodox saint . . . I do not mean to say that Clark and Holquist have not attempted to prove Baxtin's intellectual and Christian sanctity, but—and this is my major objection—hagiography is not all what is needed now . . ." ["The Baxtin Problem," 91]

According to Titunik, one must judge by the overall tenor of the work and by the reliability, precision, and care of the assertions that can be verified. And, Titunik adds, these aspects of their work are not wholly reassuring. Titunik enumerates errors in fact and documentation in the Clark/Holquist biography; see "The Baxtin Problem," 95.

52. Titunik notes that, for all the categorical assertions that "Bakhtin was a religious man" (C&H, first sentence of chap. 5), there is very little to put one's finger on. Clark and Holquist, he points out, repeatedly describe religious circles at the time, only to conclude that there is no evidence Bakhtin belonged to them; nevertheless, Titunik continues, they do not qualify their categorical claims of his religiosity. Their readers may not be aware of how much their account depends on evidence and how much depends on "supposition, speculation, and surmise" ("The Baxtin Problem," 92).

53. In "The Politics of Representation," Holquist's projected title is still *The Architectonics of Responsibility* (171).

54. We quote from pt. 4 of Nina Perlina's unpublished manuscript, "Funny Things Are Happening on the Way to the Bakhtin Forum," written while she was a fellow at the Kennan Institute in 1986–87; it will appear in *Kennan Occasional Papers* in 1988.

55. Jorge Luis Borges, "Tlön, Uqbar, Orbis Tertius," *Labyrinths: Selected Stories and Other Writings,* ed. Donald A. Yates and James E. Irby (New York: New Directions, 1964), 13.

56. Once one accepts that the relations were dialogic, another question, which we do not address here, comes into view: What are the differences between Voloshinov's and Medvedev's "monologizations" of Bakhtin and between their versions of Marxist poetics?

57. Hutcheon criticizes Morson for such an identification on p. 104 of her study, *A Theory of Parody,* from which the excerpt in the present volume is drawn.

58. Mikhail Bakhtin, "Discourse in the Novel," *The Dialogic Imagination: Four Essays by M. M. Bakhtin,* ed. Michael Holquist, trans. Caryl Emerson and Michael Holquist (Austin: University of Texas Press, 1981), 296. References in the text are to "Discourse."

59. See the first edition of the Dostoevsky book: M. M. Bakhtin, *Problemy tvorchestva Dostoevskogo* (Leningrad: Priboi, 1929), 38–41. References in the text are to PTD.

60. This argument is retained in the more familiar 1963 edition; see PDP, 24–28.

61. A reader of Bakhtin, and especially of Dostoevsky, might be tempted to reply that to focus on torture may also be to sentimentalize. Dostoevsky was also aware that victims, as well as victimizers, may participate in the sentimentalization of their own pain. If we indulge "the imagination of disaster," as Lionel Trilling observed, "we may come to assume that evil is equivalent to reality and may even come, in some distant and unconscious way, to honor it as such." See Trilling, "*Anna*

Karenina," in *Critical Essays on Tolstoy,* ed. Edward Wasiolek (Boston: G. K. Hall, 1986), 147.

62. "In rhetoric there is the unconditionally innocent and the unconditionally guilty; there is complete victory and destruction of the opponent. In dialogue the destruction of the opponent destroys that very dialogic sphere where the word lives" ("Notes," SG, 150).

Parody, History, and Metaparody

1. The significance and dynamics of the "environment" in which literature is written and read are discussed in Boris M. Ejxenbaum, "Literary Environment," in *Readings in Russian Poetics: Formalist and Structuralist Views,* ed. Ladislav Matejka and Krystyna Pomorska (Cambridge, Mass.: MIT Press, 1971), 56–65.

2. See esp. Mikhail Bakhtin, *Problems of Dostoevsky's Poetics,* trans. R. W. Rotsel (Ann Arbor: Ardis, 1973), 150–227 (henceforth PDP), and V. N. Volosinov, *Marxism and the Philosophy of Language* (henceforth *Marxism*), trans. Ladislav Matejka and I. R. Titunik (New York: Seminar, 1973), 109–59.

3. On imitation in the broader sense, and its relation to other forms of intertextuality, see Thomas M. Greene, *The Light in Troy: Imitation and Discovery in Renaissance Poetry* (New Haven: Yale University Press, 1982).

An interesting case of intertextuality is Pushkin's play *The Covetous Knight (Scenes from Chenstone's Tragi-comedy "The Covetous Knight")* — the subtitle in English in the original — a work which does not, on closer inspection, appear to be the imitation it claims to be. Assuming that Chenstone is William Shenstone, scholars have been unable to locate any Shenstone play by that title; and a number have concluded that Pushkin was deliberately engaging in "mystification," as the Soviet editors of the Jubilee edition (Moscow: Academia, 1936; 3:464) put it. They suspect an attempt to forestall interpretation of the play as a fictionalization of Pushkin's miserly father; Pushkin's characteristic metaliterary playfulness, it seems to me, may also be involved. A sort of inverse forgery, Pushkin's play does not pretend, as a forgery does, to be original when it is not, but rather to be *un*original when it is not.

4. Here again, I am identifying a class, not defining a word: the *word* 'parody,' it might be noted, also has a history of usage that does *not* entail discrediting an original (e.g., in music).

5. For example, Gilbert Highet defines parody as "imitation which, through distortion and exaggeration, evokes amusement, derision, and

sometimes scorn" (*The Anatomy of Satire* [Princeton: Princeton University Press, 1962], 69). *The Princeton Encyclopedia of Poetics* (ed. Alex Preminger, 2d ed. [Princeton: Princeton University Press, 1974]) first distinguishes between "comic p., which is close to burlesque, and literary or critical p., which follows more closely a given author's style or a particular work of art. . . . Critical p. has been defined as the exaggerated imitation of a work of art." An essay in *Poetics Today* (Ziva Ben-Porat, "Method in *Mad*ness," *PT*, 1, no. 1 – 2) defines parody as an "alleged representation, usually comic, of a literary text or other artistic object — i.e. a representation of a 'modelled reality,' which is itself already a particular representation of an original 'reality' " (247).

Neither Christopher Stone (*Parody* [London: Martin Secker, n.d.]), nor Leonard Feinberg (*An Introduction to Satire* [Ames: Iowa State University Press, 1967]), nor Dwight Macdonald (in the appendix to *Parodies: An Anthology from Chaucer to Beerbohm — and After,* ed. Dwight Macdonald [New York: Random House, 1960]) defines parody, but all seem to agree that it is a form of satire and that a good definintion "at least brings in humor" (Macdonald, *Parodies,* 557).

Russian Formalists (Shklovsky, Tynyanov, and some of their successors) have tended to waffle between definitions in terms of textual features — "devices" and devices that bare devices — and characterizations in terms of social function, the approach of the present study. Sander L. Gilman (*The Parodic Sermon in European Perspective: Aspects of Liturgical Parody from the Middle Ages to the Twentieth Century* [Wiesbaden: Franz Steiner, 1974]), who defines parody as "a literary form which is created by incorporating elements of an already existing form in a manner creating a conscious contrast," insists that features present in the text itself — the objective "description of form" rather than necessarily subjective interpretations of "motivation" or reception — must be the basis of a definition: ". . . parody can not be defined by the ends which it is thought to achieve. . . . As a workable literary term it can only be limited by a factual description of the means employed by the author" (2 – 3). I much prefer Dr. Johnson's definition: "a kind of writing in which the words of an author or his thoughts are taken and by a slight change adapted to some new purpose" (cited by Macdonald, *Parodies,* 557), which does not mention literariness or humor and does mention purpose.

6. Tynyanov's most extensive considerations of parody and its relation to literary evolution are "Dostoevskii i Gogol' (k teorii parodii)" and "O parodii," in *Poetika, istoriia literatury, kino* (Moscow: Nauka, 1977), 198 – 226, 284 – 309. The quotation is at 226.

7. As cited in Louis L. Martz, *The Poetry of Meditation: A Study of English Religious Literature of the Seventeenth Century*, 2nd ed. (New Haven: Yale University Press, 1962), 179. See the discussion of sacred parody, 184–93.

8. Henry Fielding, *"Joseph Andrews" and "Shamela"*, ed. Martin Battestin (Boston: Houghton Mifflin, 1961), from the preface to *Joseph Andrews*, 12.

9. Macdonald also includes a section of "unconscious self-parodies."

10. Leo N. Tolstoy, *What Is Art?*, trans. Aylmer Maude (New York: Bobbs-Merrill, 1960), 162.

11. For example, in Highet, *Anatomy of Satire*, 69.

12. Although I shall be primarily concerned with literary anti-genres, it should be noted that there are nonliterary anti-genres as well. Moreover, it is possible for a target genre to be nonliterary and its parody to be literary (or the reverse); and either may be literary in one period and nonliterary in another. In principle, all combinations are possible. To take a few examples, both mock epic and epic are literary; medieval parodic grammars and liturgies and their targets would seem to have been nonliterary; the parodic sermon has, like its target, changed its status, perhaps more than once. It should also be noted that the generalizations I offer regarding "classic texts" and "exemplars" in a *written* literary tradition would probably have to be modified for *oral* literary anti-genres.

On medieval parodic grammars and liturgies, see Mikhail Bakhtin, *Rabelais and His World*, trans. Helene Iswolsky (Cambridge, Mass.: MIT Press, 1968), 84–86. On the parodic sermon, see Gilman, *The Parodic Sermon* (n. 5 above).

13. *The Portable Swift*, ed. Carl Van Doren (New York: Viking Press, 1948), 403.

14. On the themes of anti-utopianism and "novelness" in Dostoevsky, see Michael Holquist, *Dostoevsky and the Novel* (Princeton: Princeton University Press, 1977). A paperback reprint is available from Northwestern University Press.

15. Bakhtin links these parodies to parodic social rituals, especially carnival, in *Rabelais and His World* (n. 12 above).

16. Ambrose Bierce, *The Devil's Dictionary* (New York: Dover Books, 1958).

17. Samuel Johnson, *Rasselas, Poems, and Selected Prose*, ed. Bertrand H. Bronson (New York: Holt Rinehart, 1958), 212–16.

18. Ibid., 233–34.

19. Mikhail Bakhtin, "Forms of Time and of the Chronotope in the Novel: Notes toward a Historical Poetics," *The Dialogic Imagination: Four Essays by M. M. Bakhtin*, ed. Michael Holquist, trans. Caryl

Emerson and Michael Holquist (Austin: University of Texas Press, 1981), 90.

20. A. S. Pushkin, *Polnoe sobranie sochinenii v desiati tomakh*, 4th ed. (Leningrad: Nauka, 1977), vol. 4, 19 (canto I, lines 460–61).

21. Mikhail Lermontov, *A Hero of Our Time*, trans. Martin Parker (Moscow: Foreign Languages, n.d.), 66.

22. Jorge Luis Borges, *Labyrinths: Selected Stories and Other Writings*, ed. Donald A. Yates and James E. Kirby, 2nd ed. (New York: New Directions, 1964), 13.

23. V. Shklovskii, "Evgenii Onegin (Pushkin i Stern)," in *Ocherki po poetike Pushkina* (Berlin: Epokha, 1923), 197–220.

24. My interpretation of the rhetorical paradox and of *The Praise of Folly* follows Walter Kaiser, *Praisers of Folly: Erasmus, Rabelais, Shakespeare* (Cambridge, Mass.: Harvard University Press, 1963); and Rosalie L. Colie, *Paradoxia Epidemica: The Renaissance Tradition of Paradox* (Princeton: Princeton University Press, 1966).

25. Desiderius Erasmus, *Moriae Encomium, or The Praise of Folly*, trans. Harry Carter (New York: Heritage, n.d.), 5–6.

26. The paradoxicalist of *The Possessed*, Kirillov, argues that the free individual is *bound* to show his or her self-will, that only the extremes of denial and atheism can be evidence of true faith, and that life only makes sense after a senseless act of suicide—that is, by an act of self-destruction that repeats the self-canceling logic of paradox.

Modern Parody and Bakhtin

1. Robert H. Brower and Earl Miner, *Japanese Court Poetry* (Stanford: Stanford University Press, 1961), 14–15.

2. See Karl Malkoff, "Allusion as Irony: Pound's Use of Dante in *Hugh Selwyn Mauberley*," *Minnesota Review* 7:81–88.

3. Walter Siegmund-Schultze, "Das Zitat im zeitgenossischen Musikschaffen: eine produktivschopferische Traditionslinie?," *Musik und Gesellschaft*, 27 (2) (1977), 73–78.

4. Cited in Donald Jay Grout, *A History of Western Music*, 3d ed. (New York: Norton, 1980), 748.

5. Cf. Peter Altmann, *Sinfonia von Luciano Berio: eine analytische Studie* (Vienna: Universal, 1977).

6. Felix Vodička, "The History of the Echo of Literary Works" in *A Prague School Reader on Esthetics, Literary Structure, and Style*, trans. and ed. Paul L. Garvin (Washington, DC: Georgetown University Press, 1964), 80.

7. Robert P. Morgan, "On the Analysis of Recent Music," *Critical Inquiry* 4 (1977): 50.

8. John Barth, "The Literature of Exhaustion," *Atlantic* (August 1967), 98–133.

9. M. M. Bachtine, *Esthétique et théorie du roman*, trans. Daria Olivier (Paris: Gallimard, 1978), 229–33.

10. Leo Steinberg, "The Glorious Company" in Jean Lipman and Richard Marshall, *Art about Art* (New York: Dutton, 1978), 21.

11. See Lipman and Marshall, *Art about Art*.

12. Richard Poirier, "The Politics of Self-Parody," *Partisan Review* 35, 339–53. Cf. Jürgen von Stackelberg, *Literarische Rezeptionsformen: Übersetzung, Supplement, Parodie* (Frankfurt: Athanäeum, 1972), 162.

13. Thomas M. Greene, *The Light in Troy: Imitation and Discovery in Renaissance Poetry* (New Haven: Yale University Press, 1982), 1.

14. Ibid., 46.

15. V. B. Grannis, *Dramatic Parody in Eighteenth-Century France* (New York: Publications of the Institute of French Studies, 1931).

16. Kenneth L. Moler, *Jane Austen's Art of Illusion* (Lincoln: University of Nebraska Press, 1968).

17. Henryk Markiewicz, "On the Definition of Literary Parody," in *To Honour Roman Jakobson* II (The Hague: Mouton, 1967), 1265.

18. Traugott Lawler, " 'Wafting Vapours from the Land of Dreams': Virgil's Fourth and Sixth Eclogues and the *Dunciad*," *Studies in English Literature 1500–1900* 14 (1974): 373–86.

19. Dean Frye, "The Question of Shakespearean 'Parody,' " *Essays in Criticism* 15 (1965): 22–26.

20. Charles Jencks, *Post-Modern Classicism: The New Synthesis* (London: Academy, 1980), 13.

21. Peter J. Rabinowitz, "Fictional Music: Toward a Theory of Listening" in *Theories of Reading, Looking and Listening*, ed. Harry R. Garvin (Lewisburg, Pa.: Bucknell University Press, 1981), 206n.

22. René Payant, "Bricolage pictural: l'art à propos de l'art; I—La Question de la citation," *Parachute* 16 (1979): 5–8; and Payant, "II—Citation et intertextualité," *Parachute* 18 (1980): 25–32.

23. René Magritte, *Ecrits complets*, ed. André Blavier (Paris: Flammarion, 1979).

24. Gary Saul Morson, *The Boundaries of Genre: Dostoevsky's "Diary of a Writer" and the Traditions of Literary Utopia* (Austin: University of Texas Press, 1981; reprint Evanston: Northwestern University Press, 1988), 48–49.

25. Bruce Alistair Barber, "Appropriation/Expropriation: Convention or Intervention," *Parachute* 33 (1983–84): 29–39.

26. Richard Foster, "Wilde as Parodist: A Second Look at *The Importance of Being Earnest*," *College English* 18 (1956): 18–23.

27. Ruth Bauerle, "A Sober Drunken Speech: Stephen's Parodies in 'The Oxen of the Sun,' " *James Joyce Quarterly* 5 (1967): 40–46.

28. Robert Boyle SJ, "Swiftian Allegory and Dantean Parody in Joyce's 'Grace,' " *James Joyce Quarterly* 7 (1970): 11–21.

29. Angus Easson, "Parody as Comment in James Joyce's 'Clay,' " *James Joyce Quarterly* 7 (1970): 75–81.

30. E. Courtney, "Parody and Literary Allusion in Menippean Satire," *Philologus* 106 (1962): 86–87.

31. Peter J. Rabinowitz, " 'What's Hecuba to us?': The Audience's Experience of Literary Borrowing," in *The Reader in the Text: Essays on Audience and Interpretation*, ed. Susan R. Suleiman and Inge Crossman, (Princeton: Princeton University Press, 1980), 241.

32. Jean Weisgerber, "The Use of Quotation in Recent Literature," *Comparative Literature* 22 (1970): 36–45.

33. For example, see Winfried Freund, *Die literarische Parodie* (Stuttgart: Metzler, 1981).

34. See Claude Abastado, "Situation de la parodie," *Cahiers du XXe Siècle* 6 (1976): 9–37; and Morson, *Boundaries,* 107 [beginning of selection in the present volume].

35. Shari Benstock, "At the Margin of Discourse: Footnotes in the Fictional Text," *PMLA* 98 (1983): 204–25.

36. Susan Stewart, *Nonsense: Aspects of Intertextuality in Folklore and Literature* (Baltimore: Johns Hopkins University Press, 1978, 1979), 185.

37. Robert Neumann, "Zur Ästhetik der Parodie," *Die Literatur* 30 (1927–28): 439–41.

38. Mikhail Bakhtin, *Rabelais and His World,* trans. Hélène Iswolsky (Cambridge, Mass.: MIT Press, 1968), 5. Subsequent references appear in the text.

39. Bachtine, *Esthétique,* 429.

40. Judith Priestman, "The Age of Parody: Literary Parody and Some Nineteenth Century Perspectives," Ph.D. dissertation (1980), University of Kent at Canterbury, 20.

41. Roland Barthes, *S/Z,* trans. Richard Miller (New York: Hill & Wang, 1974), 45.

42. Julia Kristeva, *Desire in Language,* trans. Thomas Gora, Alice Jardine, and Leon S. Roudiez (New York: Columbia University Press, 1980), 71.

43. Tuvia Shlonsky, "Literary Parody: Remarks on Its Method and Functions," in *Proceedings of the IVth Congress of the International Comparative Literature Association,* II, ed. François Jost, (The Hague: Mouton, 1966), 797–801.

44. Benjamin H. D. Buchloch, "Allegorical Procedures: Appropriation and Montage in Contemporary Art" in *Essays on [Performance] and the Cultural Politicization, Open Letter,* ed. Bruce Alistair Barber, 5th ser., nos. 5–6, 191.

45. Gérard Genette, *Introduction à l'architexte* (Paris: Seuil, 1979), 84.

46. See Harold Bloom, *The Anxiety of Influence: A Theory of Poetry* (New York: Oxford University Press, 1973); and Antoine Compagnon, *La Seconde Main ou le travail de la citation* (Paris: Seuil, 1979).

47. N. S. Josephson, "Kanon und Parodie: zu einigen Josquin-Nachahmungen," *Tijdschrifft der vereeniging voor nederlandsche muziekgeschiedanis* 25 (2) (1975): 23–32.

48. Owen Morgan and Alain Pagès, "Une pièce inconnue de Zola en 1879," *Zola: Thèmes et recherches (Cahiers de l'UGR Froissart)* 5 (1980): 91–98.

49. Harold Rosenthal and John Warrack, *Dictionary of Music* (London: Oxford University Press, 1964), 301–2.

50. Roland Barthes, *Critical Essays,* trans. Richard Howard (Evanston: Northwestern University Press, 1972), 119.

51. Ronald Sukenick, "Twelve Digressions toward a Study of Composition," *New Literary History* 6 (1975): 429–37.

52. Robert Hughes, *The Shock of the New: Art and the Century of Change* (London: BBC, 1980), 324.

53. Shlonsky, "Literary Parody," 801.

Dialogue and Dialogism

1. Michael Holquist, ed., *The Dialogic Imagination: Four Essays by M. M. Bakhtin,* trans. Caryl Emerson and Michael Holquist (Austin: University of Texas Press, 1981); Tzvetan Todorov, *Mikhail Bakhtine, le principe dialogique* with *Ecrits du cercle de Bakhtine* (Writings of the Bakhtin Circle), trans. Georges Philippenko (Paris: Seuil, 1981).

2. Leo Strauss, *Persecution and the Art of Writing* (Glencoe: Free Press, 1952), 36.

3. Bakhtin, *The Dialogic Imagination,* 354.

4. Ibid., 327–28.

5. Ibid., 278, 282.

Bakhtin and de Man

1. Such Marxist appropriations of Bakhtin have included Terry Eagleton, "Wittgenstein's Friends," *NLR* 135 (1982): 64–90; Allon White, "Bakhtin, Sociolinguistics and Deconstruction" in *The Theory of Reading*, ed. Frank Gloversmith (Brighton: Harvester, 1984), 123–46; and Alex Callinicos, "Postmodernism, Poststructuralism, Post-Marxism?" *Theory, Culture and Society* 2 (1985): 85–100. Poststructuralist appropriations include Robert Young, "Back to Bakhtin," *Cultural Critique* (Winter), 71–92; Wlad Godzich, "Foreword" to M. M. Bakhtin/P. M. Medvedev, *The Formal Method in Literary Scholarship*, trans. Albert Wehrle (Cambridge: Harvard University Press, 1985), vii–xiv. Graham Pechey offers a simultaneously Marxist and poststructuralist appropriation of Bakhtin in "Bakhtin, Marxism and Post-Structuralism," in *The Politics of Theory*, ed. Frances Barker et al. (Colchester: University of Essex Press, 1983), 234–45.

2. Paul de Man, *Blindness and Insight*, 2d ed. (Minneapolis: University of Minnesota Press, 1983), xxix–xxx. Further references cited in text as *BI*.

3. Paul de Man, *Allegories of Reading* (New Haven: Yale University Press, 1977), 299. Further references cited in text as *AR*.

4. This fragment is published in *Filisofiia i sotsiologiia nauki i tekhniki* (Moscow: Nauka, 1986) under the title "K filosofii postupka"; the editors consider this essay to predate the writing of *Avtor i geroi v esteticheskoi deiatel'nosti* (1922–24), which appears in Mikhail Bakhtin, *Estetika slovesnogo tvorchestva* (Moscow: Iskusstvo, 1979). Unfortunately, neither of these texts has as yet appeared in translation. Further references to "K filosofii postupka" will be cited in the text as *KFP*.

5. See Michael Zimmerman, *Eclipse of the Self: The Development of Heidegger's Concept of Authenticity* (Athens: Ohio University Press, 1981), 9, 15.

6. Martin Heidegger, *Being and Time*, cited in Paul Bové, *Destructive Poetics* (New York: Columbia University Press, 1980), 58. In his later writings Heidegger would progressively renounce the willful or voluntaristic aspect of this 'appropriation'; yet, as Bové argues, this aggressivity of interpretation is central to deconstructive hermeneutics.

7. Bakhtin's "other logic" is apparent in the very term *bytie-sobytie*, which suggests not only "being-as-event" but also "existence-as-coexistence"; unlike the Heideggerian event of Being as "being-uncovered-in-my-own-openness," Bakhtinian existence is purely *relational*.

8. Mikhail Bakhtin, "From Notes Made in 1970–71," in *Speech Genres and Other Late Essays*, ed. Michael Holquist, trans. Vern McGee

(Austin: University of Texas Press, 1986), 141. Further references to *Speech Genres* cited in text as *SG*.

9. According to the preface to *Blindness and Insight*, the first version of this essay was written in 1967.

10. Looking back on this essay more than a decade later, de Man will note that this new-found concept of rhetoricity, while "still uncomfortably intertwined with the thematic vocabulary of consciousness and temporality," nevertheless "signals a turn that, at least for me, has proven to be productive" (*BI*, xii).

11. Paul de Man, "Semiology and Rhetoric," *Allegories of Reading*, 19.

12. This point is discussed in Bové, *Destructive Poetics*, 80 – 81.

13. Paul de Man, "The Resistance to Theory," in *The Resistance to Theory* (Minneapolis: University of Minnesota Press, 1986), 17.

14. See esp."Problem of the Text" (*SG*, 110). The internal 'coherence' of the Bakhtin canon is, however, an issue very much open to discussion.

15. Mikhail Bakhtin, "Discourse in the Novel," in *The Dialogic Imagination*, ed. Michael Holquist, trans. Caryl Emerson and Michael Holquist (Austin: University of Texas Press, 1981), 278. Cited in text as *DI*.

16. Paul de Man, "Dialogue and Dialogism," in the present volume.

17. De Man, "The Resistance to Theory," 13.

Bakhtin's Tolstoy Prefaces

1. M. M. Bakhtin, "Predislovie. Dramaticheskie proizvedeniia L. Tolstogo," in L. N. Tolstoi, *Polnoe sobranie khudozhestvennykh proizvedenii* (Moscow-Leningrad, 1930), 11:iii – x. All references to the reprint in M. M. Bakhtin, *Literaturno-kriticheskie stat'i* (Moscow, 1986), 90 – 99. Referred to as Preface I.

2. M. M. Bakhtin, "Predislovie. (*Voskresenie* L. Tolstogo)," ibid., 13:iii – xx. All references to the reprint in M. M. Bakhtin, *Literaturno-kriticheskie stat'i*, 100 – 120. Referred to as Preface II.

On the prefaces, see K. Clark and M. Holquist, *Mikhail Bakhtin* (Cambridge and London, 1984), 154 – 156.

3. Preface I, 92.

4. Preface I, 96.

5. Ibid., 97.

6. Preface II, 100.

7. Ibid., 101.

8. Ibid., 101 – 2.

9. Ibid., 103, quoting V. I. Lenin, *Lev Tolstoi, kak zerkalo russkoi revoliutsii* (1908).

10. Ibid., 119, quoting G. V. Plekhanov, "Karl Marks i Lev Tolstoi," 1911.

11. Ibid., 108.

12. Ibid., 111.

13. Ibid., 119.

14. M. M. Bakhtin, *Problemy tvorchestva Dostoevskogo* (Leningrad: Priboi, 1929), 3–4.

15. *Problemy tvorchestva*, 213.

16. See, e.g., V. N. Voloshinov, *Marxism and the Philosophy of Language,* trans. L. Matejka and I. R. Titunik (Cambridge and London, 1986), 24: "The category of mechanical causality in explanations of ideological phenomena can most easily be surmounted on the grounds of philosophy of language." Or, in M. M. Bakhtin/P. M. Medvedev, *The Formal Method in Literary Scholarship,* trans. Albert J. Wehrle (Cambridge, Mass: Harvard University Press, 1985), 15: "Marxists often . . . move too quickly and too directly from the separate ideological phenomenon to conditions of the socio-economic environment. . . . It is just as naive to think that separate works, which have been snatched out of the unity of the ideological world, are in their isolation directly determined by economic factors as it is to think that a poem's rhymes and stanzas are fitted together according to economic causality."

17. For example, the works written before 1925: "Avtor i geroi v esteticheskoi deiatel'nosti," in M. M. Bakhtin, *Estetika slovesnogo tvorchestva* (Moscow: Iskusstvo, 1979); "K filosofii postupka," in *Filosofiia i sotsiologiia nauki i tekhniki* (Moscow: Nauka, 1986); and "Problema soderzhaniia, materiala i formy v slovesnom khudozhestvennom tvorchestve," in M. M. Bakhtin, *Voprosy literatury i estetiki* (Moscow: Khudozh. lit., 1975). [English titles of these articles are: "Author and Hero in Aesthetic Activity," "Toward a Philosophy of the Act," and "The Problem of Content, Material, and Form in Verbal Art." None are presently available in English translation; "Toward a Philosophy of the Act" is discussed at length in the introduction to the present volume.]

18. M. M. Bakhtin, *Problemy poetiki Dostoevskogo,* 2d ed. (Moscow: Sovetskii pisatel', 1963). A translation of this second edition is available as Mikhail Bakhtin, *Problems of Dostoevsky's Poetics,* ed. and trans. Caryl Emerson (Minneapolis: University of Minnesota Press, 1984).

19. Ibid., 61–62. English trans. from Emerson, 35–36.

20. Ibid., 63. English in Emerson, 36.

21. Preface I, 96.

22. Ibid.

23. Preface II, 118.

24. Ibid., 111.

25. See Clark and Holquist, 154–55.

26. Ibid., chap. 5, "Religious Activities and the Arrest."

27. This newspaper report is quoted in Pamyat', *Istoricheskii sbornik* (Paris, 1981), 4:273–74.

28. Ibid., 265.

29. "Avtor i geroi," 126.

30. Ibid., 126–127.

31. Ibid., 127. This Gospel saying is one of the sources for the Jesus Prayer ("Lord Jesus Christ, have mercy on me a sinner") which would have been well known to Bakhtin as an Orthodox Christian.

32. Ibid., 127.

33. Ibid., 112.

34. Preface I, 99.

35. Preface II, 117.

36. The epigraphs are:

"Then Peter came up and said to him, 'Lord, how often shall my brother sin against me, and I forgive him? As many as seven times?' Jesus said to him, 'I do not say to you seven times, but seventy times seven' " (Matt. 18:21–22).

"Why do you see the speck that is in your brother's eye, but do not notice the log that is in your own eye?" (Matt. 7:3).

"Let he who is without sin cast the first stone" (John 8:7).

"A disciple is not above his teacher, but everyone when he is fully taught will be like his teacher" (Luke 6:40).

See L. N. Tolstoi, *Voskresenie* (Moscow, 1948).

37. Matt. 18:1–6, 11–14, 21–33. Also Matt. 6:33. It is interesting that from Matt. 18, Tolstoy omits precisely those verses which are concerned with forgiveness through the Church. *Voskresenie*, 453–55, 456–57.

38. Preface II, 117.

39. *Voskresenie*, 455.

40. *Voskresenie*, 457–58.

41. Ibid., 458.

42. Luke 17:21. This phrase has been much debated: recent biblical scholars prefer the translation "among" to "within" for the Greek *entos*. However, it was in the tradition of the Eastern Church to understand the meaning as "within," and this rendering obviously suited Bakhtin's purposes best at this time.

43. Preface II, 117–18, quoting *Voskresenie*, 455–56.

44. Clark and Holquist, 140, 142.

45. Ibid., 140.
46. "Avtor i geroi," 38.
47. "Iz zapisei 1970–71 gg." in *Estetika,* 343.

The Tolstoy Connection in Bakhtin

1. M. M. Bakhtin, *Problemy tvorchestva Dostoevskogo* (Problems of Dostoevsky's Art) (Leningrad: Priboi, 1929). A second and much expanded edition was published in 1963 under a different title: *Problemy poetiki Dostoevskogo* (Problems of Dostoevsky's Poetics), 2d ed. (Moscow: Sovetskii pisatel', 1963). An English translation of the 1963 edition is available: M. M. Bakhtin, *Problems of Dostoevsky's Poetics,* ed. and trans. Caryl Emerson (Minneapolis: University of Minnesota Press, 1984). Subsequent references to these editions will be to *Problemy* (1929) or *Problems* (1963 in 1984 trans.).

2. This emphasis constitutes one of the major distinctions between the first and second editions of Bakhtin's book on Dostoevsky. The 1929 original is a monograph on Dostoevsky the novelist; in the 1963 revision Bakhtin sees Dostoevsky as a sort of metaphysical threshold, a watershed in novelistic consciousness. This view is evident, for example, in a fragment from M. M. Bakhtin, "Iz zapisei 1970–1971 godov" (From Notes of 1970–71), 336–73 in *Estetika slovesnogo tvorchestva* (The aesthetics of verbal art) (Moscow: Iskusstvo, 1979), 343:

Pechorin, for all his complexity and contradictoriness, seems integrated and naive when compared with Stavrogin. Pechorin has not tasted from the Tree of Knowledge. No heroes of Russian literature prior to Dostoevsky had tasted from the Tree of Knowledge of Good and Evil. Within the bounds of their novels, therefore, one could still find naive and integrated poetry, lyric, poetic landscape. They (the pre-Dostoevskian heroes) still had access to pieces (little corners) of earthly paradise, from which Dostoevsky's heroes are exiled once and forever.

These notes, written near the end of Bakhtin's life, are now available in English in M. M. Bakhtin, *Speech Genres and Other Late Essays,* trans. Vern W. McGee, ed. Caryl Emerson and Michael Holquist (Austin: University of Texas Press, 1986). Subsequent references will be to "Iz zapisei," and page numbers will refer to the Russian edition. Unless otherwise noted, all translations are mine.

3. Perhaps the earliest comprehensive statement of the Tolstoy-vs.-Dostoevsky paradigm was Dmitri Merezhkovski's *L. Tolstoi i Dostoevskii* (1900), which set up a model that was to have considerable staying power: Tolstoy is the pantheist and pagan, a "seer of the flesh," while

Dostoevsky is the great mystical Christian, a "seer of the soul." For an adequate survey in English of the positions of early influential critics, see Vladimir Seduro, *Dostoevski in Russian Literary Criticism, 1846 – 1956* (New York: Octagon Books, 1969), esp. the sections on Merezhkovski, Rozanov, Vyacheslav Ivanov, and Veresayev.

4. The phrase is from V. V. Veresayev, whose *Zhivaia zhizn'* (1911) was one of the founding works in the Tolstoy-Dostoevsky tradition. Dostoevsky, according to Veresayev, was indifferent to nature, obsessed by the sick and dying, and given to creating characters enslaved by logic. To all this the antidote was Tolstoy.

5. M. M. Bakhtin, "Forms of Time and Chronotope in the Novel," in *The Dialogic Imagination: Four Essays by M. M. Bakhtin*, ed. Michael Holquist, trans. Caryl Emerson and Michael Holquist (Austin: University of Texas Press, 1981), 249.

6. For an excellent discussion of this aspect of Tolstoy's discourse, drawing heavily on Bakhtin, see Gary Saul Morson, "Tolstoy's Absolute Language," *Critical Inquiry* 7 (1981): 667 – 87, esp. 667 – 76.

7. The Russian word for unity, *edinstvo* (from *odin/edin*, "one"), has caused Bakhtin's readers and translators some difficulty. In Bakhtin's usage the word does *not* mean unity in the sense of a fusion or conflation of discrete parts; rather, it refers more to the unit-y of something, to the fact that living wholes form an irreplaceable unit from which no part can be extracted or abstracted without violating its integrity (its responsible position in the world).

8. The essay was written in 1862, when Tolstoy was deeply involved in peasant schools on his estate. During that year, in the pages of *Sovremennik*, Tolstoy conducted a sharp polemic with Chernyshevsky on the issues of educational hierarchy, preestablished curricula, and the common people's access to universities (and yet how essentially hierarchical Tolstoy's alternative appears). See Boris Eikhenbaum, *Tolstoi in the Sixties*, trans. Duffield White (Ann Arbor: Ardis Books, 1982), 47 – 71.

9. Portions of this essay were published posthumously as "Avtor i geroi v esteticheskoi deiatel'nosti" (Author and hero in aesthetic activity) in *Estetika slovesnogo tvorchestva* (see n. 2 above). A translation by Vadim Liapunov is forthcoming from the University of Texas Press. Subsequent references to this essay will be to the Russian text, "Avtor."

10. Nina Perlina develops this possibility, using Martin Buber to "restore" the theological component of Bakhtin's system that could not receive overt expression under Soviet conditions. See Nina Perlina, "Bakhtin and Buber: The Concept of Dialogic Discourse," *Studies in Twentieth Century Literature* 9 (1984): 13 – 28.

11. See "Discourse in the Novel," in *Dialogic Imagination* (n. 5 above), 344.

12. See Vyacheslav Ivanov, "Dostoevskii i roman-tragediia," in *Borozdy i mezhi* (Furrows and boundaries) (Moscow: Musaget, 1916), 5–60; and Ivanov's *Freedom and the Tragic Life: A Study in Dostoevsky,* trans. Norman Cameron (New York: Noonday, 1951). In the latter Ivanov says, "Clearly this mode of thought is not based upon theoretical cognition, with its constant antithesis of subject and object, but upon an act of will and faith. . . . Dostoevsky has coined for this a word of his own, *proniknovenie,* which properly means 'intuitive seeing through' or 'spiritual penetration' " (26–27). For an expanded treatment, see the Russian text, 32–34.

13. It is important to understand that the Russian word *ogranichennyi* (delimited), as it is used by Bakhtin, denotes not the negative sense that "limited" has in English but the hopeful sense of "*de*limited," outlined in time and space, and therefore capable of having a point of view and generating value (34–35). Elsewhere in "Avtor" Bakhtin develops the familiar distinction between "spirit" (*dukh*) and "soul" (*dusha*): a soul, "I-for-another," is shaped in me and given final form by another, while spirit, "I-for-myself," is my self as I experience it, eternally unfinished and open to change (116–18). "The soul is the gift of my spirit to the other" (116).

14. Bakhtin, "Discourse in the Novel," in *Dialogic Imagination* (see n. 5 above), 398.

15. Leo Tolstoy, *What Is Art?,* trans. Aylmer Maude (New York: Bobbs, 1960), 140. We have secondhand evidence that Bakhtin lectured on "What Is Art" to high school students in Vitebsk (see n. 23). According to Mirkina's class notes, Bakhtin had this to say of Tolstoy's treatise: "In those places where Tolstoy strives to prove the rightness of his own views he is weak, he premeditatedly distorts, and he does not wish to understand the artists he has rejected. But moving on to the theory of empathy, he develops this theory very profoundly, although he discovers anew what had been discovered before him by Lipps" (Mirkina, 265). The German philosopher and psychologist Theodor Lipps (1851–1914) is mentioned several times by Bakhtin as a proponent of "expressive aesthetics" in "Avtor," 56–72.

16. On *Resurrection,* see "Discourse in the Novel," 344; on the end of *War and Peace,* see "Problema soderzhania, materiala i forma v slovesnom khudozhestvennom tvorchestve" (The problem of content, material, and form in verbal art), in M. M. Bakhtin, *Voprosy literatury i estetiki* (Moscow: Khudozhestvennaia literatura, 1975), 6–71.

17. In her work on this topic, Ann Shukman suggests that the Tol-

stoy prefaces are not single- but decidedly double-voiced. She points out that although these essays are among the most sociological and Marxist of Bakhtin's "own name" writings, they deal with works—the dramas and the novel *Resurrection*—that embody Tolstoy's most explicitly Christian and anarchic aspects. In an officially orthodox society Tolstoy denounced the church and invited excommunication; in an officially atheist state Bakhtin embraced the church and invited arrest. Shukman sees an overlap between Tolstoy's and Bakhtin's biographies, in the life they led as well as in the life to which they aspired. Both men were faced with the problem of sustaining belief without the institution of the church. She also sees a parallel between Tolstoy's spiritual quest, reflected in the evolution of his peasant heroes, and the fate of Bakhtin himself. For each, the dominant image became that of a wandering ascetic. If read in the guarded light of Bakhtin's religious views, the prefaces are indeed double-voiced and partly parodic texts. The prefaces, while posing as obedient exercises in monologizing Tolstoy, are perhaps also an encoded tribute to the dialogue (at times gracious, at times deadly) that both Tolstoy and Bakhtin conducted with their respective cultures. A later version of Shukman's essay was published as "Bakhtin and Tolstoy," *Studies in Twentieth Century Literature* 9 (1984): 57–74, half of which is reprinted in the present volume. Bakhtin's prefaces may be found in L. Tolstoy, *Polnoe sobranie khudozhestvennykh proizvedeneii* (Complete collected literary works), ed. Khalabaev and Eikhenbaum (Leningrad: Pechatnyi dvor, 1929), 11: iii–x, 13: iii–xx, and are translated as an Appendix to the present volume.

18. This point has been ably argued in the West under less trying political conditions. See, e.g., Gary Saul Morson, "Socialist Realism and Literary Theory," *Journal of Aesthetics and Art Criticism* 38 (1979): 121–33, where Tolstoy's aesthetics are reviewed in the context of Soviet official literature.

19. "Drafts for an Introduction" [Draft 3], Leo Tolstoy, *War and Peace*, ed. George Gibian (New York: Norton, 1966), 1365.

20. For a good treatment of Tolstoy's "expressivist" vision of the self and its origins in Rousseau and Herder, see Patricia Carden, "The Expressive Self in *War and Peace*," *Canadian-American Slavic Studies* 12 (1978): 519–34. For an instructive contrast, see Bakhtin's critique of "expressive aesthetics" in "Avtor," 55–81. For the sort of sensitive and profound attention to language constraints, inner monologue, and dialogic processes in Tolstoy that Bakhtin was unable or unwilling to provide, see Lidiia Ginzburg, *O psikhologicheskoi proze* (Leningrad: Khudozhestvennaia literatura, 1977), 317–68. It should be noted, however, that Ginzburg (as a student of Yuri Tynianov) is sympathetic to the

structuralist thinking of mature Formalism; she ultimately defines the Tolstoyan self as a system organized by a "dominant" and prefers to work with personality types as codes. Both stances were uncongenial to Tolstoy, and (in my view) to Bakhtin as well.

21. Gary Saul Morson, "Structures of Self in Dostoevsky and Tolstoy" (paper presented at the Midwest Slavic Conference, Columbus, Ohio, May 1984), 5. Tolstoy's radical contingency and its governing influence on his understanding of psychology, history, and narrative are the subject of Morson's *Hidden in Plain View: Narrative and Creative Potentials in "War and Peace"* (Stanford: Stanford University Press, 1987). The paper "Structures of Self" is integrated into chap. 7 of that book.

22. E. A. Maimin, *Pushkin: Zhizn' i tvorchestvo* (Pushkin: life and works) (Moscow: Nauka, 1981), 150–51.

23. Bakhtin's lectures have not survived, but notes on these lectures were made by one of his students, R. M. Mirkina (whose words are quoted here). From her summary, it appears that Bakhtin read a number of Tolstoy's early and late works (but not the great novels of the middle period) in terms of "I-for-myself" and "I-for-another." See R. M. Mirkina, "Konspekty lektsii M. M. Bakhtina" (Notes from Lectures by M. M. Bakhtin). *Prometei: Istoriko-biograficheskii almanach 12* (1980): 257–68, esp. 265.

24. M. M. Bakhtin, "Toward a Reworking," in *Problems* (see n. 1 above), 287, 288.

Coerced Speech and the Oedipus Dialogue Complex

1. Ian Watt, *The Rise of the Novel* (London: Chatto & Windus, 1957).

2. Robert Louis Stevenson, in "A Humble Remonstrance," quietly rejected the idea that fiction can mimic life's density, or achieve a full realism, and argued instead that the novelist as a conscious craftsman looks for formal limits, for instance the "invention (yes, invention) and preservation of a certain key in dialogue." He was in this essay dissenting (humbly) from Henry James's ambitious sense of the scope of fiction, but was at the same time to a great degree sharing James's own formalism, since James himself tended to see actual social dialogue as a kind of formless chaos, passively mirrored in the "deluge of dialogue" in popular novels. James wanted to make dialogue a steady vehicle of the action. See Robert Louis Stevenson, *Virginibus Puerisque and Other Papers* (New York: Scribners, 1918), p. 347; also, see the Preface to *The Awkward Age,* where James makes important comments on the chaos of dialogue. In the lecture "The Question of Our Speech" (Boston: Hough-

ton Mifflin, 1905), James describes common speech as a near chaos — but James's own sentences reflect on, rather than reject, that chaos. L. C. Knights, in *Explorations 3* (Pittsburgh: University of Pittsburgh Press, 1976), 24–37, argues that the main theme in James's work is "domination," and that the theme is embodied in speech and dialogue *forms* (his italics). He does not go on to say what the forms are. The domination, "pressure and coercion," in Knights's version of James's dialogue, however, have to do with themes and issues the characters discuss, not with speaking itself. The plain dramatic coercion to speak found in Scott and Conrad is unusual in James, whose scenes are generally "conversations," and whose characters, with few exceptions, want talk. Domination is apparent between them, not in primary struggle about the production of speech itself, although *The Bostonians* may be a partial exception.

3. See Mark Lambert, *Dickens and the Suspended Quotation* (New Haven: Yale University Press, 1981).

4. Stanley Rosen, *Plato's Symposium* (New Haven: Yale University Press, 1974); Kenneth Burke, *A Rhetoric of Motives* (Berkeley: University of California Press, 1969); Gilbert Pyle, *Plato's Progress* (Cambridge: Cambridge University Press, 1966).

5. *The Confidence-Man* tries to define the typical American *dialogue* scene — not exactly the same thing as the typical rhetorical scene Sacvan Bercovitch has described as jeremiad (or intense moral criticism covertly reinforcing the idea of the chosen people). The study of American dialogue and its literary representation would have to consider events such as religious meetings and talk shows. James's portrait of the precocious, ecstatic public speeches of Verena Tarrant in *The Bostonians,* and of her ambiguous forced rescue from their "phoniness" via dialogues with Basil Ransom, is one example.

6. Joseph Conrad, "Certain Aspects of the Admirable Inquiry," the Canterbury Edition of the *Complete Works* (Garden City, N.Y.: Doubleday, Page & Co., 1924), 234.

7. Gerard Jean-Aubry, *Joseph Conrad: Life and Letters,* 2 vols. (Garden City, N.Y.: Doubleday, 1927), 1:258.

8. An eloquent statement of this negative rule for the world's dialogue can be found in Leopardi's *Pensieri XXI*, which argues that since "in speaking, we feel no real or lasting pleasure unless we are allowed to speak of ourselves," it follows that the best company is that which "we have most bored," and that there are, in the universal disproportional dialogue (though this "idea of dialogue" does not shape his lyric poems), only two types of speaker, "the amiable man" who listens and the "egotistical man" who talks. See *Leopardi: Poems and Prose,* ed. Angel Flo-

res (Bloomington: Indiana University Press, 1966), 244. See also Alexandre Lazarides, *Valéry: Pour une poétique du dialogue* (Montreal: University of Montreal Press, 1978), 9–53. "La communication ne s'établit . . . que si l' 'inégalité est supposée' " (12).

9. Richard Ohmann, "Reflections on Class and Language," *The Radical Teacher*, no. 20 (n.d.), 19–22. Ohmann refers to and criticizes the work of Basil Bernstein (also criticized by Goodman) and Claus Mueller on disproportion in dialogue between classes.

10. Gilbert Ryle, *Plato's Progress* (Cambridge: Cambridge University Press, 1966). See especially chap. 4, "Dialectic," and chap. 6, "The Disappearance of the Eristic Dialogue," for discussions of Plato's dialogues as immersed in a social context of "force." Ryle's hypothesis is that Plato at first practiced, and later sublimated, the "force" of eristic dialogue, in which speakers try to drive each other into elenchus, or self-contradiction. The state, he says, itself at some point forcibly stopped the real practice, and the censorship was fruitful: "What forced Plato to find out the secret of solitary debating was the suppressing of his practice of conducting eristic Moots . . . He became a philosopher because he could no longer participate in questioner-answerer Moots, or any longer be their dramatic chronicler. No longer had the Other Voice to be the voice of another person" (208–9). That is, philosophy is sublimated forced dialogue. Ryle uses the term *force* often to describe Athenian dialogue scenes, and less quietistically than, for example, J. L. Austin, writing of "illocutionary force"; but of course he makes no cultural connection to Oedipus as the dramatic inquisitor and speech-forcer.

11. See, for example, the Last Supper in Hölderlin's "Patmos." *Friedrich Hölderlin: Poems and Fragments,* trans. Michael Hamburger (London: Routledge & Kegan Paul, 1966). Jesus' speech there is a continuous goodness that generates future speech as plenitude: "Vieles wäre zu sagen davon" (466), the poem says of Jesus' talk and death, "Much could be said of [from] it" (477). Hölderlin's own continuous syntax in this poem is itself meant to be regenerated, a continuation of Jesus' speech as the inexhaustible source of further speech in time.

12. See *The Red Badge of Courage,* chap. 3, for a brief example of speeches clustered together.

13. Bakhtin, *Problems of Dostoevsky's Poetics,* trans. R. W. Rotsel (Ann Arbor, Mich.: Ardis, 1973), 91: "Syncrisis was understood as the juxtaposition of various points of view . . . Anacrisis consisted of the means of eliciting and provoking the words of one's interlocutor, forcing him to express his opinion, and express it fully. Socrates was a great master of the anacrisis; he was able to force people to *speak,* i.e., to put into words their hazy, but stubborn, pre-formed opinions, elucidating

them by means of the word (and not by means of the plot situation as in the 'Menippean satire')." Bakhtin's emphasis on verbal, physically nonviolent coercion in his definition of *anacrisis* is not shared by the dictionaries. See, for example, *Webster's Third:* "an investigation of truth in a civil law case in which the interrogation and inquiry are often accompanied by torture." In New Testament Greek dictionaries the word seems to imply *preliminary* examination — what leads up to (*ana*) the crisis of the trial itself. Bakhtin's sublimation here of the term *anacrisis* into Socratic nonviolence is curious, since he is otherwise not usually finicky about physical life, the body, or violence. In this context the possible psychoanalytic explanation is that he is repressing, in a different way from Ryle, the connection between coercion to speak and the figure of Oedipus. Oedipus, unlike Socrates, gets others to speak by *both* verbal provocation and the threat of physical violence. In this light, Socrates' rich humor stems from his mock denial that he forces the other to speak: he does it all gently and slyly. From one perspective at least, both Oedipus and Socrates cause their own downfalls by following through — by continuing to press the inquiry and to make others speak — even after it becomes clearly dangerous to do so. Ryle argues that Plato himself was punished for conducting eristic debates — for being a speech-forcer — and that this aspect of Socrates' self-portrait in the *Apology* really belongs to Plato; but of course Ryle sees no connection to Oedipus here. The punishment of the speech-forcer is not for Bakhtin or Ryle a specific pattern: but the punished speech-forcer may indeed be a classical figure, first Oedipal and then Socratic, whom Conrad imports into the novel.

14. See Frederick Marryat, *The Phantom Ship,* in *The Works of Captain Marryat,* vol. 14 (New York: Peter Fenelon Collier, n.d.), chap. 36, and the opening chapters of *The Little Savage,* in *The Works of Captain Marryat,* vol. 17.

15. See, for example, Mickey Spillane's anticommunist novel *One Lonely Night* (New York: Signet, 1951). The paperback cover shows a naked woman hanging by her wrists. Forced questioning is of course frequent in detective novels but is also often the motif on the cover.

16. See the French translation of Bakhtin's study already cited in English: *Problèmes de la poétique de Dostoevski,* trans. Guy Verret (Lausanne: Éditions de l'Age d'Homme, 1970), 133. The phrase *rire resorbé* is clearer than its English equivalents, "reabsorbed laughter" or "muffled laughter"; it means that serious works steal or absorb comic ingredients while suppressing the laughter.

17. "The police, in the course of a persistent inquiry, could find not a single document compromising him, nor did they wrest any useful

information from him." Eloise Knapp Hay, *The Political Novels of Joseph Conrad* (Chicago: University of Chicago Press, 1963), 41.

18. Borys Conrad, *My Father: Joseph Conrad* (New York: Coward-McCann, 1970), 11–12, describes silence as the first rule in the family. Ford (*Joseph Conrad,* 21) describes how Conrad listened to him read their collaborative work aloud: "For the first chapter or two . . . he was silent. Then he became — silent. For he seemed to have about him a capacity for as it were degrees of intensity of his silence." But the contrary image of him as a good storyteller and talker can be found with equal frequency.

19. Frederick Karl, *A Reader's Guide to Joseph Conrad* (New York: Farrar, Straus, & Giroux, 1969), 155, quotes an early comparison of Conrad's plural silences to those in Maeterlinck. R. L. Megroz, *Joseph Conrad's Mind and Method* (New York: Russell & Russell, 1964; first published London: Faber & Faber, 1931), which has important comments by Conrad on language, quotes George Gissing's response: "How, in Satan's name, do you make their souls speak through their silence? Nay, it is as though the very soul of the world spoke for them — as in that voice of the sea, which makes all the world 'like a tolling bell' . . . This is your glorious power, to show man's kindred with the forces of earth . . . Only a poet can do the like" (94). Gissing's corny rhetoric seems in its way more accurate than criticism which has been made cautious by deconstructive conscience.

The Poetics of Ressentiment

An early draft of this essay was presented at a conference on narrative held at Northwestern University in May 1987. The present text has benefited significantly from the questions of the participants on that occasion, and especially from Gary Saul Morson's thoughtful response. In its full context, the discussion here will constitute part of a book-length exploration entitled *When the Carnival Turns Bitter: A Study of the Abject Hero.*

1. I have quoted from the definitions offered in the "Glossary" to M. M. Bakhtin, *The Dialogic Imagination,* ed. M. Holquist, trans. C. Emerson and M. Holquist (Austin: University of Texas Press, 1981), 426. The entire account of "Dialogism" offered in the glossary is a wonderful index of just how sweeping are the claims made for Bakhtin's favorite concepts.

2. Wayne Booth, "Introduction," in Mikhail Bakhtin, *Problems of Dostoevsky's Poetics,* ed. and trans. Caryl Emerson (Minneapolis: University of Minnesota Press, 1984), xxiv–xxv.

3. Edgar Allen Poe, "The Black Cat," in *Selected Writings*, ed. David Galloway (Baltimore: Penguin Books, 1967), 322.

4. Fyodor Dostoevsky, *Notes from Underground*, in *Notes from Underground and "The Grand Inquisitor,"* ed. and trans. Ralph E. Matlaw (New York: E. P. Dutton, 1960), 31–33. Unless otherwise noted, all future citations are from Matlaw's English translation and will be acknowledged in the body of the text.

5. Aaron Fogel, *Coercion to Speak: Conrad's Poetics of Dialogue* (Cambridge, Mass.: Harvard University Press, 1985). Fogel's critique is discussed in Caryl Emerson's illuminating essay, "Problems with Bakhtin's Poetics," which the author has been kind enough to let me read in typescript. [An expanded version of this essay appears in *Slavic and East European Journal*, no. 4 (1988).]

6. Joyce Carol Oates, *On Boxing* (New York: Dolphin/Doubleday, 1987), 12.

7. I have argued elsewhere that a similar idealization haunts Bakhtin's concept of the carnival. Indeed, both notions, the carnivalesque and the dialogic, are intimately linked and share many of the same imaginative strengths and limitations. My critique of the carnivalesque is detailed in "When the Carnival Turns Bitter: Preliminary Reflections upon the Abject Hero," in *Bakhtin: Essays and Dialogues on His Work*, ed. Gary Saul Morson (Chicago: University of Chicago Press, 1986), 99–121; and " 'O Totiens Servus': Saturnalia and Servitude in Augustan Rome," *Critical Inquiry* 13, no. 3 (Spring 1987): 450–74.

8. In this sense, I think there are important, and hitherto insufficiently explored, similarities between Bakhtin's ideas about dialogism and Jürgen Habermas's argument that human emancipation depends upon structures of undistorted communication. Habermas's analysis, however, starts from the premise that modern society is specifically antithetical to any genuine communicative ethics, and thus his texts contain a clear call for an extraliterary *praxis*. Although I am often unconvinced by the details of Habermas's arguments, his attention to the ways in which communication actually takes place—or is blocked—in daily life is a salutary corrective to the abstractions in Bakhtin. In any case, it would be interesting in the future to bring the works of these two thinkers together in a dialogue about dialogues.

9. Jorie Graham, "Cross-Stitch," in *Hybrids of Plants and of Ghosts* (Princeton: Princeton University Press, 1980), 11.

10. Emily Dickinson, *The Complete Poems of Emily Dickinson*, ed. Thomas H. Johnson (Boston: Little, Brown & Co., 1960), 143. The poem is no. 303 in Johnson's ordering of Dickinson's *oeuvre*.

11. William Shakespeare, *The Tempest*, ed. Northrop Frye (Baltimore: Penguin Books, 1959), 47 (1.2.363–64).

12. Friedrich Nietzsche, *Zur Genealogie der Moral*, pt. 1, sec. 10, in *Werke in Sechs Bänden*, ed. Karl Schlechta (München: Carl Hanser Verlag, 1966), 4:782. The English version cited is by Walter Kaufmann in *On the Genealogy of Morals and Ecce Homo* (New York: Random House/Vintage Books, 1967), 36–37.

13. Bakhtin's usefulness as an opponent of all these interrelated formalisms is well brought out in Booth's introduction to *Problems of Dostoevsky's Poetics*.

14. Sigmund Freud and Josef Breuer, "On the Psychical Mechanism of Hysterical Phenomena: Preliminary Communication," in *The Standard Edition of the Complete Psychological Works of Sigmund Freud*, trans. James Strachey (London: Hogarth Press, 1955), 2:7.

15. Sigmund Freud, *The Complete Letters of Sigmund Freud to Wilhelm Fliess*, trans. and ed. Jeffrey Masson (Cambridge, Mass.: Harvard University Press, 1985), 264.

16. Friedrich Nietzsche, *Zur Genealogie der Moral*, pt. 2, sec. 12, in *Werke in Sechs Bänden*, ed. Karl Schlechta, 4:819. The English version cited is by Walter Kaufmann in *On the Genealogy of Morals and Ecce Homo*, 77–78. The best brief discussion of Nietzsche's understanding of genealogy is Michel Foucault's essay, "Nietzsche, Genealogy, History," in the collection *Language, Counter-Memory, Practice*, ed. Donald Bouchard (Ithaca, N.Y.: Cornell University Press, 1977), 139–64.

17. Nietzsche, *Zur Genealogie der Moral*, pt. 1, sec. 10, in *Werke in Sechs Bände*, 4:782. The English version cited is by Walter Kaufmann, *On the Genealogy of Morals and Ecce Homo*, 36.

18. Given the importance, if not indeed the centrality, of *ressentiment* in modern thinking it is perhaps surprising that except for Nietzsche, so few thinkers have chosen to engage the problem directly. In a sense I think it is just to argue that *ressentiment* remains one of the last taboos of contemporary self-consciousness, a motive force for our ideas, values, and actions that, unlike sexuality, we are still reluctant to confront. Max Scheler's classic study, "über Ressentiment und moralisches Werturteil" (first published in 1912 and revised as "Das Ressentiment im Aufbau der Moralen" in 1915), is still the only post-Nietzschean account to have attained a significant stature in its own right. Scheler's work is wildly uneven and in places unintentionally comic in its eccentricity, but it also contains a number of quite remarkable formulations and insights. An English version of Scheler's book is available as *Ressentiment*, ed. Lewis Coser, trans. William Holdheim (New York: Free Press, 1961). Richard Ira Sugarman's *Rancor against Time: The Phenom-*

enology of "Ressentiment" (Hamburg: Felix Meiner Verlag, 1980) offers a competent summary and critique of Nietzsche, Scheler, and Heidegger, but its own analysis is rather pedestrian. Among the specialized studies of *ressentiment* in Nietzsche, see Amandus Altmann, *Friedrich Nietzsche: Das Ressentiment und seine Überwindung* (Bonn: Bouvier Verlag, 1977). By far the most searching treatment of the problem in modern philosophy, however, is found in the pages Heidegger devotes to Nietzsche's concept of revenge and temporality in *Was Heisst Denken* (Tübingen: Max Niemeyer Verlag, 1954), trans. by J. G. Gray as *What Is Called Thinking* (New York: Harper & Row/Colophon, 1968). My own engagement with the whole question of *ressentiment* has been greatly influenced by Heidegger's comments.

19. Cf., for example, Nietzsche's letter of February 23, 1887 to Franz Overbeck, or the one to Georg Brandes of November 20, 1888. Nietzsche also praised Dostoevsky in *Götzen-Dämmerung*, sec. 9, no. 45, and *Der Antichrist* (sec. 31).

20. Nietzsche, *Zur Genealogie der Moral*, pt. 3, sec. 15, in *Werke in Sechs Bände*, 4:869.

21. For this formulation from pt. 1, sec. 4, I have preferred Serge Shishkoff's translation, reprinted by the University Press of America (originally published by Thomas Y. Crowell Co.) in Fyodor Dostoevsky, *Notes from Underground*, ed. R. G. Durgy, trans. S. Shishkoff (New York, 1969), 14.

22. Mikhail Bakhtin, *Problems of Dostoevsky's Poetics*, 232–33.

23. See, e.g., the characteristic account of this development in Alex de Jonge, *Dostoevsky and the Age of Intensity* (London: Secker & Warburg, 1975), 12–14.

24. Ibid., 13.

25. Fyodor Dostoevsky, *The Brothers Karamazov*, ed. Ralph Matlaw, trans. Constance Garnett, rev. R. Matlaw (New York: Norton, 1976), 605.

26. Ibid., 606.

27. Ibid., 608.

28. Gary Saul Morson, "A Response to Robbins and Bernstein," unpublished text read at the Northwestern University Conference on Narrative. In his response, Morson also rightly notes that the Devil actually proposes a theory of infinite repetition that has uncanny parallels with Nietzsche's theory of eternal recurrence (cf. *The Brothers Karamazov*, 611).

29. Caryl Emerson, "Editor's Preface" to Mikhail Bakhtin, *Problems of Dostoevsky's Poetics*, xxxv.

30. Karl Marx, *The Eighteenth Brumaire of Louis Napoleon* (New York: International, 1963), 15.

31. Emile Littré, *Dictionnaire de la langue française* (Paris, 1961), 6:1447. Compare the following typical usages of the term in classical French theater:

Bérénice: Tandis qu'autour de moi votre cour assemblée
      Retentit des bienfaits dont vous m'avez comblée,
      Est-il juste, Seigneur, que seule en ce moment
      Je demeure sans voix et sans ressentiment?
      [Racine, *Bérénice*, 2.4.2–5 (Paris: Editions Pléiade, 1950), 487.]

Aristomène: Madame, je viens à vos pieds, rendre grâce à l'Amour de mes heureux destins, et vous témoigner, avec mes transports, le ressentiment où je suis des bontés surprenantes dont vous daignez favoriser le plus soumis de vos captifs. [Molière, *La Princesse d'Elide*, 4.4.1–5 (Paris: Editions Pléiade, 1971), 1:810.]

32. Friedrich Nietzsche, *Also Sprach Zarathustra*, pt. 2, "Von der Erlösung," in *Werke in Sechs Bänden*, 3:394; English version, *Thus Spoke Zarathustra*, trans. R. J. Hollingdale (Baltimore: Penguin Books, 1961), 161–62.

33. Karl Marx, *The Eighteenth Brumaire of Louis Bonaparte*, no trans. (New York: International, 1977), 15.

34. The most succinctly powerful discussion of Goya's image in its relationship to Enlightenment thought is in Jean Starobinski, *1789: The Emblems of Reason*, trans. Barbara Bray (Charlottesville: University Press of Virginia, 1982), 198.

35. See the useful article by Nicolas Moravcevich, "The Romantization of the Prostitute in Dostoevskij's Fiction," in *Russian Literature* 4, no. 3 (July 1976): 299–307, for a detailed discussion of this theme. Moravcevich outlines the long history of sentimentalizing the prostitute in Russian literature and shows how powerfully the writings of the French Romantics contributed to this tradition. Not only did Nekrasov's 1845 poem, "When from thy error, dark, degrading" derive from Hugo's 1835 lyric, "Oh! n'insultez jamais une femme qui tombe!" but such figures as Paquette in *Notre Dame de Paris* (1831) and Fantine in *Les Misérables* (1862) both had a profound effect upon Russian authors. What is most important to remember, however, is that all of these sentimental texts are as vital a part of the context for *Notes from Underground* as the more commonly discussed sources like Chernyshevsky's treatment of the theme of the redeemed whore in *What Is to Be Done?*

36. Leo Tolstoy, *Resurrection*, trans. Vera Traill (New York: Signet/New American Library, 1961), chap. 48, 164.

37. Anton Chekhov, "An Attack of Nerves," in *The Portable Chekhov*, ed. A. Yarmolinsky (New York: Penguin, 1985), 242–43.

38. Cf. Joseph Frank, *Dostoevsky: The Stir of Liberation, 1860–1865* (Princeton: Princeton University Press, 1986); Tzvetan Todorov, "Notes d'un Souterrain," in *Les Genres du Discours* (Paris, 1978), 135–60; Michael Holquist, *Dostoevsky and the Novel* (Princeton: Princeton University Press, 1977). These examples could be multiplied *ad infinitum*.

39. For this episode from pt. 2, sec. 6, I have preferred Serge Shishkoff's translation, reprinted by the University Press of America (originally published Thomas Y. Crowell Co.), in Fyodor Dostoevsky, *Notes from Underground*, ed. R. G. Durgy, trans. S. Shishkoff (New York, 1969), 93.

40. Here again I have preferred Shishkoff's translation, 120.

41. Here I must admit that there is a risk my interpretation is too optimistic. Although there is certainly a reasonable likelihood that the Underground Man's final gesture is an imitation of writers like de Sade (who, as we know from Dostoevsky's *Diary of a Writer*, fascinated both the novelist and his contemporaries), it is also possible that he is acting, for once, without a prior literary model. If so, then my interpretation is indeed far too positive, since this second alternative implies the notion that the one truly independent and original deed still available to an abject character like the Underground Man is an act of deliberate and mutually injurious cruelty to someone who is prepared to love him. Even if this were the case, of course, the next time a similar gesture takes place it would no longer contain any element of an original cruelty, but would revert to being merely a citation of *Notes from Underground*.

42. In the event, of course, Emma's reading is not nearly as secondrate as the standard comments might lead one to believe, since it includes authors like Bernardin de Saint-Pierre, Walter Scott, Chateaubriand, and Lamartine, all of whom are still studied today, although admittedly they are rarely recommended as appropriate guides for a young lady's behavior — as indeed they were not in Emma's day either.

43. For a fascinating study of this theme as applied to Flaubert's *La Tentation de Saint Antoine*, see Michel Foucault's essay, "Fantasia of the Library," in *Language, Counter-Memory, Practice*, 87–109.

44. Flaubert, *Bouvard et Pécuchet*, 389.

45. Max Scheler, *Ressentiment*, ed. Lewis A. Coser, trans. W. W. Holdheim (New York: Free Press, 1961), 66.

46. I intend to explore this theme in detail in a forthcoming book, *When the Carnival Turns Bitter: A Study of the Abject Hero*.

47. Although I have quoted the sentence in the way it has entered English usage, the actual lines are more correctly translated, "When I hear anyone talking about Culture . . . I release the safety catch of my Browning [pistol]." (The ellipsis is in the text of the play.) In any case,

the phrase is spoken by Friedrich Thiemann, a character in Johst's drama *Schlageter* (München: Albert Langen-Georg Müller Verlag, 1933), 26. *Schlageter*, dedicated to Adolf Hitler, was an enormous success in 1933 Germany, and no doubt its most provocative lines soon acquired a life of their own, independent of their original "cultural" source. For the most part, the provenance of the sentence has been forgotten entirely, and yet it rightly continues to be cited as absolutely characteristic of the fascist attitude towards culture. Such repeated citations, moreover, seem to me an interesting comment on iterability in its own right. I owe my own familiarity with Johst's text to the kind suggestion of my friend and colleague Leo Lowenthal.

48. Here I have preferred to use Serge Shishkoff's translation in Fyodor Dostoevsky, *Notes from Underground*, 124.

Preface to The Dramas

The text is translated from L. N. Tolstoy, *Polnoe sobranie khudozhestvennykh proizvedenii*, ed. K. Khalabaev and B. Eikhenbaum (Leningrad: Pechatnyi dvor, 1929), 11:iii–x.

Bakhtin's footnotes are numbered in the text and translated here without change. More precise information, available English equivalents of the reference, or later and more accessible editions are provided by the translator in brackets.

Bakhtin's footnotes (numbered in text)

1. In this regard a great deal is provided by Boris M. Eikhenbaum's book *Lev Tolstoi. Kniga I. Piatidesiatye gody* (Leningrad: Priboi, 1928) [Leo Tolstoy, Book 1. The Fifties].

[Eikhenbaum's Book 2 (*Tolstoi in the Sixties*) and Book 3 (*Tolstoi in the Seventies*) are now in English, although Book 1 has not been translated. A translation does exist, however, of Eikhenbaum's earlier, more theoretical and formalist study upon which Book 1 was based: Boris Eikhenbaum, *The Young Tolstoi*, trans. ed. Gary Kern (Ardis, 1972)].

2. See [P. I.] Biriukov, *Biografiia L'va Nik. Tolstogo* (Moscow-Petrograd: Gosizdat, 1923), 1:198.

3. Such are the convictions of Konstantin Levin, who embodies the economic and ideological quests of Tolstoy himself.

4. See "Iz vospominanii S. A. Tolstoi," *Tolstovskii Ezhegodnik* 1912, p. 19.

[An excerpt from Sofia Andreevna Tolstaia's unpublished book "My Life" which deals with Tolstoy's writing of "The Power of Darkness" (1888) and the play's difficulties with the censor. Bakhtin's reference appears to be to p. 18: "In November, after my [S. A.'s] return home, we moved to Moscow, and Lev Nikolaevich, having finished his drama, sent it off for typesetting to the firm 'The Intermediary' which sympathized with him, at the same time dreaming of its performance in folk theaters." (P. 19 discusses the reaction of the imperial family to the play.) At the end of the excerpt Sofia Andreevna mentions that her favorite production of all was the one mounted in the mid-1890s in the 'Skomorokh' folk theater in Moscow, "where there was a public of 1700, most of them the common people" (22).]

5. See *Dnevnik S. A. Tolstoi 1860 – 1891* (Moscow: izd. Sabashni-kovykh, 1928), 30. (Ed. S. L. Tolstoi.]

[Bakhtin appears to compress here two page references to the above diary. In her notebook entry for 14 February 1870 (p. 30), Sofia Andreevna mentions that her husband was much taken by the idea of writing a drama on a modern-day Ilya Muromets, "an educated and very clever man, from peasant stock, but having studied at the university." On p. 37, under the subtitle "Notes on words spoken by L. N. Tolstoi while writing" (entry for 3 March 1876), S. A. notes Tolstoy's plans for a new work in which "he will love the idea of the Russian people in the sense of a *possessing force*. And this force appeared to Lev Nikolaevich in the form of the continual resettling of Russians in new places in the south of Siberia, in the new lands to the southeast of Russia, on the White River, in Tashkent, etc."]

Translator's notes (lettered in text)

a. "Ot nei vse kachestva," lit. "From Her/It All Qualities [Flow]," translated by Louise and Aylmer Maude as "The Cause of It All" in Leo Tolstoy, *Plays* (London: Constable & Co., 1914).

The "it" in the title is probably the feminine noun vodka, but there might be other candidates. In the play, a tramp with revolutionary and progressive pretensions restrains a drunken peasant from beating his wife, only to pilfer (in his words, "expropriate") upon his departure a parcel of sugar and tea from the peasant's house. In a last-minute moral gesture the peasant gives back the parcel to the apprehended tramp, who shame-facedly refuses to accept it.

b. Tolstoy's essay "On Shakespeare and on Drama" (1903 – 4) is an exposé of the artificiality, immorality, tediousness, and lack of originality in Shakespeare's plays (with *King Lear* as exemplar). Tolstoy wrote half-a-dozen unfinished or abandoned essays on the subject of art between 1889 and the 1897–98, the year he completed his major treatise *What Is Art?* These essays are: "About Art" (two sketches, 1889), "About What Is and Is Not Art, and About When Art Is an Important Matter and When It Is Trivial" (1889), "Science and Art" (1889–91), "About Science and Art" (1891), "About That Which Is Called Art" (1896). For a selection, see *"What Is Art?" and Essays on Art* by Leo Tolstoy, trans. Aylmer Maude (London: Oxford University Press, n.d.).

    c. "A Light Shines in the Darkness" is more than autobiographical, it is almost a dramatized version of Tolstoy's diaries. Significantly, Tolstoy left the play unfinished; he began it in the 1880s and returned to it in 1900 and 1902, leaving notes for an unwritten fifth act. The first half of the play is painful in its accurate real-life references: a handsome wife of forty nurses a seventh child and complains that her husband "no longer troubles about the children, I have to decide everything myself"; the husband engages the local priest in long harangues over the corruption of the official church; meanwhile, the adolescents in the family want to get on with enjoying their life. The second half of the play seems to represent a dramatized fantasy of discipleship, centering on the brave resistance of the family's future (and ultimately ex-) son-in-law to military service, and his subsequent imprisonment and flogging.

    d. Vasily Kirillovich Syutaev (1820s?–1890s?), a peasant from Tver province who founded a religious sect based on the New Testament's doctrine of obligatory love. The "syutaevtsy" practiced personal self-perfection and neither proselytized nor respected the sacraments. The sect first attracted attention in 1876, after the local clergy lodged a legal complaint about Syutaev's refusal to christen his grandson.

    Tolstoy first met Syutaev in 1881, and thereafter Syutaev frequently visited the Tolstoy house in Moscow. (Victor Shklovsky devotes a chapter to "Tolstoy and Syutaev" in his *Lev Tolstoy* [Moscow: Progress, 1978], 524–31.) Ilya Repin's portrait of Syutaev, under the title "The Sectarian," hangs in the Tretiakov Gallery.

    e. This term of abuse (which could be rendered literally as "rich peasant and devourer of the commune") was coming into its own during Stalin's first Five Year Plan and subsequent brutal collectivization drive against the peasantry, 1928–33. Bakhtin's application of the term to Tolstoy's prerevolutionary writings is anachronistic at best, opportunistic at worst.

    f. The *narodniki* were Russian populists, active in the latter half of the 19th century, who in literature and in life sympathized with the plight of the peasants and aided them by staffing schools, hospitals, and local government institutions.

g. Gleb Ivanovich Uspensky (1843–1902), Russian populist and journalist, master of the *ocherk* or prose sketch on themes from peasant life. His early writings from the 1860s tended to be bleakly pessimistic, even nihilistic. Later, in connection with his work for the populist journal *Otechestvennye zapiski* in the early 1880s, Uspensky often idealized the peasantry; in that spirit he wrote his influential "Vlast' zemli" (The Power of the Earth) to which Bakhtin eludes.

h. This folksaying, "Kogotok uvyaz, vsei ptichke propast'," is Tolstoy's subtitle to his play "The Power of Darkness."

i. "Alyosha Gorshok" (1905), a short moral tale on the saint-like life and death of a young, cheerfully hardworking, obedient, and much abused house servant.

j. Nikolai Konstantinovich Mikhailovsky (1842–1904), essayist and leading theoretician of Russian populism. He argued for the intelligentsia's devotion to the working peasantry, the preservation of the peasant commune, and the protection of the Russian people both from capitalism and from their own potentially anarchic and demogogic impulses.

k. Ilya Muromets is a powerful, Paul Bunyan-like peasant in Slavic folk legend who was part hero, part saint. For the first thirty years of his life he was paralyzed, and then was commanded by holy men to rise, go forth, and serve Russia. He was finally killed in battle, at which time his body turned to stone.

l. In "The Fruits of Enlightenment" (1889–90), a satiric spoof on the upper-class fad for spiritualism, domestic servants impersonate spirits at a seance to facilitate the purchase of their master's land for the peasant commune.

m. From act 3, scene 2 of "The Living Corpse." Fedya Protasov speaks these lines to Prince Abrezkov, who has come to ascertain Protasov's intentions regarding his wife and infant son (whom Protasov has abandoned for a gypsy girl). Abrezkov pleads with him, unsuccessfully, to reform and return home. Protasov's wife meanwhile is being courted by a friend whom she loves, and Protasov decides to free his wife not by a shameful divorce but by feigned suicide (an idea his gypsy girlfriend gets from Chernyshevsky's *What Is to Be Done?*). But the ruse is discovered, and to prevent his wife's exile to Siberia for bigamy Protasov shoots himself at the trial.

Bakhtin considerably exaggerates the conscience-stricken and "repentant" content of this black comedy, in which licentiousness, financial irresponsibility, infidelity, and parody of Chernyshevsky's plots appear to play a much larger role than Protasov's social or moral criticisms of tsarist society.

Preface to Resurrection

The text is translated from L. N. Tolstoi, *Polnoe sobranie khudo-zhestvennykh proizvedenii,* ed. K. Khalabaev and B. Eikhenbaum, vol. 13 (Leningrad: Pechatnyi dvor, 1929): iv–xx.

Bakhtin's footnotes are numbered in the text and translated here without change, except for two omissions (where Bakhtin provides references to the Russian text of *Resurrection* in this 1929 edition). More precise information, available English equivalents of the reference, or later and more accessible editions are provided by the translator in brackets.

Bakhtin's footnotes (numbered in text)

1. For this reason Tolstoy, in many respects close to the Slavophiles, was at the same time both comprehensible and close (closer than Turgenev) to the declassé intelligentsia of the 1850s and sixties, to Chernyshevsky, Nekrasov, and others, who were able to hear in his work kindred social tones.

[Bakhtin ignores here—as he does in the preface to vol. 11—the powerful polemic that Tolstoy waged *against* Chernyshevsky in the 1860s on questions of social organization and popular education; see Boris Eikhenbaum, *Tolstoi in the Sixties,* trans. Duffield White (Ann Arbor: Ardis, 1982), chap. 5].

2. "Lev Tolstoi kak zerkalo russkoi revoliutsii" [Leo Tolstoy as the mirror of the Russian Revolution] (1908), *O Tolstom. Literaturno-kriticheskii sbornik* (Moscow-Leningrad: Gosizdat, 1928), 5.

[Bakhtin's citation of this essay, the most famous of seven journalistic pieces on Tolstoy that Lenin wrote between 1908 and 1910, would have been almost mandatory in the Soviet context. The essay is widely anthologized; for a recent translation by Boris Sorokin, see Edward Wasiolek, ed., *Critical Essays on Tolstoy* (Boston: J. K. Hall, 1986), 20–24.]

3. See *Dnevnik Sofii Andreevny Tolstoi, 1860–1891* [The Diary of Sofia Andreevna Tolstoy] (Izd. Sabashnikovykh, 1928), 40.

[S. A.'s entry for 25 October 1877. Tolstoy is discussing plans for a new (post-*Anna Karenina*) novel which would involve the adventures of the third and favorite son of a prosperous peasant. In the first part of the novel this son resolves to study and eventually mixes in educated circles; in the second part "there will be a resettled peasant, a Russian Robinson, who will settle on the new lands (the Samara steppes) and will begin afresh a new life there, full of petty, indispensable human necessities." It is at this point that Tolstoy comments on the difficulty of describing the peasant way of life.]

4. Ibid., 30.

[S. A.'s entry for 14 February 1870. On Ilya Muromets, see trans. note k. to Tolstoy preface no. 11.]

5. *Dnevnik Sofii Andreevny Tolstoi*, 37.

[S. A.'s entry for 3 March 1876. See Bakhtin's n. 5 to Tolstoy preface no. 11.]

6. See *Anna Karenina*, pt. 7, chap. 3. Izd. Giz. 1928, 2:209.

[In this chapter Levin, in Moscow for his wife's confinement, discusses Russian agriculture with an old friend, now a professor, and an economic specialist. The professionals consider the problem of the farm laborer conventionally, "from the standpoint of capital, wages, and rent." Levin, who is writing his own book on agriculture, considers the laborer as an organic whole with a special relationship to the land—one due, Levin says, to the Russian peasant's "consciousness of his vocation to populate vast, unoccupied tracts in the east."]

7. Four fragments have been published. See vol. 3 of the present edition.

8. On this point, see Plekhanov, "Karl Marks i Lev Tolstoi" (1911), in the above-mentioned handbook [n. 2 above], 64ff.

[Georgy Plekhanov (1856–1918), Marxist revolutionary theorist, critic, and sociologist of art. In this 20-page essay, Plekhanov argues that Tolstoy, *contra* the dialectical materialist Marx, was a "metaphysical idealist," by which he meant a sort of binary thinker whose mind worked best in closed oppositions and "absolute consistency." Criticizing Tolstoy's doctrine of nonviolent resistance to evil and his stand against capital punishment, Plekhanov insists that absolute judgments about good and evil cannot be made in the real (and relative) world. When they are, absolute negation results, which works in the interests of the "hangmen" and "oppressors of the people."]

9. See the present vol., p. 158.

[Passage cited as per chap. 55 of the Maude Translation (1916) in Leo Tolstoy, *Resurrection* (New York: W. W. Norton, 1966), 202–3. The text has been slightly adjusted to accord more literally with the passage Bakhtin cites, which appears not to be from the standard published text (as per the Jubilee Edition of Tolstoy's works, 32:183–84) but from a published variant (see 32:454). In its final sentence [given below], the Jubilee Edition text is considerably *more* suspicious of revolutionary commitment than is the version Bakhtin cites: "It was clear that she considered herself a heroine ready to sacrifice her life for the success of her cause; yet she could hardly have explained what that cause was, or in what its success consisted."

10. See *Dnevnik* [The Diary], 34.

[The only diary previously cited by Bakhtin is Sofia Andreevna's, and there is no reference on that page (written in 1873) to this passage on *Resurrection* (begun fifteen years later). Bakhtin perhaps had some edition of Tolstoy's diary in mind. The quotation in the text is from Tolstoy's entry of 17 May 1896, where he is copying into his diary points from his notebooks. See *Tolstoy's Diaries*, vol. 2, ed. and trans. R. F. Christian (New York: Charles Scribner's Sons, 1985), 427.]

11. See *Dnevnik*, 7.

[Here too Bakhtin seems to be referring to some edition of Tolstoy's diaries. The period he has in mind is most likely November 1885 through the spring of 1886, when Tolstoy notes several attempts to rethink the novel, to "begin it with her," etc.]

12. See Plekhanov's article, "Karl Marx i Lev Tolstoi" [n. 8], 76.

13. If this weren't so, it would be necessary to throw overboard from the ship of artistic literature a good half of all French and English novels.

Translator's notes (lettered in text)

a. Bakhtin discusses Tolstoy's "Three Deaths" as an exemplary monologic work—that is, as a work with only one true center of consciousness—in his second (1963) edition of the book on Dostoevsky (Mikhail Bakhtin, *Problems of Dostoevsky's Poetics* [Minneapolis: University of Minnesota Press, 1984], 69–73). The story does not figure into his original 1929 version of the Dostoevsky book (published almost simultaneously with these Tolstoy prefaces), but Bakhtin's later discussion of it in the revised edition is very much in the spirit of this preface, which might have served as a sketch.

b. Reference is to the so-called Decembrist Revolt of 14 December, 1825, an abortive demonstration on Senate Square in St. Petersburg against the Russian monarchy, organized by various highborn liberal and radical dissident groups during the confusion of the interregnum following Alexander I's death.

c. Bakhtin's attempts to link the text we now know as *Resurrection* with Tolstoy's plans for a "peasant novel" are at best strained. Although it is true that Tolstoy hoped someday to write on the peasant-colonizers, and also that he envisioned an epic sequel to *Resurrection* in which Nekhludov lived "as a peasant" (diary entry for 23 June 1900), the actual novel published in 1899 contains very little of this theme. If anything, the following diary entry (24 October 1895) is characteristic: "Took up

Resurrection again, and was convinced that it's all bad, that the centre of gravity is not where it ought to be, that the land question is a distraction and a weakness, and will turn out to be weak itself . . ." (as cited in *Tolstoy's Diaries,* vol. 2, ed. and trans. R. F. Christian [New York: Charles Scribner's Sons, 1985], 419).

d. "For Each Day" was Tolstoy's third and final attempt, undertaken in the last decade of his life, to compose, from his own and others' writings, a book or calendar of daily readings based on his moral world view (earlier attempts were "Thoughts of Wise Men" and "A Circle of Reading"). About half of these entries were approved for print during Tolstoy's lifetime; the entire 12-month set of readings were published for the first time only in the Jubilee Edition, vols. 43–44 (1929, 1932).

e. "Field of vision" or "conceptual horizon" (*krugozor*) will become an important concept for Bakhtin in the early 1930s, when he extends the insights of his book on Dostoevsky into a theory of the novel.

f. The effectiveness of the Russian phrase *sud nad sudom* is difficult to translate; *sud* means *both* court and judgment (with overtones of the biblical *Strashnyi sud,* "Last [lit. Terrible] Judgment"). Equally possible equivalents of the phrase would therefore be: "a court passing judgment on a court," "judgment on/over judgment."

g. The technique Bakhtin attributes to Tolstoy here is *ostrannenie,* "defamiliarization," a literary device made famous by the Formalist critic Victor Shklovsky, who frequently noted its use by Leo Tolstoy.

h. People's Will, or *Narodnaya volya,* was the radical revolutionary group active in the 1870s and responsible for the assassination of Emperor Alexander II in 1881.

i. From an entry for 5 January 1897: "Began to re-read *Resurrection,* and gave it up in disgust when I got as far as *his* decision to marry. It's all untrue, made-up and weak. it's difficult to put right something that's flawed. To put it right it will be necessary: 1) to describe her feelings and life and his alternately. And in her case positively and seriously, and in his case negatively and sardonically [lit. "with a smirk."]. I doubt if I'll finish it. It's all very flawed." Cited as per *Tolstoy's Diaries,* 2:439.

j. Note the traces here of Bakhtin's ruminations, in his early manuscripts, on the relationship between authoring and love. See the prefatory essay "Introduction: Rethinking Bakhtin," in the present vol., 24–25.

k. For another discussion of this passage, see Michael André Bernstein's article in the present vol., 216.

l. The opening sentence of chap. 3. The Maude translation (see n. 9), 10, is "literalized" here to accord more closely with Bakhtin's reference to specific phrases.

m. Reference is to the final page of the novel, where Nekhlyudov, rejected by Katyusha, turns to the Gospels and is transformed by the Parable of the Laborers in the Vineyard.

n. Reference is to Tolstoy's 300-page essay on the essence of religious experience, "The Kingdom of God Is within You," written in the early 1890s.

Contributors

MICHAEL ANDRÉ BERNSTEIN, Professor of English and Comparative Literature at the University of California at Berkeley, is the author of *The Tale of the Tribe: Ezra Pound and the Modern Verse Epic* (Princeton University Press, 1980), of *Prima Della Rivoluzione* (a collection of poems; National Poetry Foundation, University of Maine, 1984), and of numerous articles on modern poetry and on literary theory. An earlier essay on Bakhtin, "When the Carnival Turns Bitter: Preliminary Reflections on the Abject Hero," appeared in the *Critical Inquiry* "Forum on Bakhtin" (December 1983).

The late PAUL DE MAN was Professor of Comparative Literature at Yale University. Among his best known works are *Blindness and Insight: Essays in the Rhetoric of Contemporary Criticism* (Oxford University Press, 1971), *Allegories of Reading: Figural Language in Rousseau, Nietzsche, Rilke, and Proust* (Yale University Press, 1979), and *The Resistance to Theory* (University of Minnesota Press, 1986).

CARYL EMERSON, Professor of Slavic Languages and Literatures and of Comparative Literature at Princeton University, is the author of *Boris Godunov: Transpositions of a Russian Theme* (Indiana University Press, 1986) and of articles on Russian literature, Russian opera and vocal music, and literary theory. Her essay "The Inner Word and Outer Speech: Bakhtin, Vygotsky, and the Internalization of Language" appeared in *Critical Inquiry* "Forum" (December 1983).

She is also editor and translator of Bakhtin's *Problems of Dostoevsky's Poetics* (University of Minnesota Press, 1984), the co-translator of *The Dialogic Imagination: Four Essays by M. M. Bakhtin* (University of Texas Press, 1981), and co-editor of Bakhtin, *Speech Genres and Other Late Essays* (University of Texas Press, 1986).

AARON FOGEL, Associate Professor of English at Boston University, is the author of *Coercion to Speak: Conrad's Poetics of Dialogue* (Harvard University Press, 1985). He is currently writing a study of demography and representation in modern prose and poetry.

LINDA HUTCHEON, Professor of English and Comparative Literature at the University of Toronto, is the author of *Narcissistic Narrative: The Metafictional Paradox* (Wilfrid Laurier University Press, 1980; paperback edition, Methuen, 1984); *Formalism and the Freudian Aesthetic: The Example of Charles Mauron* (Cambridge University Press, 1984); *A Theory of Parody: The Teachings of Twentieth-Century Art Forms* (Methuen, 1985); *A Poetics of Postmodernism: History, Theory, Fiction* (Routledge, 1988); and *The Canadian Postmodern: A Study of Contemporary English-Canadian Fiction* (Oxford University Press, 1988).

GARY SAUL MORSON, Professor of Slavic Languages and Comparative Literature at Northwestern University, is the author of *The Boundaries of Genre: Dostoevsky's "Diary of a Writer" and the Traditions of Literary Utopia* (University of Texas Press, 1981; paperback edition, Northwestern University Press, 1988); *Hidden in Plain View: Narrative and Creative Potentials in "War and Peace"* (Stanford University Press, 1987), and numerous articles on literary theory and Russian prose.

He is also the editor of *Literature and History: Theoretical Problems and Russian Case Studies* (Stanford University Press, 1986), of the "Forum on Bakhtin" in *Critical Inquiry* (December 1983), and of *Bakhtin: Essays and Dialogues on his Work* (University of Chicago Press, 1986).

MATHEW ROBERTS holds a Master's Degree in Russian Literature from Cornell University, and is currently a doctoral candidate in the Program in Comparative Literature and Theory at Northwestern University. He is the author of "Bakhtin and Jakobson" (forthcoming in *Slavic and East European Journal*, 1989).

ANN SHUKMAN, editor of *Russian Poetics in Translation*, is the author of *Literature and Semiotics: A Study of the Writings of Yu. M.*

Lotman (North-Holland, 1977). She has edited *Bakhtin School Papers* (Holdan, 1984), *The Semiotics of Russian Culture: Ju. M. Lotman, B. A. Uspenskij* (Michigan Slavic Contributions, 1984), and several other volumes devoted to contemporary Russian literary theory.

Index

The following abbreviations are used: B = Bakhtin; V = Voloshinov; M = Medvedev; D = Dostoevsky; T = Tolstoy.